International 'Criminal' Responsibility

In the course of the 20th and 21st centuries, major offences committed by individuals have been subject to progressive systematisation in the framework of international criminal law. Proposals developed within the context of the League of Nations coordinated individual liability and State responsibility. By contrast, international law as codified after World War II in the framework of the United Nations embodies a neat divide between individual criminal liability and State aggravated responsibility. However, conduct of State organs and agents generates dual liability. Through a critical analysis of key international rules, the book assesses whether the divisive approach to individual and State responsibility is normatively consistent. Contemporary situations, such as the humanitarian crises in Syria and Libya, 9/11 and the Iraq wars demonstrate that the matter still gives rise to controversy: a set of systemic problems emerge. The research focuses on the substantive elements of major offences, notably aggression, genocide, core war crimes, core crimes against humanity and terrorism, as well as relevant procedural implications.

The book is a useful resource for practitioners, policymakers, academics, students, researchers and anyone interested in international law and politics.

Ottavio Quirico is a Senior Lecturer in the School of Law at the University of New England in Australia, an Honorary Lecturer at the Centre for European Studies of the Australian National University and an Alumnus of the European University Institute.

Routledge Research in International Law

Available:

Unilateral Acts
A History of a Legal Doctrine
Betina Kuzmarov

Regional Developmentalism through Law
Establishing an African Economic Community
Jonathan Bashi Rudahindwa

China's One Belt One Road Initiative and Private International Law
Edited by Poomintr Sooksripaisarnkit and Sai Ramani Garimella

Transnational Terrorist Groups and International Criminal Law
Anna Marie Brennan

Confronting Cyberespionage Under International Law
Oğuz Kaan Pehlivan

Russian Discourses on International Law
Sociological and Philosophical Phenomenon
Edited by P Sean Morris

Backstage Practices in Transnational Law
Lianne Boer and Sofia Stolk

International 'Criminal' Responsibility
Antinomies
Ottavio Quirico

For a full list of titles in this series, visit https://www.routledge.com/Routledge-Research-in-International-Law/book-series/INTNLLAW

International 'Criminal' Responsibility

Antinomies

Ottavio Quirico

Routledge
Taylor & Francis Group
NEW YORK AND LONDON

First published 2019
by Routledge
605 Third Avenue, New York, NY 10017

and by Routledge
2 Park Square, Milton Park, Abingdon, Oxon, OX14 4RN

First issued in paperback 2021

Routledge is an imprint of the Taylor & Francis Group, an informa business

Library of Congress Cataloging-in-Publication Data
Names: Quirico, Ottavio, author.
Title: International 'criminal' responsibility: antinomies / Ottavio Quirico.
Description: New York, NY: routledge, 2019. |
Series: Routledge research in international law |
Includes bibliographical references and index.
Identifiers: LCCN 2018051616 (print) | LCCN 2018051764 (ebook) |
ISBN 9781315104256 (ebk) | ISBN 9781138098916 (hbk)
Subjects: LCSH: Criminal liability (International law) |
Crimes against humanity.
Classification: LCC KZ7075 (ebook) | LCC KZ7075 .Q57 2019 (print) |
DDC 345/.04—dc23
LC record available at https://lccn.loc.gov/2018051616

Typeset in Galliard
by codeMantra

ISBN 13: 978-1-03-224147-0 (pbk)
ISBN 13: 978-1-138-09891-6 (hbk)

DOI: 10.4324/9781315104256

'A State is called the coldest of all cold monsters'
Friedrich Nietzsche, *Thus Spoke Zarathustra*

Ghisleriorum Collegio gratus

Foreword

International 'criminal' responsibility: this book is an exceptionally rigorous scientific investigation of a modern field of law rife with technical complexity.

The issue of State 'criminal' responsibility has been discussed since the adoption of the Treaty of Versailles, around a hundred years ago. The Treaty simultaneously addressed the liability of Germany as a State and that of its Emperor, Wilhelm II of Hohenzollern, as an individual. In the 1920s, legal commentators invoked the establishment of a special jurisdiction with competence over individuals, and possibly States, for criminal offences. In the last quarter of the 20th century, the Statute of the International Criminal Court was approved after the international community experienced a troubled and complex period. At the same time, the UN International Law Commission (ILC) developed its work on the codification of 'international crimes' attributable to either natural persons or States.[1]

Within the context of the Draft Articles on State Responsibility, the ILC outlined a dualistic approach to State wrongful acts, distinguishing offences that affect one or more States in the context of bilateral and multilateral relations from breaches concerning the international community as a whole.[2] The expression 'international community as a whole' has become part of positive law. As is well known, the concept is based on Article 53 of the Vienna Convention on the Law of Treaties, which governs peremptory international norms having by their very nature a universal scope of application. In spite of the imperfection and incompleteness of the ILC's work on the issue, which I have considered in detail elsewhere,[3] it is possible to identify a certain 'progress' in international law as concerns

1 See, in particular, Roberto Ago, Fifth Report on State Responsibility: The Internationally Wrongful Act of the State, Source of International Responsibility, UN Doc A/CN.4/291 and Add.1 and 2 (1976) 2(1) *YBILC* 54, para 155; ILC, Report to the General Assembly on the Work of the Thirty-Fifth Session, UN Doc A/38/10 (1983) 2(2) *YBILC* 14, paras 50 and 54; Id, Report to the General Assembly on the Work of the Forty-Eight Session, UN Doc A/51/10 (1996) 2(2) *YBILC* 60.

2 ILC, Report to the General Assembly on the Work of the Fifty-Third Session, UN Doc A/56/10 (2001) 2(2) *YBILC* 112.

3 Pierre-Marie Dupuy, 'The Deficiencies of the Law of State Responsibility Relating to Breaches of "Obligations Owed to the International Community as a Whole": Suggestions for Avoiding

both the legal technique and the political 'consciousness of nations', which underpin the international community as a 'legal construct'.[4]

The matter has been enriched by the jurisprudence of the International Criminal Tribunal for the Former Yugoslavia (ICTY) and its Appeals Chamber. Particularly in the initial phase, the jurisprudence of the ICTY was dynamic as concerns the overlap between the responsibility of a State and that of an individual acting on its behalf. Evidence has in fact proved that the relationship between the two forms of responsibility is quite strict and has arisen to a greater or lesser extent in different cases.[5] The International Court of Justice has shown extreme prudence in approaching the question, notably in its 2007 judgment delivered in the case concerning the *Application of the Genocide Convention*:[6] only to a limited extent can it be said that the decision has contributed to shedding light on the overlap between individual and State responsibility.

Nonetheless, political developments, which the law should in principle frame and, more properly, normatively regulate, have led to what can be called the 'renewed frequency of barbarism'. The second Balkan war ended a century that began with the tragic events of the first. Despite UN membership, there has been an increase in the number of States where major offences against international humanitarian law and human rights have been committed, either internally or vis-à-vis other countries. The phenomenon has evolved together with the development of international terrorism, which has recently culminated in the humanitarian crises in Iraq and Syria.

This framework essentially raises the question of the effectiveness of fundamental principles and rules of international law, which have long been established and are still subject to progressive evolution, as shown by the aforementioned developments in the case law of international jurisdictions. Respect for the international rule of law is at stake. This is all the more troublesome in light of the fact that particularly serious offences are increasingly often supported by rough and seditious political declarations, involving countries that contributed to establishing the international legal order at the end of World War II.

In light of these developments, it is critical that lawyers undertake studies on the precise content of aggravated breaches of positive international law and their procedural implications, in order to elucidate the regime, or regimes, of State responsibility and consistency with individual regimes. This is a demanding and urgent task, as much as an indispensable one. Ottavio Quirico has developed such a study with great competence. He has completed this work with an intellectual

Obsolescence of Aggravated Responsibility', in Antonio Cassese, *Realizing Utopia: The Future of International Law* (OUP, 2012) 214-219.

4 Pierre-Marie Dupuy, 'L'unité de l'ordre juridique international' (2002) 297 *RCADI* 9.

5 See, for instance, *Tadić*, IT-94-1, Trial Chamber, Judgment of 7 May 1997, 217, para 606.

6 *Application of the Convention on the Prevention and Punishment of the Crime of Genocide (Bosnia and Herzegovina v Yugoslavia)* [2007] ICJ Rep 43.

rigour that is equalled only by the practical and theoretical openness and importance of his methodical investigation.

Any reader will be grateful to the author.

Pierre-Marie Dupuy

Emeritus Professor
Université Panthéon-Assas, Paris 2
Graduate Institute of International and Development Studies, Geneva
International Arbitrator
2015 ASIL Manley Hudson Award

Contents

Cases

Documents

1926

1927

1928

1929

1935

1937

1944

1945

1946

1947

1948

1949

1971

1973

1974

1976

1977

1978

1980

1981

1982

1983

1984

1985

1992

1993

1994

1995

1996

1997

1998

1999

2000

2003

2004

2005

2006

2007

2008

2009

2010

2011

2012

2013

2014

2015

2016

2017

2018

Abbreviations

AFDI	Annuaire français de droit international
AJIL	American Journal of International Law
An Der Int	Anuario de derecho internacional
ASIL Proc	Proceedings of the American Society of International Law
Aust YBIL	Australian Yearbook of International Law
Austrian J Pub Intl L	Austrian Journal of Public and International Law
Berkeley J Intl L	Berkeley Journal of International Law
BFSP	British and Foreign State Papers
Br J Crim	British Journal of Criminology
BYBIL	British Yearbook of International Law
Case W Res J Intl L	Case Western Reserve Journal of International Law
Col L Rev	Columbia Law Review
Col J Transnatl L	Columbia Journal of Transnational Law
Cornell Intl LJ	Cornell International Law Journal
Crim LF	Criminal Law Forum
Crit Crim	Critical Criminology
Denv J Intl L & Pol	Denver Journal of International Law and Policy
Geo JIL	Georgetown Journal of International Law
GRP	Global Responsibility to Protect
Harv ILJ	Harvard International Law Journal
Hastings Intl & Comp L Rev	Hastings International and Comparative Law Review
ICLQ	International and Comparative Law Quarterly
IJHR	International Journal of Human Rights
ILQ	International Law Quarterly
ILR	International Law Reports
Ind JICL	Indonesian Journal of International and Comparative Law
Intl CLR	International Criminal Law Review
IRRC	International Review of the Red Cross

It YBIL	Italian Yearbook of International Law
JC&SL	Journal of Conflict and Security Law
JHR	Journal of Human Rights
JICJ	Journal of International Criminal Justice
Law & Contemp Probs	Law and Contemporary Problems
LJIL	Leiden Journal of International Law
LNOJ	League of Nations Official Journal
LRTWC	Law Reports of Trials of War Criminals
Mel JIL	Melbourne Journal of International Law
Mich St ILR	Michigan State International Law Review
Min L Rev	Minnesota Law Review
NILR	Netherlands International Law Review
Nordic JIL	Nordic Journal of International Law
NYBIL	Netherlands Yearbook of International Law
NYU JILP	New York University Journal of International Law and Policy
Off Gaz CCG	Official Gazette Control Council for Germany
Pal YBIL	Palestine Yearbook of International Law
RBDI	Revue belge de droit international
RCADI	Recueil des cours de l'Académie de droit international de La Haye
RDI	Rivista di diritto internazionale
RDISPD	Revue de droit international et de science politique et diplomatique
RDPC	Revue de droit pénal et de criminologie
RGDIP	Revue générale de droit international public
RIDP	Revue internationale de droit pénal
Santa Clara JIL	Sanat Clara Journal of International Law
Stan L Rev	Stanford Law Review
Utr L Rev	Utrecht Law Review
Vand J Transnatl L	Vanderbilt Journal of Transnational Law
Wash UGSLR	Washington University Global Studies Law Review
Yale JIL	Yale Journal of International Law
Yale LJ	Yale Law Journal
YBIIL	Yearbook of the Institute of International Law
YBILC	Yearbook of the International Law Commission

add	addendum
art	article
CAT	Convention against Torture and Other Cruel, Inhuman or Degrading Treatment or Punishment
ch	chapter
CUP	Cambridge University Press

DAISOFCJ	Draft Articles on the Immunity of State Officials from Foreign Criminal Jurisdiction
DASR	Draft Articles on State Responsibility for Internationally Wrongful Acts
DCCPSM	Draft Code of Crimes against the Peace and Security of Mankind
DCOPSM	Draft Code of Offences against the Peace and Security of Mankind
doc	document
ECOSOC	Economic and Social Council
ed	editor
edn	edition
EU	European Union
ff	and following
GA	General Assembly
HRC	Human Rights Council
ICC	International Criminal Court
ICJ	International Court of Justice
ICJ Rep	Reports of the International Court of Justice
ICLA	International Criminal Law Association
ICTR	International Criminal Tribunal for Rwanda
ICTY	International Criminal Tribunal for the Former Yugoslavia
IIL	Institute of International Law (Institut de droit international)
ILC	International Law Commission
ILM	International Legal Materials
ILO	International Labour Organisation
IMT	International Military Tribunal
IMTFE	International Military Tribunal for the Far East
ISI	Islamic State of Iraq
ISIL	Islamic State of Iraq and The Levant
ISIS	Islamic State of Iraq and Syria
LN	League of Nations
MICT	Mechanism for the International Criminal Tribunals
n	note
n^{o}	number
NATO	North Atlantic Treaty Organisation
OUP	Oxford University Press
Para	paragraph
PCEICC	Preparatory Committee on the Establishment of an International Criminal Court
PCIJ	Permanent Court of International Justice
princ	principle

reg	regulation
Res	Resolution
s	section
SC	Security Council
SCSL	Special Court for Sierra Leone
SFRY	Social Former Republic of Yugoslavia
STL	Special Tribunal for Lebanon
tit	title
tr	translation
UK	United Kingdom
UN	United Nations
UNCIO	United Nations Conference on International Organisation
UNCLOS	United Nations Convention on the Law of the Sea
UNDCPICC	United Nations Diplomatic Conference of Plenipotentiaries on the Establishment of an International Criminal Court
UNMIK	United Nations Mission in Kosovo
UNTS	United Nations Treaty Series
US	United States
USSR	Union of Soviet Socialist Republics
VCLT	Vienna Convention on the Law of Treaties
VCLTIO	Vienna Convention on the Law of Treaties between States and International Organisations or between International Organisations
vol	volume
wg	working group

Introduction

Context

In the course of the 20th century, international law progressively framed major violations committed by individuals as criminal offences. This process started at the beginning of the century with scholarly initiatives and was subsequently institutionalised via the League of Nations. Such proposals coordinated individual liability with State criminal responsibility, from a 'monistic' perspective, and aimed in particular to establish a Criminal Chamber of the Permanent Court of International Justice (PCIJ).[1]

After World War II, individual criminal responsibility was severed from State responsibility, taking a divergent path within the framework of the United Nations (UN). As to individual responsibility, following the input of the International Military Tribunals in Nuremberg (IMT) and the Far East (IMTFE), in the 1950s the UN International Law Commission (ILC) produced two draft Statutes for an International Criminal Court (ICC).[2] However, work on the issue was then suspended pending the definition of State aggression, which was only outlined in 1974.[3] The ILC resumed the codification of individual criminal responsibility in the 1980s, via the Draft Code of Crimes against the Peace and Security of Mankind (DCCPSM). The Code, which was finalised in 1996,[4] prompted the parallel adoption of a Draft Statute for an ICC in 1994.[5] The Statute provided the basis for any subsequent work by UN Committees, in view

1 Secretary General, Historical Survey of the Question of International Criminal Jurisdiction, Memorandum, UN Doc A/CN.4/7/Rev.1 (1949) 8 ff.

2 Committee on International Criminal Jurisdiction, Report, Annexe: Draft Statute for an International Criminal Court, UN Doc A/AC.48/4 (1952) 46(1) *AJIL Suppl* 1–11; Id, Report, Annexe: Revised Draft Statute for an International Criminal Court, UN General Assembly Ninth Session Supplement n° 12 A/2645 (1954) 23–26.

3 General Assembly, Definition of Aggression, UN Doc A/RES/3314 (XXIX), 14 December 1974.

4 ILC, Report to the General Assembly on the Work of the Forty-Eighth Session, UN Doc A/51/10 (1996) 2(2) *YBILC* 17–56.

5 Id, Report to the General Assembly on the Work of the Forty-Sixth Session, UN Doc A/49/10 (1994) 2(2) *YBILC* 26–67.

of the drafting of an international treaty, which was finally adopted in 1998 and entered into force in 2002.[6]

Following the adoption of the Convention on the Prevention and Punishment of the Crime of Genocide in 1949,[7] State responsibility was first systemically considered in the 1950s from the standpoint of injury to aliens.[8] A more holistic approach emerged in the 1970s, when the ILC addressed the issue as a 'secondary' consequence of the 'primary' law of treaties.[9] In the first phase of the project (1972–1996), the Commission discussed the possibility of regulating major wrongful acts as 'State crimes'.[10] The second phase of the work (1996–2001), however, led to relinquishing this stance, so as to finally characterise major wrongful acts as serious breaches of peremptory norms.[11] Most scholars thus refer to 'State aggravated Responsibility'.[12] Others, however, still rely on the notion of a 'State crime'.[13] Eventually, the ILC's Draft Articles on State Responsibility for Internationally Wrongful Acts (DASR) were submitted to the attention of States,[14] but they have not yet led to the adoption of a binding treaty.

The IMT held that '[c]rimes under international law are committed by men, not by abstract entities'.[15] However, the Tribunal made such a statement to reject the argument that only States are responsible under international law and considered that 'international law imposes duties and liabilities upon individuals as well as upon States'.[16] Within the context of its work on the DCCPSM, twice the ILC debated the possibility of linking individual and State criminal liability, but the Commission eventually disregarded the option without developing a critical normative analysis:[17] are there any loopholes in such a regulatory approach?

6 Rome Statute of the International Criminal Court, adopted 17 July 1998, 2187 UNTS 90, in force 1 July 2001.
7 'Genocide Convention', adopted 9 December 1948, 78 UNTS 278, in force 12 January 1951.
8 Francisco García-Amador, Report on International Responsibility, UN Doc A/CN.4/96 (1956) 2(2) *YBILC* 173–231.
9 Roberto Ago, Third Report on State Responsibility: The Internationally Wrongful Act of the State, Source of International Responsibility, UN Doc A/CN.4/246 and Add.1–3 (1971) 2(1) *YBILC* 202, para 15.
10 ILC, Report (1996) 60.
11 Id, Report to the General Assembly on the Work of the Fifty-Third Session, UN Doc A/56/10 (2001) 2(2) *YBILC* 112.
12 Beatrice Bonafè, *The Relationship between State and Individual Responsibility for International Crimes* (Martinus Nijhoff, 2009) 17.
13 Andreas Zimmermann and Michael Teichmann, 'State Responsibility for International Crimes', in André Nollkaemper and Harmen van der Wilt (eds), *System Criminality in International Law* (CUP, 2009) 299 and 312; Nigel White, 'Responses of Political Organs to Crimes by States', ibid, 315.
14 ILC, Report (2001) 25, paras 72–73.
15 IMT, Judgment of 1 October 1946 (1947) 41(1) *AJIL* 221.
16 Ibid 220.
17 ILC, Report to the General Assembly on the Work of the Thirty-Fifth Session, UN Doc A/38/10 (1983) 2(2) *YBILC* 13–15, paras 45–61; ILC, Report to the General Assembly on the Work of the Thirty-Sixth Session, UN Doc A/39/10 (1984) 2(2) *YBILC* 11, para 32.

Some scholars have pointed out that research on the relationship between individual criminal liability and State aggravated responsibility is 'very modest' and 'many fundamental questions remain open.'[18] Others have underscored that international instruments 'do not provide any guidance as to how overlaps, interplay or contradiction between the two regimes can be resolved'.[19] Some commentators think that the notion of a 'State crime' is essential to 'close the loopholes and overcome the inconsistencies of the current system.'[20] Antônio Cançado Trindade concludes that international law should not 'keep on intending to elude' the question of the crime of a State.[21] Article 58 of the 2001 DASR and Article 25(4) of the ICC Statute currently provide that State responsibility and individual responsibility are without prejudice to one another. Situations such as the humanitarian crisis in Syria confirm that critical problems are far from being resolved.[22]

This book aims to shed light on the consistency between individual criminal responsibility and State aggravated responsibility in international law, via a systemic analysis of relevant regulatory instruments. The research is conceived of as a normative study on the substantive elements of individual and State offences as well as relevant procedural implications. A key component is attribution of responsibility, given that State responsibility arises from the conduct of its organs and agents and is therefore based on individual liability: the same conduct generates dual responsibility.

Analysis

The research is underpinned by the basic distinction between 'primary' and 'secondary' norms, which is key to both individual and State responsibility. According to Hans Kelsen, 'primary norms' are those prohibiting specific conduct, such as the obligation prohibiting aggression.[23] 'Secondary norms' outline sanctions applying to violations of primary norms, such as the duty to provide reparation in the case of aggression.[24] In the view of Herbert Hart, 'secondary norms' regulate power, that is, the 'ability to vary legal relations (rights and duties)'.[25]

18 André Nollkaemper, 'Systemic Effects of International Responsibility for International Crimes' (2010) 8(1) *Santa Clara JIL* 316.

19 Philippa Webb, 'Binocular Vision: State Responsibility and Individual Criminal Responsibility for Genocide', in Larissa Van Den Herik and Carsten Stahn (eds), *The Diversification and Fragmentation of International Criminal Law* (Brill, 2012) 120.

20 Joachim Wolf, 'Individual Responsibility and Collective State Responsibility for International Crimes: Separate or Complementary Concepts under International Law?', in Bartłomiej Krzan (ed), *Prosecuting International Crimes: A Multidisciplinary Approach* (Brill, 2016) 52.

21 Antônio Augusto Cançado Trindade, 'Complementarity between State Responsibility and Individual Responsibility for Grave Violations of Human Rights: The Crime of State Revised', in Maurizio Ragazzi (ed), *International Responsibility Today* (Brill, 2005) 268.

22 Nina Jørgensen, 'The Concept of State Crimes in the Context of the Syrian Crisis' (2015) 18 *Pal YBIL* 175.

23 Hans Kelsen, *General Theory of Norms* (1979, Clarendon Press, tr Michael Hartney, 1991) 142.

24 Ibid.

25 Herbert Hart, *The Concept of Law* (1961, OUP, 3rd edn, 2012) 94.

Within this framework, according to Willem Riphagen, 'tertiary norms' govern measures of enforcement following the breach of a sanction.[26] In sum, from a temporal perspective (t), the research is based on the following slightly adapted schematic pattern:

(t_1) Primary procedural norms (sources)
→ Primary substantive norms (obligations) → Breach
→ (t_2) Secondary procedural norms (dispute settlement)
→ Secondary substantive norms (sanctions) → Breach
→ (t_3) Tertiary procedural norms (enforcement)

Along these lines, the book includes three chapters. The first chapter has a historical focus, the second considers the breach of a primary norm and the third one analyses its implications from the standpoint of secondary and tertiary norms.

Chapter 1 explores the historical evolution of regulatory initiatives in the matter of State and individual responsibility. Key steps in this development are the pre-World War II projects for a Universal Criminal Code, a Criminal Chamber of the PCIJ and a Permanent Court of International Criminal Justice. The research then moves to considering regulatory initiatives undertaken after World War II, particularly within the context of the UN. Core instruments include the Charters, Statutes and projects for *ad hoc* international criminal tribunals and the ICC, the Genocide Convention, the ILC's DCCPSM, the UN Charter,[27] the ILC's DASR, UN General Assembly Resolution 3314 (XXIX) on the Definition of Aggression and the UN Draft Comprehensive Convention against International Terrorism.[28] The analysis shows how these regulatory initiatives moved from coordinating to disjoining individual and State responsibility.

Chapter 2 focuses on the breach of a primary norm, that is, the offence. The research first considers the common general elements of individual and State breaches. Within this context, the analysis underscores the non-severable *erga omnes* nature of individual and State violations. Furthermore, the research considers the attribution of conduct of individual organs and agents to the State, either objectively or via negligence and intent. In light of such a theoretical framework, the chapter explores the nexus between individual and State responsibility for specific dual *erga omnes* offences, notably aggression, core war crimes, core crimes against humanity, genocide and terrorism.

Chapter 3 focuses on the secondary implications of the offence in terms of dispute settlement, sanctions and enforcement. The research thus considers UN procedures, notably those centred on the Security Council, State countermeasures and other dispute settlement and implementation mechanisms, in parallel

26 Willem Riphagen, Fourth Report on the Content, Forms and Degrees of International Responsibility (Part 2 of the Draft Articles), UN Doc A/CN.366 and Add.1 (1983) 2(1) *YBILC* 8, para 33.
27 Adopted 26 June 1945, 1 UNTS XVI, in force 24 October 1945.
28 UN Doc A/59/894, 12 August 2005.

with domestic and international criminal jurisdictions. This analysis singles out intersections between the different procedures for individual and State responsibility in the case of dual *erga omnes* offences. The research further assesses the implications of such a theoretical framework by considering critical practical situations, notably the Bosnian genocide; humanitarian crises in the Former Yugoslavia, Libya and Syria; the Iraq wars and counterterrorism in Afghanistan, Syria and Iraq.

In sum, the research critically assesses regulation, scholarly opinions and case law reported mostly in English and French, covering around 100 years of the history of international law, from the end of the 19th century to the beginning of the 21st century. Whilst it does not provide universal coverage of relevant references, this approach ensures a minimum essential basis. Indeed, work undertaken on individual and State responsibility prior to World War II is abundantly available in French, whereas work undertaken after World War II is largely accessible in English. By bringing together pre- and post-World War II studies, the book aims to provide a comprehensive perspective on core mechanisms of the international legal system. The research thus aims to shed light on the question to what extent the multilateral dimension of the law of State responsibility is 'just a dream based on an optimistic vision [...] or [whether] there is still a chance to make this dream a reality in the future'.[29]

29 Pierre-Marie Dupuy, 'The Deficiencies of the Law of State Responsibility Relating to Breaches of "Obligations Owed to the International Community as a Whole": Suggestions for Avoiding the Obsolescence of Aggravated Responsibility', in Antonio Cassese (ed), *Realizing Utopia: The Future of International Law* (OUP, 2012) 214.

1 From monism to dualism

Introduction

The criminal responsibility of natural persons developed during the course of the 20th century. On the one hand, this has led to the adoption of international instruments that (transnationally) harmonise domestic crimes, criminal procedures and sanctions, such as the International Convention for the Suppression of Terrorist Bombings.[1] On the other hand, the trend has prompted the adoption of international instruments that outline international crimes, procedures and sanctions, particularly the Statute of the ICC. The two layers interact, with respect to both substance and procedure.[2]

Critical instruments have also been adopted in the matter of State responsibility, which sometimes qualifies as 'criminal' and at other times as 'aggravated'. Thus, for instance, the Genocide Convention regulates genocide with respect to both individual and State conduct. However, whilst some commentators talk about 'State criminality',[3] most writers are hesitant to go beyond the recognition of State responsibility as 'aggravated'.[4] Such an approach initially developed from the 17th century along the lines of the perception of war as being State aggravated conduct, which has subsequently extended to other acts,[5] such as genocide and terrorism. Hesitation and discontinuous terminology arise from the equal sovereign nature of States in international law, whereby the horizontal character of sovereignty clashes with the vertical centralisation of criminal law and procedure.

This chapter provides a historical overview of key regulation, *de lege lata* and *ferenda*, in the matter of individual criminal responsibility and State aggravated,

1 Adopted 15 December 1997, 2149 UNTS 256, in force 23 May 2001.

2 Neil Boister, 'Transnational Criminal Law?' (2003) 14(5) *EJIL* 962; André Nollkaemper and Harmen van der Wilt, 'Conclusions and Outlook', in Nollkaemper and Van Der Wilt, *System Criminality* (2009) 344 and 352–353; Linda Carter, Mark Ellis and Charles Jalloh, *The International Criminal Court in an Effective Global Justice System* (Edward Elgar, 2016) 16 ff.

3 Zimmermann and Teichmann, 'State Responsibility' (2009) 299.

4 Nina Jørgensen, *The Responsibility of States for International Crimes* (OUP, 2000) 35; Bonafè, *The Relationship* (2009) 17.

5 Hugo Grotius, *On the Law of Peace and War* (1625, CUP, Stephen Neff ed, 2012) 301 ff.

or criminal, responsibility, under particular and general international law. The analysis not only presents the different regulatory initiatives from a historical perspective, but also explores them through a substantive and procedural legal lens. The aim is to highlight how the two forms of responsibility have evolved pre- and post-World Wars I and II. The study follows a chronological order, which underscores the controversial evolution of the relationship between individual and State responsibility. Within this framework, basic common strands emerge, whereby consistent initiatives are contextually explained, such as regulation prompted by the League of Nations or the Draft Code of Offences against the Peace and Security of Mankind (DCOPSM) developed by the UN ILC. The plurality of approaches helps to underscore the evolution of the theoretical concepts that underpin the different regulatory initiatives, notably as concerns the universal scope and nature of the obligations breached by aggravated, or criminal, responsibility of natural persons and States.

1.1 Monism: coordinating individual and State responsibility prior to World War II

1.1.1 The dawn of criminal responsibility in international law: proposals for a universal criminal code (1860–1919)

The first proposal for an international criminal court goes back to Gustave Moynier, President of the International Committee of the Red Cross (ICRC). Moynier suggested the establishment of an international criminal jurisdiction to adjudicate upon and prevent breaches of the 1864 Geneva Convention for the Amelioration of the Condition of the Wounded in Armies in the Field.[6] Different initiatives followed at the beginning of the 20th century, aiming to define a system for international criminal law from the standpoint of both substance and procedure. Notably, Moynier's proposal is part of the progressive codification of the rules on the peaceful settlement of international disputes and the regulation of the law of war via the Hague Conventions of 1899 and 1907,[7] which built upon core regulation embedded in the 1964 Geneva Convention. These projects constitute the background for codification developed after World Wars I and II.

After the end of World War I, on 25 January 1919 the Paris Peace Conference held in Versailles established a Commission to assess the responsibility of individuals allegedly accountable for the facts that took place during the war. The Commission submitted a Report envisaging the establishment of an international criminal tribunal.[8] As a follow-up, the Conference adopted Article 227 of the

6 Adopted 22 August 1864, in force 22 June 1865. See Christopher Hall, 'The First Proposal for a Permanent International Criminal Court' (2010) 322 *IRRC* 60 ff.

7 Available at https://ihl-databases.icrc.org/applic/ihl/ihl.nsf/vwTreaties1949.xsp.

8 Commission on the Responsibility of the Authors of the War and on Enforcement of Penalties, Report to the Preliminary Peace Conference: Excerpts (1919), in Secretary General, Historical Survey (1949) 47–52.

Versailles Treaty,[9] which arraigned William II of Hohenzollern, former German Emperor, for waging war as 'a supreme offence against international morality and the sanctity of treaties'.[10] A 'special tribunal', comprising five judges appointed by the United States (US), Great Britain, France, Italy and Japan, had jurisdiction over the offence. By contrast, Articles 228 and 229 established the trial of other war criminals by military tribunals of the Allied and Associated Powers. According to Hans Kelsen, the acceptance of such provisions by Germany signified recognition of individual criminal responsibility for acts of State.[11] However, the Netherlands refused to extradite the Emperor and Germany refused to surrender officials accused of war crimes. The Allied Powers therefore agreed to the officers being judged by the Supreme Court of Leipzig, so as not to destabilise the newly established Republic of Weimar. The Court only convicted twelve officers with light sentences.[12]

A bilateral approach to invocation of State responsibility characterises this historical period, based on the principle of reparation. However, some scholars suggested the establishment of an aggravated regime of responsibility, whereby breaches of *erga omnes* obligations were supposed to trigger collective State reaction and aggravated sanctions, including adequate satisfaction, fines and assurances of non-repetition.[13] In this respect, the Treaty of Versailles imposed on Germany sanctions under Articles 159–213 that some scholars considered to be mainly aimed at punishing State criminality, notably for aggressive war, for instance, the obligations to demobilise and reduce armed forces under Article 159.[14] Furthermore, Articles 11 and 16 of the Covenant of the League of Nations qualified war as an *erga omnes* breach, affecting 'the whole League' and entailing specific sanctions, such as the severance of financial and trade relations. The Council of the League was mandated to coordinate the collective enforcement of these sanctions.

1.1.2 Interwar coordination (1920–1939)

1.1.2.1 Triggering initiatives within the League of Nations

Following the experience of World War I, different initiatives were undertaken within and outside the League of Nations in order to establish a system of

9 Adopted 28 June 1919, in force 10 January 1920.

10 Kirsten Sellars, 'The First World War, Wilhelm II and Article 227: The Origin of the Idea of "Aggression" in International Criminal Law', in Claus Creß and Stefan Barriaga (eds), *The Crime of Aggression: A Commentary* (CUP, 2017) 34 ff.

11 Hans Kelsen, *Peace through Law* (1944, North Carolina Press, Garland Edition, 1973) 109–110.

12 Julio Barboza, 'International Criminal Law' (1999) 278 *RCADI* 33–34.

13 Elihu Root, 'The Outlook for International Law' (1916) 10(1) *AJIL* 7–11; Amos Peaslee, 'The Sanction of International Law' (1916) 10(2) *AJIL* 335–336; Georg Nolte, 'From Dionisio Anzilotti to Roberto Ago: The Classical International Law of State Responsibility and the Traditional Primacy of a Bilateral Conception of Inter-State Relations' (2002) 13(5) *EJIL* 1087–1088.

14 Charles Fenwick, 'Germany and the Crime of the World War' (1929) 23(4) *AJIL* 815; Nolte, 'From Dionisio Anzilotti' (2002) 1089–1090.

international criminal law. Within the context of its work on the establishment of a PCIJ under Article 14 of the Covenant of the League, an Advisory Committee of Jurists put forward a first project. In 1920, the President of the Committee proposed the adoption of a Recommendation to the Council and the General Assembly of the League on the institution of a High Court of International Justice. This would have had competence 'for the purpose of trying crimes against international public order, and against the universal law of nations' (Article 3).[15] The Court could adjudicate upon a referral by the Assembly or Council of the League of Nations (Article 4).

> Article 3
> The High Court of Justice shall be competent to try crimes constituting a breach of international public order or against the universal law of nations, referred to it by the Assembly or by the Council of the League of Nations.
>
> Article 4
> The Court shall have the power to define the nature of the crime, to fix the penalty and to decide the appropriate means of carrying out the sentence.

More generally, the possibility was envisaged of establishing the compulsory competence of the PCIJ after exhaustion of diplomatic means,[16] which was nonetheless eventually abandoned in favour of consensual jurisdiction under Article 36 of the PCIJ Statute. This approach followed critiques by France and the United Kingdom (UK), which considered it dangerous to allow States to act unilaterally in court against one another.[17] Eventually, the Council and Assembly of the League of Nations decided that the question of State criminal responsibility was not ready for definition and submitted it to the attention of institutions specialised in international law in view of a Conference on the topic.[18]

Later proposals suggested the institution of an international criminal court with competence over both individual and State responsibility, as well as the responsibility of other legal persons.[19] In 1923, the Draft Treaty on Mutual Assistance prepared by the Commission on Armaments of the League of Nations qualified

15 See the text of the proposal in Secretary General, Historical Survey (1949) 9–10. For a scholarly opinion, see Henri Donnedieu De Vabres, 'La Cour permanente de justice internationale et sa vocation en matière criminelle' (1924) 1 *RIDP* 175–201.

16 See Frances Kellor and Antonia Hatvanj, *Security against War* (MacMillan, 1924) 458 ff.

17 Ibid 461 ff.

18 Lord Phillimore, 'An International Criminal Court and the Resolution of the Committee of Jurists' (1922–23) 3 *BYBIL* 84; James Leslie Brierly, 'Do We Need an International Criminal Court?' (1927) 8 *BYBIL* 81.

19 On the development of projects for the institution of an international criminal court between 1919 and 1930, see Manley Hudson, 'The Proposed International Criminal Court' (1938) 32(3) *AJIL* 549–551.

war as a 'State crime' and envisaged collective countermeasures.[20] The Treaty, however, never entered into force. In 1924, the Fifth Assembly of the League of Nations adopted the Geneva Protocol for the Pacific Settlement of International Disputes,[21] which qualified war as an 'international crime'. Similarly, the League of Nations Resolution relative to Wars of Aggression of 24 September 1927 banned aggressive war as a means to resolve inter-State disputes and qualified it as an 'international crime'.[22] In 1928, when the Kellogg-Briand Pact declared war an instrument of 'criminal policy',[23] Henri Donnedieu De Vabres posited that the creation of an international criminal court was necessary to prevent and repress the crime of aggression.[24]

1.1.2.2 Establishing the Fundamental Principles of an International Legal Code for the Repression of International Crimes

In 1925, based on a Report by Professor Vespasian Pella the 13th Conference of the Inter-Parliamentary Union adopted a Resolution on the Criminality of Aggressive War and International Repression.[25] The Resolution mandated a Sub-Committee to consider the causes of aggressive war and prepare the preliminary draft of an International Legal Code for the Repression of International Crimes, the Fundamental Principles of which were outlined in an Annexe.[26] Principles 1 and 9(B)(a) criminalised State conduct, such as 'aggressive war' or 'raising effectives or arming beyond the limits laid down in conventions or treaties', and individual conduct such as the 'declaration by a sovereign of a war of aggression'. Principle 2 linked individual and State aggression. Principle 4 further provided that 'offences committed by States or by individuals' should have been 'laid down and penalties provided for in advance in enactments drawn in precise terms', based on 'the principle *nulla poena sine lege*'. Furthermore, Principles 10 and 13 envisaged the institution of a Criminal Chamber within the PCIJ, having jurisdiction over individuals, whilst the Chambers of the Court in combined session had competence over State responsibility. Principle 11 instituted an International Public Prosecutor's Department and conferred preliminary investigations

20 Adopted 15 October 1923, LN Doc A.111.1923.1.

21 Adopted 2 October 1924, LN Doc C.606.M.211.1924.IX.

22 LN Doc A.119.1927.IX, (1927) 8 LNOJ Spec Supp 51, 155.

23 General Treaty for Renunciation of War as an Instrument of National Policy, adopted 27 August 1928, 94 LNTS 57, in force 25 July 1929.

24 Henri Donnedieu De Vabres, *Les principes modernes du droit pénal international* (Sirey, 1928, republished by Pantheon-Assas, 2004) 418. See also Florian Jeßberger, 'The Modern Doctrinal Debate on the Crime of Aggression', in Claus Kreß and Stefan Barriaga, *The Crime* (2017) 289–290.

25 Inter-Parliamentary Union, Resolution on the Criminality of Wars of Aggression and the Organization of International Repressive Measures, in Secretary General, Historical Survey (1949) 70.

26 Fundamental Principles of an International Legal Code for the Repression of International Crimes, in Secretary General, Historical Survey (1949) 71–74.

and the preparation of evidence to *ad hoc* commissions of enquiry set up to discharge police duties.

Principle 8(A) did not establish a clear distinction between sanctions and countermeasures and thus classified as sanctions the withdrawal of treaty rights as well as resort to the use of force. Interestingly, some sanctions addressed nationals of the responsible State abroad, for instance, sequestration of property (Principle 8(A)(b)). In the case of violent aggression, the Council of the League of Nations had an executive role with respect to 'urgent counter police measures' and 'decisions' adopted by the PCIJ, in cooperation with all States of the League (Principles 16 and 17). The Council also had an executive function with respect to the judgments of the Court (Principle 16(2)). Individual sanctions included primary obligations such as imprisonment, fines and exile, as well as accessory sanctions, such as the incapacity to hold diplomatic functions abroad (Principle 8(B)).

1.1.2.3 Individual initiatives for a comprehensive International Criminal Code

In 1925, Professor Quintiliano Saldaña published a Draft Project for an International Criminal Code.[27] The Code criminalised State aggression, the use of force (Article 43) and other wrongful acts to be defined according to the *nullum crimen sine lege* principle (Articles 3, 4 and 44). Saldaña further considered for States the categories of crimes against humanity and war crimes.[28] The Code applied the same principles to crimes committed by natural persons.

Saldaña grounded State responsibility in the classical principle that the conduct of an organ or agent of the State generates dual liability (Article 41),[29] based on negligence and intent (Article 44). Consequently, the Project envisaged the competence of the PCIJ to adjudicate upon the criminal responsibility of individuals (Article 23) and that of the Council of the League of Nations or the PCIJ over State crimes (Article 57).[30] Article 96 vested the Council of the League of Nations with the power to decide upon the adoption of preliminary measures against criminal States, so as to impose orders for cessation of conduct threatening world peace. Preliminary measures included demilitarisation, warning, evacuation, arms control, armistice and occupation under Articles 96–102. These measures were additional to those imposed upon individuals, including restrictions such as pre-emptive detention and bail under Articles 104–108.

27 Quintiliano Saldaña, Avant-Projet de Code pénal international – Partie générale (1925) 10(5) *RCADI* 387–422.

28 Id, 'La justice pénale internationale', ibid 298–307.

29 Id, Avant-Projet (1925) 403, Partie générale, Livre Premier (L'infraction criminelle et sa répression internationale, Titre premier (L'infraction), ch IV (L'infraction en rapport aux personnes), Première section (L'État délinquant), art 41 (Responsabilité directe de l'État)).

30 See also Saldaña, 'La justice' (1925) 10(5) *RCADI* 348, 358–359 and 366–369.

The Project established economic sanctions, social sanctions and military sanctions against a criminal State, without drawing a clear distinction between sanctions and enforcement measures:

> Article 57
> Sanctions imposed by the Council (or the PCIJ) on delinquent States include:
> a) Economic, commercial and financial sanctions;
> b) Social, diplomatic and legal sanctions;
> c) Military, naval and aerial sanctions.[31]

Economic sanctions included the interruption of commercial and financial relations (Article 58), compensation for breaching the law of war (Article 59), embargo (Article 60), other economic restrictions (Articles 61–62), reparation for repressive war (Article 63) and reparation for breaching international obligations (Article 64).

Social sanctions encompassed the interruption of diplomatic relations (Article 65) and personal relations (Article 66), nullity of treaties (Article 67), exclusion from the League of Nations (Article 68), suspension of treaties and conventions (Article 69) and prohibition of access to jurisdictional remedies for nationals of the responsible State (Article 70).

Military sanctions notably included collective war against an aggressor State, however safeguarding political independence and territorial integrity (Articles 70–73).

With regard to individuals, the Project outlined sanctions against liberty and rights. Sanctions against liberty included the prohibition of entry into territory and stay (Article 77), forced domicile (Article 78), arrest at domicile (Article 79), imprisonment (Articles 80–87), deportation (Article 88) and expulsion (Article 89). Sanctions against rights included disqualification from civil and political rights (Articles 91–92), from a profession or from acting in court (Article 93), fines (Article 94) and confiscation (Article 95).

The Project also vested the Council of the League of Nations with executive and decisional power on the implementation of criminal sanctions against States under Articles 50, 109–110 and 112. Consequently, under Articles 113–114 the Project abolished countermeasures as a means to enforce sanctions. Articles 71–72 also required that the State Members of the League of Nations would have to make available necessary military forces for implementing the decisions of the Court.[32]

31 Translation by the author.
32 Saldaña, Avant-Projet (1925) 405, Partie générale, art 50 (Aggravation de la responsabilité de l'État – Résistance passive), 411–412, arts 71 and 72 (Répression ou châtiment militaire (La guerre-peine)).

1.1.2.4 The ICLA's Draft Statute for a Criminal Chamber of the PCIJ and the Global Repressive Code

In 1925, within the context of the work of the International Criminal Law Association (ICLA), Judge Megalos Caloyanni proposed a Draft Statute for the PCIJ.[33] Under Article 25 of the Draft Statute, the Court had competence on war crimes and crimes against humanity. As a follow-up, in 1926 the ICLA proposed the establishment of the criminal competence of the PCIJ in the matter of State responsibility.[34] The proposal further prompted Caloyanni to develop its initial project into the Statute of the ICC, adjudicating separately upon the criminal responsibility of States and individuals (Preliminary Article) for war crimes and other internationally defined crimes (Article 21).[35] Article 22 of the Statute envisaged the possibility of a declaratory judgment, not imposing a sanction, or the imposition of the sanctions of reparation and fines. In the matter of enforcement, Article 37 of the Statute proposed that any State Party implement the decisions and orders of the Court upon request:

> Article 37 (Enforcement of the Judgments and Orders of the Court)
> Judgments delivered by the Court are enforced by the State of nationality of the person or, if the person is Stateless, by the State of residence [...]
> A judgment or order against the State is enforced upon request by any contracting State.

In 1927, the ICLA adopted a Draft Statute for an ICC, slightly adapting the Caloyanni proposal.[36]

In 1928, Professor Vespasian Pella proposed a Draft Statute for a Criminal Chamber of the PCIJ, within the context of the ICLA.[37] Article 35 of the Draft Statute provided that a Criminal Chamber of the PCIJ had jurisdiction over crimes committed by States or their nationals. The Chamber would have had exclusive competence over individual crimes triggering an international armed conflict, thus excluding domestic jurisdiction.[38] Articles 20–27 established that either the Council of the League of Nations seized by a State or a State authorised by the Council could bring a case to the attention of the

33 ICLA, Projet de Statut pour la Cour permanente de justice internationale criminelle, by Megalos A Caloyanni (1925) II *RIDP* 314–325.

34 Id, Voeux adoptés par le Congrès de Bruxelles (1926) III *RIDP* 462–464.

35 ICLA, Statut de la Cour criminelle internationale, by Megalos A Caloyanni (1926) III *RIDP* 469–491.

36 Secretary General, Historical Survey (1949) 61, Annexe 4.

37 ICLA, Projet de Statut pour la création d'une Chambre criminelle au sein de la Cour Permanente de Justice Internationale, by Vespasian Pella (1928) V *RIDP* 293–307, also reproduced in Vespasian Pella, *La guerre-crime et les criminels de guerre – Réflexions sur la justice pénale internationale ce qu'elle est et ce qu'elle devrait être* (Sottile and Pedone, 1946) Annexe I, 129–144.

38 Pella, *La guerre-crime* (1946) 123.

Criminal Chamber of the PCIJ.[39] Under Article 40, the Council could develop preliminary inquiries with the support of special commissions, whereby a political phase preceded the judicial one.[40] Articles 16 and 56(2) established a prosecution organ, including three members, for investigations concerning State responsibility.[41] Pella also envisaged the institution of supportive international police organs or investigative commissions for collecting evidence.[42] Articles 65 and 67 allowed proceedings *in absentia*. Under Article 1, the Project integrated the Covenant of the League of Nations and could have later integrated the UN Charter.[43]

In the case of proceedings addressing exclusively individuals but raising the possibility of State responsibility, Article 31 of the Draft Statute compelled the Criminal Chamber of the PCIJ to suspend action and refer a case to the Council of the League of Nations. This provision clearly raised the question of a possible overlap between individual and State liability. However, Pella had in mind a distinction between 'individual criminal law', concerning natural persons, and 'interstate criminal law'.[44] Under Article 28, the Project also envisaged for a directly injured State the possibility of acting as a civil party in proceedings before the Criminal Chamber of the PCIJ to obtain reparation.[45] Article 64 subjected decisions against States to revision, according to Article 61 of the PCIJ Statute. The decisions of the Court were compulsory and notified to the Council, which was entrusted to decide on necessary enforcement measures:

> Article 68
> Decisions delivered by the Court are compulsory. They are notified to the Council of the League of Nations,* which takes international measures necessary to apply sanctions against States.
>
> *Security Council

The Project thus outlined a system whereby the Council fundamentally had executive functions and was largely subject to the jurisdictional power of the Criminal Chamber of the PCIJ.

39 Vespasian Pella, Rapport sur un Projet de Statut d'une Cour criminelle internationale présenté au Conseil de direction de l'Association internationale de droit pénal (1928) V *RIDP* 287–288.

40 ICLA, Projet de Statut (1928) 139–144, ch V, arts 40–49, ch VI, arts 50–63, ch VII, arts 64–70.

41 See also Vespasian Pella, De l'influence d'une juridiction criminelle internationale, Report to the ICLA Brussels Congress (1926) III *RIDP* 415–417.

42 Pella, De l'influence (1926) 417–418.

43 Vespasian Pella, 'La codification du droit pénal international' (1952) 56(3) *RGDIP* 339–340 and 425–428.

44 He actually distinguished 'international criminal law' ('*droit international pénal*') from 'inter-State criminal law' ('*droit pénal inter-étatique*'). See Vespasian Pella, 'La répression des crimes contre la personnalité de l'État'(1930) 33(3) *RCADI* 818–820.

45 See also Pella, 'La codification' (1952) 448–450.

In 1935, Professor Pella further drafted the Project for a Global Repressive Code as a substantive complement to the Draft Statute for the ICC.[46] The Code posited that the 'criminal law of the future' be underpinned by the concept of 'plural responsibility', involving natural and legal persons, for crimes regarded as breaches of *erga omnes* obligations protecting the fundamental interests of the international community:[47]

> Title 1, Chapter 2
> International offences and responsible persons
> 2. Responsible persons: (a) States; (b) natural persons; (c) national and international legal persons.[48]

The Code established a list of 12 State crimes, notably aggression (1), which Pella considered a form of collective criminality,[49] and violent acts against other States that could qualify as terrorism (6):

> Title 2, Chapter 1
> State offences
> 1. The crime of aggressive war consists of the fact that a State commits first one of the following acts: a) declaring war to another State; b) invasion by a State armed forces of the territory of another State, with or without a declaration of war; c) attack, by the ground, naval or aerial forces of a State, of the territory, ships or aircraft of another State, with or without a declaration of war; e) supporting on its territory armed bands which invade the territory of another State, or refusing to take on its territory all the measures available to deprive such bands of any aid or protection, despite a request of the invading State [...]
> 6. The fact that a State tolerates on its territory or provides aid or assistance to any individuals or organisations preparing offences against the interest of another State, notably: a) offences against life or liberty of either foreign Heads of State or Members of the Government, or political, administrative or judicial bodies of a foreign State; b) attacks against public foreign or international buildings, railways, aircraft and other means of communication; c) association in view of committing such offences.[50]
>
> ...

46 ICLA, Plan d'un Code répressif mondial, by Vespasian Pella (1935) 12(4) *RIDP* 348, reproduced in Vespasian Pella, *La guerre-crime* (1946) Annexe II, 145–156.
47 Pella, *La guerre-crime* (1946) 35 and 51–52.
48 Translation by the author.
49 Secretary General, Draft Code of Offences against the Peace and Security of Mankind, Memorandum by Vespasian Pella (ICLA President), UN Doc A/CN.4/39 (1950) 2(2) *YBILC* 293, para 35.
50 Translation by the author.

The same acts gave rise to the responsibility of individuals:

> Title 2, Chapter 2
> Offences committed by individuals
> 1. The fact of a Head of State or other qualified persons of taking the initiative of or preparing the execution of acts under sections 1–12 of the previous Chapter, as well as any association or agreement in view of the commission of such acts.[51]

The Code also criminalised other legal entities for some of these acts, notably in connection with aggression. The crime of aggression was indeed critical to the establishment of a comprehensive system of international criminal law:[52]

> Title 2, Chapter 3
> Offences committed by legal entities other than States
> Offences can be committed by non-State legal persons, first and foremost the fact of facilitating the preparation or execution of an act under sections 1, 2, 4 and 11 of chapter 1 [State offences].[53]

These rules envisaged international criminal law as the discipline that 'in view of the defence of the international order, determines crimes against the peace and security of mankind, consequent sanctions and conditions for the responsibility of individuals, States and other legal persons'.[54] Thus, according to Pella:

> [P]rospective international criminal law ['*droit pénal de l'avenir*', as opposed to 'classical' international criminal law] is the ramification of public international law that outlines the offences, establishes sanctions and conditions for the responsibility of individuals and States. It encompasses the substantive and formal rules that govern the exercise of the repression of acts committed by States or individuals, upsetting the public international order and harmony among people.[55]

51 Translation by the author. See also Pella, *La guerre-crime* (1946) 16, 32–33, 49 and 57.
52 Jeßberger, 'The Modern Doctrinal Debate' (2017) 292.
53 Translation by the author. It was later considered that acts committed during World War II proved the responsibility of non-State legal entities. A note to tit 2, ch 3 of the Code republished in 1946 indeed provided:

> Relevant documents were discovered concerning the activity of certain German legal persons. Among those having subsidiaries abroad, several were responsible for grave breaches, notably espionage. Others facilitated or organised atrocious experimentation on human beings in concentration camps.

On criminal sanctions addressing legal entities under international law, see Secretary General, Draft Code (1950) 320, para 80. See also Pella, 'La codification' (1952) 347.
54 Secretary General, Draft Code (1950) 294, para 36, translation by the author.
55 Vespasian Pella, *La criminalité collective des États et le droit pénal de l'avenir* (Imprimerie de l'État de Romanie, 2nd edn, 1926) 168, n 103, translation by the author.

These were the foundations of a 'new', 'universal' and 'interstate' criminal law, which Pella meaningfully defined as 'public international criminal law'.[56]

Under the Code, criminal sanctions for States included: (a) diplomatic sanctions, such as the prohibition of diplomatic relations; (b) legal sanctions, such as the prohibition of standing before international tribunals; (c) economic sanctions, such as economic isolation, and (d) other sanctions, such as the disqualification from participation in international organisations, temporary occupation and loss of independence.[57] These were inspired by sanctions established under Article 16(1) of the Covenant of the League of Nations.

The Code also outlined security measures against the responsible State, so as to ensure non-repetition, including obligations such as the destruction of strategic infrastructure, destruction and control of military industry, confiscation of armaments, reduction of military contingents, financial control, establishment of demilitarised zones, education control and control of State activities.[58] These measures were based on different constraints imposed on Germany under the Treaty of Versailles, notably according to Articles 31–117 (Political Clauses for Europe), Articles 118–158 (Rights and Interests of Germany outside Europe) and Articles 428–453 (Guarantees).

The Code also established sanctions against non-State legal entities. These included admonition, fines and security measures, prohibition of establishing subsidiary companies abroad, disqualification from specific activities, capital restraint, special surveillance and dissolution.[59] Sanctions against natural persons included admonition, fines, warning, disqualification from diplomatic functions, deprivation of liberty, as well as security measures, such as the prohibition of access to specific territories or disqualification from a particular profession.[60]

With respect to enforcement, the Code did not outline any precise proceedings, but envisaged a difference between the responsibility of individuals, States and other legal persons.[61] Indeed, Pella conceived of the Code as complementary to the Statute for a Criminal Chamber of the PCIJ.[62] The Code should have had the same normative effectiveness as the Covenant of the League of Nations or the UN Charter, binding all State Members of these Organisations.[63] In order to make enforcement measures effective, the Code also compelled the limitation of armaments, notably by criminalising the recruitment of militaries and military education beyond authorisation.[64]

56 Pella, 'La codification' (1952) 339–340. See also Joseph Dautricourt, 'Nature et fondement du droit pénal universel' (1949–50) 30(10) *RDPC* 1023–1061.
57 Tit 4, ch 1, s 1.
58 Tit 4, ch 1, s 2.
59 Tit 4, ch 3. See also Secretary General, Draft Code (1950) 320, para 80.
60 Tit 4, ch 2.
61 Tit 4, ch 4.
62 Tit 3, ss 1–4.
63 Pella, *La guerre-crime* (1946) 127.
64 Tit 2, ch 1, s 3.

In 1929, working for the ICLA Judge Albert Levitt elaborated another Project for an International Criminal Code.[65] The proposal mostly criminalised aggressive war and related violent acts, including a violation of the obligation to punish natural persons responsible for such acts (Article 1). The Project established the jurisdiction of a permanent Court over a State upon referral by another State under Article 6. It thus created the compulsory jurisdiction of the Court over State crimes, independently from the Council of the League of Nations (Articles 1–10). The Code provided a detailed list of sanctions for State crimes under Article 9(1), including the suspension of diplomatic relations, economic relations, other treaty rights and embargoes. Under Article 6(9), economic sanctions were also conceived of as enforcement measures.

In 1937, a Conference of 13 States organised within the context of the League of Nations adopted a Convention for the Creation of an ICC,[66] based on the 1935 Code proposed by Pella. The Court would have had jurisdiction over terrorism committed by individuals as defined in the contemporaneous Convention for the Prevention and Punishment of the Crime of Terrorism.[67] This Treaty committed States not to facilitate and to criminalise specific acts, such as murder, when directed against a State and aiming to create terror (Articles 1 and 2). According to Pella, the competence of the Court should have been extended to all crimes threatening international security.[68] These Conventions were not ratified and thus never entered into force, because of the events that preceded World War II.[69]

1.2 Dualism: disjoining individual and State responsibility after World War II

1.2.1 Between coordination and disjunction (1940–1960)

1.2.1.1 Peace through law? UN procedures and the critical role of the Security Council

At the end of World War II, some scholars clearly affirmed the existence of different degrees of State responsibility, distinguishing bilateral and multilateral breaches from *erga omnes* violations, with particular regard to aggressive war and

65 ICLA, Projet de Code pénal international, by Albert Levitt (1929) 6(1) *RIDP* 33–46.

66 Adopted 16 November 1937, Final Proceedings of the International Conference on the Suppression of Terrorism, League of Nations, Doc C.548.M.385.1937.V, Part I(2).

67 Adopted 16 November 1937, Final Proceedings of the International Conference on the Suppression of Terrorism, League of Nations, Doc C.548.M.385.1937.V, Part I(1). See Constantin Eustathiadès, 'La Cour pénale internationale pour la répression du terrorisme et le problème de la responsabilité internationale des États' (1936) 43(1) *RGDIP* 389–393; Philip Marshall Brown, 'International Criminal Justice' (1941) 35(1) *AJIL* 119–120.

68 Pella, *La guerre-crime* (1946) 121.

69 Hudson, 'The Proposed International Criminal Court' (1938) 551–554.

genocide.[70] Against this background, in 1944 Hans Kelsen proposed a Covenant of a Permanent League for the Maintenance of Peace and Annexed Treaty Stipulations Establishing Individual Responsibility for Violations of International Law.[71] These were conceived of as complementary instruments providing a model for the drafters of the UN Charter, in the wake of the Dumbarton Oaks agreements and preparatory work for the Charter.[72] The project is particularly interesting because it coordinates non-judicial institutions, notably the Council and General Assembly of the League, with an ICC, having jurisdiction over both individuals and States for war and war crimes. To a certain extent, Kelsen subordinated the executive action of the Council to the jurisdiction of the Court.

Under Article 31 of the Covenant proposed by Kelsen, the Court of the League had compulsory jurisdiction, upon referral by a State. In the case of war or retaliation, Article 35 of the Covenant established the competence of the Court to determine State responsibility upon request by the injured State or the Council. However, the same provision conferred on the Council the power to order consequent military and economic sanctions:

> Sanctions against Member States
> Article 35
> Should any member of the League resort to war or reprisals against another Member in disregard of its obligation under Article 34 the Court shall, on the request of the injured Member or of the Council, decide the question whether the accused Member has violated the Covenant. In accordance with the decision the Council shall order the necessary economic or military sanctions against the Member declared responsible for the violation.

Article 36(2) of the Covenant consequently established the competence of the Council, possibly upon request by the Court, to adopt countermeasures in the case of a breach of a sanction. This system conferred a large decisional role on the Council that the judicial power of the Court constrained only in part. However, Article 36(3) of the Covenant vested the Court with the power to make decisions on executive matters, in the case of a State opposing the execution of a decision:

> Execution
> Article 36
> 1. All orders and decisions of the Court and the Council must be executed in full good faith by the Member State designated in the order or decision.

70 Philip Jessup, *A Modern Law of Nations: An Introduction* (Macmillan, 1948) 12; Nolte, 'From Dionisio Anzilotti' (2002) 1095.

71 Kelsen, *Peace* (1973) 127 ff, Annexes 1 and 2.

72 The Dumbarton Oaks Proposals for a General International Organization to be Subject of the United Nations Conference at San Francisco, April 25, 1945 (US Government Printing Office, 1944), http://www.idaillinois.org/cdm/ref/collection/isl3/id/9851.

2. If a Member State does not fulfil this obligation the Council shall, at the request of the Court or on its own initiative, order the necessary measures destined to assure the execution.
3. In the event the Member State concerned should object to the order or decision to be executed excess of jurisdiction, the matter shall be settled by a decision of the Court.

The establishment of an ICC with jurisdiction over natural persons was conceived of as a way to 'complete' State responsibility.[73] The Court would have thus had competence to adjudicate upon the criminal responsibility of individuals acting as State organs or agents, after delivering a decision on State non-criminal responsibility and its enforcement, according to Article 35(a) and (d) of the Treaty Stipulations on Individual Responsibility. Individual crimes particularly concerned violations of the law of warfare under Article 35(b) and consequent sanctions included measures such as forfeiture of office, loss of the capacity to hold public office as well as political rights under Article 35(d)(2) of the Stipulations. The Council was however vested with a right to pardon under Article 35(k). By virtue of Article 35(i) of the Stipulations, Member States were compelled to deliver individuals under their jurisdiction to the Court, thus ensuring cooperation and the presence of the accused at the process.

Practice did not see the establishment of an international criminal court, but only that of the United Nations. In fact, *ad hoc* military tribunals or domestic courts tried crimes associated with World War II. The UN Charter was adopted in 1945, following the Dumbarton Oaks proposals and work in San Francisco. The Charter establishes fundamental universal principles, banning aggression, promoting human rights and establishing procedures centred on the Security Council for State aggravated responsibility. In this context, negotiation, conciliation and jurisdictional means are the preferred avenues for dispute settlement under Chapter VI of the UN Charter for both aggravated and non-aggravated State responsibility. Specifically, a dispute can be brought to the attention of the General Assembly or the Security Council under UN Charter Article 35(2). However, the Security Council has a major power of initiative under Chapter VI. Furthermore, the Council is key to addressing State aggravated responsibility in the case of a threat to or breach of the peace or an act of aggression under Chapter VII of the Charter, entailing countermeasures that can go as far as to involve the use of armed force.

In light of this framework, when the UN Charter was adopted some scholars posited the existence of State aggravated responsibility for aggression and assumed it allowed the adoption of centralised or decentralised general countermeasures, regardless of proportionality.[74] Within such a context, reaction to

73 Ibid 115.

74 Josef Kunz, 'Individual and Collective Self-Defense in Article 51 of the Charter of the United Nations' (1947) 41(4) *AJIL* 874–876; Hans Kelsen, 'Collective Security and Collective Self-Defence under the Charter of the United Nations' (1948) 42(4) *AJIL* 784; Leland Goodrich and

aggression in self-defence under UN Charter Article 51 was regarded as a form of secondary exclusion of State criminal responsibility.[75] Along these lines, by means of Resolution 380 (V) of 17 November 1950, meaningfully concerning 'Peace through Deeds', the UN General Assembly stated that 'any aggression' is 'the gravest of all crimes against peace and security throughout the world'.[76]

1.2.1.2 The IMT, IMTFE, Nuremberg principles and Draft Code of Offences against the Peace and Security of Mankind

In 1943, the London International Assembly drafted a Statute for an International Criminal Court. The Court would have had competence over war crimes committed by natural persons either in wartime or connected with the preparation, waging or prosecution of war. Such jurisdiction would have been complementary with respect to that of domestic jurisdictions (Articles 1 and 2).[77] In 1944, the UN War Crimes Commission presented a Project for the creation of a UN Tribunal, with jurisdiction over war crimes committed by natural persons.[78] A permanent court was not established. By contrast, in 1945 the history of international law recorded the London Agreement,[79] establishing the IMT in Nuremberg.[80] This was followed shortly after by the creation of the IMTFE in Tokyo.[81]

The IMT Charter is a milestone in international criminal law. Article 6 of the Charter established the jurisdiction of the Tribunal over the major war criminals of the European Axis countries 'whether as individuals or as members of organisations', for committing crimes against peace, war crimes and crimes against humanity.[82] The Tribunal could convict leaders, organisers, instigators and accomplices participating in the formulation or execution of a common plan or conspiring to commit such crimes. Under Article 7, official positions did not afford a justification. According to Article 9, the Tribunal could declare the criminal nature of any group or organisation, which would then allow national jurisdictions to prosecute individuals for affiliation under Article 10.[83]

Edvard Hambro, *Charter of the United Nations: Commentary and Documents* (Stevens, 2nd edn, 1949) 302.

75 Secretary General, Draft Code (1950) 318, para 77.

76 General Assembly, Peace through Deeds, UN Doc A/RES/380 (V), 17 November 1950, para 1.

77 Secretary General, Historical Survey (1949) 97 ff, Annexe 9.B.

78 Ibid 112 ff, Annexe 10; Clyde Eagleton, 'Punishment of War Criminals by the United Nations' (1943) 37(3) *AJIL* 495–499.

79 Adopted 8 August 1945, 251 UNTS 280.

80 Charter of the IMT, adopted 8 August 1945, 251 UNTS 284.

81 Charter of the IMTFE, adopted 19 January 1946, 1589 Treaties and Other International Acts Series 20. On the institution of an international criminal jurisdiction from 1920 to 1945, see Arthur Kuhn, 'International Criminal Jurisdiction' (1947) 41(2) *AJIL* 430–431.

82 George Finch, 'The Nuremberg Trial and International Law' (1947) 41(1) *AJIL* 20–37; Quincy Wright, 'The Law of the Nuremberg Trial' (1947) 41(1) *AJIL* 38–72.

83 Desislava Stoitchkova, *Towards Corporate Liability in International Criminal Law* (Intersentia, 2010) 59–60.

The same principle applied before military tribunals established under Article II(1)(d) of Control Council Law No 10.[84] However, the principle of imputation in criminal association was complicity, not the responsibility of a legal entity as such.[85] Thus, the IMT criminalised the *Reich* Cabinet, the Leadership Corps of the Nazi Party, SS, SD, SA, Gestapo and the General Staff and High Command of the German Armed Forces as criminal organisations, based on complicity by association.[86] Nonetheless, it is interesting to note that a non-criminal legal text, the Protocol of Proceedings of the Potsdam Conference adopted on 2 August 1945, provided for the suppression of Nazi criminal organisations (Principle II.A.3.i.b.iii).[87] This measure concerned legal persons as such, rather than individuals. As regards individuals, under Articles 27 and 28 of the IMT Charter penalties ranged from death to confiscation or any other 'just' punishment and were reviewed and carried out by the Control Council for Germany under Article 29. The IMT only afforded a unique procedural instance, excluding appeals, with possibility of proceedings *in absentia* under Article 12.

The Charter of the IMTFE followed that of the Nuremberg Tribunal as a model, but without specific provisions on the criminal nature of organisations. Under Article 5 of its Charter, the Tribunal tried major war criminals in the Far East. Under Article 17, the Supreme Commander for the Allied Powers reviewed and executed judgments.[88] Whilst some scholars argue that the IMT and IMTFE were the first steps to criminalise States,[89] legally speaking States were excluded from proceedings as legal entities.

Despite this exclusive approach, it is considered that certain sanctions imposed on the Axis Powers, notably Germany and Japan, mainly had a punitive nature for aggressive war and related crimes. This would have been the case of occupation, control of economic and political activities or destruction of military industry under the Protocol of Proceedings of the Yalta Conference of 11 February 1945[90] and the Protocol of Proceedings of the Potsdam Conference of 2 August 1945. Notably, the Protocol of Proceedings of the Potsdam Conference provided for the complete disarmament and demilitarisation of Germany

84 Punishment of Persons Guilty of War Crimes, Crimes against Peace and against Humanity, 20 December 1945 (1946) 3 *Off Gaz CCG* 50–55.

85 Henri Donnedieu De Vabres, 'Le procès de Nuremberg devant les principes modernes du droit pénal international' (1947) 70(1) *RCADI* 543–562; Nina Jørgensen, 'Criminality of International Organisations under International Law', in Nollkaemper and Van der Wilt, *System Criminality* (2009) 204–206.

86 *Göring* et al, IMT Nuremberg, Judgment of 1 October 1946, in *Trial of Major War Criminals before the International Military Tribunal* (1947) vol 1, 80 ff.

87 Protocol of the Proceedings of the Berlin Conference, approved 2 August 1945 (1947) 1(3) *ILQ* 418.

88 See the judgment of the Tokyo Tribunal of 12 November 1948 in John Pritchard, Sonia Zaide and Donald Cameron Watt (eds), *The Tokyo War Crimes Trial* (Garland, 1981) vol 22, paras 48,415 ff.

89 Descheemaeker, 'Le tribunal militaire international des grands criminels de guerre' (1946) 50(1) *RGDIP* 287–288; Secretary General, Draft Code (1950) 318, para 78.

90 Signed 11 February 1945, 148 BSP 80, in force 11 February 1945.

(Article II.A.3.i), the reform of Germany in view of its democratisation (Article II.A.7–9), the control of the German economy in order to eliminate its war potential (Article II.A.11–19) and of the German navy and Merchant Marines (Article IV.A and B). These indeed seem to be security measures preventing repetition of aggressive war.[91]

In the wake of the IMT and IMTFE, by means of Resolution 95 (I) of 11 December 1946 the UN General Assembly affirmed the principles of international law recognised in the Charter of the Nuremberg Tribunal and the Judgment of the Tribunal.[92] In 1947, by means of Resolution 177(II) the UN General Assembly gave mandate to the ILC to formulate such principles,[93] and, upon this basis, to further prepare a Draft Code of Offences against the Peace and Security of Mankind.[94]

In 1949, the Geneva Conventions on the law of war codified the notion of 'war crimes'.[95] These instruments do not preclude further national legislation, since States may enact law criminalising any (serious) breach of international humanitarian law.[96] In the case of an armed conflict of an international character, opposing two or more States, the Geneva Conventions establish a list of grave breaches of international humanitarian law. The Conventions further compel States to provide effective criminal sanctions against the perpetrators, so that breaches such as wilful killing, torture or intensive destruction of property necessarily qualify as war crimes.[97] Jurisdiction over these offences is universal, which means that any State has the ability to prosecute, regardless of the territory where a breach is committed (*locus commissi delicti*), the nationality of the perpetrator and that of the victim. Furthermore, these crimes are subject to the principle *aut dedere aut judicare*, compelling a State to either prosecute a suspect or hand him over to the authorities of another State for prosecution.[98]

91 Secretary General, Draft Code (1950) 321, para 81. See also André Gros, 'La condition juridique de l'Allemagne' (1946) 50(1) *RGDIP* 75–78.

92 General Assembly, Affirmation of the Principles of International Law Recognised by the Charter of the Nuremberg Tribunal, UN Doc A/RES/1/95, 11 December 1946.

93 Id, Formulation of the Principles Recognized in the Charter of the Nuremberg Tribunal and in the Judgment of the Tribunal, UN Doc A/RES/177 (II), 21 November 1947.

94 Secretary General, The Statute and Judgment of the Nuremberg Tribunal, Memorandum, UN Doc A/CN.4/5 (1949) 11 ff.

95 Geneva Convention (I) on Wounded and Sick in Armed Forces in the Field, 75 UNTS 31, Geneva Convention (II) on Wounded, Sick and Shipwrecked of Armed Forces at Sea, 75 UNTS 85, Geneva Convention (III) on Prisoners of War, 75 UNTS 135, Geneva Convention (IV) on the Protection of Civilians in Time of War, 75 UNTS 287, adopted 12 August 1949, in force 21 October 1950.

96 Yves Sandoz, 'The Dynamic but Complex Relationship between International Penal Law and International Humanitarian Law', in José Doria, Hans-Peter Gasser and Cherif Bassiouni (eds), *The Legal Regime of the International Criminal Court* (Brill, 2009) 1053–1054. In the sense that only serious violations of the law of armed conflicts qualify as war crimes, see *Tadić*, IT-94-1, Appeals Chamber, Decision on the Defence Motion for Interlocutory Appeal on Jurisdiction, 2 October 1995, para 94.

97 Geneva Convention I arts 49–51, Geneva Convention II arts 50–52, Geneva Convention III arts 129–131, Geneva Convention IV arts 146–148. See also Jean-Marie Henckaerts and Louise Doswald-Beck, *Customary International Humanitarian Law* (CUP, 2005) vol 1, 568 ff.

98 Ibid 604–611.

In 1950, the ILC formulated seven Nuremberg Principles,[99] concerning the international criminal responsibility of natural persons for crimes against peace, war crimes and crimes against humanity, regardless of their official position, superior orders and domestic law:

> Principle VI
> The crimes hereinafter set out are punishable as crimes under international law:
> (a) Crimes against peace:
> (i) Planning, preparation, initiation or waging of a war of aggression or a war in violation of international treaties, agreements or assurances;
> (ii) Participation in a common plan or conspiracy for the accomplishment of any of the acts mentioned under (i).
> (b) War crimes:
> Violations of the laws or customs of war which include, but are not limited to, murder, ill-treatment or deportation to slave-labour or for any other purpose of civilian population of or in occupied territory, murder or ill-treatment of prisoners of war, of persons on the seas, killing of hostages, plunder of public or private property, wanton destruction of cities, towns, or villages, or devastation not justified by military necessity.
> (c) Crimes against humanity:
> Murder, extermination, enslavement, deportation and other inhuman acts done against any civilian population, or persecutions on political, racial or religious grounds, when such acts are done or such persecutions are carried on in execution of or in connection with any crime against peace or any war crime.

The Principles constitute the core of international criminal law and underpin the development of the entire matter, including the current Statute of the ICC. During preparatory work, Henri Donnedieu De Vabres submitted a study to the ILC, proposing to subject crimes embedded in the Nuremberg principles to the competence of a Criminal Chamber established within the International Court of Justice (ICJ). The Chamber would have thus had jurisdiction over aggression, war crimes and crimes against humanity committed by Sates and their officials and agents:

> 1. Jurisdiction conferred on a criminal chamber to be established as part of the International Court of Justice. This would deal with:
> [...]

99 Jean Spiropoulos, Formulation of the Nürnberg Principles, UN Doc A/CN.4/22 (1950) 2 *YBILC* 191.

(b) Indictments for crimes against peace (the crime of aggression in all its forms) brought against a State or its constitutionally responsible rulers.
(c) Indictments for crimes against humanity which might be brought against a State or its constitutionally responsible rulers.[100]

Along the lines of the work of the ILA and ICLA, the idea was to have a jurisdiction complementing the Nuremberg Principles, so as to avoid criticism addressing the IMT and IMTFE as *ad hoc* Tribunals only partially representing the international community.[101] Based on the 1937 Convention on the Creation of an ICC, the proposal merged jurisdiction over States and individuals. The proposal coordinated the action of a Prosecutor and that of the UN Security Council and vested any interested governments with a power of initiative. The final Principles did not embed these proposals.

Based on the Nuremberg Principles, in 1951 the ILC adopted the first DCOPSM.[102] In 1954, the ILC adopted a second version of the Code.[103] In this context, international crimes committed by natural persons, notably State authorities, included aggression, State-sponsored terrorism, inhumane acts and violations of the laws and customs of war (1951 and 1954 DCOPSM Article 2). Article 2(6) defined terrorism as:

> The undertaking or encouragement by the authorities of a State of terrorist activities in another State, or the toleration by the authorities of a State of organized activities calculated to carry out terrorist acts in another State.

The 1954 DCOPSM also included the crime of genocide in Article 2(10), along the lines of the definition outlined in the Convention for the Prevention and Punishment of the Crime of Genocide.

The DCOPSM did not follow the suggestions of Vespasian Pella, who envisaged the responsibility of natural persons, as well as States and non-State legal entities, under an international criminal jurisdiction,[104] along the lines of the

100 Secretary General, Historical Survey (1949) 119, Annexe 11. In favour of the establishment of a permanent criminal court with jurisdiction over individuals and States, but independent from the ICJ, see Kuhn, 'International Criminal Jurisdiction' (1947) 432–433.
101 See F B Schick, 'The Nuremberg Trial and the International Law of the Future' (1947) 41(4) *AJIL* 775.
102 ILC, Report to the General Assembly on the Work of the Third Session, UN Doc A/CN.4/48 (1951) 2 *YBILC* 133. See also Charles Fenwick, 'Draft Code of Offences against the Peace and Security of Mankind' (1952) 46(1) *AJIL* 98–100; Pitman Potter, 'Offences against the Peace and Security of Mankind', ibid, 101–102.
103 ILC, Report to the General Assembly on the Work of the Sixth Session, UN Doc A/2693 (1954) 2 *YBILC* 150. See also Jean Spiropoulos, Draft Code of Offences against the Peace and Security of Mankind, Third Report, UN Doc A/CN.4/85 (1954) 2 *YBILC* 112–122.
104 Jean Spiropoulos, Report on the Draft Code of Offences against the Peace and Security of Mankind, UN Doc A/CN.4/25 (1950) 2(1) *YBILC* 261, paras 53–55.

proposals put forward in 1928 and 1935.[105] UN General Assembly Resolutions 897 (IX) of 14 December 1954 and 1186 (XII) of 11 December 1957 suspended work on the DCOPMS,[106] pending the definition of aggression, which was the core crime of the project. Indeed, in 1952 and 1954 by means of Resolutions 688 (VII) and 895 (IX) the UN General Assembly had entrusted a Special Committee to define aggression.[107]

1.2.1.3 The Genocide Convention and the proposals for an international criminal jurisdiction

By means of Resolution 96 (I) of 11 December 1946,[108] the UN General Assembly mandated the Economic and Social Council (ECOSOC) to develop studies in view of the drafting of a Convention on the Crime of Genocide. In 1947, the Assembly restated the mandate via Resolution 180 (II), affirming that 'genocide is an international crime entailing national and international responsibility on the part of individuals and States'.[109] Based on the preparatory work of the Secretary General and the *Ad Hoc* Committee on Genocide,[110] the ECOSOC submitted a project to the General Assembly in 1948, including the jurisdiction of an international criminal court. When the text was submitted to the attention of the Sixth Committee of the General Assembly, some members envisaged the insertion of a clause on the ICJ jurisdiction over State responsibility for genocide.[111]

Article I of the text eventually adopted by means of UN General Assembly Resolution 260 (III) of 9 December 1948,[112] which entered into force in 1951, defines genocide as 'a crime under international law'. The Convention establishes the jurisdiction of the State where the crime was committed or that of an international criminal court accepted by State Parties (Article VI). It is considered that the ICC and possibly *ad hoc* Tribunals created after the entry into force of the Genocide Convention fulfil the requirements outlined in Article VI.[113] Article VIII allows State Parties to call upon UN organs

105 Secretary General, Draft Code (1950) 282–283, paras 4–7.

106 General Assembly, Draft Code of Offences against the Peace and Security of Mankind, UN Doc A/RES/897 (IX), 14 December 1954; Id, UN Doc A/RES/1186 (XII), 11 December 1957.

107 General Assembly, Question of Defining Aggression, UN Doc A/RES/688 (VII), 20 December 1952; Id, UN Doc A/RES/895 (IX), 4 December 1954.

108 Id, The Crime of Genocide, UN Doc A/RES/96 (I), 11 December 1946.

109 Id, Draft Convention on Genocide, UN Doc A/RES/180 (II), 21 November 1947, preamble.

110 Secretary General, Historical Survey (1949) 33 ff, 120 and 142, Annexes 12 and 14.

111 Ibid 43.

112 General Assembly, Prevention and Punishment of the Crime of Genocide, UN Doc A/RES/260 (III), 9 December 1948.

113 *Application of the Convention on the Prevention and Punishment of the Crime of Genocide (Bosnia and Herzegovina v Yugoslavia)* [2007] ICJ Rep 227, para 445; Webb, 'Binocular Vision' (2012) 126–127 and 134.

to take action under the UN Charter to prevent and suppress genocide.[114] Article IX establishes the compulsory jurisdiction of the ICJ with respect to State responsibility:

> Article IX
> Disputes between the Contracting Parties relating to the interpretation, application or fulfilment of the present Convention, including those relating to the responsibility of a State for genocide or for any of the other acts enumerated in article III, shall be submitted to the International Court of Justice at the request of any of the parties to the dispute.

Despite the letter of Articles I, III and IX of the Convention, it is controversial whether these rules provide a positive answer to the question as to whether a State can be held criminally responsible.[115]

In its advisory opinion in *Reservations to the Genocide Convention*, the ICJ upheld the *erga omnes* nature of the prohibition of genocide as a 'crime under international law', which is 'binding on States, even without any conventional obligation'.[116] The Court later confirmed this stance in the *Bosnian Genocide* case,[117] where the ICJ was called upon to determine whether the subject matter of State responsibility for genocide falls within the scope of Article IX of the Genocide Convention.[118] The Court noted that Article IX 'does not exclude any form of State responsibility'.[119] Judge Kreća dissented, confining action under Article IX to a 'meta-legal' interpretation of questions arising from the Convention, thus excluding State responsibility.[120] However, the ICJ further upheld the possibility of holding a State responsible for genocide in the subsequent *Croatian Genocide* case.[121]

Preparatory work discloses a contentious approach and leaves room for envisaging the relationship between individual and State responsibility from a criminal or non-criminal perspective. In fact, the UK proposed that 'criminal responsibility for any act of genocide as specified in Articles II and IV' should 'extend not only to all private persons or associations, but also to *States*,

114 Some scholars, however, underscore that this provision does not explicitly mention procedures under UN Charter ch VII (see Roberto Ago, Fifth Report on State Responsibility: The Internationally Wrongful Act of the State, Source of International Responsibility, UN Doc A/CN.4/291 and Add.1 and 2 (1976) 2(1) *YBILC* 38, para 115).

115 Stefan Glaser, 'L'État en tant que personne morale est-il pénalement responsable?' (1948–1949) 29(5) *RDPC* 425–452.

116 *Reservations to the Convention on the Prevention and Punishment of the Crime of Genocide* [1951] ICJ Rep 23.

117 *Application of the Convention*, Preliminary Objections [1996] ICJ Rep 615–616, para 31.

118 Ibid 614, paras 27 ff.

119 Ibid 616, para 32. See also Webb, 'Binocular Vision' (2012) 123–124.

120 *Application of the Convention* [1996] Dissenting Opinion Kreća, 769, para 104.

121 *Application of the Convention on the Prevention and Punishment of the Crime of Genocide (Croatia v Serbia)* [2015] ICJ Rep 45, para 85.

governments, or organs or authorities of the State or government, by whom such acts are committed'.[122] Based on these premises, according to some commentators Article IX could lead to envisaging the creation of an international criminal court with jurisdiction over State crimes.[123] However, scholars have mostly argued that Article IX does not recognise State criminal responsibility, but only State international responsibility.[124] Given the open scope of the initial mandate of the ILC, such a divisive interpretation represents a turning point for the subsequent evolution of individual criminal responsibility and State aggravated responsibility.

Endorsing the Genocide Convention, by means of Resolution 260/1948 the UN General Assembly entrusted the ILC to study the possibility of establishing an international criminal court with competence over genocide and related crimes committed by natural persons.[125] Following the positive advice of the ILC, which was favourable to the institution of a criminal court independent from the ICJ, by means of Resolution 489 (V) of 12 December 1950 the UN General Assembly established a Committee for an International Criminal Court,[126] which presented a project in 1951.[127] By means of Resolution 687 (VII) of 5 December 1952, the Assembly established a new Committee,[128] which submitted a Project for an ICC Statute in 1953.[129] Following the Nuremberg approach, Article 25 of the Projects proposed in 1951 and 1953 established the jurisdiction of the Court exclusively over natural persons, including heads of

122 Hirad Abtahi and Philippa Webb, *The Genocide Convention: The* Travaux Préparatoires (Martinus Nijhoff Publishers, 2008) 1986, emphasis added. See also Nina Jørgensen, *The Responsibility* (2000) 36–38; Kevin Aquilina and Klejda Mulaj. 'Limitations in Attributing State Responsibility under the Genocide Convention' (2018) 17(1) *JHR* 125–126.

123 Yuen-Li Liang, 'Notes on Legal Questions Concerning the United Nations – The Question of the Establishment of an International Criminal Jurisdiction' (1949) 43(3) *AJIL* 478 ff; Vespasian Pella, 'Towards an International Criminal Court' (1950) 44(1) *AJIL* 51.

124 For a review of scholarly opinions, see Jørgensen, *The Responsibility* (2000) 35 ff. See also Antonio Cassese, 'On the Use of Criminal Law Notions in Determining State Responsibility for Genocide' (2007) 5(4) *JICJ* 878; Webb, 'Binocular Vision' (2012) 122.

125 General Assembly, Prevention and Punishment of the Crime of Genocide, UN Doc A/RES/3/260, 9 December 1948, Part B.

126 Id, International Criminal Jurisdiction, UN Doc A/RES/489 (V), 12 December 1950.

127 Committee on International Criminal Jurisdiction, Draft Statute (1952) 1 ff. For a scholarly viewpoint, see Yuen-Li Liang, 'Notes on Legal Questions Concerning the United Nations – The Question of the Establishment of an International Criminal Jurisdiction: The First Phase' (1952) 46(1) *AJIL* 73–88; Quincy Wright, 'Proposal for an International Criminal Court', ibid, 60–72; George Finch, 'Draft Statute for an International Criminal Court', ibid, 89–98.

128 General Assembly, International Criminal Jurisdiction, UN Doc A/RES/687 (VII), 5 December 1952.

129 Committee on International Criminal Jurisdiction, Revised Draft Statute (1954) 23. For a scholarly viewpoint, see Pierre-Marie Carjeu, 'Quelques aspects du nouveau Projet de Statut des Nations Unies pour une juridiction criminelle internationale' (1956) 60(3) *RGDIP* 401–425.

States or governmental agents.[130] In 1953, by means of Resolutions 898 (IX) of 14 December 1954[131] and 1187 of 11 December 1957[132] the UN General Assembly suspended work on the ICC Statute, pending the definition of aggression and the achievement of the DCOPSM.[133]

1.2.2 Defining aggression, State crimes and underlying concepts (1960–1980)

1.2.2.1 Non-institutional initiatives

Pending the definition of aggression, no initiatives were undertaken within the UN on individual crimes. Private initiatives registered the institution of an ICC by Lord Bertrand Russell in 1966. The Court carried out major proceedings in Roskilde in 1967 and Stockholm in 1974 to try crimes committed during the Vietnam War. Meeting in Rome in 1974, the Court tried human rights violations committed in South-America. Following the model of the Russell Tribunal, a War Tribunal on Iraq assessed the invasion of 2003. These tribunals have no effective power but are sociologically relevant initiatives.[134]

During this time, some scholars delved into the distinction between State ordinary responsibility, having a bilateral nature, and State aggravated responsibility, regarded as a violation of an *erga omnes* obligation vis-à-vis the entire international community, possibly having a criminal nature.[135] Other commentators envisaged a more sophisticated tripartite distinction, whereby aggression constituted the most serious State offence, triggering self-defence under UN Charter Article 51, the response of the UN Security Council and expulsion of the aggressor from the UN under UN Charter Article 6. Sanctions for aggression encompassed reparation, suspension of treaty rights and assurances of non-repetition. A second category of offences included breaches of State sovereignty, setting off countermeasures by the injured State not involving the use of force and UN recommendations in view of cessation of unlawful conduct. The third category encompassed ordinary State offences, triggering reparation and proportionate bilateral countermeasures.[136] With particular regard to aggression, some scholars underscored the possibility for a State of acting in self-defence without a prior demand for reparation, including the use of force and

130 Constantin Eustathiadès, 'Les sujets du droit international et la responsabilité internationale – Nouvelles tendances' (1953) 84(3) *RCADI* 454–456.

131 General Assembly, International Criminal Jurisdiction, UN Doc A/RES/898 (IX), 14 December 1954.

132 Id, UN Doc A/RES/1187 (XII), 11 December 1957.

133 On work for the institution of an international criminal court prior to the definition of aggression, see Gerhardt Grebing, 'La création d'une Cour pénale internationale: bilan et perspectives' (1974) 45(3–4) *RIDP* 435–452.

134 Ken Coates, 'Russell Tribunals', http://www.russfound.org/The_Spokesman/KCTrib104.html.

135 Georg Nolte, 'From Dionisio Anzilotti' (2002) 1094–1097.

136 Ago, Fifth Report (1976) 50, para 153.

collective countermeasures.[137] Within this framework, according to a particular stance breaches of peremptory norms would have been State crimes, including aggression, slavery, piracy, crimes against humanity and violations of the right to self-determination of peoples, possibly entailing *actio popularis.*[138]

1.2.2.2 Peremptory norms (jus cogens), erga omnes *obligations and State crimes*

In 1969, the adoption of the Vienna Convention on the Law of Treaties (VCLT)[139] led to establishing the notion of a 'peremptory norm', belonging to the realm of *jus cogens.* VCLT Article 53 provides:

> Treaties Conflicting with a Peremptory Norm of General International Law ('*jus cogens*')
> A treaty is void if, at the time of its conclusion, it conflicts with a peremptory norm of general international law. For the purposes of the present Convention, a peremptory norm of general international law is a norm accepted and recognized by the international community of States as a whole as a norm from which no derogation is permitted and which can be modified only by a subsequent norm of general international law having the same character.

Article 53 of the 1986 Vienna Convention on the Law of Treaties between States and International Organisations or between International Organisations (VCLTIO) later replicated the same rule.[140] The norm does not provide a definition of *jus cogens*, but only deals with its implications in terms of validity of treaties, from the standpoint of the sources of international law. Specifically, the notion of *jus cogens* entails for States universal obligations essential for the whole international community.[141]

In 1970, the ICJ elaborated the notion of an obligation vis-à-vis 'the international community as a whole', that is, *erga omnes*, via a well-known *obiter dictum* in *Barcelona Traction*:

> An essential distinction should be drawn between the obligations of a State towards the international community as a whole, and those arising vis-à-vis

137 Ian Brownlie, *International Law and the Use of Force by States* (Clarendon Press, 1963) 252 ff; Rosalyn Higgins, *The Development of International Law through the Political Organs of the United Nations* (OUP, 1963) 208.

138 Roberto Ago, Fifth Report (1976) 50, para 141.

139 Adopted 23 May 1969, 1155 UNTS 331, in force 27 January 1980.

140 Adopted 21 March 1986, UN Doc A/CONF.129/15, not yet in force.

141 Roberto Ago, 'Droit des traités à la lumière de la Convention de Vienne – Introduction' (1971) 134(3) *RCADI* 323–324; Christian Tomuschat, 'Obligations *Erga Omnes* for States without or against Their Will' (1993) 241(4) *RCADI* 223; Thomas Weatherall, Jus Cogens: *International Law and Social Contract* (CUP, 2015) 6–8 and 29.

> another State in the field of diplomatic protection. By their very nature the former are the concern of all States. In view of the importance of the rights involved, all States can be held to have a legal interest in their protection; they are obligations *erga omnes* [...]
>
> Such obligations derive, for example, in contemporary international law, from the outlawing of acts of aggression, and of genocide, as also from the principles and rules concerning the basic rights of the human person, including protection from slavery and racial discrimination.[142]

Although the Court did not refer to '*jus cogens*', from the standpoint of a right, constructing an obligation '*erga omnes*' as a duty owed to the 'international community as a whole' necessarily has implications for peremptory norms, in light of the correlation between duties and rights.[143] In this respect, scholars are divided. In fact, some commentators assume that only *jus cogens* would include *erga omnes* obligations.[144] Others maintain that the notion of *jus cogens* is more limited than that of *erga omnes* obligations, based on the derogability of the duty: some *erga omnes* obligations may be derogated from, as a sum of bilateral duties.[145]

In 1970, the UN General Assembly adopted Resolution 2625 (XXVI), declaring the Principles of International Law concerning Friendly Relations and Co-operation among States in Accordance with the Charter of the United Nations.[146] Principle 1 of the Declaration 'solemnly proclaims' that '[a] war of aggression constitutes a crime against the peace, for which there is responsibility under international law.' Along similar lines, Article 5(2) of Resolution 3314 (XXIX) on the Definition of Aggression adopted by the Assembly on 14 December 1974 states that '[a] war of aggression is a crime against international peace' and 'gives rise to international responsibility.'[147] Whether

142 Barcelona *Traction, Light and Power Company, Limited (New Application: 1962) (Belgium v Spain) Second Phase* [1970] ICJ Rep 32, paras 33–34. See also Maurizio Ragazzi, *The Concept of International Obligation* Erga Omnes (Clarendon Press, 1997) 2–3; Paolo Picone, 'Distinction between *Jus Cogens* and Obligations *Erga Omnes*', in Enzo Canizzaro (ed), *The Law of Treaties beyond the Vienna Convention* (OUP, 2011) 414–415.

143 Wesley Newcomb Hohfeld, 'Some Fundamental Legal Conceptions as Applied in Judicial Reasoning' (1913–14) 23(1) *Yale LJ* 30 and 33; Hans Kelsen, *Pure Theory of Law* (1934, Peter Smith, tr Max Knight, 1989) 127.

144 Pierre-Marie Dupuy, 'Observations sur la pratique récente des "sanctions" de l'illicite' (1983) 87(3) *RGDIP* 536; Christian Dominicé, 'The International Responsibility of States for Breach of Multilateral Obligations' (1999) 10(2) *EJIL* 358–359; Weatherall, Jus Cogens (2015) 10–11.

145 Bruno Simma, 'From Bilateralism to Community Interest in International Law' (1994) 250(6) *RCADI* 300; José Acosta Estévez, 'Normas de *ius cogens*, efecto *erga omnes*, crimen internacional y la téoria de los círculos concéntricos' (1995) 11 *An Der Int* 13; Picone, 'Distinction' (2011) 415–416.

146 General Assembly, Declaration on Principles of International Law concerning Friendly Relations and Co-operation among States in Accordance with the Charter of the United Nations, UN Doc A/RES/2625 (XXVI), 24 October 1970.

147 A/RES/3314 (XXIX), Annexe, art 5(2).

responsibility for aggression is only 'criminal' as concerns individuals or also with regard to States is a debated question.[148] In fact, the text of Article 5(2) was purposely left open.[149] However, combining the definition of responsibility for aggression as 'criminal' under Resolutions 2625 (XXVI) and 3314 (XXIX) with the *erga omnes* nature of aggression in light of the *obiter dictum* of the ICJ in *Barcelona Traction* leads to concluding that there is a link between *erga omnes* obligations and State aggravated offences. Based on the relationship between *erga omnes* obligations and *jus cogens*, it ought to be inferred that there is also a link between State aggravated responsibility and peremptory norms. Further considering the *erga omnes* scope of State aggravated offences and countermeasures, Jan Hendrik Willem Verzijl posited the emergence of an embryonic form of State criminal responsibility for aggression and related offences, notably core war crimes and crimes against humanity.[150] This approach was complemented by the ideas of those scholars who supported the concept of *actio popularis* in international law.[151]

Concerning individual responsibility, two Additional Protocols to the 1949 Geneva Conventions were adopted in 1977.[152] Article 85 of Additional Protocol I confirms the notion of 'war crimes' embedded in the four Geneva Conventions. Additional Protocol II is particularly concerned with non-international armed conflicts. The definition of a non-international armed conflict is a thorny question.[153] Fundamentally, according to Article 1(1) of Additional Protocol II non-international armed conflicts take place thoroughly within the boundaries of a State and involve 'governmental forces and dissident armed forces or other organised armed groups'. Furthermore, under Article 1(2) of Additional Protocol II non-international armed conflicts are different from 'internal disturbances and tensions, such as riots, isolated and sporadic acts of violence or other acts of similar nature', which have a lower level of intensity.[154]

148 Pierre-Marie Dupuy, 'International Criminal Responsibility of the Individual and International Responsibility of the State', in Antonio Cassese, Paola Gaeta and John Jones (eds), *The Rome Statute of the International Criminal Court* (OUP, 2002) 1088; Bonafè, *The Relationship* (2009) 111–112.

149 Thomas Bruha, 'The General Assembly's Definition of an Act of Aggression', in Kreß and Barriaga, *The Crime* (2017) 167.

150 Jan Hendrik Willem Verzijl, *International Law in Historical Perspective* (Martinus Nijhoff, 1973) vol 6, 741–742.

151 Brigitte Bollecker-Stern, *Le préjudice dans la théorie de la responsabilité internationale* (Pedone, 1973) 83 ff.

152 Additional Protocol I to the Geneva Conventions, 1125 UNTS 3, Additional Protocol II, 1125 UNTS 609, adopted 8 June 1977, in force 7 December 1978.

153 Robert Kolb, *Advanced Introduction to International Humanitarian Law* (Edward Elgar, 2014) 22.

154 *Tadić* (1995) para 70; *Akayesu*, ICTR-96-4, Trial Chamber, Judgment of 2 September 1998, para 620; *Rutaganda*, ICTR-96-3, Trial Chamber, Judgment of 6 December 1999, 43, para 93; *Dordević*, IT-05-87/1-T, Trial Chamber, Judgment of 23 February 2011, 609, para 1522; *Lubanga Dyilo*, ICC-01/04-01/06, Trial Chamber, Public Judgment Pursuant to Article 74 of

Although non-international armed conflicts are not subject to all the rules of international humanitarian law applying to international armed conflicts, they are covered by Article 3 common to the Geneva Conventions, establishing critical standards of protection rooted in the right to life and principles of humanity, and related war crimes. Serious violations of Article 3 common to the Geneva Conventions and Additional Protocol II are considered to be subject to criminal sanctions.[155] Furthermore, the difference between international and non-international armed conflicts has progressively narrowed. In order to grant an extensive application of international humanitarian law, non-international armed conflicts have indeed been 'internationalised'.[156] At the same time, domestic and international courts have identified customary international humanitarian law rules applicable to both international and non-international armed conflicts, particularly Geneva customary law aiming to protect civilians and Hague customary law restraining methods and means of warfare.[157] Accordingly, serious violations of international humanitarian law, notably breaches of Article 3 common to the Geneva Conventions and Additional Protocol II, such as wilful killing and torture, should be subject to compulsory criminal jurisdiction, regardless of whether they are committed in international or non-international armed conflicts.[158]

1.2.2.3 State crimes under Article 19 of the ILC's 1980 Draft Articles on State Responsibility

In the 1970s, the ILC started to work on a comprehensive codification of State responsibility under the guidance of Special Rapporteur Roberto Ago, developing the previous work of Garcia-Amador on State Responsibility for Injury to Aliens from a more general perspective.[159] The DASR were conceived of as a codification of secondary international law complementing the VCLTs as a codification of primary international law, along the lines of the Kelsenian categorisation of legal norms.[160] The DASR initially included three parts: (1) origin

the Statute, 14 March 2012, 242, para 533; *Haradinaj*, IT-04-84bis-T, Trial Chamber, Judgment of 29 November 2012, 393, para 144.

155 Gauthier De Beco, 'War Crimes in International versus Non-International Armed Conflicts: New Wine in Old Wineskins?' (2008) 8(1) *Intl CLR* 321; Marco Sassòli, 'Humanitarian Law and International Criminal Law', in Antonio Cassese (ed), *The Oxford Companion to International Criminal Justice* (OUP, 2009) 112.

156 Notably, when (a) another State intervenes in an internal conflict with its armed forces, or (b) some of the participants in an internal armed conflict act on behalf of another State (*Tadić*, IT-94-1-A, Appeals Chamber, Judgment of 15 July 1999, 34, para 84).

157 *Rutaganda* (1999) 41, para 88; *Strugar*, IT-01-42, Trial Chamber, Judgment of 31 January 2005, 115, para 261. See also Kolb, *Advanced Introduction* (2014) 34.

158 *Furundžija*, IT-95-17/1, Trial Chamber, Judgment of 10 December 1998, 18, para 43, 60, para 156.

159 See the Reports of Garcia-Amador in *YBILC* 1956–1961.

160 Ago, Third Report (1971) 203, para 15; Eric David, 'Primary and Secondary Rules', in James Crawford, Alain Pellet, Simon Olleson and Kate Parlett (eds), *The Law of International Responsibility* (OUP, 2010) 28.

of international responsibility; (2) content, forms and degrees of responsibility and (3) dispute settlement.[161]

Garcia-Amador envisaged a distinction between State criminal and non-criminal responsibility and raised the issue of coordinating the former with individual responsibility.[162] However, it is Roberto Ago who first included such a categorisation in the text of Draft Article 18 in his 1976 Fifth Report to the ILC on State Responsibility.[163] Article 18 clearly distinguished aggression as the most serious State crime from criminal breaches of self-determination, human rights and common resources:

> Article 18 (Content of the International Obligation Breached)
>
> 1. The breach by a State of an existing international obligation incumbent upon it is an internationally wrongful act, regardless of the content of the obligation breached.
> 2. The breach by a State of an international obligation established for the purpose of maintaining international peace and security, and in particular the breach by a State of the prohibition of any resort to the threat or use of force against the territorial integrity or political independence of another State, is an 'international crime'.
> 3. The serious breach by a State of an international obligation established by a norm of general international law accepted and recognized as essential by the international community as a whole and having as its purpose:
>   (a) respect for the principle of the equal rights of all peoples and of their right of self-determination; or
>   (b) respect for human rights and fundamental freedoms for all, without distinction based on race, sex, language or religion; or
>   (c) the conservation and the free enjoyment for everyone of a resource common to all mankind
>   is also an 'international crime'.
> 4. The breach by a State of any other international obligation is an 'international delict'.

Aggression thus emerged as the international crime 'par excellence', within the context of a tripartite categorisation also including other State crimes and international delicts.[164] Ago assumed that such a distinction had existed in international law since at least 1939.[165] In this respect, the ILC underscored that '[t]he idea of an international criminal law of States had long been established,

161 Ago, Third Report (1971) 201, para 7.

162 Francisco García-Amador, 'State Responsibility in the Light of the New Trends of International Law' (1955) 49(3) *AJIL* 345–346; García-Amador, Report (1956) 180, para 36, 182–183, paras 46–53.

163 Ago, Fifth Report (1976) 54, para 155.

164 Ibid, para 154; ILC, Summary Records of the Twenty-Eighth Session, UN Doc A/CN.4/SER.A/1976 (1976) 1 *YBILC* 58, para 24, 66, para 45.

165 ILC, Summary Records (1976) 90, para 33.

both in international practice and judicial decisions and in legal opinion.'[166] Some members of the ILC pointed out that the existence of a dual regime of State criminal and non-criminal responsibility under Article 18 was well-established in international law;[167] others assumed that the distinction fostered 'much needed' international law development, particularly in light of the notion of *jus cogens*.[168] The Commission highlighted the importance of progressive international law development in the matter of 'the distinction between different categories of international offences and the content and degrees of responsibility'.[169] This was considered of 'exceptional importance' and comparable to the 'explicit recognition of the category of rules of *jus cogens* in the codification of the law of treaties.'[170] The notion of a 'State crime' should have allowed the establishment of corresponding sanctions and enforcement procedures.[171]

Following the proposal of Article 18 by Ago, in 1976 the ILC adopted Article 19 of the First Part of the Draft Articles, including aggression and other State crimes under Article 19(3) and outlining the general principles of State crimes under Article 19(2).[172] In 1980, the ILC approved the First Part of the Draft Articles, including Article 19, confirming a clear distinction between State responsibility for 'crimes' and delicts'. Article 19 outlined a dual type of liability, whereby crimes constituted a smaller circle within the broader context of ordinary responsibility:

> Article 19 (International Crimes and International Delicts)
> 1. An act of a State which constitutes a breach of an international obligation is an internationally wrongful act, regardless of the subject-matter of the obligation breached.
> 2. An internationally wrongful act which results from the breach by a State of an international obligation so essential for the protection of fundamental interests of the international community that its breach is recognized as a crime by that community as a whole constitutes an international crime.

166 Ibid 88, para 21.
167 Ibid.
168 Ibid 70, paras 23 and 25, 82, para 28.
169 ILC, Report to the General Assembly on the Work of the Twenty-Eighth Session, UN Doc A/31/10 (1976) 2(1) *YBILC* 73, para 77.
170 Ibid 122, para 73. See also ILC, Summary Records (1976) 67, para 4, 69, para 17, 85, para 3, where it is stated that 'Article 18 played a very important role in the draft; it was one of the pillars on which the whole law of State responsibility rested.'
171 ILC, Summary Records (1976) 91, para 34.
172 See the adoption of a modified text of art 18 in ILC, Summary Records (1976) 239, para 3. This eventually became the text of art 19 of the First Part of the DASR adopted by the Commission (ILC, Report (1976) 75). See also Sixth Committee, Report to the General Assembly on the Work of the ILC of Its Twenty-Eighth Session, UN Doc A/31/370 (1976) 55–56, paras 154–155.

3. Subject to paragraph 2, and on the basis of the rules of international law in force, an international crime may result, inter alia, from:
   (a) a serious breach of an international obligation of essential importance for the maintenance of international peace and security, such as that prohibiting aggression;
   (b) a serious breach of an international obligation of essential importance for safeguarding the right of self-determination of peoples, such as that prohibiting the establishment or maintenance by force of colonial domination;
   (c) a serious breach on a widespread scale of an international obligation of essential importance for safeguarding the human being, such as those prohibiting slavery, genocide and apartheid;
   (d) a serious breach of an international obligation of essential importance for the safeguarding and preservation of the human environment, such as those prohibiting massive pollution of the atmosphere or of the seas.
4. Any internationally wrongful act which is not an international crime in accordance with paragraph 2 constitutes an international delict.[173]

Crimes were thus characterised by three main features: (1) the *erga omnes* scope of the obligation breached, (2) its fundamental importance and (3) the gravity of the breach. With respect to the *erga omnes* scope of the obligation breached, Article 19(2) was partly based on the notion of *jus cogens* under the 1969 VCLT and partly on the 1970 *obiter dictum* of the ICJ on *erga omnes* obligations in *Barcelona Traction*.[174]

Concerning specific crimes, in light of the evolution of State responsibility Article 19 codified and progressively developed international practice established after World Wars I and II, notably as concerns aggression and genocide.[175] Along the lines of the 1972 Stockholm Declaration on the Human Environment, the ILC quite progressively also considered that massive environmental offences affect fundamental peremptory obligations.[176] The ILC held that Article 19(3) constituted an embryonic international criminal code.[177] Furthermore, the Commission underscored that State criminal responsibility was distinct from the criminal responsibility of individuals acting as State organs or agents.[178]

173 ILC, Report to the General Assembly on the Work of the Thirty-Second Session, UN Doc A/35/10 (1980) 2(2) *YBILC* 32.

174 Ago, Fifth Report (1976) 28 ff, paras 89 ff; ILC, Summary Records (1976) 75, paras 18–20; ILC, Report (1976) 109, para 33; Giorgio Gaja, 'Obligations *Erga Omnes*, International Crimes and *Jus Cogens*: A Tentative Analysis of Three Related Concepts', in Joseph Weiler, Antonio Cassese and Marina Spinedi (eds), *International Crimes of States* (Walter de Gruyter & Co, 1989) 156–160.

175 ILC, Summary Records (1976) 89, para 25; ILC, Report (1976) 97, para 6, 101, para 15.

176 Id, Report (1976) 101–102, para 15. See also Hans-Martien Ten Napel, 'The Concept of International Crimes of States: Walking the Thin Line between Progressive Development and Disintegration of the International Legal Order' (1988) 1(2) *LJIL* 155.

177 ILC, Summary Records (1976) 64, para 29.

178 Ibid 73, para 7, 79 ff, paras 6 ff, 89, para 25; ILC, Report (1976) 118–119, para 59.

1.2.3 Codifying dualism (1980–2001)

1.2.3.1 The ICLA's Project for a comprehensive International Criminal Code

Prompted by the evolution of institutional work in the matter of State responsibility and the imminent resumption of the DCOPSM after aggression had been defined, in the 1980s the ICLA resumed work on an international criminal code and jurisdiction. Within this framework, in 1981 Professor Cherif Bassiouni completed the Project of an International Criminal Code.[179] In 1987, a Draft Statute for an ICC complemented a revised version of the Project.[180] Along the lines of the 1935 Proposal drafted by Pella, the Code asserted the 'plural responsibility' of States, individuals and other legal persons for crimes under international law in Article IV(1.3) of the General Part.[181] Within this framework, the principle that individual conduct of State organs or agents generates dual responsibility underpinned imputation under Article V(2) of the General Part:[182]

> General Part – Article V(2) (State Responsibility)
>
> 2.1.1. A State is responsible for any crime committed on its behalf, behest or benefit by a person in authority [...]
>
> 2.1.2. Conduct is attributed to a State if it is performed by persons or groups acting in their official capacity, who under the domestic law of that State possess the authority to make decisions for the State or any political subdivision thereof or possess the status of organs, agencies or instrumentalities of that State or a political subdivision thereof.

Under Article V(1.4.1) of the General Part, the Code spelled out in detail the criminal responsibility of legal entities other than a State, including governmental and non-governmental organisations.

According to Article III of the General Part, the Project established the universal jurisdiction of an international criminal court, overcoming the limited scope of application of a treaty necessary to make the Code compulsory. Article VIII(1.1) of the General Part provided that immunities could not grant an excuse before the ICC. In order to ensure the presence of the accused in Court, Article XI of the General Part of the Project established a State obligation to deliver persons under investigation to the Court, overriding any political exceptions or extradition clauses. The Court had jurisdiction over States and other

179 ICLA, Projet de Code pénal international, by Cherif Bassiouni (1981) 52(1–2) *RIDP* 97–236.

180 Cherif Bassiouni, *A Draft International Criminal Code and Draft Statute for an International Criminal Tribunal* (Martinus Nijhoff, 1987) 81–212.

181 On the extension of the jurisdiction of the ICC to legal persons, see Otto Triffterer, 'Efforts to Recognize and Codify International Crimes' (1989) 60(1–2) *RIDP* 61–66.

182 See Ahmed Fathi Sorour, 'Quelques remarques sur la partie générale du projet de code pénal international' (1981) 52(3–4) *RIDP* 509–510.

legal persons under Articles IV and V of the Code, as confirmed by Article XIV of the 1987 Draft Statute of the ICC.

Article VIII(3) of the General Part established for non-State legal entities sanctions including fines or other duties, according to the principle of proportionality. Article VIII(4) of the General Part established for States the sanction of a fine vis-à-vis the international community. The same rule created for the ICC the possibility of imposing cessation or equivalent corrective sanctions preventing repetition, without prejudice to the sanctions imposed under the UN Charter:

> General Part – Article VIII(3) (Penalties for States)
>
> 4.1. Penalties for States which are responsible for crimes under Article V, Section 2 of this Code shall consist of fines and other sanctions assessed on the basis of proportionality, without prejudice to compensation for damage and interests.
>
> 4.2. Such fines shall be due by States, provided they do not critically impair the economic viability of the State.
>
> 4.3. The determination and assessment of fines against a State shall be made by the International Criminal Tribunal and the enforcement of such fines shall be by and through the United Nations.
>
> 4.4. The provisions of this Article are without prejudice to the rights and duties of the United Nations to impose sanctions against a State as provided for in the United Nations Charter.
>
> 4.5. Special remedies - No provisions under this Article prevent the International Criminal Court from invoking its inherent judicial power to impose upon a State cessation of conduct in breach of the Code or to determine equitable injunctions in view of the correction of previous violations and to prevent their repetition.

The Special Part of the Code established a list of crimes falling concurrently under the jurisdiction of domestic criminal courts and the ICC, including aggression, war crimes, crimes against humanity, genocide and terrorism.[183] The Code thus envisaged a system coordinating domestic and international criminal jurisdictions.

This Project is the most recent and accomplished attempt to establish a monistic system of international criminal responsibility for natural persons, States and non-State legal entities from the standpoint of both substance and procedure.

1.2.3.2 Achieving the Draft Code of Crimes against the Peace and Security of Mankind

After adopting the text on the definition of aggression in 1974, the UN General Assembly made the DCOPSM a priority in its work programme in 1978 via Resolution 33/97.[184] In 1981, the Assembly again conferred on the ILC the task

183 ICLA, Projet de Code pénal international, Partie spéciale (1981) 99–163.

184 General Assembly, Draft Code of Offences against the Peace and Security of Mankind, UN Doc A/RES/33/97, 16 December 1978.

of drafting the DCOPSM by means of Resolution 36/106.[185] After considering 13 reports by the Special Rapporteur on the issue, Mr Doudou Thiam, in 1991 the ILC adopted a first text of the DCCPSM, including 26 articles.[186] In 1996, the ILC adopted a second text, including 20 articles,[187] thus achieving around 20 years of work spread over a time period of 50 years.

Similar to the 1991 Draft Code, the final version of the DCCPSM only focuses on the responsibility of natural persons (Article 2), possibly acting as State organs (Article 7). Article 4 further specifies that the Code is without prejudice to State responsibility. Notably, along the lines of the Nuremberg Principles, Articles 1–15 outline a general theory, Articles 16–20 define specific offences and Articles 8–12 define basic procedural principles.[188] Specific offences include aggression, necessarily entailing State responsibility (Article 16), genocide, based on the definition outlined in the Genocide Convention (Article 17), crimes against humanity instigated or directed by a government or by any organisation or group (Article 18), crimes against UN and associated personnel (Article 19) and war crimes (Article 20).[189] Some war crimes, such as the 'transfer by the Occupying Power of parts of its own civilian population into the territory it occupies' under Article 20(c)(i), necessarily involve the State.

The 1991 DCCPSM also included the crimes of intervention (Article 17), mercenarism (Article 23), international terrorism (Article 24) and wilful and severe damage to the environment (Article 26). 'Exceptionally serious war crimes' and 'systemic or mass violations of human rights' were prohibited under Articles 21 and 22. Article 24 outlined international terrorism as a crime involving a State context:

> Article 24 (International terrorism)
> An individual who as an *agent or representative of a State* commits or orders the commission of any of the following acts:
> - undertaking, organizing, assisting, financing, encouraging or tolerating acts against another State directed at persons or property and of such a nature as to create a state of terror in the minds of public figures, groups of persons or the general public [...] shall, on conviction thereof, be sentenced [to...].[190]

185 General Assembly, Draft Code of Offences against the Peace and Security of Mankind, UN Doc A/RES/36/106, 10 December 1981.

186 ILC, Report to the General Assembly on the Work of the Forty-Third Session, UN Doc A/46/10 (1991) 2(2) *YBILC* 94–97.

187 Id, Report (1996) 17–56.

188 Robert Rosenstock, 'The Forty-Eighth Session of the International Law Commission' (1997) 91(2) *AJIL* 365–370.

189 See Doudou Thiam, Thirteenth Report on the Draft Code of Crimes against the Peace and Security of Mankind, UN Doc A/CN.4/466 (1995) 2(1) *YBILC* 38 ff; Jean Allain and John Jones, 'A Patchwork of Norms: A Commentary on the 1996 Draft Code of Crimes against the Peace and Security of Mankind (1997) 8(1) *EJIL* 108 ff.

190 Emphasis added. See also Timothy McCormack and Gerry Simpson, 'The ILC's Draft Code of Crimes against the Peace and Security of Mankind: An Appraisal of the Substantive Provisions' (1994) 5(1) *Crim LF* 34–36.

In the course of preparatory work for the DCCPSM, the ILC debated the possibility of including in the Code Article 19 of the 1976 DASR, outlining State crimes. The idea was to coordinate individual and State responsibility, assuming that they could not operate in isolation from one another. In this regard, Cherif Bassiouni considered that individual and State criminal responsibility are tightly interwoven, raising questions such as whether or not individual liability is a necessary condition for State responsibility or how to shape reciprocal relations and sanctions.[191]

It was thus argued that individuals cannot commit crimes, such as aggression, without the State and that excluding responsibility under DASR 19 would entail State impunity. It was also assumed that sanctions for State crimes could include obligations such as fines and moral duties:

> The problem is to determine to which subjects of law international penal responsibility may be attributed: to individuals only or to States and other entities as well? Article 19 of part 1 of the draft articles on State responsibility prepared by the Commission indicates which internationally wrongful acts of a State constitute international crimes and delicts [...] The prevailing opinion was that the criminal responsibility of the State must be recognized and set forth in the draft. In support of this view, it was argued that offences against the peace and security of mankind were often committed by States and, indeed in many cases, could only be committed by States – for example, aggression, apartheid or annexation. Failure to recognize the State as a subject of criminal law would simply mean allowing those offences to go unpunished. It was also emphasized that it would be regrettable not to derive from article 19 all the legal consequences entailed by the principle stated therein, and that a system of sanctions adapted to the nature of States would appear to be altogether conceivable: moral or financial sanctions, among many others.[192]

Eventually, however, by reason of the 'uncertainty' still surrounding the notion of a 'State crime', the ILC exclusively focused on individual responsibility, temporarily disregarding State responsibility, without developing a critical normative analysis:

> With regard to the content *ratione personae,* the Commission took the view that its efforts *at this stage* should be devoted exclusively to the criminal responsibility of *individuals.* This approach was dictated by the uncertainty still attaching to the problem of the criminal responsibility of States [...] the question of international criminal responsibility should be limited, *at least at the present stage*, to that of individuals.[193]

191 Cherif Bassiouni, *Introduction to International Criminal Law* (Martinus Nijhoff, 2nd edn, 2013) 107.

192 ILC, Report (1983) 14, paras 50 and 54.

193 Ibid 15, paras 55–60; ILC, Report (1984) 11, para 32, emphasis added.

In his Third Report on the DCCPSM, Mr Thiam underscored that State crimes under Article 19 of the First Part of the DASR approved in 1980 constituted core offences under the Code:

> [T]he definition of an international crime given in article 19 of part 1 of the draft articles on State responsibility encompasses offences against the peace and security of mankind [...] It is true that all international crimes are characterized by the breach of an international obligation that is essential for safeguarding the fundamental interests of mankind. But some interests should be placed at the top of the hierarchical list. These are international peace and security, the right of self-determination of peoples, the safeguarding of the human being and the preservation of the human environment [...]
>
> Offences against the peace and security of mankind might therefore be defined in the following way:
>
> Offences against the peace and security of mankind are international crimes which result from:
>
> (a) a serious breach of an international obligation of essential importance for the maintenance of international peace and security;
> (b) a serious breach of an international obligation of essential importance for safeguarding the right of self-determination of peoples;
> (c) a serious breach on an extensive scale of an obligation of essential importance for safeguarding the human being;
> (d) a serious breach on an extensive scale of an obligation of essential importance for the safeguarding and preservation of the human environment.
>
> It will be noted that the provisional list of offences against the peace and security of mankind, established by the Commission at its thirty-sixth session, can fit perfectly into any subparagraph of this definition.[194]

Alternatively, the Special Rapporteur proposed a definition of the crimes against the peace and security of mankind based on *jus cogens*:

> Of course, a more synoptic definition might be proposed along the following lines:
>
> Any breach of an international obligation recognized as such by the international community as a whole is an offence against the peace and security of mankind.
>
> This second definition has the advantage of being brief and concise, but it does not sufficiently emphasize the various subject-matters to which a breach of the obligation in question may apply. The first definition, although long, has the merit of being coherent. It takes as its starting-point the same

194 Doudou Thiam, Third Report on the Draft Code of Crimes against the Peace and Security of Mankind, UN Doc A/CN.4/387 (1985) 2(1) *YBILC* 70–71, paras 61–64.

> approach and formulation as article 19 [of the DASR]. It emphasizes the two elements that are at the basis of a criminal transgression: the subjective element (the opinion of the international community) and the objective element (the subject-matter of the obligation violated). In this respect, it is more analytical. It will be for the Commission to assess the respective merits of the two formulas and make a choice.[195]

Along the lines of coordination, Article 5 of the Code proposed by Thiam in 1994 stated that '[p]rosecution of an individual for a crime against the peace and security of mankind does not relieve a State of any responsibility under international law for an act or omission attributable to it.'[196] Some members of the Sixth Committee of the General Assembly later expressed the view that 'all crimes against the peace and security of mankind were to be considered as crimes under international law and entailing both the criminal responsibility of their perpetrators and also State responsibility.'[197]

Whilst the DCCPSM is mainly concerned with substantive law, it cannot be separated from the international criminal court, which it ideally complements.[198] The eighth, ninth and tenth Reports of Doudou Thiam also deal with the question of an international criminal court and the eleventh Report includes a Draft Statute for the ICC as an organ of the UN.[199] Article 8 of the 1996 DCCPSM thus provided for the establishment of an ICC, combined with the domestic

195 Ibid 71, paras 65–66.

196 Doudou Thiam, Twelfth Report on the Draft Code of Crimes against the Peace and Security of Mankind, UN Doc A/CN.4/460 (1994) 2(1) *YBILC* 101–102, paras 41–48.

197 Sixth Committee of the General Assembly, Topical Summary of the Discussion Held during the Fiftieth Session of the General Assembly on the Report of the ILC of Its Forty-Seventh Session, UN Doc A/CN.4/472/Add.1 (1996) 20, para 75. See also ILC, Report to the General Assembly on the Work of the Forty-Seventh Session, UN Doc A/50/10 (1995) 2(2) *YBILC* 18, para 50, 49–50, para 270; Sixth Committee, Topical Summary, UN Doc A/CN.4/472 (1996) 19, paras 65–68:

> While it was recognised that the interplay between State responsibility and individual responsibility was unclear, the point was made that, where the individual was a government functionary acting on behalf of the State, State responsibility would probably arise in addition to individual responsibility in respect of acts by the individual which constituted crimes against the peace and security of mankind.

198 ILC, Report (1994) 26–27, para 91. For a scholarly viewpoint, see Benjamin Ferencz, 'An International Criminal Code and Court: Where They Stand and Where They're Going' (1992) 30(2) *Col J Transnatl L* 375–399.

199 Doudou Thiam, Eighth Report on the Draft Code of Crimes against the Peace and Security of Mankind, UN Doc A/CN.4/430 and Add.l (1990) 2(1) *YBILC* 36 ff; Id, Ninth Report on the Draft Code of Crimes against the Peace and Security of Mankind, UN Doc A/CN.4/435 and Add.1 (1991) 2(1) *YBILC* 41 ff; Id, Tenth Report on the Draft Code of Crimes against the Peace and Security of Mankind, UN Doc A/CN.4/442 (1992) 2(1) *YBILC* 51–58; Id, Eleventh Report on the Draft Code of Crimes against the Peace and Security of Mankind, UN Doc A/CN.4/449 (1993) 2(1) *YBILC* 111–124. The considerations of the ILC on the Draft Statute proposed by Mr Thiam are embedded in ILC, Report to the General Assembly on the Work of the Forty-Fifth Session, UN Doc A/48/10 (1993) 2(2) *YBILC* 14–20, paras 21–100.

application of the principle *aut dedere aut judicare* under Article 9. By virtue of Article 8, the ICC necessarily adjudicated upon aggression, overriding national jurisdictions. With respect to the jurisdiction of the Court, preparatory work envisaged the necessity of allowing proceedings *in absentia*. This was considered essential for the functioning of the Court to be effective, since ensuring the presence of the accused in international criminal proceedings depends on the uncertainties of State cooperation.[200]

1.2.3.3 Ad hoc *international and hybrid tribunals*

In the 1990s, the practice developed of establishing *ad hoc* international and hybrid criminal tribunals.[201] Thus, by means of Resolutions 827/1993[202] and 955/1994[203] the UN Security Council established *ad hoc* the ICTY and ICTR, which are complemented by the Mechanism for the International Criminal Tribunals (MICT).[204] Hybrid UN jurisdictions include the Extraordinary Chambers in the Courts of Cambodia,[205] the Special Tribunal for Lebanon (STL),[206] the Special Court and Residual Special Court for Sierra Leone (SCSL),[207] as well as the tribunals created by special UN Missions in Kosovo,[208] East Timor[209] and the Central African Republic.[210] The Special Tribunal established by the

200 Thiam, Eleventh Report (1993) 121–122, paras 93–96.

201 Sarah Williams, *Hybrid and Internationalized Criminal Tribunals: Selected Jurisdictional Issues* (Hart, 2012) 189 ff; Robert Cryer, Håkan Friman, Darryl Robinson and Elizabeth Wilmshurst, *An Introduction to Criminal Law and Procedure* (CUP, 3rd edn, 2014) 127 ff.

202 Security Council, International Tribunal for the Former Yugoslavia, UN Doc S/RES/827, 25 May 1993.

203 Id, Establishment of the International Criminal Tribunal for Rwanda (ICTR) and Adoption of the Statute of the Tribunal, UN Doc S/RES/955, 8 November 1994.

204 UN International Residual Mechanism for Criminal Tribunals, http://www.unmict.org/en.

205 General Assembly, Khmer Rouge Trials, UN Doc A/RES57/228, 27 February 2003; Agreement between the United Nations and the Royal Government of Cambodia Concerning the Prosecution under Cambodian Law of Crimes Committed during the Period of Democratic Kampuchea, 6 June 2003.

206 Security Council, Middle East: Agreement between the United Nations and the Lebanese Republic on the Establishment of a Special Tribunal for Lebanon and Statute of the Special Tribunal for Lebanon, UN Doc S/RES/1757, 30 May 2007.

207 Security Council, Sierra Leone, UN Doc S/RES/1315, 14 August 2000; Agreement between the United Nations and the Government of Sierra Leone on the Establishment of a Special Court for Sierra Leone and Statute of the Tribunal, 16 January 2002.

208 Security Council, Kosovo, UN Doc S/RES/1244, 10 June 1999; UNMIK Regulation 6/2000 as Amended by Regulation 34/2000 on the Appointment and Removal from Office of International Judges and International Prosecutors.

209 Security Council, East Timor, UN Doc S/RES/1272, 25 October 1999; UNTAET, Establishment of Panels with Exclusive Jurisdiction over Serious Criminal Offences, REG/2000/15.

210 President of the UN Security Council, Statement, UN Doc S/PRST/2017/9, 13 July 2017, 1; Loi organique 15.003, Création, organisation et fonctionnement de la Cour pénale spéciale, 3 June 2015.

Coalition for Iraq in 2003 is an example of a hybrid court created by States.[211] All these jurisdictions only have competence over natural persons.

Along the lines of the Nuremberg Principles, the ICTY had jurisdiction over grave breaches of the 1949 Geneva Conventions, laws and customs of war, genocide and crimes against humanity committed in the Socialist Former Republic of Yugoslavia (SFRY) since 1991 (ICTY Statute Articles 1–4). The ICTR had jurisdiction over genocide, crimes against humanity and core war crimes common to the Geneva Conventions and Additional Protocol II, including acts of terrorism, committed in Rwanda between 1 January 1994 and 31 December 1994 (ICTR Statute Articles 1–4). ICTY Statute Article 7(2) and ICTR Statute Article 6(2) excluded the excuse of acting in an official capacity. Furthermore, ICTY Statute Article 7(3) and ICTR Statute Article 6(1) allowed prosecuting superiors and subordinates. However, official agents were only responsible via complicity under ICTY Statute Article 7 and ICTR Statute Article 6, whilst legal entities as such were not. Following recommendations by the UN Secretary General,[212] ICTY and ICTR proceedings included two instances, therefore allowing appeals, unlike the IMT and IMTFE of Nuremberg and Tokyo. The ICTR ceased to operate in 2015 and the ICTY in 2017: the MICT still carries out residual functions.

In 1998, the ICTY delivered a critical decision in the case of *Furundžija*, clarifying the nature and scope of the prohibition of torture in international law and the relationship between *erga omnes* and peremptory obligations. Following the *obiter dictum* of the ICJ in *Barcelona Traction*, the ICTY regarded obligations *erga omnes* as universal duties owed to the international community as a whole. Along the lines of VCLT and VCLTIO Article 53, the Tribunal qualified the prohibition of torture not only as an *erga omnes* obligation but also as *jus cogens*, entailing universal jurisdiction:

> [T]he prohibition of torture imposes upon States obligations *erga omnes*, that is, obligations owed towards all the other members of the international community, each of which then has a correlative right. In addition, the violation of such an obligation simultaneously constitutes a breach of the correlative right of all members of the international community and gives rise to a claim for compliance accruing to each and every member, which then has the right to insist on fulfilment of the obligation or in any case to call for the breach to be discontinued [...] Because of the importance of the values it protects, this principle has evolved into a peremptory norm or *jus cogens*, that is, a norm that enjoys a higher rank in the international hierarchy than treaty law and even 'ordinary' customary rules [...] Clearly, the *jus cogens* nature of the prohibition against torture articulates the notion that

211 Iraqi Governing Council, Statute of the Iraqi Special Tribunal, 10 December 2003.

212 Secretary General, Report Pursuant to Paragraph 2 of Security Council Resolution 808, UN Doc S/25704, 3 May 1993, 29, para 116.

> the prohibition has now become one of the most fundamental standards of the international community [...] Furthermore, at the individual level, that is, that of criminal liability, it would seem that one of the consequences of the *jus cogens* character bestowed by the international community upon the prohibition of torture is that every State is entitled to investigate, prosecute and punish or extradite individuals accused of torture, who are present in a territory under its jurisdiction.[213]

Among hybrid tribunals, which include local and international judicial personnel and apply domestic and international law,[214] on 30 May 2007 the UN Security Council established the Special Tribunal for Lebanon under Chapter VII of the UN Charter, via Resolution 1757. This Tribunal is of particular interest, because it has concurrent competence over persons responsible for the attack of 14 February 2005 that resulted in the death of former Lebanese Prime Minister Rafiq Hariri and in the death or injury of other persons, as well as connected acts (STL Statute Article 1). Under Article 2 of the Statute, these acts are prosecuted as 'acts of terrorism, crimes and offences against life and personal integrity, illicit associations and failure to report crimes and offences, including the rules regarding the material elements of a crime, criminal participation and conspiracy'.

1.2.3.4 Achieving the Statute of the International Criminal Court

In 1981, after resuming work on the DCCPSM the ILC was confronted with the question of resuming work on the establishment of an international criminal court, which had been interrupted in 1953, pending the definition of aggression. By means of Resolutions 44/39 of 4 December 1989,[215] 45/41 of 28 November 1990[216] and 46/54 of 9 December 1991,[217] the UN General Assembly invited the ILC to examine the question of the establishment of an ICC. In particular, Resolution 44/39 prompted the ILC to consider the establishment of the ICC within the framework of the DCCPSM.[218] The ILC thus resumed work on the establishment of an ICC in the 1990s, which was further supported by events such as the conflicts in the SFRY and Rwanda.[219]

213 *Furundžija* (1998) 58–60, paras 151, 153–154 and 156.
214 Williams, *Hybrid* (2012) 58.
215 General Assembly, International Criminal Responsibility of Individuals and Entities Engaged in Illicit Trafficking in Narcotic Drugs across National Frontiers and Other Transnational Criminal Activities, UN Doc A/RES/44/39, 4 December 1989.
216 Id, Report of the International Law Commission on the Work of Its Forty-Second Session, UN Doc A/RES/45/41, 28 November 1990.
217 Id, Report of the International Law Commission on the Work of Its Forty-Third Session, UN Doc A/RES/46/54, 9 December 1991.
218 A/RES/44/39, para 1.
219 ILC, Report to the General Assembly on the Work of the Forty-Second Session, UN Doc A/45/10 (1990) 2(2) *YBILC* 19 ff, paras 93 ff.

Within the context of the DCCPSM, based on the Draft Statute included in the eleventh Report of Special Rapporteur Thiam,[220] in June 1993 the ILC established a Working Group on a Draft Statute for an ICC, chaired by Professor James Crawford. The Working Group submitted a Project to the Commission on 21 July 1993.[221] On this basis, the ILC achieved a first Draft Statute and submitted it to the attention of the General Assembly in 1994.[222] The 1994 Draft Statute envisaged the ICC as either an organ of the UN or a separate jurisdiction, having competence exclusively over natural persons for genocide, aggression, serious breaches of the laws and customs of armed conflicts, crimes against humanity and 'exceptionally serious crimes of international concern' (Article 20).[223] An Annexe to the Draft Statute outlined 'exceptionally serious crimes of international concern', including offences such as those under Article 1 of the 1970 Convention for the Suppression of Unlawful Seizure of Aircraft[224] and Article 2 of the 1973 Convention on the Prevention and Punishment of Crimes against Internationally Protected Persons, Including Diplomatic Agents.[225]

By means of Resolution 49/53,[226] in 1994 the UN General Assembly established an *Ad Hoc* Committee to study the main questions raised by the ICC Statute and work with a view to a Conference of Plenipotentiaries. The Committee submitted its final Report to the Assembly in 1995.[227] In the meantime, a group of experts from the ICLA and Max Planck Institute prepared a Draft Statute alternative to that of the ILC.[228]

In 1995, by means of Resolution 50/46 the UN General Assembly created a Preparatory Committee to develop the fundamental questions highlighted by the ILC in the 1994 Draft Statute.[229] The Committee worked from 1996 to 1998 and submitted a Draft Statute to the Conference of Plenipotentiaries,[230]

220 Thiam, Eleventh Report (1993) 111.

221 ILC, Report (1993) 100–132. See also James Crawford, 'The ILC's Draft Statute for an International Criminal Tribunal' (1994) 88(1) *AJIL* 140–152.

222 ILC, Report (1994) 18 ff. See also James Crawford, 'The ILC Adopts a Statute for an International Criminal Court' (1995) 89(2) *AJIL* 404–416.

223 See Bradley Berg, 'The 1994 ILC Draft Statute for an ICC: A Principled Appraisal of Jurisdictional Structure' (1996) 28(2) *Case W Res J Intl L* 226.

224 Adopted 16 December 1970, 860 UNTS 105, in force 14 October 1971.

225 Adopted 14 December 1973, 1035 UNTS 168, in force 20 February 1977.

226 General Assembly, Establishment of an International Criminal Court, UN Doc A/RES/49/53, 9 December 1994).

227 *Ad Hoc* Committee on the Establishment of an ICC, Report to the General Assembly, UN Doc A/50/22, 6 September 1995.

228 ICLA, ISISC and MPI, Draft Statute for an ICC – Alternative to the ILC Draft (Siracusa Draft) (1995).

229 General Assembly, Establishment of an International Criminal Court, UN Doc A/RES/50/46, 11 December 1995.

230 Preparatory Committee on the Establishment of an International Criminal Court (PCEICC), Report to the General Assembly, vol 1 (Proceedings of the Preparatory Committee during March-April and August 1996) UN Doc A/51/22, 13 September 1996); Id, Report to the General Assembly, vol 2 (Compilation of Proposals) UN Doc A/51/22/A, 13 September 1996; Id, Draft Statute and Draft Final Act, Report to the General Assembly, UN Doc

which adopted the Statute on 17 July 1998.[231] The Conference also established a Preparatory Commission for the ICC, which was mandated to adopt complementary instruments, including the Elements of Crimes and a definition of aggression.[232]

The Rome Statute of the ICC entered into force on 12 July 2001, establishing an *ex ante* system of criminal law and procedure (ICC Statute Article 24(1)). To a large extent, the Statute codifies the development of international criminal law that had taken place in the course of the 20th century.[233] However, the Statute also fosters progressive international law development.[234] Articles 21–33 of the Statute outline a general theory of international crimes, Articles 5–9 define specific crimes included in the jurisdiction of the Court, Articles 1–4, 10–20 and 34–128 outline the procedure and Article 77 regulates sanctions.

Under Article 5 of the ICC Statute, international crimes within the jurisdiction of the Court include genocide, crimes against humanity, war crimes and aggression. The Statute only embedded aggression in 2012 under Article 8bis, including a set of conditions triggering effective jurisdiction under Articles 15bis and 15ter.[235] Accordingly, the Assembly of States Parties to the ICC effectively activated the jurisdiction of the Court over aggression as of 17 July 2018.[236] In 1996, the Preparatory Committee also envisaged including the crime of terrorism within the jurisdiction of the ICC,[237] encompassing offences against aviation, maritime safety and protected persons according to the Annexe to Article 20(e). Article 5(1)(e) of the 1998 Draft Statute for the ICC also sought to outline a comprehensive definition of terrorism.[238] Eventually, the crime of terrorism was excluded from the Statute, notably because of the impossibility of outlining a uniform and precise definition of the crime.[239] Furthermore, decentralised national prosecution seemed to be a more appropriate response.[240]

A/CONF.183/2/Add.1, 14 April 1998. See also Cherif Bassiouni, 'Observations Concerning the 1997–1998 Preparatory Committee's Work' (1996–97) 25(2) *Denv J Intl L & Pol* 397–422.

231 United Nations Diplomatic Conference of Plenipotentiaries on the Establishment of an International Criminal Court (UNDCPICC), Final Act, UN Doc A/CONF.183/10, 17 July 1998.

232 Ibid 8–10, paras 1–11.

233 Reynald Ottenhoff, 'L'Association internationale de droit pénal et la création de la Cour pénale internationale: de l'utopie à la réalité' (2002) 73(1–2) *RIDP* 16 ff.

234 Leena Grover, *Interpreting Crimes in the Statute of the International Criminal Court* (CUP, 2014) 23–24.

235 ICC Statute Review Conference, The Crime of Aggression, RC/Res.6, 11 June 2010.

236 ICC Assembly of States Parties, Activation of the Jurisdiction of the Court over the Crime of Aggression, ICC-ASP/16/Res.5, 14 December 2017, 1, para 1; Claus Kreß, 'On the Activation of ICC Jurisdiction over the Crime of Aggression' (2018) 16(1) *JICJ* 15.

237 PCEICC, Report, A/51/22 (1996) 26, paras 106–107.

238 Id, Draft Statute (1998) 27–28, art 5 (Crimes within the Jurisdiction of the Court: Terrorism).

239 Mahnoush Arsanjani, 'The Rome Statute of the International Criminal Court' (1999) 93(1) *AJIL* 29; Aviv Cohen, 'Prosecuting Terrorists at the International Criminal Court: Reevaluating an Unused Legal Tool to Combat Terrorism' (2012) 20(2) *Mich St ILR* 254.

240 Ibid.

According to Article 25(1) of its Statute, the ICC only has competence over natural persons, regardless of their rank, including complicity (Article 25(3)), provided they are nationals of a State Party or committed a crime in the territory of a State Party (Article 12). *Mens rea* requires intent, whilst negligence is exceptional (ICC Statute Article 30).[241] Along the lines of the Nuremberg Principles, under ICC Statute Article 27 official capacity does not exclude responsibility.

The ICC Statute does not vest the Court with jurisdiction over legal entities as such. Notably, the Court does not have jurisdiction over States. During preparatory work, the possibility was envisaged of establishing the jurisdiction of the Court not only over natural persons, but also over legal persons. In fact, the proposals elaborated by the Preparatory Committee in 1996 foreshadowed the criminal responsibility of legal persons, save States, for acts of their agencies or representatives.[242] Corresponding sanctions included fines, dissolution, prohibition of professional or social activities, closure and confiscation.[243] Similarly, the Draft Statute submitted by the Preparatory Committee to the Conference of Plenipotentiaries in 1998 envisaged the responsibility of legal persons, save States, under Article 23.[244] Article 76 of the 1998 Draft Statute established corresponding sanctions, along the lines of Article 46-bis of the 1996 Draft Statute, including 'appropriate forms of reparation'.[245] The proposal was eventually rejected, fundamentally because not all State Parties to the ICC Statute envisage the responsibility of legal persons domestically.[246]

A brief comparative perspective shows that some States, for instance, Germany, Italy, Poland, Russia and Sweden, still follow the classical principle *societas delinquere non potest* and do not recognise the criminal responsibility of legal persons. More and more jurisdictions, however, have accepted the notion of corporate criminal liability, including State and non-State entities.[247] This is the case, for instance, of Australia, where the 1995 Criminal Code Act embeds a set of provisions on the criminal liability of corporate bodies in general.[248] Under US federal legislation, criminal responsibility applies to an 'organisation', that is, a 'person other than an individual',[249] including 'corporations, partnerships, associations, joint stock companies, unions, trusts, pension funds, unincorporated organisations, governments and political subdivisions thereof, and non-profit

241 See also PCEICC, Report, A/51/22 (1996) 45, para 200; PCEICC, Draft Statute (1998) 55–56, art 29.
242 Id, Report, A/51/22/A (1996) 80 (Part 3-bis (General Principles of Criminal Law), art B (Individual Criminal Responsibility), proposal 2 (Physical Persons and Juridical Persons)).
243 Ibid 234, art 47bis (Penalties Applicable to Juridical Persons).
244 PCEICC, Draft Statute (1998) 48–49 (Article 23[5]: Individual Criminal Responsibility).
245 Ibid 121–122 (Article 76: Penalties Applicable to Legal Persons).
246 PCEICC, Report, A/51/22 (1996) 44, para 194.
247 Stoitchkova, *Towards Corporate Liability* (2010) 7–8.
248 Australia Criminal Code Act (1995) ch 2, div 12.1(1), providing that the Criminal Code 'applies to bodies corporate in the same way as it applies to individuals'.
249 18 US Code ch 1, para 18.

organizations.'[250] Similarly, Section 2 of the Canadian Criminal Code extends criminal liability to 'organisations', that is, 'a public body, body corporate, society, company, firm, partnership, trade union or municipality' or an 'association of persons' with a 'common purpose and operational structure'.[251] Within this context, a first approach equally considers natural and legal persons, criminalising organisations for the same offences as individuals. The Australian Criminal Code thus affirms that 'a body corporate may be found guilty for any offence, including one punishable by imprisonment.'[252] A second method is legislating on organisational liability for specific offences either via provisions governing particular crimes or under general criminal provisions. For instance, according to the French Criminal Code corporate criminal liability only applies when there is an express mention 'in the law or in a Regulation.'[253]

With regard to State responsibility, some scholars underscore that individual crimes outlined in the ICC Statute largely overlap with State crimes under Article 19 of the ILC's 1996 DASR.[254] In this respect, during preparatory work for the ICC Statute a provision was envisaged establishing that individual criminal responsibility 'did not absolve the State of any of its responsibility'.[255] Article 25(4) of the ICC Statute eventually asserts that 'no provision [...] relating to individual criminal responsibility shall affect the responsibility of States under international law.' Some scholars argue that a tension underpins this rule, whereby '[t]he apparent historical inevitability and moral appeal of individual criminal responsibility is undermined by the temptations of collective responsibility.'[256]

The ICC procedure is based on the accusatorial model. Unlike the ICTY and ICTR, under Article 17 of its Statute the competence of the ICC is complementary to that of domestic courts. Appeals are allowed under ICC Statute Articles 81–85 and revision under Article 84. Since the effectiveness of the Court largely depends on State support, ICC Statute Articles 86–102 regulate in detail international cooperation and assistance, with a particular emphasis on the surrender of persons and collection of evidence. ICC Statute Article 63(1) excludes proceedings *in absentia*,[257] although the ILC's 1994 Draft Statute and the 1996 and 1998 Draft Statutes proposed by the *Ad Hoc* Committee and Preparatory

250 US Sentencing Guidelines Manual (2016) para 8A1.1, https://www.ussc.gov/guidelines.
251 Criminal Code of Canada, RSC (1985) ch C-46, s 2.
252 Australia Criminal Code Act (1995) ch 2, div 12(1)(2).
253 Code pénal (1994) art 121–2, translation by the author. See also Cristina de Maglie, 'Models of Corporate Criminal Liability in Comparative Law' (2005) 4(3) *Wash UGSLR* 551–552.
254 Joe Verhoeven, 'Vers un ordre répressif universel? Quelques réflexions' (1999) 45 *AFDI* 61. See also ss 1.2.2.3 and 1.2.3.5.
255 PCEICC, Report, A/51/22 (1996) 44, para 192.
256 Gerry Simpson, 'Men and Abstract Entities: Individual Responsibility and Collective Guilt in International Criminal Law', in Nollkaemper and Van der Wilt, *System Criminality* (2009) 86.
257 See Mohammad Hadi Zakerhossein and Anne-Marie De Brouwer, 'Diverse Approaches to Total and Partial *in Absentia* Trials by International Criminal Tribunals' (2015) 26(2) *Crim LF* 192.

Committee envisaged the possibility of trials *in absentia*.[258] Concerning enforcement, a State designated by the Court carries out the execution of imprisonment (ICC Statute Article 103), whereas State Parties implement fines and confiscation according to domestic procedures (ICC Statute Article 109).

1.2.3.5 From 'State crimes' to 'serious breaches of peremptory norms' in the ILC's Draft Articles on State Responsibility

The First Part of the ILC's DASR adopted in 1980, including Article 19 on State crimes, was complemented by the Second and Third Parts on the consequences of internationally wrongful acts provisionally adopted in 1996. Willem Riphagen and Gaetano Arangio-Ruiz, respectively Second and Third Rapporteur on the issue, worked on the substantive and procedural implications of State responsibility, including crimes.

Riphagen led the Commission to draft a few provisions, including Articles 5, 14 and 15 of DASR Part Two.[259] Article 5 provided that, in the case of a State crime, 'all other States' of the international community would be injured. Article 14(1)–(2) outlined specific consequences of State crimes: it compelled non-recognition of the legality of a situation created by the offence and established an obligation not to render aid or assistance to the responsible State, as well as mutual assistance in these respects. Furthermore, Article 14(3)–(4) subjected such consequences to the primacy of the procedures and obligations under the UN Charter. Concerning the crime of aggression, Article 15 further specified the additional nature of consequences under the DASR with respect to the procedures under the UN Charter. Article 4(b) of the Third Part of the DASR submitted by Riphagen to the ILC in his Seventh Report in 1986 established the possibility for a State of unilaterally resorting to the ICJ after invoking State criminal responsibility and failing to reach a consensual solution.[260]

Gaetano Arangio-Ruiz developed in detail the Second and Third Parts of the DASR, paying particular attention to the implications of State crimes in terms of sanctions and dispute settlement in his Fifth, Sixth, Seventh and Eight Reports.[261] Notably, Article 16 of the Second Part of the DASR envisaged the

258 ILC, Report (1994) 53–54, Commentary to art 37; PCEICC, Report, A/51/22 (1996) 54, para 254, art 37 (Trial in the Presence of the Accused); PCEICC, Draft Statute (1998) 99 ff, art 63 (Trial in the Presence of the Accused).

259 Willem Riphagen, Sixth Report on the Content, Forms and Degrees of International Responsibility (Part 2 of the Draft Articles) and 'Implementation' (*Mise en oeuvre*) of International Responsibility and the Settlement of Disputes (Part 3 of the Draft Articles), UN Doc A/CN.4/389 (1985) 2(1) *YBILC* 5, 13 and 14.

260 Id, Seventh Report on State Responsibility, UN Doc A/CN.4/397 and Add.1 (1986) 2(1) *YBILC* 4–5.

261 Gaetano Arangio-Ruiz, Fifth Report on State Responsibility, UN Doc A/CN.4/453 and Add.1–3 (1993) 2(1) *YBILC* 30 ff; Id, Sixth Report on State Responsibility, UN Doc A/CN.4/461 and Add.1–3 (1994) 2(1) *YBILC* 18 ff; Id, Seventh Report on State Responsibility,

exclusion of proportionality in reparation for State crimes.[262] Procedurally, Article 18(1)(e) compelled States to implement the principle *aut dedere aut judicare* against individuals committing a crime against the peace and security of mankind triggering State responsibility.[263] Article 18(1)(f) obliged States to participate in the implementation of measures taken by an international organisation against a criminal State.[264] Critically, Article 19 established the possibility for a State to unilaterally resort to the ICJ in the case of a State crime, upon authorisation by the UN Security Council or General Assembly:

> Article 19
>
> 1. Any State Member of the United Nations Party to the present Convention claiming that an international crime has been or is being committed by one or more States shall bring the matter to the attention of the General Assembly or the Security Council of the United Nations in accordance with Chapter VI of the Charter of the United Nations.
> 2. If the General Assembly or the Security Council resolves by a qualified majority of the Members present and voting that the allegation is sufficiently substantiated to justify the grave concern of the international community, any Member State of the United Nations Party to the present Convention, including the State against which the claim is made, may bring the matter to the International Court of Justice by unilateral application for the Court to decide by a judgment whether the alleged international crime has been or is being committed by the accused State ...[265]

Article 20 coordinated these procedures with proceedings under the UN Charter:

> Article 20
>
> The provisions of the articles of the present part are without prejudice to:
>
> (a) Any measures decided upon by the Security Council of the United Nations in the exercise of its functions under the provisions of the Charter;
> (b) The inherent right of self-defence as provided in Article 51 of the Charter.[266]

Article 7 of the Third Part of the DASR proposed by Arangio-Ruiz further established that the State victim of the breach of a sanction imposed for an

---

UN Doc A/CN.4/469 and Add.1 and 2 (1995) 2(1) *YBILC* 7–31; Id, Eighth Report on State Responsibility, UN Doc A/CN.4/476 and Add.1 (1996) 2(1) *YBILC* 1–8.

262 Arangio-Ruiz, Seventh Report (1995) 29, para 140.

263 Ibid 29–30.

264 Ibid 30.

265 Ibid.

266 Ibid.

international crime could unilaterally resort to the ICJ, subject to a failure to settle the matter via arbitration.[267]

Article 19 of the First Part of the ILC's DASR approved in 1980, governing State crimes, was eventually embedded in the first complete version of the Draft Articles approved by the ILC in 1996.[268] In this context, continental scholars observe that Article 19 was a crucial provision, codifying international practice.[269] By virtue of corresponding Article 40(3), a crime was conceived of as an *erga omnes* breach, affecting all States of the international community. Under Articles 51–53, consequences included the exclusion of proportion in reparation, non-recognition of the legality of a situation created by a crime, the obligation not to render aid or assistance to the responsible State, and mutual assistance in the application of measures aiming to eliminate the consequences of a crime. According to Article 39, this framework was subject to the provisions of the UN Charter concerning the maintenance of peace and security. In the view of Arangio-Ruiz, this norm critically reinforced the power of the UN Security Council in the matter of State responsibility.[270] By contrast, proposals on the establishment of compulsory jurisdiction were not included in the 1996 DASR.

Whether Article 19 established a criminal regime for State responsibility remains dubious. Indeed, Article 19 distinguished 'crimes' from 'delicts', but the latter are also considered to trigger (minor) criminal responsibility domestically.[271] The terminology is inspired by the distinction between aggravated and ordinary responsibility in Roman law,[272] but is not particularly helpful to shed light on the nature of liability.[273] In any case, the terminology of Article 19 certainly aimed to establish a dualistic regime for State responsibility.[274] The provision, however, raised the sceptical reaction of several States. For instance, the US held that the notion of a 'State crime' has no support in customary international law and does not foster positive international law

267 Ibid 31, para 147.

268 ILC, Report (1996) 60.

269 Giuseppe Palmisano, 'Les causes d'aggravation de la responsabilité des États et la distinction entre "crimes" et "délits" internationaux' (1994) 98(3) *RGDIP* 632; Acosta Estévez, 'Normas' (1995) 22.

270 Gaetano Arangio-Ruiz, 'The "Federal Analogy" and UN Charter Interpretation: A Crucial Issue' (1997) 8(1) *EJIL* 24–25; Id, 'Fine prematura del ruolo preminente di studiosi italiani nel progetto di codificazione della responsabilità degli Stati: specie a propositio di crimini internazionali e dei poteri del Consiglio di sicurezza' (1998) 81(1) *RDI* 117 and 121.

271 ILC, Summary Records (1976) 68, para 8, 71, para 34; ILC, Report to the General Assembly on the Work of the Fiftieth Session, UN Doc A/53/10 (1998) 2(2) *YBILC* 71–72, para 292. See also Georges Abi-Saab, 'The Uses of Article 19' (1999) 10(2) *EJIL* 346; Marina Spinedi, 'La responsabilité de l'État pour "crime": une responsabilité pénale ?', in Hervé Ascensio, Emmanuel Decaux and Alain Pellet, *Droit international pénal* (Pedone, 1st edn, 2000) 102.

272 ILC, Report (1976) 121–122, para 72.

273 Alain Pellet, 'Remarques sur une révolution inachevée: le Projet d'articles de la CDI sur la responsabilité des États' (1996) 42 *AFDI* 22–23.

274 Abi-Saab, 'The Uses' (1999) 346.

development.[275] For the UK, the concept of a 'State crime' was a major obstacle to the adoption of the Draft Articles.[276] The Spanish Government considered that there is no international definition of 'State crimes'.[277] According to the Canadian Government, the absence of a precise definition of a 'State crime' prevented the acceptance of the notion.[278] However, other States, such as Germany, underscored the significance of the notion of a 'State crime' for the purpose of protecting rules that are essential for the peaceful coexistence of States.[279] Czechoslovakia pointed out the *erga omnes* nature of State criminal offences.[280]

Under the guidance of the Fourth Rapporteur on State Responsibility, James Crawford, the ILC debated the destiny of Article 19 within the context of the division of the DASR into four parts: (1) the internationally wrongful act of a State, (2) the content of responsibility, (3) implementation and (4) general provisions. Whilst some scholars considered it crucial to maintain Article 19 in the text of the DASR,[281] others envisaged its suppression.[282] Favouring suppression, Crawford fostered the notion of a 'serious breach of an *erga omnes* obligation', that is, a duty owed to the international community as a whole,[283] triggering general countermeasures.[284] Along these lines, Article 41 included in Part II

275 ILC, Comments and Observations Received from Governments on State Responsibility, UN Doc A/CN.4/488 and Add.1–3 (1998) 2(1) *YBILC* 100, para 3(b).

276 Ibid, para 10.

277 ILC, Comments and Observations of Governments on Part 1 of the Draft Articles on State Responsibility for Internationally Wrongful Acts, UN Doc A/CN.4/351 and Add.1–3 (1982) 2(1) *YBILC* 17, para 4.

278 ILC, Observations and Comments of Governments on Chapters I, II, and III of Part 1 of the Draft Articles on State Responsibility for Internationally Wrongful Acts, UN Doc A/CN.4/328 and Add.1–4 (1980) 2(1) *YBILC* 94, para 5.

279 Id, Comments and Observations of Governments on Part 1 of the Draft Articles on State Responsibility for Internationally Wrongful Acts, UN Doc A/CN.4/414 (1988) 2(1) *YBILC* 4, para 35.

280 Id, Comments of Governments on Part 1 of the Draft Articles on State Responsibility for Internationally Wrongful Acts, UN Doc A/CN.4/342 and Add.l–4 (1981) 2(1) *YBILC* 73, para 7. For an overview of questions raised by art 19, see ILC, Report (1998) 64 ff, paras 241 ff.

281 Arangio-Ruiz, Eighth Report (1996) 2, paras 3–8; ILC, Report (1998) 69, para 276; Abi-Saab, 'The Uses' (1999) 347; Andrew Jacovides, 'State Responsibility: Reflections on the International Law Commission's Draft Articles' (2000) 94 *ASIL Proc* 296.

282 James Crawford, First Report on State Responsibility, UN Doc A/CN.4/490 and Add.1–7 (1998) 2(1) *YBILC* 22 ff, paras 87 ff; ILC, Report (1998) 66 ff, paras 252 ff, notably 69, paras 275 and 277. See also James Crawford, 'The Internationalization of Criminal Law: Remarks' (1995) 89 *ASIL Proc* 301; Derek William Bowett, 'Crimes of State and the 1996 Report of the International Law Commission on State Responsibility' (1998) 9(1) *EJIL* 173.

283 Crawford, First Report (1998) 23, paras 92–93; James Crawford, Third Report on State Responsibility, UN Doc A/CN.4/507 and Add.1–4 (2000) 2(1) *YBILC* 32 ff, paras 96 ff. See also James Crawford, 'International Crimes of States', in Crawford, Pellet, Olleson and Parlett, *The Law* (2010) 413.

284 Crawford, Third Report (2000) 108, art 51; Crawford, 'International Crimes' (2010) 412; James Crawford, *State Responsibility: The General Part* (CUP, 2013) 390–394.

of the DASR provisionally adopted by the ILC in 2000 replaced 'State crimes' under prior Article 19:

> Chapter III
> Serious Breaches of Essential Obligations to the International Community
> Article 41 (Application of This Chapter)
> 1. This chapter applies to the international responsibility arising from an internationally wrongful act that constitutes a serious breach by a State of an obligation *owed to the international community as a whole* and essential for the protection of its fundamental interests.
> 2. A breach of such an obligation is serious if it involves a gross or systematic failure by the responsible State to fulfil the obligation, risking substantial harm to the fundamental interests protected thereby.[285]

Eventually, Article 40 of the DASR approved by the ILC in 2001 focuses on *jus cogens*:[286]

> Chapter III
> Serious Breaches of Obligations under Peremptory Norms of General International Law
> Article 40 – Application of This Chapter
> 1. This chapter applies to the international responsibility which is entailed by a serious breach by a State of an obligation arising under a peremptory norm of general international law.
> 2. A breach of such an obligation is serious if it involves a gross or systematic failure by the responsible State to fulfil the obligation.[287]

Thus, the ILC's DASR do not outline specific breaches of peremptory norms, withdrawing the list of offences embedded in Article 19(3) of the ILC's 1996 DASR, nor do they clarify the secondary *erga omnes* structure of peremptory obligations outlined in VCLT and VCLTIO Article 53. Article 41 simply follows the notion of *jus cogens* established in the primary rules of international law.[288] However, Alain Pellet maintains that, at least with respect to the definition of

285 ILC, Report to the General Assembly on the Work of the Fifty-Second Session, UN Doc A/55/10 (2000) 2(2) *YBILC* 69, emphasis added.

286 Eric Wyler, 'From "State Crime" to Responsibility for "Serious Breaches of Obligations under Peremptory Norms of General International Law"' (2002) 13(5) *EJIL* 1156; Crawford, 'International Crimes' (2010) 410.

287 ILC, Report (2001) 112. See also James Crawford, Fourth Report on State Responsibility, UN Doc A/CN.4/517 and Add.1 (2001) 2(1) *YBILC* 12 ff, paras 43 ff, emphasis added.

288 James Crawford, Pierre Bodeau and Jacqueline Peel, 'The International Law Commission's Draft Articles on State Responsibility: Toward Completion of a Second Reading' (2000) 94(4) *AJIL* 673.

the offence, breaches of *jus cogens* under Article 40 entail the violation of an *erga omnes* obligation and are therefore grounded in the pattern envisaged in Article 19 of the 1996 DASR.[289]

Draft Article 41 outlines the 'particular' consequences of a serious breach of a peremptory norm of international law, which apply in addition to cessation, non-repetition and reparation under Part II. Such consequences are therefore supposed to distinguish the aggravated regime of State responsibility from the standpoint of secondary rules:

> Article 41
> Particular Consequences of a Serious Breach of an Obligation under This Chapter [Peremptory Norms of General International Law]
> 1. States shall cooperate to bring to an end through lawful means any serious breach within the meaning of article 40.
> 2. No State shall recognize as lawful a situation created by a serious breach within the meaning of article 40, nor render aid or assistance in maintaining that situation.
> 3. This article is without prejudice to the other consequences referred to in this part and to such further consequences that a breach to which this chapter applies may entail under international law.[290]

The suppression of the notion of a 'State crime' from the standpoint of the offence eventually led to abandoning the meaningful procedural consequences envisaged by Arangio-Ruiz from the viewpoint of implementation.

The 2001 DASR were submitted to the attention of States and should have led to a conference of plenipotentiaries, with a view to the adoption of a treaty on State responsibility.[291] This nevertheless has not (yet) happened, and thus for the time being the Articles only constitute soft law.[292] The UN General Assembly is indeed still considering the possibility of adopting the DASR as a binding convention.[293] It is questionable whether the 2001 DASR, which do not embed the notion of a 'State crime', are fully consistent with international practice. In fact, with particular regard to aggression and genocide, different international instruments might be interpreted as supporting the criminal nature of such offences. This is notably the case of UN General Assembly Resolution 2625 (XXVI) on Friendly Relations and Co-operation among Nations and Resolution 3314 (XXIX) on the Definition of Aggression, as well as the

289 Alain Pellet, 'Les articles de la CDI sur la responsabilité de l'État pour fait internationalement illicite: suite - et fin?' (2002) 48 *AFDI* 15–16.
290 ILC, Report (2001) 113–114.
291 Ibid 25, paras 72–73.
292 Crawford, *State Responsibility* (2013) 90–92.
293 General Assembly, Responsibility of States for Internationally Wrongful Acts, UN Doc A/RES/71/133, 13 December 2016.

1948 Genocide Convention.[294] Some scholars define such responsibility as '*sui generis*',[295] others propose a review of the text of the Genocide Convention so as to clarify that not only individuals, but also States, can be held criminally responsible.[296] In this regard, it has been underscored that the use of the word 'crime' in international legal instruments would only have the aim of stigmatising aggravated offences, so that international law would not (yet) recognise State criminal responsibility.[297] However, on the one hand, stigma is a specific element of criminality,[298] on the other, in legal texts words have precise literal and contextual implications by virtue of VCLT and VCLTIO Article 31. Noting that advances in the area move back and forth, Cançado Trindade concludes that State aggravated responsibility has both a civil and criminal nature.[299]

1.2.4 Genocide, aggression and terrorism still in search of identity (2001–2019)

1.2.4.1 Genocide in the jurisprudence of the ICJ: the 'second death' of State crimes?

The ICJ delivered its final judgment in the *Bosnian Genocide* case on 26 February 2007, deciding on the responsibility of Serbia and Montenegro for genocidal acts committed in Bosnia.[300] Following the stance taken in the 1993 decision on preliminary objections,[301] the Court held that Article IX of the Convention involves not only the State obligations to legislate, prosecute or extradite so as to prevent and punish the crime of genocide, but also the duty not to commit genocide.[302] The ICJ indeed confirmed that the effect of Article I of the Genocide Convention is to 'prohibit States from themselves committing genocide'.[303] However, the Court ultimately did not uphold the criminal nature of State responsibility for genocide.[304] This approach is certainly influenced by the abandonment of State criminal responsibility in the 2001 DASR. In this respect, Pierre-Marie Dupuy considered that the ICJ 'did not cross the Rubicon', thus determining the 'second death' of the 'crimes of States':[305]

294 Dupuy, 'International Criminal Responsibility' (2002) 1088 and 1093; Wolf, 'Individual Responsibility' (2016) 49.
295 Webb, 'Binocular Vision' (2012) 121.
296 Aquilina and Mulaj, 'Limitations' (2018) 135.
297 Anne-Laure Vaurs Chaumette, *Les sujets du droit international pénal* (Pedone, 2009) 227–228.
298 David Caron, 'State Crimes in the ILC Draft Articles on State Responsibility: Insights from Municipal Experience with Corporate Crimes' (1998) 92 *ASIL Proc* 308–309.
299 Cançado Trindade, 'Complementarity' (2005) 257 and 263.
300 *Application of the Convention* [2007] ICJ Rep 43.
301 See s 1.2.1.3.
302 *Application of the Convention* [2007] 106–107, para 152.
303 Ibid 113, para 166, 118–119, para 179.
304 Ibid 116, para 173.
305 Pierre-Marie Dupuy, 'A Crime without Punishment' (2016) 14(4) *JICJ* 880.

> Genocide, the Court recalled in the judgment, similar to aggression, is a crime of State. However, the ICJ stopped short of taking the final step of finding that this State was 'criminal' with respect to the Srebrenica events. As if struck dumb, the Judges stepped away at the very last hurdle and refused to conclude in favour of the international criminal responsibility of the State.[306]

Nonetheless, the ICJ has not been fully consistent with this negative approach throughout the judgment. In fact, the Court considered the possibility that Serbia and Montenegro be held responsible for 'complicity' in the genocidal acts committed by the Republika Srpska, in practice a branch of the Serb Army operating in the Bosnian territory. Whilst it eventually excluded complicity in the case in issue, in light of a direct State prohibition on committing genocide the Court maintained that a State can be held responsible for 'complicity' in genocide.[307] Given the absence of the concept of 'complicity' in the codification of State responsibility, the ICJ applied a classical criminal law concept to State liability, thus 'sitting on two stools, by combining public international law and criminal law categories'.[308]

Following its previous jurisprudence,[309] the ICJ highlighted 'the significance of the *jus cogens* character' of the norms regulating genocide and other violations of human rights, as well as 'the *erga omnes* character of the relevant obligations'.[310] The ICJ thus confirmed the correlation existing between peremptory rights and universal obligations, which the ICTY previously underscored particularly in *Furundžija* with respect to the prohibition of torture.

Concerning the subjective link between individual and State responsibility, the ICJ held that the establishment of the former is not a *conditio sine qua non* for determining the latter.[311] The Court thus approached from a dualistic perspective the concerns raised by the ICTY in *Tadić*, where the Tribunal held:

> [T]he continued, indirect involvement of the Government of the Federal Republic of Yugoslavia (Serbia and Montenegro) in the armed conflict in the Republic of Bosnia and Herzegovina [...] gives rise to issues of State responsibility beyond the scope and concern of this case [individual liability].[312]

306 Ibid 891.

307 *Application of the Convention* [2007] 119–120, para 182, 200 ff, paras 381 ff, 216–217, paras 418 ff.

308 Cassese, 'On the Use' (2007) 881. See also Marina Aksenova, *Complicity in International Criminal Law* (Hart, 2017) 178 ff.

309 *Reservations to the Convention* [1951] 23; *Application of the Convention* [1996] 615–616, para 31; *Armed Activities on the Territory of the Congo (New Application: 2002) (Democratic Republic of the Congo v Rwanda)* [2006] ICJ Rep 31, para 64.

310 *Application of the Convention* [2007] 120, para 185.

311 Ibid 119–120, para 182.

312 *Tadić*, IT-94-1, 217, Trial Chamber, Judgment of 7 May 1997, para 606.

However, the ICJ addressed the question without considering analytically the relationship between individual and State conduct, but 'pragmatically' based on procedural matters, notably the impossibility of ensuring the presence of accused natural persons at trial.[313] Furthermore, in practice the ICJ was highly deferential to the findings of the ICTY in assessing State responsibility,[314] raising doubts as to whether 'a State will ever be held responsible for genocide outside the parameters of the prior convictions of individual perpetrators'.[315] In this respect, scholars consider that, rather than 'duality', individual liability generates the 'subalternity' of State responsibility.[316]

The ICJ confirmed the stance taken in the *Bosnian Genocide* case in the judgment subsequently delivered in 2015 in the dispute concerning the *Application of the Genocide Convention* between Croatia and Serbia, under Article IX of the Convention.[317] Adjudicating upon the alleged responsibility of Serbia for committing genocide against Croatians in the territory of Croatia and the counter-claim submitted by Serbia on the responsibility of Croatia for committing genocide against Serbians in the Krajina Region, the ICJ held both States not responsible.[318] Specifically, the Court reached this conclusion based on the absence of the required persecutory intent.[319]

In its argumentation in the second case concerning the *Application of the Genocide Convention*, the ICJ confirmed that 'State responsibility and individual criminal responsibility are governed by different legal régimes and pursue different aims.'[320] However, the ICJ considered a significant factor the fact that 'the ICTY Prosecutor has never charged any individual on account of genocide against the Croat population'.[321] Furthermore, the Court reasoned that 'no high-ranking Croatian civilian or military officer has been found guilty of genocide by the ICTY'.[322] Most significantly, in the course of the dispute the Court applied the same 'beyond reasonable doubt' standard of proof that applies to natural persons in order to determine State persecutory intent. In fact, for State persecutory intent to exist the Court required that it be the 'only reasonable inference' to be drawn from a pattern of Serb acts constituting the *actus reus*

313 *Application of the Convention* [2007] 119, paras 180–182. See also Webb, 'Binocular Vision' (2012) 128–129.

314 See, for instance, *Application of the Convention* [2007] 132, para 217, 155, para 277, 166, para 296.

315 Richard Goldstone and Rebecca Hamilton, '*Bosnia v Serbia*: Lessons from the Encounter of the International Court of Justice with the International Criminal Tribunal for the Former Yugoslavia' (2008) 21(1) *LJIL* 103. See also Webb, 'Binocular Vision' (2012) 128 and 144–145.

316 Mark Drumbl, 'Accountability for System Criminality' (2010) 8(1) *Santa Clara JIL* 379.

317 *Application of the Convention* [2015] ICJ Rep 3.

318 Ibid 153–154, para 524.

319 Ibid 128–129, paras 441–442, 152, para 515.

320 Ibid 61, para 129.

321 Ibid 128, para 440.

322 Ibid 133–134, para 461.

of genocide.[323] Even more explicitly, the Court held that such a criterion is the same as that applied by the ICTY to assess the responsibility of natural persons.[324] It is actually unclear why the ICJ applied the ultimate standard of proof that is based on the presumption of innocence in order to determine State *mens rea*. In fact, such a standard is meant to counterbalance the particularly serious implications of individual criminal liability in terms of sanctions, but should not suit a separate regime of State responsibility, if it pursues 'different aims'.[325] Scholars have thus noted that, despite the theoretical divide, '[i]n practice, State responsibility appears more dependent on the establishment of individual responsibility than it should be.'[326]

1.2.4.2 Aggression and terrorism: developments in the ICC Statute and beyond

Concerning aggression, in 2010 the ICC Statute eventually included in Article 8bis the definition outlined in Resolution 3314 (XXIX) adopted by the UN General Assembly in 1974. At least from the standpoint of conduct, there is therefore overlap between individual and State liability.[327] Such a substantive relationship entailed the adoption of particular provisions governing the institutional and procedural relations between the ICC, States and the UN Security Council. Notably, Article 15bis regulates the jurisdiction of the Court when a State submits a case or the Prosecutor investigates *proprio motu* under Article 13(a) and (c) of the ICC Statute. Article 15ter governs the jurisdiction of the Court when the Security Council submits a case under Article 13(b) of the ICC Statute. This approach is consistent with Article 5(2) initially embedded in the Statute of the ICC adopted in 1998, which established the jurisdiction of the Court in conformity with relevant provisions of the UN Charter. It is unclear, however, how the Council and the Court will coordinate with one another.

After the failed adoption of the 1937 Convention for the Prevention and Punishment of the Crime of Terrorism and the related Treaty on an ICC, terrorism has faced scattered development.[328] The 1991 DCCPSM outlined terrorism as an individual crime committed in a State context and centred on violent conduct and political purposes. By contrast, the proposals for including terrorism in the ICC Statute in 1996 and 1998 focused exclusively on natural persons, particularly based on different transnational conventions. Such transnational

323 Ibid 128, para 440.
324 Ibid 67, para 148.
325 Beatrice Bonafè, 'Reassessing Dual Responsibility for International Crimes' (2016) 73 *Seqüência* 22 and 33. See also Aquilina and Mulaj, 'Limitations' (2018) 132.
326 Bonafè, 'Reassessing' (2016) 36.
327 Dapo Akande and Antonios Tzanakopoulos, 'The Crime of Aggression in the ICC and State Responsibility' (2017) 58 *Harv ILJ (Online)* 34.
328 Kimberley Trapp, *State Responsibility for International Terrorism* (OUP, 2011) 252 ff; Shadi Adnan Alshdaifat, *International Law and the Use of Force against Terrorism* (Cambridge Scholars Publishing, 2017) 49 ff.

conventions, for instance, the International Convention for the Suppression of Terrorist Bombings[329] and the Convention for the Suppression of Unlawful Acts against the Safety of Civil Aviation,[330] are currently positive law on the matter. Article 2 of the UN Draft Comprehensive Convention against International Terrorism seeks to single out a uniform definition of the offence. In 2011, the STL took a critical step towards a consistent definition of terrorism under general international law, outlining the offence as a customary prohibition:

> [A] number of treaties, UN resolutions, and the legislative and judicial practice of States evince the formation of a general *opinio juris* in the international community, accompanied by a practice consistent with such *opinio*, to the effect that a customary rule of international law regarding the international crime of terrorism, at least in time of peace, has indeed emerged. This customary rule requires the following three key elements: (i) the perpetration of a criminal act (such as murder, kidnapping, hostage-taking, arson, and so on), or threatening such an act; (ii) the intent to spread fear among the population (which would generally entail the creation of public danger) or directly or indirectly coerce a national or international authority to take some action, or to refrain from taking it; (iii) when the act involves a transnational element.[331]

Conclusion

Key steps in the evolution of international criminal responsibility include different proposals elaborated prior to World War I and within the context of the League of Nations prior to World War II. This work addresses the criminal responsibility of natural persons, States and non-State legal entities. From the viewpoint of substance, the projects developed in this period underscore an essential identity between individual and State criminal acts, whereby the conduct of State organs or agents generates dual liability, with a particular focus on aggression, terrorism and the use of force. From the standpoint of procedure, coordination emerges between the two forms of responsibility. Several proposals support the establishment of a Criminal Chamber within the PCIJ with jurisdiction over both individual and State liability, not necessarily entailing uniform proceedings. Concretely, in 1937 these projects resulted in the adoption of a Convention against terrorism committed by natural persons and a complementary treaty on an international criminal court, which nonetheless never entered into force.

Such proposals paved the way for the adoption of critical instruments after World War II. Whilst in the 1980s ICLA initiatives developed a monistic

329 Adopted 15 December 1997, 2149 UNTS 256, in force 23 May 2001.
330 Adopted 23 September 1971, 974 UNTS 177, in force 26 January 1973.
331 *Ayyash* et al, STL-11-01/I, Appeals Chamber, Interlocutory Decision on the Applicable Law: Terrorism, Conspiracy, Homicide, Perpetration, Cumulative Charging, 16 February 2011, 49–50, para 85.

approach, whereby the same jurisdiction should have ideally adjudicated upon individual and State criminal responsibility, institutional work clearly evolved in a dualistic sense. Individual criminal responsibility developed around aggression, war crimes, crimes against humanity, genocide and terrorism. It evolved from the IMT and IMTFE to the ICC, via the DCOPSM, several draft Statutes for an ICC and *ad hoc* international and hybrid tribunals. Although the question of the relationship between individual and State responsibility arose in this context, these instruments only concern individual responsibility, uncoordinated with State responsibility, mostly in light of the uncertainty of the notion of a 'State crime'. The limits of aggregate responsibility are therefore those of complicity in criminal association.

Concerning State responsibility, UN General Assembly Resolution 2625 (XXVI) on Friendly Relations and Co-operation among Nations and Resolution 3314 (XXIX) on the Definition of Aggression establish the responsibility of States for aggression, which now matches individual criminal responsibility under the ICC Statute as amended in 2012. However, procedurally it is difficult to envisage how concretely the ICC and the UN Security Council will coordinate with one another in the matter. The 1948 Genocide Convention establishes not only the responsibility of the State for the same genocidal conduct as that of natural persons, but also the compulsory jurisdiction of the ICJ over State liability. Particularly in light of this practice, soft law, notably the ILC's DASR, criminalised State breaches of *erga omnes* obligations from 1976 to 1996. However, in 2001 the DASR degraded State criminal responsibility to aggravated responsibility for a 'serious' breach of a 'peremptory norm', along the lines of VCLT and VCLTIO Article 53. The 2001 DASR are therefore silent on the question of State criminal responsibility. The subsequent jurisprudence developed by the ICJ in the cases concerning the *Application of the Genocide Convention*, involving Bosnia, Croatia and Serbia, demonstrates that the question is far from being definitively settled.

2 Breach of a primary norm

Offence

Introduction

The historical analysis developed in Chapter 1 shows that some individual criminal offences digressed from giving rise to State criminal responsibility to generating State aggravated responsibility in international law. This chapter explores offences that generate such a dual responsibility, by means of a two-step investigation. First, the analysis focuses on the critical common elements of dual offences, particularly through the lens of peremptory obligations and attribution of liability to responsible persons. Second, in light of the systemic analysis of the common elements of dual offences, the investigation considers specific breaches that generate serious dual responsibility, notably the prohibition of aggression, genocide, core war crimes, core crimes against humanity and terrorism.

This chapter underscores commonalities between State aggravated responsibility and individual criminal responsibility from the standpoint of the general concepts underpinning the different offences. In this respect, the study focuses first on the objective elements of the violation, considering its structure and content. Furthermore, the analysis takes into account the nature of unlawful conduct. Second, the subjective elements of the violation are discussed. In this regard, the chapter considers the principle that individual conduct of State organs or agents is attributed to the State itself and to what extent the criteria applying to individual *mens rea* also apply to the State.

Focusing on key regulatory instruments, the analysis considers specific offences giving rise to serious dual responsibility. Notably, supranational criminal law directly regulates international crimes for natural persons, including penalties, whereby the reference is the Statute of the ICC. Furthermore, international law can play a 'transnational' role in defining individual domestic crimes. In particular, by means of treaties, such as the Genocide Convention, States can outline compulsory directives for criminalising specific conduct in national legal orders. The domestic definition of crimes and penalties is thus harmonised, but ultimately left to States. Harmonisation also applies to conduct that is criminalised at the supranational level, as in the case of genocide, which is an international crime under both the Genocide Convention and the ICC Statute. There is therefore overlap between crimes that are regulated at the supranational level and domestically harmonised crimes. The same international instruments can also define State aggravated responsibility. For instance, the Genocide Convention outlines not only the responsibility of individuals, but also that of States for genocidal conduct of its organs or agents, within the context of the general rules on State responsibility embedded in the DASR. The definition of war crimes and crimes against humanity outlined in the ICC Statute also provides a basis to define State aggravated offences.

The analysis developed in this chapter ultimately aims to identify possible overlaps and differences between individual criminal responsibility and State aggravated responsibility from the standpoint of the breach of a primary norm in international law, addressing the general elements of the offence and specific violations.

2.1 Core substantive elements of the offence

2.1.1 The obligations breached by State aggravated offences

2.1.1.1 Serious breaches of peremptory norms (jus cogens: *2001 DASR 40)*

Two elements are critical to defining the aggravated regime of State responsibility under the ILC's 2001 DASR 40:

1. The peremptory character of the obligation breached
2. A 'serious breach', that is, a 'gross or systematic' failure to comply with a peremptory obligation

The peremptory nature of the obligation breached (1) outlines its non-derogability. In fact, VCLT and VCLTIO Article 53 defines a peremptory norm as a non-derogable rule accepted as such by the international community as a whole. Whilst in the past scholars noted that States did not conduct themselves as though peremptory obligations existed, before or after the entry into force of the VCLT,[1] currently the notion of *jus cogens* is well-established in international law, although its content is not clearly defined.[2]

The 'seriousness' of the breach entails a 'gross or systematic failure to comply' with the obligation in question (2).[3] More specifically, the ILC considered that 'systematic' means 'carried out in an organized and deliberate way'.[4] The term

1 Charles De Visscher, 'Positivisme et "*jus cogens*"' (1971) 75(1) *RGDIP* 7. See also ILC, Summary Records (1976) 17, para 33.
2 Weatherall, Jus Cogens (2015) 7 and 200–201.
3 ILC, Report (2001) 113, para 8; Crawford, *State Responsibility* (2013) 380–381. See also Paola Gaeta, 'The Character of the Breach', in Crawford, Pellet, Olleson and Parlett, *The Law* (2010) 425–426.
4 ILC, Report (2001) 113, para 8.

'gross' refers to 'the intensity of the violation or its effects' and 'denotes violations of a flagrant nature'.[5] The 'systematic' or 'gross' nature of the violation is to be determined based on 'the scope and number of individual violations' and 'the gravity of their consequences for the victims'.[6] Furthermore, the ILC clarified that the 'seriousness' of a breach refers to 'the intent to violate the norm'.[7] This stance supports a fault-based approach to State responsibility, as opposed to objective liability. The ILC also pointed out that '[t]he terms [gross or systematic] are not of course mutually exclusive' so that 'serious breaches will usually be both systematic and gross.'[8] This makes it clear that a violation that is both 'gross' and 'systematic' or either 'gross' or 'systematic' triggers State aggravated responsibility.[9]

Therefore, we can summarise the regime of State aggravated responsibility under the 2001 DASR as follows:

1 Peremptory character of the obligation breached
2 Gross (intent + scope and number of violations, consequences for victims) and/or systematic (intent + organised) failure to comply

On this basis, scholars have underscored that, similar to domestic law, where the highest societal interests define the content of criminal responsibility, the notion of *jus cogens*, which is the only hierarchical principle in international law, defines the content of State aggravated responsibility. Therefore, even if 2001 DASR 40 erased the notion of a 'State crime' embedded in 1996 DASR 19, the 'ghost' of criminal responsibility would still 'haunt' the Draft Articles.[10] Cançado Trindade thus points out that '[*a*]*ggravated* responsibility is precisely that which corresponds to a crime of State.'[11] Iain Scobbie identifies violations under 2001 DASR 40 with system criminality in international law.[12] In this regard, studying Article 40 and its normative implications within the 2001 DASR requires an 'archaeological' investigation, in the sense that Article 40 and related norms reveal concealed traces of State crimes embedded in Article 19 of the 1996 DASR and related rules.

Other scholars consider that Article 41 of the DASR proposed in 2000, which was grounded in the concept of *erga omnes* obligations,[13] embedded the essence of State criminal responsibility posited in 1996 DASR 19, without explicitly

5 Ibid.
6 Ibid.
7 Ibid.
8 Ibid.
9 Ibid.
10 Crawford, Fourth Report (2001) 12, para 43; Pierre-Marie Dupuy, 'Quarante ans de codification du droit de la responsabilité internationale des États: un bilan' (2003) 107(2) *RGDIP* 329.
11 Cançado Trindade, 'Complementarity' (2005) 264.
12 Iain Scobbie, 'Assumptions and Presuppositions: State Responsibility for System Crimes', in Nollkaemper and Van der Wilt (eds), *System Criminality* (2009) 274–275 and 277.
13 See s 1.2.3.5.

mentioning State crimes.[14] In this respect, the ILC specified that the violation of an *erga omnes* obligation affects not only all States of the international community, but also all other subjects, including individuals and non-State entities.[15] Pierre-Marie Dupuy considers 2000 DASR 41 'more coherent' than 2001 DASR 40.[16] However, in this context the Fourth Special Rapporteur on State Responsibility, James Crawford, rejected the notion of 'exceptionally serious wrongful acts' proposed during preparatory work,[17] which could have been interpreted as a reference to State crimes.[18]

Whilst from the viewpoint of the general definition there is at least overlap, and possibly also considerable commonality between serious breaches of *jus cogens* under 2001 DASR 40 and 1996 DASR 19(2), the suppression of specific hypotheses of State criminal conduct excludes the notion of a 'State crime'. In fact, it is not impossible to identify conduct that triggers State aggravated responsibility under 2001 DASR 40 based on customary international law, particularly, as we shall see,[19] aggression, genocide, core war crimes, core crimes against humanity and prospectively terrorism.[20] However, a critical principle of criminal law is *nullum crimen sine lege*, which would require that State crimes be explicitly singled out in a coherent normative text, notably a treaty as the natural outcome of the DASR. In the absence of such a clear definition, it is impossible to elaborate a regime for State criminal responsibility. Indeed, from the very beginning of its work the ILC underscored that, even assuming that State crimes coincide with serious breaches of peremptory norms, it would still be necessary to precisely identify such violations.[21] In this respect, it should not be forgotten that the ILC envisaged the DASR as a codification treaty for State responsibility complementing the primary rules established by the VCLT and VCLTIO. It is well known that, thus far, the Draft Articles have not become a binding instrument and for the time being therefore they only provide guidance as soft law.[22]

14 Sixth Committee of the General Assembly, Topical Summary of the Discussion Held during the Fifty-Fifth Session on the Work of the ILC of Its Fifty-Second Session, UN Doc A/CN.4/513 (2001) 20, para 92.
15 Ibid 21, para 99; ILC, Report (2000) 20, para 49. See also Antônio Augusto Cançado Trindade, *International Law for Humankind: Towards a New* Jus Gentium (Brill, 2nd edn, 2013) 317.
16 Dupuy, 'L'unité de l'ordre juridique international' (2002) 297 *RCADI* 367.
17 Sixth Committee of the General Assembly, Topical Summary of the Discussion Held during the Fifty-Fourth Session on the Work of the ILC of Its Fifty-First Session, UN Doc A/CN.4/504 (2000) 10, para 23.
18 Crawford, First Report (1998) 78, paras 51 and 81–87; ILC, Report (1998) 66–67, para 256.
19 Section 2.1.1.5.
20 ILC, Report (2001) 112–113, paras 4–6; James Crawford, *The International Law Commission's Articles on State Responsibility: Introduction, Text and Commentaries* (CUP, 2002) 245–246; Asif Hameed, 'Unravelling the Mystery of *Jus Cogens* in International Law' (2013) 84(1) *BYBIL* 57; Weatherall, Jus Cogens (2015) 209 ff.
21 ILC, Summary Records (1976) 1 *YBILC* 84, para 40. See also Antoine Ollivier, 'International Criminal Responsibility of the State', in Crawford, Pellet, Olleson and Parlett, *The Law* (2010) 710.
22 See s 1.2.3.5.

Other non-binding instruments, such as a declaration by the UN General Assembly, seem to be unsuitable to establish a regime of State criminal responsibility, owing to their non-binding nature.[23] However, this should not prevent the adoption of a binding regime for State criminal responsibility *erga omnes contractantes*, by means of a particular treaty, in accordance with 2001 DASR 48(1)(a).[24]

2.1.1.2 Linking jus cogens *and* erga omnes *obligations (VCLT and VCLTIO Article 53 and 2001 DASR 40, 42, 48 and 54)*

From a State perspective, the most important norm on *jus cogens* is VCLT and VCLTIO Article 53. This rule defines *jus cogens* from the standpoint of the theory of treaties. The purpose of the VCLT and VCLTIO is to regulate the sources of international law, conclusion of treaties and their effectiveness. Therefore, Article 53 does not outline a straightforward definition of *jus cogens*, but rather defines its impact on the validity of treaties.[25]

The first part of VCLT and VCLTIO Article 53 establishes that a treaty does not produce any effects in the case of a conflict with a peremptory norm (1). Furthermore, a peremptory norm belongs to general international law (2). Therefore, peremptory norms have two features: a non-derogable nature and a universal scope.[26] The second part of VCLT and VCLTIO Article 53 defines the non-derogable and universal nature of peremptory norms.[27]

'Universality' is defined from the standpoint of the acceptance and recognition of the norm, based on power and consensus.[28] Under VCLT and VCLTIO Article 53, a rule is general when the 'international community of States as a whole' recognises it. This formulation has given rise to different interpretations. It could be read as a reference to all States, but preferably it is interpreted as a reference to the consensus of the majority of States, including the most powerful ones.[29]

23 James Crawford, 'Revisiting the Draft Articles on State Responsibility' (1999) 10(2) *EJIL* 443, note 32.

24 Id, First Report (1998) 9, paras 39–42; ILC, Report (1998) 63–64, paras 231–235; Crawford, Fourth Report (2001) 6–7, paras 22–26; Sixth Committee, Report to the General Assembly on the Work of the ILC of Its Fifty-Third Session, UN Doc A/56/589 (2001) 5–6. See also James Crawford, 'On Re-Reading the Draft Articles on State Responsibility' (1998) 92 *ASIL Proc* 299; Giorgio Gaja, 'Should all References to International Crimes Disappear from the ILC's Draft Articles on State Responsibility?' (1999) 10(2) *EJIL* 369; Chusei Yamada, 'Revisiting the International Law Commission's Draft Articles on State Responsibility', in Ragazzi, *International Responsibility* (2005) 119; Hugh Thirlway, *The Sources of International Law* (OUP, 2014) 150.

25 Lauri Hannikainen, *Peremptory Norms* (Jus Cogens) *in International Law* (Finnish Lawyers' Publishing, 1988) 1–3; Hameed, 'Unravelling' (2013) 56–57; Weatherall, Jus Cogens (CUP, 2015) 6.

26 Thirlway, *The Sources* (2014) 160. Concerning 'universality', the expression '*jus cogens*' is literally problematic, because it means 'peremptory law' (or 'right')', thus encompassing 'non-derogability', but not 'universality'.

27 See the text of art 53 in s 1.2.2.2.

28 Antonio Gómez Robledo, 'Le *ius cogens* international' (1981) 172(3) *RCADI* 105; Hameed, 'Unravelling' (2013) 58.

29 Giorgio Gaja, '*Jus Cogens* beyond the Vienna Convention' (1981) 172(3) *RCADI* 283; Hannikainen, *Peremptory Norms* (1988) 4 and 209 ff; Hameed, 'Unravelling' (2013) 62.

The 'peremptory nature' of *jus cogens* is outlined in terms of non-derogability. In fact, States cannot modify peremptory norms bilaterally or multilaterally, and thus *jus cogens* is *jus non dispositivum*.[30] The perspective is again that of power, that is, the relationship between States and a right in issue. However, the temporal angle changes with respect to the definition of 'universality'. In fact, Article 53 defines 'universality' by considering the time when a rule comes into existence via general recognition (t_1). As of this time, it is impossible to modify that rule, so that 'non-derogability' is defined with respect to the time elapsing from the establishment of the rule onwards ($t_1 \rightarrow$). This time is not necessarily unlimited, because under VCLT and VCLTIO Article 53 a peremptory norm 'can be modified' by means of 'a subsequent norm of general international law having the same character'. The expression 'same character' indicates that a peremptory norm_1 (*cogens*) can only be modified by a subsequent peremptory norm_2 (*cogens*), which comes into existence when the international community achieves consensus, according to the definition of 'universality'.

The definition of *jus cogens* is wholly based on the notion of 'power', in light of primary procedural norms. VCLT and VCLTIO Article 53 specifies that '*jus cogens*' includes non-derogable rules recognised as such by the majority of States.[31] It is possible to outline the temporal model of a peremptory norm (*cogens*) as follows:

Majority consensus (t_1)
→ non-derogable norm_1
→ majority consensus (t_2)
→ non-derogable norm_2

In other words, States cannot bilaterally repeal *jus cogens*, which, once established, is therefore non-derogable. This means that the consensus of the majority of States is necessary not only for the establishment of a peremptory norm, but also to vary or remove it.

Since the definition of *jus cogens* is based on power from the standpoint of primary procedural norms, it does not focus on the substantive structure of peremptory rules. VCLT and VCLTIO Article 53 does not say that a peremptory norm establishes a universal obligation. It is only possible to infer universality implicitly from the nature of *jus cogens* as a non-bilaterally derogable duty. In fact, the majority of States might accept a non-derogable rule that only binds two States or a few of them. It is indeed impossible to explain the scope of a norm in terms of non-derogability, which defines the incapacity of modifying a rule bilaterally.[32]

30 Gómez Robledo, 'Le *ius cogens*' (1981) 92; Acosta Estévez, 'Normas' (1995) 4–5; Thirlway, *The Sources* (2014) 144; Weatherall, Jus Cogens (2015) 4; Robert Kolb, *Peremptory International Law* – Jus Cogens (Hart, 2015) 2.
31 Weatherall, Jus Cogens (2015) 5–6.
32 Gómez Robledo, 'Le *ius cogens*' (1981) 92–93.

Interestingly, VCLT and VCLTIO Article 66(a) provides that, if a dispute concerning the application or interpretation of Article 53 is not resolved within twelve months, any of the parties can submit it to the ICJ, unless the litigants find an agreement on arbitration. This seems to introduce the possibility of unilaterally resorting to the ICJ in the case of a conflict concerning a peremptory norm.[33] However, in practice the ICJ tends to separate *jus cogens* from compulsory jurisdiction.[34]

The DASR entail a link between primary and secondary rules.[35] Given that the law of treaties embeds the notion of *jus cogens*, rules on State responsibility develop its implications. Fundamentally, the idea is that the law of treaties mostly concerns primary procedural norms (power), whereas the law of State responsibility focuses on primary substantive norms (obligations), secondary procedural rules (dispute settlement), secondary substantive norms (sanctions) and tertiary procedural rules (enforcement). Temporally, the DASR shift the focus from the sources (t_1) to the structure of primary and secondary substantive obligations, as well as related procedures ($t_1 \rightarrow$).[36] More specifically, within the 2001 DASR rules included in Part 1 (Internationally Wrongful Act of the State) address conduct in breach of a primary substantive norm. Norms embedded in Part 2 (Content of the International Responsibility) outline sanctions and are thus secondary substantive rules. Part 3 norms (Implementation of the International Responsibility of a State) regulate invocation of responsibility (secondary procedural norms) and countermeasures (tertiary procedural norms).

Because of the complementarity between the law of treaties and State responsibility, the 2001 DASR provide supplementary evidence on the nature of *jus cogens* outlined in the VCLT and VCLTIO. Chapter 3 of the DASR includes Articles 40 and 41 and specifically addresses '[s]erious [b]reaches of [o]bligations under [p]eremptory [n]orms of [g]eneral [i]nternational [l]aw'. Article 40(1) outlines the specific consequences of a serious breach of an obligation arising under a peremptory norm of general international law. The perspective is no longer that of primary procedural norms, that is, power, but the violation of an existing obligation. Normative terminology underscores this change by referring to the obligation arising under a peremptory norm that is already in place, not to the recognition of a peremptory norm. However, Article 40(1) does not outline the structure of *jus cogens* and Article 40(2) specifies that Article 40 only addresses 'serious' breaches of *jus cogens*.

Although DASR 40 does not explicitly add anything to the definition of *jus cogens* under VCLT and VCLTIO Article 53, it is possible to implicitly retrieve information by systemically considering the implications of Article 40 within the framework of the 2001 DASR. In fact, from the standpoint of secondary

33 Orakhelashvili, *Peremptory Norms in International Law* (OUP, 2006) 490 ff.
34 *Armed Activities* [2006] 32, para 64; *Application of the Convention* [2007] 104, para 147.
35 See s 1.2.2.3.
36 Orakhelashvili, *Peremptory Norms* (2006) 80; Robert Kolb, *The International Law of State Responsibility: An Introduction* (Edward Elgar, 2017) 57.

procedural norms DASR 42(b) and 48(1)(b) provide that, in the case of a breach of an obligation 'owed to the international community as a whole', all States can invoke responsibility. As concerns secondary substantive rules, DASR 33(1) establishes that a sanction is an obligation that can bind a State vis-à-vis 'the international community as a whole'. With regard to tertiary rules, DASR 54 provides for all States the possibility of adopting enforcement measures if the obligation breached binds a State vis-à-vis the international community as a whole. Whilst none of these rules explicitly mention *jus cogens*, there is a clear overlap with the notion of an *erga omnes* obligation, given that the breach of a peremptory obligation directly or indirectly affects all States and possibly non-State subjects of the international community.[37] In fact, Crawford underscored that *erga omnes* obligations are 'virtually coextensive' with peremptory norms.[38]

2.1.1.3 Serious breaches of erga omnes *obligations: 1996 DASR 19 and 40*

The ILC's 1996 DASR were more specific than the 2001 DASR with respect to the nature of a State crime. Article 19(2) outlined the general criteria for defining State criminal responsibility, whilst Article 19(3) further spelled out specific protected interests, thus defining a 'general theory' and 'specific offences' entailing State criminal responsibility.

Article 19(2) provided that a State crime involves the 'breach by a State of an international obligation so essential for the protection of fundamental interests of the international community (1)' that is 'recognized as a crime by that community as a whole' (2). Similar to *jus cogens*, this norm was based on power and normative recognition (t_1),[39] not on the structure of the obligation and its breach ($t_1 \rightarrow$).[40] Thus, the definition of international crimes was not based on the scope of the obligation breached and its non-derogability (primary substantive rule),

37 On the identity between obligations 'owed to the international community as a whole' under 2001 DASR 48(1)(b) and *erga omnes* obligations, see James Crawford, *The International Law Commission* (2002) 278; Iain Scobbie, 'The Invocation of Responsibility for the Breach of "Obligations under Peremptory Norms of General International Law"' (2002) 13(5) *EJIL* 1209 ff; Crawford, *State Responsibility* (2013) 368; Thirlway, *The Sources* (2014) 143.

38 Crawford, Third Report (2000) 34, para 106(a).

39 On the similar definition of State crimes and *jus cogens*, see Gaja, '*Jus Cogens*' (1981) 300; Abi-Saab, 'The Uses' (1999) 341; Jørgensen, *The Responsibility* (2000) 100–104. On the necessary relationship between ILC's 1996 DASR 19(2) and VCLT and VCLTIO art 53, see Ago, Fifth Report (1976) 31–33, paras 99–101, 52–53, para 149; ILC, Summary Records (1976) 57, paras 20–21, 60, para 37, 61, para 4, 64, para 24, 65, para 37, 68, para 13, 71, para 36, 83, para 34, 241, para 16, 251–252, para 41; ILC, Report (1976) 94–95, paras 16–17, 119, para 61, 113, para 73; Sixth Committee, Report to the General Assembly on the Work of the ILC of Its Thirtieth Session, UN Doc A/33/419 (1978) 54, para 152; Riphagen, Sixth Report (1985) 18, para 31.

40 Giorgio Gaja, '*Jus Cogens*' (1981) 300; Roberto Ago, 'The Concept of "International Community as a Whole": A Guarantee to the Notion of State Crimes', in Weiler, Cassese and Spinedi, *International Crimes* (1989) 252–253.

so that eventually DASR 19(2) only defined *jus cogens* from the standpoint of primary procedural rules.

The first criterion was merely objective and provided that the interest protected by the obligation must be a fundamental condition for a State crime to exist.[41] The second parameter was strictly linked to the former and established that the international community as a whole should recognise the importance of the protected interest.[42] These conditions applied jointly and underscored that crimes offend the most important interests protected in society. The general nature of such conditions allowed flexibility, so as to include or exclude interests based on the evolution of societal needs,[43] although this has been criticised as a source of uncertainty.[44]

Based on these premises, according to a first scholarly interpretation the concept of a State crime under DASR 19(2) was nothing other than the secondary implication of *jus cogens* under VCLT and VCLTIO Article 53 as a primary norm.[45] State crimes would have thus been serious violations of peremptory norms. A serious breach of a peremptory norm would have entailed a derogation from the ordinary regime of State responsibility under Draft Article 19, in the same way as Article 53 derogates from the bilateral and multilateral regime of treaties. Criminal sanctions would have been the secondary equivalent of nullification in the field of primary rules, because of a breach of the 'international public order'.[46] In the absence of a strict normative hierarchy, *jus cogens* would have singled out superior interests necessitating criminal protection.[47] From this perspective, the possibility of introducing the faculty of unilateral recourse to the ICJ envisaged during preparatory work for the text of 1996 DASR 19 was in line with unilateral action for interpreting *jus cogens* under VCLT and VCLTIO Article 66(a). However, according to a different interpretation, State crimes may exist outside *jus cogens.*[48]

In order to fully understand the structure of the obligation breached by a State crime, it is necessary to read Article 19 in conjunction with 1996 DASR 40.[49] Article 40(3) substantively established that, in the case of a State crime 'all other States' of the international community would be injured.[50] Article 40

41 Ago, Fifth Report (1976) 13, para 32; ILC, Report (1976) 87, para 2, 120–121, paras 63–67.
42 ILC, Report (1976) 97, para 6; John Quigley, 'The International Law Commission's Crime-Delict Distinction: A Toothless Tiger?' (1988) 66(2) *RDISPD* 118–120.
43 ILC, Summary Records (1976) 63, para 19, 66, para 43.
44 Pellet, 'Remarques' (1996) 21.
45 Cançado Trindade, 'Complementarity' (2005) 263.
46 Pierre-Marie Dupuy, 'Le fait générateur de la responsabilité internationale des États' (1984) 188(5) *RCADI* 56–57; Dominicé, 'The International Responsibility' (1999) 359.
47 Ago, Fifth Report (1976) 32, paras 99 ff; ILC, Report (1976) 119–120, para 62; Acosta Estévez, 'Normas' (1995) 19; Cançado Trindade, 'Complementarity' (2005) 264.
48 ILC, Summary Records (1976) 17, paras 33–36, 71, para 23.
49 Article 40 adopted in 1996 is essentially based on the text of art 5 proposed in 1985 by Willem Riphagen (see Riphagen, Sixth Report (1985) 5 ff; ILC, Report to the General Assembly on the Work of the Thirty-Seventh Session, UN Doc A/40/10 (1985) 2(2) *YBILC* 25–27).
50 ILC, Report (1998) 72, paras 296–297.

thus complemented Article 19 by focusing on the structure of the obligation breached as an *erga omnes* duty.[51] A State crime would affect the correlated rights of all States of the international community other than the offender. In this respect, scholars have pointed out that the fact that a State crime affects 'humanity', and thus 'the international community as a whole', justifies a separate regime of responsibility.[52] Article 40(3) thus replicated on a universal scale the principle of the general reaction to the breach of an obligation *erga omnes contractantes* embedded in 1996 DASR 40(2)(e)–(f), which complemented VCLT and VCLTIO Article 60.[53] Under 1996 DASR 40(3), all States of the international community were affected as the 'injured' and 'victims' of a State crime.[54] Thus, unlike 2001 DASR 48, 1996 DASR 40(3) did not distinguish between 'injured' and 'non-injured States'. However, despite the different terminology as concerns 'injured' and 'non-injured' States, 1996 DASR 40 was the equivalent of 2001 DASR 48.

In light of the decisive observation that it would breach an *erga omnes* obligation, a State crime overlaps with a breach of *jus cogens*. This feature is akin to criminal responsibility under domestic law, whereby a crime is an offence against the community as such, not just a breach of the right of a single individual.[55] However, considering the specific horizontal nature of international law, whilst, in light of its scope, the notion of a State crime could not be broader than that of *jus cogens*, the latter might well be broader than the former.[56] It is indeed possible to assume that the breach of a peremptory norm is a simple 'delict', not entailing State criminal responsibility,[57] as in the case, for instance, of the breach

51 Id, Report (1995) 118 ff, paras 273 ff. See also Dominicé, 'The International Responsibility' (1999) 362, note 27; Gaja, 'Should All References' (1999) 367; Pierre-Marie Dupuy, 'A General Stocktaking of the Connections between the Multilateral Dimension of Obligations and Codification of the Law of Responsibility' (2002) 13(5) *EJIL* 1069–1070.

52 ILC, Summary Records (1976) 69, para 14, 88, para 22. See also Max Gounelle, 'Quelques remarques sur la notion de "crime international de l'État" et sur l'évolution de la responsabilité internationale de l'État', in Daniel Bardonnet *et al* (eds), *Le droit international: unité et diversité* (Pedone, 1981) 320; Pellet, 'Remarques' (1996) 19–20.

53 David Bederman, 'Article 40 (2) (E) and (F) in the ILC Draft Articles on State Responsibility: Standing of Injured States under Customary International Law and Multilateral Treaties' (1998) 92 *ASIL Proc* 291–294. On the relationship between VCLT and VCLTIO art 60 and 1996 DASR 40, see Marina Spinedi, 'From One Codification to Another: Bilateralism and Multilateralism in the Genesis of the Codification of the Law of Treaties and the Law of State Responsibility' (2002) 13(5) *EJIL* 1103–1106.

54 Gaja, 'Should All References' (1999) 368.

55 Acosta Estévez, 'Normas' (1995) 20; Dominicé, 'The International Responsibility' (1999) 358.

56 Gaja, 'Obligations' (1989) 159; Geoff Gilbert, 'The Criminal Responsibility of States' (1990) 39(2) *ICLQ* 354–355; Acosta Estévez, 'Normas' (1995) 19; Abi-Saab, 'The Uses' (1999) 348; Pemmaraju Sreenivasa Rao, 'International Crimes and State Responsibility', in Ragazzi, *International Responsibility* (2005) 79.

57 Sixth Committee of the General Assembly, Topical Summary of the Discussion Held during Its Fifty-Third Session on the Work of the ILC of Its Fiftieth Session, UN Doc A/CN.4/496 (1999) 16, para 115.

of the obligation to safeguard embassy archives.[58] The breach of an *erga omnes* obligation is therefore a condition necessary to define State crimes, but not a sufficient one.[59]

2.1.1.4 Fundamental obligations

Concerning specific State crimes, 1996 DASR 19(3) provided that an international crime might result, 'inter alia', from specific breaches, subject to Article 19(2) and on the basis of the rules of international law in force.[60] In more detail, Article 19(3) provided that a crime would result from 'a serious breach of an international obligation of essential importance' for international peace and security, the right to self-determination, human beings and the environment.[61] In other words, via Article 19(3) the ILC defined the essential obligations breached by international crimes and further provided some examples of breaches of such obligations.[62] To a large extent, Article 19(3) covered the examples of breaches of peremptory norms given by the ILC in its 1996 Report to the UN General Assembly.[63] This was of course a first attempt to outline a list of State crimes in a written document, since it is impossible to establish a regime of international criminal responsibility by

58 ILC, Summary Records (1976) 74, para 13. Similarly, on a particular scale, it is necessary to envisage non-criminal violations of obligations *erga omnes contractantes*, notably under 1996 DASR 40(1) and VCLT art 60(2), allowing all State parties to a treaty to suspend or terminate its application (Abdelkader Yahi, 'La violation d'un traité: l'articulation du droit des traités et du droit de la responsabilité internationale' (1993) 26(2) *RBDI* 442–446). Thus, for instance, art 26 of the Constitution of the International Law Organisation (ILO: Treaty of Versailles, Part XIII) allows a State to act in the interest of the law before the ILO against a State that does not adequately implement an ILO Convention (Dominicé, 'The International Responsibility' (1999) 355–356).

59 ILC, Summary Records (1976) 74, para 12. See also ILC, Report (2000) 31, para 128.

60 Id, Summary Records (1976) 72, para 31.

61 On the relationship between ss 2 and 3 of art 19, see Ago, Fifth Report (1976) 53, paras 150–151. Some members of the ILC proposed to prohibit under art 19 all conduct 'inconsistent with the Purposes of the United Nations' (ILC, Summary Records (1976) 70, paras 21 and 27, 73–74, para 9).

62 ILC, Summary Records (1976) 66, para 44, 89–90, para 28, where Ago posited that 'if they [the essential rules of the international community] could not at present be formulated as precisely as the rules of internal criminal law, the obligations whose breach constituted an international crime should at least be defined as closely as possible'.

63 ILC, Report to the General Assembly on the Second Part of the Seventeenth Session and on the Eighteenth Session, UN Doc A/6309/REV.1 (1966) 2(1) *YBILC* 247–248, paras 1 and 3:

> Some members of the Commission felt that there might be advantage in specifying, by way of illustration, some of the most obvious and best settled rules of *jus cogens* [...] [e]xamples suggested included (a) a treaty contemplating an unlawful use of force contrary to the principles of the Charter, (b) a treaty contemplating the performance of any other act criminal under international law, and (c) a treaty contemplating or conniving at the commission of acts, such as trade in slaves, piracy or genocide, in the suppression of which every State is called upon to co-operate.

means of examples.[64] It has indeed been pointed out that the approximate list of crimes embedded in Article 19(3) should have been more correctly included in the commentary to the text of Article 19 than in the rule itself.[65]

Only 'serious' breaches of obligations 'of primary importance' constituted State crimes under Article 19(3), based, in particular, on the scale of the violation.[66] Scholars, however, have underscored that the 'seriousness' of the breach duplicates the required 'widespread' character of the infringement.[67]

Article 19(3)(a) of the 1996 DASR qualified aggression as a 'serious breach of an international obligation of essential importance for the maintenance of international peace and security',[68] hence a State crime. This approach followed the UN Charter, notably Article 1(1) and the Preamble, in line with Chapter II(2) and (4) of the Dumbarton Oaks Proposals,[69] which consider peace to be the most important interest protected under international law.[70] In this context, the term 'aggression' was exclusive of economic aggression, so as not to blur the distinction between aggression and intervention.[71] Otto Triffterer particularly underscored the dual nature of criminal responsibility for aggression, concerning both the State and its organs or agents.[72] Interestingly, during preparatory work some members of the ILC proposed to include the notion of 'war crimes' in Article 19(3)(a), consistently with the 1954 DCOPSM. This stance foreshadowed a link between war crimes and aggression, particularly because there can be no individual responsibility for war crimes without State aggressive war.[73]

Article 19(3)(b) of the 1996 DASR qualified the 'maintenance by force of colonial domination' as a 'serious breach of an international obligation of essential importance for safeguarding the right of self-determination of peoples', hence a State crime. The reference in this case was UN Charter Article 1(2), which further established a link with the maintenance of peace,[74] along the lines of

64 ILC, Summary Records (1976) 84, para 39. See also Pierre-Marie Dupuy, 'Observations sur le "crime international de l'État"' (1980) 84(2) *RGDIP* 468; Bowett, 'Crimes' (1998) 167; Dominicé, 'The International Responsibility' (1999) 357, note 13.

65 Abi-Saab, 'The Uses' (1999) 342.

66 ILC, Report (1976) 120, para 66; ILC, Summary Records (1976) 72–74, paras 2, 4, 5 and 11, 82, para 26, 87, para 16; Krystyna Marek, 'Criminalizing State Responsibility' (1978–79) 14(2) *RBDI* 475–478.

67 Paola Gaeta, 'The Character' (2010) 422–424.

68 On the openness of offences against peace under 1996 DASR 19(3)(a), see Bowett, 'Crimes' (1998) 167.

69 United Nations Dumbarton Oaks Proposals (1944) ch II(2) and (4).

70 According to the ICJ, '[t]he primary place ascribed to international peace and security is natural, since the fulfilment of the other purposes will be dependent upon the attainment of that basic condition' (*Certain Expenses of the United Nations (Article 17, Paragraph 2, of the Charter) (Advisory Opinion)* [1962] ICJ Rep 168).

71 ILC, Report (1976) 121, para 68; ILC, Summary Records (1976) 69, para 10. But see ILC, Summary Records (1976) 62, para 7, 66, para 40.

72 Otto Triffterer, 'Prosecution of States for Crimes of State' (1996) 67(1–2) *RIDP* 346.

73 ILC, Summary Records (1976) 71, para 32.

74 Ago, Fifth Report (1976) 36, para 110.

Chapter I(1) of the Dumbarton Oaks Proposals.[75] The example of colonial domination was grounded in the historical importance of decolonisation, particularly in the aftermath of World War II, although this is currently no longer an issue. The State crime matched the individual crime of colonialism embedded in the 1991 DCCPSM, which was nevertheless withdrawn in the final version of the Code adopted in 1996.[76] By contrast, the right to self-determination remains fundamental, to the extent that it underpins the concept of State sovereignty and all human rights, according to Article 1 of the International Covenant on Civil and Political Rights (ICCPR)[77] and Article 1 of the International Covenant on Economic, Social and Cultural Rights (ICESCR).[78]

Article 19(3)(c) of the 1996 DASR classified as an international crime conduct such as 'slavery, genocide and apartheid' in 'breach on a widespread scale of an international obligation of essential importance for safeguarding the human being'. The basis for this rule was Article 1(3) of the UN Charter, along the lines of the Dumbarton Oak Proposals (Chapter IX, Section A-1).[79] The 'widespread scale' of the violation involved State planning and thus outlined the context of collective responsibility. Also these offences were in breach of the fundamental necessity of preserving peace in international relations, like violations under Article 19(3)(a) and (b), which therefore shared a common ground.[80]

Article 19(3)(d) of the 1996 DASR defined 'massive pollution of the atmosphere or the sea' as 'a serious breach of an international obligation of essential importance for the safeguarding and preservation of the human environment', therefore a State crime.[81] This section reinforced environmental protection,[82] along the lines of instruments such as the 1972 Stockholm Declaration and 1992 Rio Declaration, which respectively recognise a fundamental right to environmental protection and sustainable development. Furthermore, Article 30 of the 1974 Charter of Economic Rights and Duties of States[83] and Article 192 of

75 United Nations Dumbarton Oaks Proposals (1944) ch I(1).

76 According to art 18 of the 1991 DCCPSM, colonialism is the fact of '[a]n individual who as leader or organizer establishes or maintains by force or orders the establishment or maintenance by force of colonial domination or any other form of alien domination contrary to the right of peoples to self-determination as enshrined in the Charter of the United Nations'. On the link between individual and State responsibility concerning the crime of colonial domination, see Anouche Beaudouin, 'Le maintien par la force d'une domination coloniale', in Ascensio, Decaux and Pellet, *Droit* (2000) 432 ff.

77 Adopted 16 December 1966, 999 UNTS 171, in force 23 March 1976.

78 Adopted 16 December 1966, 993 UNTS 3, in force 3 January 1976.

79 Dumbarton Oak Proposals (1944) ch IX, s A-1. For a critical approach to the broad definition of crimes against humanity under 1996 DASR 19(3), see Bowett, 'Crimes' 167.

80 ILC, Summary Records (1976) 68, para 7.

81 Id, Report (1976) 109, paras 31 ff; Id, Summary Records (1976) 71, para 22.

82 Sixth Committee of the General Assembly, Topical Summary of the Discussion Held during the Fifty-First Session on the Work of the ILC of Its Forty-Eighth Session, UN Doc A/CN.4/479/Add.1 (1997) 9, para 18.

83 General Assembly, Charter of Economic Rights and Duties of States, UN Doc A/RES/29/3281, 12 December 1974.

the 1982 UN Convention on the Law of the Sea (UNCLOS)[84] compel States to respect the environment and marine environment.

DASR 19(3)(d) anticipated the separate opinion of Judge Weeramantry in *Gabčíkovo-Nagymaros*, underscoring the *erga omnes* nature of the obligation to respect the environment.[85] This approach entailed general procedural implications in terms of environmental impact assessment that the ICJ subsequently underscored in *Pulp Mills on the River Uruguay*.[86] Nonetheless, the ILC also highlighted the difficulty of criminalising environmental offences committed by natural persons within the framework of the DCCPSM, save in time of war.[87] Given the principle according to which State responsibility is grounded in individual conduct, it would not be easy to explain a shift in the degree of responsibility for the individual and the State.

It must be assumed that 1996 DASR 19 outlined a scale of decreasing gravity from aggression to environmental crimes. Furthermore, each criminal class embedded a decreasing scale of gravity between, for instance, actual and threatened aggression.[88] More specifically, the ILC aimed at dividing the first three categories of crimes, that is, the most serious ones, from environmental pollution as a less serious offence, which should entail different sanctions, notably non-punitive damages.[89]

With the exception of environmental pollution, the list embedded in 1996 DASR 19 relied on *jus cogens* and *erga omnes* obligations, particularly as outlined by the ICJ in *Barcelona Traction*, notably with respect to aggression, self-determination and human rights.[90] The ILC also envisaged the possibility of including economic crimes in Article 19, but eventually rejected the option.[91] This signals that, whilst the notion of *jus cogens* was certainly a source of inspiration for State crimes, the concept of a State crime could have become a source of information for the definition of *jus cogens*. Indeed, Roberto Ago considered it necessary not to leave the notion of a State crime 'vague' under secondary international rules, unlike that of *jus cogens* under primary international rules.[92] Therefore, whilst DASR 19 is different from VCLT and VCLTIO Article 53, from the standpoint of both the general definition of State crimes and specific offences, there is consistent overlap between the two notions.

84 Adopted 10 December 1982, 1833 UNTS 3, in force 16 November 1994.

85 *Gabčíkovo-Nagymaros Project (Hungary v Slovakia)* [1997] ICJ Rep 7, Separate opinion Weeramantry, 88.

86 *Pulp Mills on the River Uruguay (Argentina v Uruguay)* [2010] ICJ Rep 83, para 204.

87 Christian Tomuschat, Document on Crimes against the Environment, UN Doc ILC(XLVIII)/DC/CRD.3 (1996) 2(1) *YBILC* 21 ff.

88 ILC, Summary Records (1976) 58–59, para 27, whereby a parallel is established between the scale of gravity of domestic crimes and that of international crimes; Willem Riphagen, Preliminary Report on State Responsibility, UN Doc A/CN.4/330 (1980) 121, para 67.

89 ILC, Summary Records (1976) 86, paras 7–8.

90 See s 1.2.2.2.

91 ILC, Summary Records (1976) 83, para 34.

92 See the opinion of Roberto Ago in ILC, Summary Records (1976) 74, paras 14–15, 89, para 28.

In sum, in order to define State crimes, 1996 DASR 19, in conjunction with DASR 40(3), relied on four fundamental criteria: (1) a State crime breached an *erga omnes* obligation and thus affected all States of the international community; (2) such an obligation should have been essential to the protection of the fundamental interests of the international community; (3) the breach of the obligation should have been 'serious' and (4) the offence should have been specifically established, for instance, aggression.[93] The first three criteria defined an embryonic theory of State criminal responsibility in international law,[94] whilst the fourth principle outlined an embryonic special part of State criminal responsibility.[95] It is interesting to note that criteria (1)–(3) also apply under 2001 DASR 40, which nonetheless withdraws principle (4).[96] This approach, however, eliminates the notion of a 'State crime', which is narrower than that of *jus cogens*, and thus establishes a uniform regime of aggravated responsibility for different offences such as aggression, human rights violations and failure to protect embassy archives.

On a particular scale, the adoption of a binding regime for State aggravated responsibility *erga omnes contractantes* would have been possible under 1996 DASR 40(2)(e) and (f).[97] Creating a particular regime and then universalising it by means of State practice might have been a better way to proceed in order to establish the concept of State criminal responsibility in international law. Introducing such a progressive notion in a treaty that was supposed to codify general international law indeed encountered the foreseeable opposition of State representatives and ultimately led to its rejection.[98]

93 ILC, Report (1998) 146, para 293. See also Alain Pellet, 'Can a State Commit a Crime? Definitely, Yes!' (1999) 10(2) *EJIL* 430.

94 On the limits of art 19, see Crawford, First Report (1998) 10, paras 46–49.

95 See the Opinion of Paul Reuter in ILC, Summary Records (1976) 245, para 62:

> [A]rticle 18 [of the 1976 DASR can be regarded] methodologically, as a pointer which would dominate the work of the Commission but did not commit it to drawing up either a general regime of international crimes or, still less, a penal definition of a particular crime.

ILC, Report (1976) 117–118, para 54:

> It is therefore inconceivable that the Commission, even if it so wished, could limit its task to establishing in the draft articles a supposedly general regime of responsibility valid for all internationally wrongful acts, leaving it to international custom or particular conventional instruments to lay down the regime, or rather regimes, of responsibility applicable to international "crimes".

Riphagen, Fourth Report (1983) 10 ff, paras 50 ff. See also Crawford, 'On Re-Reading' (1998) 296–297; Abi-Saab, 'The Uses' (1999) 342.

96 Pellet, 'Les articles' (2002) 15–16.

97 Bederman, 'Article 40' (1998) 291 ff.

98 Barboza, 'International Criminal Law' (1999) 100:

> We are, then, dealing, with a *de lege ferenda* exercise or, if preferred, one of progressive development of the law. Such being the case, caution must be had in proposing the incorporation in the draft articles on State responsibility of a notion which might very well lead to the collapse of the whole project. From that point of view, the separation of State crimes from States responsibility seems advisable.

2.1.1.5 Jus cogens, erga omnes *obligations and State responsibility in international case law*

International case law is critical to understanding the notion of *jus cogens*. Notably, some decisions of international courts disclose overlap between obligations *erga omnes* and *jus cogens*. The ICJ is better acquainted with the concept of '*erga omnes* obligation' than '*jus cogens*'. In this respect, the basic statement is the *obiter dictum* in the *Barcelona Traction* judgment, where *erga omnes* obligations, particularly the prohibition of aggression, genocide and core crimes against humanity, are considered duties 'towards the international community as a whole', so that 'all States can be held to have a legal interest in their protection.'[99] In a few cases, however, the ICJ established a tight link between *erga omnes* obligations and *jus cogens*.

Notably, in *Military and Paramilitary Activities in and against Nicaragua* the ICJ assumed that the prohibition on the use of force embedded in Article 2(4) of the UN Charter is a 'universal norm' and a 'principle of *jus cogens*'.[100] According to the interpretation put forward in *Armed Activities on the Territory of the Congo*, a 'universal norm' is an '*erga omnes* obligation',[101] and therefore the peremptory prohibition of aggression overlaps with *erga omnes* obligations.

In its advisory opinion in *Legal Consequences of the Construction of a Wall in the Occupied Palestinian Territory*,[102] the ICJ applied the consequences of a breach of a peremptory norm to the violation of an *erga omnes* obligation. In fact, concerning the 'obligations *erga omnes* [...] to respect the right of the Palestinian people to self-determination' and 'certain [Israeli] obligations under international humanitarian law', the ICJ considered that 'all States are under an obligation not to recognise the illegal situation' resulting from a violation.[103] The Court further held that States 'are under an obligation not to render aid or assistance in maintaining the situation' resulting from the breach.[104] This approach is in line with breaches of *jus cogens* under 2001 DASR 41. Similarly, in the advisory opinion in *Legality of the Threat or Use of Nuclear Weapons* the ICJ referred to the jurisprudence of the Nuremberg Tribunal and held that 'many rules of humanitarian law' must 'be observed by all States whether or not they have ratified the conventions that contain them, because they constitute intransgressible principles of international customary law'.[105] According to the ICJ, key principles of international humanitarian law include the protection of civilians

99 *Barcelona Traction* [1970] 32, para 33. See also s 1.2.2.2.

100 *Military and Paramilitary Activities in and against Nicaragua (Nicaragua v US)* [1986] ICJ Rep 100, para 190.

101 *Armed Activities* [2006] 31–32, para 64.

102 *Legal Consequences of the Construction of a Wall in the Occupied Palestinian Territory (Advisory Opinion)* [2004] ICJ Rep 136.

103 Ibid 199–200, paras 155 and 159.

104 Ibid 200, para 159. See also Crawford, 'International Crimes' (2010) 411–413.

105 *Legality of the Threat or Use of Nuclear Weapons (Advisory Opinion)* [1996] ICJ Rep 257, para 79. See also ILC, Report (2001) 113, para 5.

and civilian objects and the obligation not to cause unnecessary suffering to combatants.[106] These are particularly protected by means of individual criminal prohibitions under Article 3 common to the 1949 Geneva Conventions. This approach was later confirmed in the cases on the *Application of the Genocide Convention*, where the ICJ held that obligations 'protecting human rights in armed conflicts' are 'peremptory norms' or 'obligations which protect essential humanitarian values, and which may be owed *erga omnes*'.[107]

Approaching the prohibition of the crime of genocide in light of its previous jurisprudence,[108] in *Armed Activities on the Territory of the Congo* the ICJ considered that 'the principles underlying the [Genocide] Convention [...] are recognized by civilized nations as binding on States, even without any conventional obligation.'[109] This determines 'the universal character both of the condemnation of genocide and of the co-operation required in order to liberate mankind from such an odious scourge'.[110] Thus, 'the rights and obligations enshrined by the Convention are rights and obligations *erga omnes*.'[111] Therefore, the prohibition of genocide is a (universally recognised) *erga omnes* obligation that implies the (*erga omnes*) duty for all States to cooperate and end its violation. Once again, the Court applied to the breach of an *erga omnes* obligation the secondary implications outlined in 2001 DASR 41 for the violation of a peremptory norm. Furthermore, in this dispute the Court explicitly qualified the prohibition of genocide as a norm of *jus cogens*.[112] Along the same lines, in the cases on the *Application of the Genocide Convention* the ICJ underscored the peremptory and *erga omnes* nature of the prohibition of genocide.[113]

Even more explicitly, in *Furundžija* the ICTY tackled the notions of *erga omnes* obligation and *jus cogens* head-on from the standpoint of States. The Tribunal held that the prohibition of torture 'imposes upon States obligations *erga omnes*' and 'has evolved into a peremptory norm or *jus cogens*' in international law.[114] The status of the prohibition of torture as a peremptory norm entails, according to the ICTY, a connection with the 'law of enforcement', by reason of the importance of the protected values.[115] Such a status also implies 'a higher rank in the international hierarchy than treaty law and even "ordinary" customary rules'.[116] This involves the nullity of any acts (of power) allowing torture.

106 *Legality of the Threat* [1996] 257, para 78.
107 *Application of the Convention* [2007] 104, para 147; *Application of the Convention* [2015] 45, para 85.
108 *Reservations to the Convention* [1951] 23; *Application of the Convention* [1996] 616, para 31.
109 *Armed Activities* [2006] 31–32, para 64.
110 Ibid.
111 Ibid.
112 Ibid.
113 *Application of the Convention* [2007] 120, para 185; *Application of the Convention* [2015] 45, para 85. See also ss 1.2.1.3 and 1.2.4.1.
114 *Furundžija* (1998) 58–59, paras 151 and 153. See further s 1.2.3.3.
115 *Furundžija* (1998) 59, para 153.
116 Ibid.

Furthermore, this would 'signal to all members of the international community [...] that the prohibition of torture is an absolute value from which nobody must deviate'.[117] Therefore, a link subsists between the non-derogability of *jus cogens* and the universal nature of its violation. The ICTY also analytically regarded the prohibition of torture as an *erga omnes* obligation binding a State vis-à-vis 'all the other members of the international community, each of which then has a correlative right'.[118] Moreover, the violation of this *erga omnes* obligation 'simultaneously constitutes a breach of the correlative right of all members of the international community', so that it 'gives rise to a claim for compliance accruing to each and every member'.[119] In light of the *obiter dictum* of the ICJ in *Barcelona Traction*, the ICTY therefore defined the prohibition of torture as an obligation 'owed to the international community as a whole', in the sense that it is *erga omnes*. Furthermore, such an obligation entails correlative rights for all the members of the international community, whose breach generates a universal claim for compliance. These considerations are relevant to 2001 DASR 42(b) and 48(1)(b), which posit the existence of obligations 'owed to the international community as a whole' and invocation of responsibility by all States. In *Questions Relating to the Obligation to Prosecute or Extradite*, the ICJ confirmed the peremptory nature of the prohibition of torture.[120]

2.1.2 Individual criminal responsibility, jus cogens *and* erga omnes *obligations*

2.1.2.1 From criminals to crimes: erga omnes *responsibility in the ICC Statute*

Natural persons have limited legal personality under (public) international law: they have rights and duties, but not the ability to create and vary legal rules. Individuals therefore have no power within the international legal system. Since VCLT and VCLTIO Article 53 addresses States, primary procedural rules afford no definition of *jus cogens* with respect to natural persons. Therefore, the question arises as to whether the notion of *jus cogens* affects the sphere of individual criminal responsibility at the international level.

Positive international law does not embed a specific reference to international crimes committed by individuals as breaches of *jus cogens*, or of *erga omnes* obligations.[121] In fact, these notions have been formulated within the context of classical inter-State law, not with respect to individual responsibility. However,

117 Ibid 59, para 154.
118 Ibid 58, para 151.
119 Ibid.
120 *Questions Relating to the Obligation to Prosecute or Extradite (Belgium v Senegal)* [2012] ICJ Rep 457, para 99.
121 Cherif Bassiouni, 'International Crimes: *Jus Cogens* and *Obligatio Erga Omnes*' (1996) 59(4) *Law & Contemp Probs* 66; Weatherall, Jus Cogens (2015) 11–12.

contrary to State aggravated responsibility, individual crimes are clearly identified in binding international instruments, particularly the Statute of the ICC. It is therefore possible to single out implicit overlaps within the context of international practice and regulatory instruments.

From the IMT established in Nuremberg to the ICTR, *ad hoc* jurisdictions have addressed the punishment of '(major) war criminals'[122] or 'persons responsible for serious violations of international humanitarian law'.[123] In this context, the focus is on the perpetrator of the crime, not on the structure of the obligation infringed. The DCCPSM takes into account 'crimes under international law', without any further specification as to their structure.[124]

The ICC Statute does not explicitly mention '*jus cogens*' and '*erga omnes* obligations', but its Preamble states that the 'most serious crimes of concern to the international community as a whole must not go unpunished.' More specifically, ICC Statute Article 5 qualifies genocide, crimes against humanity, war crimes and aggression as 'the most serious crimes of concern to the international community as a whole'. The focus thus shifts from the perpetrator to the victim of the crime and the structure of the obligation infringed. Some scholars read this statement as an affirmation that individual crimes embedded in the ICC Statute are breaches of *jus cogens.*[125] Others assume that such crimes necessarily entail a 'State environment'.[126] Whilst the expression is not particularly analytical, it can certainly be interpreted as a reference to *erga omnes* obligations, whose breach necessarily affects all the subjects of the international community. This entails that at least some international crimes committed by individuals are in breach of peremptory obligations.[127]

2.1.2.2 Erga omnes *responsibility in the case law*

The considerations developed by the ICTY in *Furundžija* with respect to the notions of '*erga omnes* obligations' and '*jus cogens*' concerning the prohibition of torture apply not only to the State, but also to natural persons. In fact, in light of the observation that the prohibition of torture 'imposes upon States obligations *erga omnes*',[128] the ICTY held that the *jus cogens* status of the prohibition of

122 See art 6 of the Charter of the Nuremberg Tribunal (1945) and art 5 of the Charter of the IMTFE (1946).

123 See art 1 of the Statute of the ICTY (1993) and art 1 of the Statute of the ICTR (1994).

124 See art 1 of the DCCPSM (1996), in ILC, Report (1996) 14.

125 Bassiouni, 'International Crimes' (1996) 68. According to Dupuy, ICC Statute art 5 and VCLT and VCLTIO art 53 are based on the same logic, so much so that 'international criminal law' would have a 'privileged relation' with respect to 'peremptory norms' (see Pierre-Marie Dupuy, 'Normes internationales pénales et droit impératif (*jus cogens*)', in Ascensio, Decaux and Pellet, *Droit* (Pedone, 2nd edn, 2012) 85–86).

126 Wolf, 'Individual Responsibility' (2016) 20–21.

127 Stefan Kadelbach, 'Genesis, Function and Identification of *Jus Cogens* Norms' (2015) 46 *NYBIL* 163. See also Władysław Czapliński, '*Jus Cogens*, Obligations *Erga Omnes* and International Criminal Responsibility', in Doria, Gasser and Bassiouni, *The Legal Regime* (2009) 410–420.

128 *Furundžija* (1998) 58, paras 151 and 153.

torture 'signals to all members of the international community and the *individuals* [...] that the prohibition of torture is an absolute value from which nobody must deviate'.[129] Therefore, the ICTY flags up the non-derogability of *jus cogens* and the *erga omnes* nature of a violation committed by an individual.

Applying the jurisprudence developed by the ICJ on *jus cogens* with respect to State responsibility,[130] it ought to be assumed that the crime of aggression is in breach of a peremptory norm also from the standpoint of natural persons. In fact, individual responsibility under ICC Statute Article 8bis is based on State responsibility under Resolution 3314 (XXIX) and the ICJ clearly upheld the *erga omnes* nature of the prohibition of aggression in *Barcelona Traction*, as well as its peremptory character in *Nicaragua*.[131] The same reasoning applies to core war crimes and crimes against humanity,[132] which are defined at the individual level and also trigger State responsibility, in light of the cases of the *Wall*, [133] *Nuclear Weapons*,[134] *Genocide Convention*[135] and *Obligation to Prosecute or Extradite*.[136] An identical argument can be put forward for the crime of genocide, in light of the cases of *Barcelona Traction*,[137] *Reservations to the Genocide Convention*,[138] *Armed Activities on the Territory of the Congo*[139] and *Application of the Genocide Convention*.[140] The ICJ has held that *erga omnes* duties enshrined in the Genocide Convention imply that 'each State' has 'the *obligation* to prevent and *punish* the crime of genocide'.[141] The word 'punishment' refers to criminal sanctions and necessarily concerns individual liability. Furthermore, the ICTY qualified the prohibition of genocide as a peremptory norm with respect to individuals in *Krstić*, *Tolimir* and *Karadžić*.[142] In *Kupreskić*, the ICTY held that 'most norms of international humanitarian law, in particular those prohibiting war crimes, crimes against humanity and genocide are also peremptory norms of international law or *jus cogens*.'[143]

129 Ibid 59, para 154, emphasis added.
130 See s 2.1.1.5.
131 *Barcelona Traction* [1970] 32, para 34; *Military and Paramilitary Activities* [1986] 100, para 190.
132 Auriane Botte, 'Redefining the Responsibility to Protect Concept as a Response to International Crimes' (2015) 19(8) *IJHR* 1030–1031.
133 *Legal Consequences* [2004] 199–200, paras 155–159.
134 *Legality of the Threat* [1996] 257, para 79.
135 *Application of the Convention* [2007] 104, para 147; *Application of the Convention* [2015] 45, para 85.
136 *Questions* [2012] ICJ Rep 457, para 99.
137 *Barcelona Traction* [1970] 32, para 34.
138 *Reservations to the Convention* [1951] 23.
139 *Armed Activities* [2006] 31–32, para 64.
140 *Application of the Convention* [1996] 616, para 31; *Id* [2007] 120, para 185; *Id* [2015] 45, para 85.
141 *Application of the Convention* [1996] 616, para 31, emphasis added.
142 *Krstić*, IT-98-33-T, Trial Chamber, Judgment of 2 August 2001, 189, para 541; *Tolimir*, IT-05-88/2-T, Trial Chamber, Judgment of 12 December 2012, 325, para 733; *Karadžić*, IT-95-5/18-T, Judgment of 24 March 2016, 202, para 539.
143 *Kupreskić*, IT-95-16, Trial Chamber, Judgment of 14 January 2000, 203, para 520.

Recent case law and regulation supports the view that the prohibition of terrorism is part of *jus cogens* and therefore belongs to the realm of *erga omnes* obligations. Notably, within the context of international humanitarian law in *Galić* the ICTY held that the prohibition of terrorism constitutes 'a peremptory norm of customary international law'.[144] The STL also implicitly upheld the *jus cogens* nature of the prohibition of terrorism in time of peace.[145] In *Réunion Aérienne v Socialist People's Libyan Arab Jamahiriya*, the French Court of Cassation adjudicated on the bombing of a French airliner over Niger that resulted in the death of 170 people in September 1989.[146] In the particular circumstances of the dispute, the Court excluded State responsibility before domestic courts based on jurisdictional immunity. However, the Court recognised that 'the prohibition on acts of terrorism can be ranked as a *jus cogens* norm of international law, which takes precedence over other rules of international law and can constitute a legitimate restriction on jurisdictional immunity.'[147] Furthermore, Canadian legislation underscores that:

> [T]he prohibition against terrorism, as well as the prevention, repression and elimination of terrorism, are peremptory norms of international law (*jus cogens*) accepted and recognized by the international community of States as a whole as norms from which no derogation is possible.[148]

Scholars confirm the peremptory nature of aggression, genocide, crimes against humanity and war crimes.[149] Bassiouni critically assumes that 'a *jus cogens* crime is characterised explicitly or implicitly by State policy or conduct', which 'distinguishes *jus cogens* crimes from other international crimes'.[150]

2.1.3 State aggravated responsibility, individual criminal responsibility, **jus cogens** *and (non-severable)* **erga omnes** *obligations*

2.1.3.1 (Non-severable) erga omnes *obligations as* jus cogens

Positive rules outline *jus cogens* from the viewpoint of primary procedural norms at the State level. In contrast, they do not provide much information about

144 *Galić*, IT-98-29-T, Trial Chamber, Judgment of 5 December 2003, para 98.

145 *Ayyash* et al (2011) 91 and 104.

146 *Réunion Aérienne v Socialist People's Libyan Arab Jamahiriya*, 09-14743, French Court of Cassation, Judgment of 9 March 2011 (2012) 150 *ILR* 630.

147 Ibid 634.

148 Act to Amend the State Immunity Act and the Criminal Code (Deterring Terrorism by Providing a Civil Right of Action against Perpetrators and Sponsors of Terrorism), SC 2007, Canada, preamble (cited in Weatherall, Jus Cogens (2015) 249, n 294).

149 Lyal Sunga, *The Emerging System of International Criminal Law* (Kluwer, 1997) 246; Bassiouni, *Introduction* (2013) 240.

150 Bassiouni, 'International Crimes' (1996) 69; Id, *Introduction* (2013) 242.

jus cogens from the standpoint of primary and secondary substantive rules, as well as secondary and tertiary procedural rules, with respect to both States and natural persons. However, this does not mean that peremptory norms are irrelevant to such categories of legal thinking. The case law of the ICJ underscores a link between *jus cogens*, considered from the viewpoint of primary procedural rules, and *erga omnes* obligations relevant to primary and secondary substantive rules, as well as secondary and tertiary procedural rules. Furthermore, the ICTY has established an implied link between the non-derogability of *jus cogens*, the universal impermissibility of its breach, the universality of a violation of an *erga omnes* obligation and general implementation. Nonetheless, neither the ICJ nor the ICTY has clearly articulated the structure of such a link.

This line of reasoning shows that, within the context of general international law, two categories of international norms emerge: obligations *erga omnes* and peremptory obligations (*jus cogens*). These particularly encompass the prohibition of aggression, genocide, core war crimes, core crimes against humanity, notably torture, and prospectively terrorism. However, the distinctive features of these obligations and the way in which they relate to one another are not clearly articulated. Scholars usually assume that either obligations *erga omnes* and *jus cogens* are identical or that *jus cogens* defines a smaller circle within the context of the larger framework outlined by *erga omnes* obligations.[151] A careful analysis as regards the structure of international legal obligations can help to shed light on the question.

Obligations *erga omnes* and *jus cogens* belong to the realm of general international law. General international obligations bind a natural or legal person vis-à-vis all other subjects within the international community. Some subjects are the 'primary beneficiaries' of the obligation, whereas others are the 'secondary beneficiaries'. For instance, within the context of the prohibition of genocide, a group of people is the primary beneficiary of the duty-right in issue, whereas States are the secondary beneficiaries.[152] Owing to the basic correlation between duties and rights,[153] in principle a general obligation, *omnium* and *erga omnes*, generates universal rights. In fact, the *erga omnes* obligation of A and B vis-à-vis C matches the *erga omnes* right of C vis-à-vis A and B. That said, it is suitable, or rather necessary, to logically distinguish non-severable general obligations from severable general obligations.

151 André de Hoog, 'The Relationship between *Jus Cogens*, Obligations *Erga Omnes* and International Crimes: Peremptory Norms in Perspective' (1991) 42(2) *Austrian J Pub Intl L* 202; Antonio Cassese, 'The Character of the Violated Obligation', in Crawford, Pellet, Olleson and Parlett, *The Law* (2010) 417; Picone, 'Distinction' (2011) 412; Weatherall, Jus Cogens (2015) 10. See also s 1.2.2.2.

152 Linos-Alexandre Sicilianos, 'The Classification of Obligations and the Multilateral Dimension of the Relations of International Responsibility' (2002) 13(5) *EJIL* 1132; Weatherall, Jus Cogens (2015) 31.

153 Hohfeld, 'Some Fundamental Legal Conceptions' (1913–14) 30 and 33; Id, 'Fundamental Legal Conceptions' (1916–17) 26(8) *Yale LJ* 710.

A non-severable general obligation is a bundle of indivisible obligations that a legal person has vis-à-vis all other legal persons within the international community, that is, a unitary duty. In this respect, Gaetano Arangio-Ruiz considered:

> [T]he concept of *erga omnes* obligation is not characterized by the importance of the interest protected by the norms – this aspect being typical of *jus cogens* – but rather by the 'legal indivisibility' of the content of the obligation, namely by the fact that the rule in question provides for obligations which bind simultaneously each and every addressee with respect to all others. This legal structure is typical not only of peremptory norms, but also of other norms of general international law and of a number of multilateral treaty rules (*erga omnes partes* obligations).[154]

Since they are not severable, general indivisible obligations are non-derogable by means of bilateral or multilateral consent. Furthermore, in the case of a breach, all (State and non-State) subjects of the international community should be allowed to invoke the responsibility of the injurer and enforce sanctions.[155] In other words, a non-severable *erga omnes* obligation jointly binds a subject vis-à-vis all the other subjects of the international legal system as a unitary duty, or a set of interdependent claim-obligation relations. Consequently, a subject cannot regulate such a duty without the consent of all the subjects enjoying correlative rights. Furthermore, a serious violation of such an obligation simultaneously breaches correlative universal claims. This obligation is necessarily *erga omnes*, which means that it is binding vis-à-vis the international community as a whole, according to the terminology of the ICJ, because it cannot be split into separate bilateral obligations.[156]

Since it is non-derogable, a non-severable *erga omnes* obligation fulfils the necessary criteria to be considered peremptory under VCLT and VCLTIO Article 53: it necessarily belongs to *jus cogens*.[157] In fact, if a State is bound by a

154 Gaetano Arangio-Ruiz, Fourth Report on State Responsibility, UN Doc A/CN.4/444 and Add.1–3 (1992) 2(1) *YBILC* 34, para. 92. See also Oliver Lopes Peña, 'Counter-claims and Obligations *Erga Omnes* before the International Court of Justice' (1998) 9(4) *EJIL* 732; Gaja, 'Obligations' (1989) 156; Weatherall, Jus Cogens (2015) 10.

155 Kadelbach, 'Genesis' (2015) 163.

156 According to Ago, an *erga omnes* obligation is a single obligation binding a State vis-à-vis the international community as a unitary legal person (see Roberto Ago, 'Obligations *Erga Omnes* and the International Community', in Weiler, Cassese and Spinedi, *International Crimes* (1989) 238). Nevertheless, this hypothesis is problematic, because the international community should also include the obliged State (see Anne-Laure Vaurs Chaumette, 'The International Community as a Whole', in Crawford, Pellet, Olleson and Parlett, *The Law* (2010) 1024).

157 Pellet, 'Can a State?' (1999) 429; Orakhelashvili, *Peremptory Norms* (2006) 45, 68 and 242, who further identifies unitary *erga omnes* obligations and *jus cogens*; Cassese, 'The Character' (2010) 416. In this regard, Riphagen speaks of a 'fusion' of interstate relations (see Willem Riphagen, 'State Responsibility: New Theories of Obligation in Interstate Relations', in Ronald St John MacDonald and Douglas Millar Johnston (eds), *The Structure and Process of International Law* (Martinus Nijhoff, 1983) 609–610). See also Sicilianos, 'The Classification' (2002)

unitary obligation vis-à-vis all the other States of the international community, that State cannot vary the obligation bilaterally by way of consent with one State or a few States. In order to repeal such an obligation, the obliged State needs the consensus of all the other States of the international community. This means that the obligation cannot be modified, unless all States agree to repeal it.[158] It can thus be concluded that a non-severable general obligation and correlative rights are necessarily *erga omnes* and *cogentes*, notably including the prohibition of aggression, genocide, core war crimes, core crimes against humanity and prospectively terrorism.[159]

By contrast, a general severable obligation is a bundle of divisible obligations that a natural or legal person has vis-à-vis all other subjects in international law. Since it is divisible, a general severable obligation is subject to derogation by means of bilateral and multilateral consent. In the case of a breach, only bilaterally or multilaterally injured State and non-State persons can invoke and enforce responsibility. Thus, a severable *erga omnes* obligation binds separately a subject vis-à-vis all the others in international law. A severable *erga omnes* obligation is a non-unitary duty, including a set of severable bilateral claim-obligation relations. Consequently, from the standpoint of power, a divisible *erga omnes* obligation is subject to derogation via the consent of one or some of the subjects having corresponding rights. Moreover, the breach of such an obligation only violates the correlative claim of a directly injured person. An example is the obligation to respect the freedom of the high seas.

The element that makes an obligation universal and divisible rather than indivisible is its content, that is, the interest protected via compelled negative or positive conduct.[160] Non-severable universal obligations protect such fundamental interests that their breach allows all the subjects of the international community to invoke compliance. By contrast, severable obligations protect less important interests, which allow for bilateral or multilateral protection:

1 Non-severable general obligation
→ non-derogable
→ universal breach
2 Severable general obligation
→ derogable
→ multilateral/bilateral breach

1136–1137; Vaurs Chaumette, 'The International Community' (2010) 1025; Weatherall, Jus Cogens (2015) 11.

158 Thomas Kleinlein, 'Jus Cogens as the "Highest Law"? Peremptory Norms and Legal Hierarchies' (2015) 46 *NYBIL* 192. See also Gaja, '*Jus Cogens*' (1981) 281. Orakhelashvili concludes that 'the *erga omnes* character of obligations under general international law is consequential upon the peremptory character of the norms under which those obligations are stipulated' (Orakhelashvili, *Peremptory Norms* (2006) 270).

159 Erika De Wet, '*Jus Cogens* and Obligations *Erga Omnes*', in Dinah Shelton (ed), *Oxford Handbook of International Human Rights Law* (OUP, 2013) 555; Weatherall, Jus Cogens (2015) 200.

160 Dominicé, 'The International Responsibility' (1999) 356–357.

The same distinction between divisible and indivisible obligations applies, *mutatis mutandis*, to multilateral regimes, whereby scholars speak of obligations *erga omnes contractantes*.[161]

The analysis of general international legal obligations shows that confusion between obligations '*erga omnes*' and '*jus cogens*' is unsuitable. In fact, the expression '*erga omnes*' means 'vis-à-vis everyone', and thus it should designate not only peremptory obligations (*cogentes*), but also non-peremptory obligations (*non-cogentes*). By assuming that *erga omnes* obligations are general and non-severable obligations, it becomes linguistically difficult to define the category of general and severable obligations.[162]

2.1.3.2 *State aggravated offences and individual criminal offences as breaches of (non-severable)* erga omnes *obligations*

From the standpoint of State aggravated responsibility, 2001 DASR 42(b) and 48(1)(b) posit the notion of obligations 'owed to the international community as a whole' (*erga omnes*). This expression certainly includes the case of an obligation unitarily binding a State vis-à-vis all the other States of the international community, which is peremptory. Articles 42(b) and 48(1)(b) thus complement 2001 DASR 40 and 41, allowing universal invocation of responsibility by all States.[163] This is thus the nature of the obligations breached by State aggression, genocide, core war crimes, core crimes against humanity and prospectively terrorism.[164]

With respect to 2001 DASR 40 and 41, this entails:

1 Peremptory nature of the obligation breached by a State (*jus cogens*)
State non-severable *erga omnes* obligation → non-derogable
Prohibition of aggression, genocide, core war crimes, core crimes against humanity, prospectively terrorism

161 Christian Tams, *Enforcing Obligations* Erga Omnes *in International Law* (CUP, 2005) 125–128; Ulf Linderfalk, 'International Legal Hierarchy Revisited: The Status of Obligations *Erga Omnes*' (2011) 80(1) *Nordic JIL* 11; Daniel Costelloe, *Legal Consequences of Peremptory Norms in International Law* (CUP, 2017) 24.

162 The same reasoning applies to particular multilateral obligations, which can be either divisible or indivisible. By contrast, bilateral obligations are necessarily derogable, since the consent of two parties is sufficient to modify them.

163 Orakhelashvili argues that violations of *jus cogens* have an *erga omnes* scope ('objective unlawfulness') and entail universal invocation of responsibility (Orakhelashvili, *Peremptory Norms* (2006) 71–72 and 242).

164 See, for instance, the opinion of Denmark on part 2, ch 3 of the 2001 DASR:

> Chapter III, concerning serious breaches of essential obligations to the international community, is an acceptable compromise to settle the earlier distinction between 'delicts' and 'crimes'. The essential point is not the terminology, though the word 'crime' in the context of State responsibility may give rise to false implications. The essential point is that some violations such as aggression and genocide are such an affront to the international community as a whole that they need to be distinguished from other violations.

(ILC, State Responsibility: Comments and Observations Received from Governments, UN Doc A/CN.4/515 and Add.1–3 (2001) 2(1) *YBILC* 44).

2 Serious State breach
Gross (intent + scope and number of violations, consequences for victims) and/or systematic (intent + organised) failure to comply
→ State *erga omnes breach*

Similarly, 1996 DASR 19 and 40 outlined the following pattern:

1 Non-severable *erga omnes* nature of the obligation breached by a State
State non-derogable obligation (*jus cogens*)
Prohibition of aggression, right to self-determination, core human rights, massive environmental pollution
2 Serious State infringement
→ State *erga omnes breach*

Concerning individuals, the expression 'crimes of concern to the international community as a whole' embedded in the Preamble to the ICC Statute necessarily includes the case of a crime conceived of as the violation of a non-severable *erga omnes* obligation. In fact, if an obligation binds unitarily an individual vis-à-vis all the other subjects of the international community, it is necessarily compelling vis-à-vis the international community as a whole. A grave breach of such an obligation infringes correlative universal claims. Therefore, an international crime can be seen as the individual violation of a non-severable *erga omnes* obligation, which is necessarily peremptory (*cogens*).[165] In light of international practice, this should be the nature of core war crimes and crimes against humanity, genocide, aggression and prospectively terrorism:

> Core individual international crime in breach of a non-severable *erga omnes* obligation
> Aggression, genocide, core war crimes, core crimes against humanity, prospectively terrorism

Such a restrictive approach to the range of individual international crimes breaching non-severable *erga omnes* obligations allows the identification of core individual crimes that have the same structure as State aggravated offences.[166] This addresses the concerns of the ILC, which underscored the necessity of adopting a restrictive interpretation of the relationship between individual criminal responsibility and State aggravated responsibility:

> [I]t is not necessarily true that any 'crime under international law' committed by one of its organs for which the perpetrator is held personally liable to punishment, despite his capacity as a State organ, must automatically be considered not only as an internationally wrongful act of the State concerned, but also as an act entailing a 'special form' of responsibility for that State.[167]

165 In favour of the conception of international crimes as violations of *jus cogens*, see Cançado Trindade, 'Complementarity' (2005) 262; Orakhelashvili, *Peremptory Norms* (2006) 288. See also the ILC, Report (1966) 248, para 3.
166 Sunga, *The Emerging System* (1997) 246; Dupuy, 'Normes' (2012) 85; Wolf, 'Individual Responsibility' (2016) 49.
167 ILC, Report (1976) 103–104, para 21.

2.2 Attribution of responsibility

2.2.1 Dual conduct

2.2.1.1 Attributing aggravated responsibility to the State based on conduct of its organs or agents: absolute identity?

Attribution of aggravated responsibility to the State involves a regulatory system for attaching specific wrongful conduct to a particular legal entity.[168] These rules are the same norms that apply to ordinary responsibility. The 2001 DASR govern the issue in Articles 4–11. These norms closely follow the principles established in 1996 DASR 5–15. Thus, a State is responsible for positive or negative conduct of its organs and agents, including cyber acts.[169] Conduct of a natural person acting on behalf of the State is therefore attributed to the State itself. Whilst such conduct is naturally individual, it is also legally attributed collectively to the State.[170] In fact, the organ or agent of a State is either part of the State itself or acts on its behalf, and therefore his conduct is 'organically' attributed to the State.[171] Such a principle applies to lawful conduct as well as conduct that is contrary to international legal obligations, including fundamental non-severable *erga omnes* obligations. In this regard, Cançado Trindade speaks of 'complementarity' between individual and State responsibility, which are 'ineluctably intertwined'.[172]

Aggravated responsibility is therefore attributed to the State based on a vicarious approach, beginning with the individual and moving to the State. In this respect, it is interesting to observe that the IMT, IMTFE, ICTY and ICTR only adjudicated upon the responsibility of individuals acting as State organs or agents, not as private persons, although their Charters and Statutes allowed the prosecution of natural persons acting in their private capacity. This is essentially owed to the fact that international criminal proceedings ordinarily target high-ranking State organs and agents, whilst domestic jurisdictions mostly try lower-ranking persons and private individuals.

168 Luigi Condorelli, 'L'imputation à l'État d'un fait internationalement illicite: solutions classiques et nouvelles tendances' (1984) 189(6) *RCADI* 19 ff; Crawford, *State Responsibility* (2013) 113.

169 Michael Schmitt, *Tallin Manual 2.0 on the International Law Applicable to Cyber Operations* (CUP, 2017) 84 ff, rules 14–15; Kriangsak Kittichaisaree, *Public International Law of Cyberspace* (Springer, 2017) 36–40.

170 Roberto Ago, 'Le délit international' (1939) 68(2) *RCADI* 174 and 186; Id, Third Report on State Responsibility, UN Doc A/CN.4/246 and Add.1–3 (1971) 2(1) *YBILC* 233, para 107; Crawford, First Report (1998) 33, para 146; Id, *State Responsibility* (2013) 115.

171 According to Ago, natural persons acting as State organs would not have a status independent from the State in international law (Ago, 'Le délit' (1939) 186). See also Djamchid Momtaz, 'Attribution of Conduct to the State: State Organs and Entities Empowered to Exercise Elements of Governmental Authority', in Crawford, Pellet, Olleson and Parlett, *The Law* (2010) 237 and 239.

172 Cançado Trindade, 'Complementarity' (2005) 258 and 260–262.

International law relies on domestic law to identify State organs. Therefore, a State determines its organs, which can then act in the international sphere in the exercise of their functions. International law acknowledges the internal organisation of a State as such, so that international rules refer to domestic norms in order to identify the subjects who are able to express the will of the State in the international sphere.[173] Conduct of a State organ in the exercise of his functions is attributed to the State, even if it is *ultra vires*. Vice versa, conduct of a State organ outside the exercise of his functions cannot be attributed to the State.[174] This principle is embedded in 2001 DASR 4 and 5:

> Article 4 (Conduct of organs of a State)
> 1. The conduct of any State organ shall be considered an act of that State under international law, whether the organ exercises legislative, executive, judicial or any other functions, whatever position it holds in the organization of the State, and whatever its character as an organ of the central Government or of a territorial unit of the State.
> 2. An organ includes any person or entity which has that status in accordance with the internal law of the State.

The same regulation was embedded in 1996 DASR 5–6. In this respect, all State organs can act in breach of international law, regardless of their position within the hierarchy and type of functions. Therefore, any organs belonging to the legislative, executive or judiciary can act in breach of international law and trigger State aggravated responsibility.[175] In fact, the State is considered to be a unitary entity in international law, regardless of its internal divisions.[176] Furthermore, conduct of both superior and subordinate organs can be attributed to the State.[177] Similarly, conduct of decentralised organs generates State responsibility in the same way as that of centralised organs.[178]

This approach matches the trend of those domestic legislations, such as the US and Australia, where, with respect to corporate liability, all individuals who act on behalf of a legal entity are considered to be its 'agents'. For instance, the Australian Criminal Code Act provides that '[i]f a physical element of the offense is committed by an employee, agent or officer of a body corporate acting within the actual or apparent scope of his or her employment, or within his or

173 Ago, 'Le délit' (1939) 187; Id, Third Report (1972) 237, para 199; Kolb, *The International Law* (2017) 76.
174 Ago, 'Le délit' (1939) 198; Id, Third Report (1972) 241, para 129; Crawford, *State Responsibility* (2013) 136–137.
175 Crawford, *State Responsibility* (2013) 118.
176 *Lagrand (Germany v US)*, Request for the Indication of Provisional Measures [1999] ICJ Rep 16, para 28; Crawford, *State Responsibility* (2013) 123–124.
177 Ago, Third Report (1972) 249, para 151, 253, para 160; Crawford, *The International Law Commission* (2002) 95; Kolb, *The International Law* (2017) 74.
178 Crawford, First Report (1998) 34, para 158; Crawford, *The International Law Commission* (2002) 95; Kolb, *The International Law* (2017) 74.

her apparent authority, the physical element must also be attributed to the body corporate.'[179]

However, the opposite opinion has also been formulated that only unlawful acts of high-ranking officials would generate State aggravated responsibility.[180] Certainly, from the standpoint of international responsibility, unlawful conduct of State leaders by nature facilitates establishing a link between individual criminal responsibility and State aggravated responsibility, particularly in the case of aggression.[181] A similar model applies in some domestic legal systems, such as Canada, France and Finland, where it is considered that only acts committed by high-ranking managers in the exercise of their functions are attributable to a legal entity.[182] However, this approach has been criticised because it generates low deterrence.[183] Furthermore, the DASR do not embed such a distinction, which is also problematic with respect to acts of torture or genocide committed by subordinates in the State hierarchy.

A State is also responsible for conduct of agents participating in the exercise of its power, according to 2001 DASR 5–6 and 9–11, which correspond to 1996 DASR 7–10 and 12–15. Furthermore, a State is responsible for conduct of persons acting on the instructions of, or under the direction or control of, a State under 2001 DASR 8.[184] In this respect, the case law developed by the ICJ and ICTY with regard to human rights violations, notably genocide, is critical to determining the criteria for attributing individual conduct to the State.

In *Nicaragua*, the ICJ adjudicated upon the attribution to the US of human rights violations committed by the *Contras* during a counter-revolution that led to the destabilisation of the government led by Augusto Sandino. The ICJ applied the restrictive 'effective control' test in order to determine the attributability to the US of conduct of the rebel group *Contras.*[185] The Court thus considered insufficient for the purposes of imputation the 'financing, organising, training, supplying and equipping of the *Contras*, the selection of its military or paramilitary targets, and the planning of the whole of its operation'.[186]

Subsequently, in *Tadić* the ICTY dealt with human rights violations committed by the army of the Republika Srpska commanded by General Ratko Mladić.[187] In particular, the ICTY assessed responsibility for the genocide that

179 Australian Criminal Code Act (1995) Part 2.5, Division 12.2.

180 Nollkaemper, 'Concurrence between Individual Responsibility and State Responsibility in International Law' (2003) 52(3) *ICLQ* 632–633.

181 See ss 2.3.1.1 and 2.3.1.2.

182 *TESCO Supermarkets, Ltd v Nattrass* [1972] AC 153; Code pénal (1994) arts 121–122. Celia Wells, 'Corporate Criminal Responsibility', in Stephen Tully (ed), *Research Handbook on Corporate Criminal Responsibility* (Edward Elgar, 2005) 152.

183 De Maglie, 'Models' (2005) 554–555.

184 Luigi Condorelli and Claus Kreß, 'The Rules of Attribution: General Considerations', in Crawford, Pellet, Olleson and Parlett, *The Law* (2010) 229.

185 *Military and Paramilitary Activities* [1986] 64–65, para 115.

186 Ibid 65, para 116.

187 See s 1.2.4.1.

took place in Srebrenica, which caused the death of more than 8,000 people. The Tribunal applied the broader 'overall control' test, based on the criterion of 'equipping and financing [...] coordinating or helping in the general planning'.[188] Thus, the Tribunal rejected the need for 'instructions for the commission of specific acts' and held that human rights violations committed by the armed forces of the Republika Srpska were attributable to the Former Republic of Yugoslavia.[189]

Eventually, in the *Bosnian Genocide* case the ICJ adjudicated upon the same facts as the ICTY in *Tadić*, but it did so in order to determine State responsibility, not individual responsibility. The ICJ applied the very narrow criterion of 'complete dependence', based on a factual evaluation of the position of the agent as a 'mere instrument' of the State.[190] As a consequence, the Court excluded the attribution to the SFRY of genocidal acts committed in Bosnia by agents of the Republika Srpska.[191]

In the specific hypothesis of an aggravated act of a State organ or agent inconsistent with both domestic law and international law, the question arises as to whether the State can be held responsible. Article 3 of the 2001 DASR, which is based on corresponding 1996 DASR 4, provides that international law determines the unlawfulness of an act. Whilst the same provision only explicitly refers to acts domestically characterised as lawful, it is considered that the domestic unlawfulness of an act or omission does not affect its unlawfulness under international law, as confirmed by 2001 DASR 7 and 1996 DASR 10.[192]

Within such a framework, it is unclear whether aggression, genocide, core war crimes, core crimes against humanity and terrorism committed by an individual acting on behalf of the State infringe the same non-severable *erga omnes* obligations imposed upon the State, or rather different ones. The question is crucial, but has been given scant attention in the case law and scholarly work. In light of the fact that conduct of an individual acting on behalf of the State generates dual responsibility, it can be assumed that individual aggression, genocide, core war crimes, core crimes against humanity and prospectively terrorism breach the same indivisible *erga omnes* prohibitions imposed on both the individual and the State.[193] In this respect, Arangio Ruiz held:

> The individual crime will easily appear to be so closely connected with the reprehensible conduct of other organs that the individual crime will be recognized as a crime of State of the same or very similar denomination. Two factors may frequently concur in making such an outcome inevitable. One is

188 *Tadić* (1999) 49–50, para 122, 56, para 131.
189 Ibid 56, para 131.
190 *Application of the Convention* [2007] 205, para 392.
191 Ibid 214, para 413. See, in more detail, s 3.2.4.1.
192 Ago, Third Report (1972) 242, para 133; Crawford, 'Revisiting' (1999) 440; Id, *State Responsibility* (2013) 136.
193 Bonafè, 'Reassessing' (2016) 21.

> that the infringed rule is basically identical in both cases, as is also the dimension of the wrongful act or acts, i.e. the actions or omissions constituting the 'objective' or 'external' element of the crime. The other factor relates to the so-called 'internal' or 'psychological' element, namely the wilful intent (*dolus*).[194]

This view is based on the identical content of peremptory rules addressing the State and the individual. Those scholars who assume that individual crimes and State crimes are identical in international law formulate the same assumption.[195]

Other scholars, however, assume that individual conduct breaches obligations that are different from State obligations, despite sharing identical content. This approach is based on the idea that the sources of individual and State responsibility are different norms.[196] Furthermore, a separate approach is supported by the observation that sanctions for individual criminal responsibility are obligations different from those applying to State responsibility.[197] Concerning the sources of international obligations, it is possible to object that international law defines aggression at the individual level by means of a reference to the State prohibition. The prohibition of genocide originally stems for both individuals and States from Article III of the Genocide Convention. State responsibility for core war crimes, crimes against humanity and terrorism originates from norms addressing natural persons.[198] Concerning sanctions, it is not impossible to posit that a breach of the same primary substantive norm by the State and its organs or agents generates different secondary substantive rules, based on the nature of the responsible person.

Whatever approach is preferred,[199] the obligations breached proscribe the same conduct,[200] which affects the same victims, in light of their non-severable *erga omnes* scope.

2.2.1.2 Individual responsibility for international crimes: mens rea

ICC Statute Article 30 spells out in detail the mechanisms for attributing criminal responsibility to an individual, following classical domestic rules. In fact,

194 Arangio-Ruiz, Seventh Report (1995) 27, para 124.

195 ILC, Report (1983) 13 ff, para 46 ff; Thiam, Third Report (1985) 70–71, paras 61–63; Beaudouin, 'Le maintien' (2000) 431.

196 Christian Dominicé, 'La question de la double responsabilité de l'État et de son agent', in Emile Yakpo and Tahar Boumedra (eds), *Liber amicorum Judge Mohammed Bedjaoui* (Kluwer, 1999) 152.

197 Ibid 146.

198 See ss 2.3.1–2.3.5.

199 According to Akande and Tzanakopoulos, '"core crimes" are not addressed merely to individuals but are also related to the same (or substantially similar) obligations imposed on States' (Akande and Tzanakopoulos, 'The Crime' (2017) 33).

200 Nollkaemper, 'Systemic Effects' (2010) 332.

imputation is based on intent and knowledge.[201] Fundamentally, intent (*dolus*) entails attribution of unlawful conduct that a natural person envisaged (knowledge) and willingly implemented (intention). Consequently, negligence (*culpa*) entails imputation of unlawful conduct in the absence of either knowledge or intention. In the absence of intention, there will be advertent negligence, whilst in the absence of knowledge there will be inadvertent negligence.

Advertent negligence is quite close to recklessness (*dolus eventualis*),[202] because an individual perceives the consequences of his conduct as a mere possibility. However, whilst in the case of recklessness the perpetrator would accept the risk of the consequences of his conduct, in the case of advertent negligence he would not accept such a risk. The difference, nonetheless, is subtle and not universally accepted.[203] Indeed, the 1996 and 1998 Draft ICC Statutes simply envisaged awareness of potential consequences as a source of negligence.[204]

Gross negligence is usually required for criminal responsibility. Negligence is different from strict, or objective, liability, to the extent that it entails for an individual the possibility of correctly envisaging the elements of the crime (avoidable mistake), whilst such a possibility is excluded in the case of objective liability (unavoidable mistake):[205]

Knowledge + intention
→ intent (*dolus*)
Knowledge + intention as awareness of the risk of a desired consequence
→ recklessness (*dolus eventualis*)
Knowledge + no intention as awareness of the risk of a non-desired consequence
→ advertent negligence (*culpa*)
No (but possible) knowledge + no intention
→ inadvertent negligence (*culpa*)
No (but impossible) knowledge + no intention
→ objective (strict) liability

201 Iryna Marchuck, *The Fundamental Concept of Crime in International Criminal Law* (Springer, 2014) 127; Donald Piragoff and Darryl Robinson, 'Article 30: Mental Element', in Otto Triffterer and Kai Ambos (eds), *Commentary on the Rome Statute of the International Criminal Court* (Nomos, 3rd edn, 2016) 1117.

202 In favour of the identification of *dolus eventualis* and *recklessness*, see *Stakić*, IT-97-24, Trial Chamber, Judgment of 31 July 2003, 166, para 587; Antonio Cassese, *International Criminal Law* (OUP, 3rd edn, 2013) 46, note 15.

203 *Blăskić*, IT-95-14, Trial Chamber, Judgment of 3 March 2000, 52, para 152, mentioning 'reckless acts' and 'recklessness which may be likened to serious criminal negligence', 157, para 474, 190, para 562; *Blăskić*, IT-95-14, Appeals Chamber, Judgment of 29 July 2004, 14–15, para 40.

204 PCEICC, Report, A/51/22A (1996) Part 3bis, General Principles of Criminal Law, Article H (*Mens rea*) 92; Id, Draft Statute (1998) Article 29 (*Mens rea* – Mental Element) 55–56.

205 Stefan Glaser, 'Culpabilité en droit international pénal' (1960) 99(1) *RCADI* 485–492; Herbert Hart, 'Negligence, *Mens Rea* and Criminal Responsibility', in Anthony Guest (ed), *Oxford Essays in Jurisprudence* (OUP, 1961) 33 ff; Cassese, *International Criminal Law* (2013) 41–43.

On this basis, ICC Statute Article 30 provides:

> Article 30 (Mental element)
> 1. Unless otherwise provided, a person shall be criminally responsible and liable for punishment for a crime within the jurisdiction of the Court only if the material elements are committed with intent and knowledge.
> 2. For the purposes of this article, a person has intent where:
>   (a) In relation to conduct, that person means to engage in the conduct;
>   (b) In relation to a consequence, that person means to cause that consequence or is aware that it will occur in the ordinary course of events.
> 3. For the purposes of this article, 'knowledge' means awareness that a circumstance exists or a consequence will occur in the ordinary course of events. 'Know' and 'knowingly' shall be construed accordingly.

Based on ICC Statute Article 30(2)–(3), intent and knowledge concern (positive or negative) conduct, consequences, hence the causal nexus, and circumstances.[206] By contrast, intent and knowledge are not concerned with the unlawfulness of conduct, that is, the breach of an international obligation. In fact, ICC Statute Article 32(2) provides that a mistake of law does not exclude responsibility, save when it is a factual element of the crime.

Intent, that is *dolus*, is therefore the ordinary criterion for the imputation of aggression, war crimes, crimes against humanity and genocide to an individual. Negligence, by contrast, is not mentioned in ICC Statute Article 30. However, negligence may provide an exceptional basis for imputation when specific norms of the ICC Statute and related texts, notably the Elements of Crimes, mention it ('unless otherwise provided').[207] The introduction to the Elements of Crimes (Section 7) and preparatory work for the ICC Statute confirm this approach.[208]

206 Roger Clark, 'The Mental Element in International Criminal Law: The Rome Statute of the ICC and the Elements of Offences' (2001) 12(3) *Crim LF* 299 and 303–307; Piragoff and Robinson, 'Article 30' (2016) 1122 and 1114; Geert-Jan Alexander Knoops, Mens Rea *at the International Criminal Court* (Brill, 2017) 36–39.

207 Albin Eser, 'Mental Elements – Mistake of Fact and Mistake of Law', in Cassese, Gaeta and Jones, *The Rome Statute* (2002) 898; Gerhard Werle and Florian Jeßberger, *Principles of International Criminal Law* (OUP, 3rd edn, 2014) 179 and 192.

208 Article 29 of the 1998 Draft Statute provided:

> [For the purposes of this Statute and unless otherwise provided, *where this Statute provides that a crime may be committed recklessly*, a person is reckless with respect to a circumstance or a consequence if: (a) the person is aware of a risk that the circumstance exists or that the consequence will occur; (b) the person is aware that the risk is highly unreasonable to take; [and][(c) the person is indifferent to the possibility that the circumstance exists or that the consequence will occur].
>
> emphasis added

The related commentary underscored that 'there was no reason for rejecting the concept of commission of an offence also through negligence, in which case the offender shall be liable only when so prescribed by the Statute' (PCEICC, Draft Statute (1998) Article 29 (*Mens rea* – Mental Element) 55–56). Article 29 was almost literally based on art H of the 1996 Draft Statute:

Accordingly, ICC Statute Article 32(1) provides that a mistake of fact, necessarily excluding knowledge, and thus intent, does not automatically exclude negligence. Furthermore, negligence can exceptionally apply as a principle of imputation under all complementary sources of international law envisaged in ICC Statute Article 21.

The approach whereby intent is the main criterion of imputation follows Article 2(3)(a) of the 1996 DCCPSM. The Genocide Convention also refers to the 'intent to destroy, in whole or in part, a national, ethnical, racial or religious group' (Article II). The Convention against Torture and Other Cruel, Inhuman or Degrading Treatment or Punishment (CAT)[209] mentions 'intentionally inflicted' severe pain or suffering (Article 1). The Convention for the Suppression of Terrorist Bombings punishes whoever 'intentionally delivers, places, discharges or detonates an explosive or other lethal device' (Article 2). More generally, the Nuremberg Principles establish that '[a]ny person who commits or is accomplice in an act which constitutes a crime under international law is responsible therefore and liable to punishment.'[210]

Although it only applies residually, negligence still plays an important role within the context of individual imputation. Indeed, advertent negligence, or possibly recklessness, is fundamental to determine knowledge of the widespread or systematic character of an attack directed against civilian population in crimes against humanity.[211] Concerning war crimes, advertent negligence, or recklessness, plays a critical role in determining individual liability with respect to a gross or systematic failure to comply with core obligations under international humanitarian law.[212] Indeed, the ICTY held that individual responsibility in such circumstances subsists when planning can be envisaged in terms of probability and acceptance of risk.[213] Similarly, in *Lubanga Dyilo* the ICC required for imputation that 'the suspect and the other co-perpetrators [...] clearly or expressly accepted the idea that implementing the common plan would result in the realisation of the objective elements of the crime.'[214] More restrictively, in *Katanaga*

'[u]nless otherwise provided, a person is only criminally responsible and liable for punishment for a crime under this Statute if the physical elements are committed with intent [or] and knowledge [, whether general or specific or as the substantive crime in question may specify]'. The related commentary specified that 'a definition of recklessness, [is] to be used only where the Statute explicitly provides that a specific crime or element may be committed recklessly. In all situations, the general rule [...] is that crimes must be committed intentionally and knowingly' (PCEICC, Report, A/51/22A (1996) Part 3bis, General Principles of Criminal Law, Article H (*Mens rea*) 92).

209 Adopted 10 December 1984, 1465 UNTS 84, in force 26 June 1987.

210 Spiropoulos, Formulation (1950) 181, princ I.

211 Thomas Weigend, 'Problems of Attribution in International Criminal Law' (2014) 12 *JICJ* 253–266, 255; Mohamed Elewa Badar and Sara Porro, 'Rethinking the Mental Elements in the Jurisprudence of the ICC', in Carsten Stahn, *The Law and Practice of the International Criminal Court* (OUP, 2015) 651 ff.

212 Werle and Jeßberger, *Principles* (2014) 189–190.

213 *Blăskić* (2000) 83, para 251, 84, paras 255 and 257; *Blăskić* (2004) 16, para 41.

214 *Lubanga Dyilo*, ICC-01/04-01/06-803, Pre-Trial Chamber, Decision on the Confirmation of Charges, 29 January 2007, 123, para 364.

the ICC held that, whilst 'absolute certainty that [a] consequence will occur in future [...] by definition is impossible to prove', it cannot be assumed that 'the drafters of the [ICC] Statute intended to include awareness of the existence of a mere likelihood or possibility.'[215]

ICC Statute Article 33 confirms the relevance of negligence for the purpose of imputation, since it provides that the absence of knowledge of a superior order that is non-manifestly unlawful, and could thus be known, triggers responsibility. However, this threshold, which exceptionally entails the relevance of the ignorance of the law for the purpose of imputation, in derogation from ICC Statute Article 32(2), only applies to aggression and war crimes.[216] In fact, an order to commit crimes against humanity and genocide is necessarily considered to be manifestly unlawful under ICC Statute Article 33(2), triggering intentional responsibility.

Moreover, under Article 28(1) of the ICC Statute, a military superior is responsible for crimes committed by subordinates under his effective control, whether he 'knew' or 'should have known' that a crime was (about to be) committed.[217] This is a clear reference to negligence as a principle of imputation.[218] By contrast, under ICC Statute Article 28(2) a non-military superior is responsible if he knew or 'consciously disregarded information' that a crime was (about to be) committed, entailing wilful blindness, which is an extreme form of recklessness. In this respect, however, the ICC Statute does not seem to codify general international law, since ICTY Statute Article 7(3) and ICTR Statute Article 6(3) applied the 'had reason to know' standard to both military and non-military superiors. The case law of international tribunals has interpreted analytically such a standard so as to embrace both negligence and wilful blindness.[219] In practice, the ICTY applied the same standard, that is, negligence, to both military and non-military superiors.[220] The ICTR sometimes required wilful blindness for non-military superiors and sometimes a case-by-case assessment, not excluding negligence.[221] It is therefore preferable to interpret the standard 'consciously disregarded information' under ICC Statute Article 28(2) in light of the notion of 'constructive

215 *Katanga*, ICC-01/04-01/07, Trial Chamber, Judgment Pursuant to Article 74 of the Statute, 7 March 2014, 289–290, paras 775–777.

216 Knoops, Mens Rea (2017) 92 and 161.

217 *Kayshema and Ruzindana*, ICTR-95-I, Trial Chamber, Judgment of 21 May 1999, 86–87, paras 226–228; *Blăskić* (2000) 98, paras 309 ff; *Dordević* (2011) 730, para 1886; *Bemba Gombo*, ICC-01/05-01/08, Trial Chamber, Judgment of 21 March 2016, 80, para 170. See also Piragoff and Robinson, 'Article 30' (2016) 1118.

218 Kai Ambos, 'Command Responsibility and *Organisationsherrschaft*: Ways of Attributing International Crimes to the "Most Responsible"', in Nollkaemper and Van der Wilt, *System Criminality* (2009) 137.

219 *Krnojelac*, IT-97-25, Appeals Chamber, Judgment of 17 September 2003, 29, para 59; *Dordević* (2011) 731, para 1886.

220 *Delalić* et al, IT-96-21, Trial Chamber, Judgment of 16 November 1998, 131 ff, paras 355 ff, notably 134, para 363, 140, para 378; *Dordević* (2011) 729, para 1884.

221 *Akayesu* (1998) para 491; *Kayshema and Ruzindana* (1999) 86–87, para 228.

knowledge', according to which a person 'could not not know', and thus 'necessarily knew', because of the manifest nature of the crimes committed by subordinates.[222] Constructive knowledge is close to the 'should have known' standard, entailing negligence as a minimum threshold for imputation.[223]

2.2.2 Attributing individual criminal conduct to the State

2.2.2.1 Individual mens rea *versus State objective responsibility?*

It has been acknowledged that the fact that the same conduct generates two distinct forms of responsibility simultaneously, that is, that of the individual and vicariously that of the State, inevitably establishes a link between individual criminal conduct and State aggravated responsibility.[224] On this basis, Cançado Trindade concludes that a crime should be imputable to both a State organ or agent and the State itself.[225] This raises the question as to whether it is consistent to introduce a distinction between individual criminal liability and State non-criminal responsibility. In other words, if the State is responsible for conduct of its organs and agents that qualifies as 'criminal', is it correct to classify State responsibility simply as 'aggravated'?

As we have seen,[226] the question as to whether only individuals can be held criminally responsible, or also States can, has been the focus of scholarly debate for a long time and has given rise to different interpretations. The main obstacle in attributing the criminal responsibility of an individual to the State is the principle of *mens rea*. In fact, unlike an individual, it is assumed that the State, as a collective, would not be able to have knowledge and intention.[227] The argument excludes *mens rea* based on the principle *societas delinquere non potest*, according to which it would be impossible to apply the *mens rea* of those in government or in charge of the affairs of a State to the State itself as a legal entity and its population.[228] Not being capable of negligence, *a fortiori* a State would be unable to have intent, which is fundamentally required for the commission of individual crimes affecting non-severable *erga omnes* obligations.[229] This would exclude criminal responsibility at the State level, in accordance with the tendency to

222 *Blăskić* (2000) 159–160, para 478.
223 *Kordić and & Čerkez*, IT-95-14/2, Trial Chamber, Judgment of 26 February 2001, 129, para 437.
224 Arangio-Ruiz, 'Fine prematura' (1998) 123.
225 Cançado Trindade, 'Complementarity' (2005) 259.
226 Chapter 1.
227 ILC, Report (1995) 49, para 266. Critically, see Dupuy, 'International Criminal Responsibility' (2002) 1095.
228 ILC, Report (1994) 144–145, paras 291–294; ILC, Report (2000) 57, paras 349–350; De Maglie, 'Models' (2005) 548; Albin Eser and Felix Rettenmeier, 'Criminality of Organizations: Lessons from Domestic Law – A Comparative Perspective', in Nollkaemper and Van Der Wilt, *System Criminality* (2009) 235.
229 Gilbert, 'The Criminal Responsibility' (1990) 356–357.

only establish international criminal courts with jurisdiction over individuals, not over States.[230] It would thus be necessary to assume that there is a discrepancy between the responsibility of the organ or agent acting for the State and the State itself, including the population living in a specific territory.

More specifically, taking into account domestic obligations would compel embracing the theory of State objective responsibility for conduct of its organs or agents, which would apply to both State aggravated and ordinary responsibility. Dionisio Anzilotti proposed the doctrine of State objective responsibility, fundamentally based upon domestic law. Indeed, Anzilotti argued that, if a State organ or agent acts consistently with domestic law, but contrary to international law, it would have no knowledge and intention with respect to the breach of international law, which would necessarily lead to positing State objective responsibility.[231] If a State organ or agent acts in breach of both domestic law and international law, the State could not be held to have knowledge and intention, because the conduct of the organ or agent is inconsistent with the State order.[232]

However, Roberto Ago showed that individual knowledge and intention apply with respect to international law, not based on domestic law, for instance, with regard to the prohibition of genocide, and it is on this basis that State knowledge and intention should be determined.[233] In the author's view, individual knowledge and intention should be determined with regard to the factual elements of the offence, not considering the domestic or international obligation breached, which is a mere matter of legality with respect to both the individual and the State.[234] Therefore, if an individual acting as a State organ or agent forcibly transfers the members of a group, intention rather than negligence should be determined based on whether or not that individual envisaged such conduct and intentionally carried it out, or could have envisaged such conduct and its consequences. This assessment should not involve the perception of the conformity of forcibly transferring the members of a group with domestic or international law. The same principles should underpin State responsibility. On this basis, it is possible to conclude that intent and knowledge should apply to the State in the same way as to the individual.[235]

From a comparative perspective, excluding State criminal responsibility based on objective liability can be criticised on the basis that some domestic legal systems apply the principle of corporate criminal liability objectively, in the absence of *mens rea*.[236] Article 121-2 of the French Criminal Code thus

230 Glaser, 'Culpabilité' (1960) 483; ILC, Report (1994) 138–139, paras 240–242.

231 Dionisio Anzilotti, *Cours de droit international* (Sirey, 1929, re-published by Panthéon-Assas, 1999) 470 and 500.

232 Ibid 470–471 and 501. See also Hans Kelsen, *General Theory of Law and State* (Russell & Russell, 1961) 362.

233 Ago, 'Le délit' (1939) 482.

234 See s 2.2.1.2.

235 Ago, 'Le délit' (1939) 492–493 and 498.

236 De Maglie, 'Models' (2005) 555.

provides that 'legal persons [...] are criminally liable [...] for offences committed on their behalf by their organs or representatives.'[237] This implies that, when the *actus reus* and *mens rea* of the offence are established with reference to a natural person acting on behalf of a legal entity, it would only be necessary to prove a relationship between the *actus reus* and the activity carried out on behalf of the organisation, excluding the necessity of proving collective *mens rea*.[238] On this basis, Cançado Trindade concludes that a State *delinquere potest*.[239]

2.2.2.2 *Individual and State* mens rea?

Assuming that a State can have *mens rea* in the same way as an individual,[240] conduct of a State organ or agent should be attributed to the State based on knowledge and intention.[241] The ICJ particularly endorsed this approach in the cases concerning the *Application of the Genocide Convention*, where the Court upheld the necessity of proving *dolus specialis* at the State level to determine collective responsibility under the Convention.[242] Some scholars speak, in this regard, of a 'collective psychology':[243] the collective should not be allowed to shift criminal responsibility for offences committed in its name to mere individuals.[244] Collective responsibility would have a pre-emptive effect, to the extent that it would avert acquiescence and compel the population of a State to thwart the commission of crimes by its leaders.[245] Along these lines, Article 44 of the Draft Project for an International Criminal Code proposed by Quintiliano Saldaña established State responsibility for the breach of an international obligation for either intent or negligence.[246] Article VI(3) of the General Part of the 1981 ICLA Project of an International Criminal Code established the *mens rea*

237 This is known as '*responsabilité par ricochet*', translation by the author.

238 Markus Dubber and Tatjana Hörnle, *Criminal Law: A Comparative Approach* (OUP, 2014) 336.

239 Cançado Trindade, 'Complementarity' (2005) 259–260.

240 ILC, Report (1994) 139, para 243. See also Crawford, *State Responsibility* (2013) 61.

241 Gilbert, 'The Criminal Responsibility' (1990) 348–349; Arangio-Ruiz, Seventh Report (1995) 123–124, para 122; Cançado Trindade, 'Complementarity' (2005) 264.

242 *Application of the Convention* [2007] 121, para 187; *Application of the Convention* [2015] 66, para 145.

243 Saldaña, 'La justice' (1925) 297–298; Secretary General, Draft Code (1950) 316–317, para 72; Anamika Twinam Ghoshal and Nikos Passas, 'State and Corporate Drivers of Global Dysnomie: Horrendous Crimes and the Law', in Greg Barak (ed), *International Handbook of the Crimes of the Powerful* (Routledge, 2015) 106.

244 ILC, Report (1994) 139, para 244. See also Hersch Lauterpacht, 'Règles générales du droit de la paix' (1937) 62(4) *RCADI* 351; Andrea Gattini, 'A Historical Perspective: From Collective to Individual Responsibility and Back', in Nollkaemper and Van der Wilt, *System Criminality* (2009) 108 and 115–116; Eser and Rettenmeier, 'Criminality' (2009) 235; Nollkaemper, 'Systemic Effects' (2010) 314, 320–321 and 323.

245 Secretary General, Draft Code (1950) 316, para 70; Drumbl, 'Accountability' (2010) 380–381.

246 Saldaña, 'Avant-Projet' (1925) 404, art 44.

of the individual, State and other legal persons based on intent, knowledge or negligence.[247]

In this context, one criticism concerns the fact that sanctions for State aggravated responsibility affect the State as such, including its population.[248] This was the case of the sanctions imposed on Germany and Japan after World War II as a consequence of the crimes committed by their organs and agents. Therefore, it is arguably more appropriate to consider the State negligently or intentionally responsible, hence subject to international sanctions, rather than imposing sanctions on objectively responsible people.[249] Indeed, in light of similar considerations, several domestic legal orders have overcome the principle *societas delinquere non potest*, for instance, Australia, Canada, Denmark, Finland, the Netherlands, the UK and the US. In these States, the *actus reus* and *mens rea* of the individual acting on behalf of a legal entity are vicariously attributed to the entity itself.[250] Furthermore, domestic legal systems commonly acknowledge the tortious and contractual responsibility of legal persons and attribute it to organisations based on intent and knowledge.[251]

Some States determine the *mens rea* of a legal entity based on the identification doctrine, following a bottom-up approach. Identification, also known as the '*alter ego*' doctrine, posits that the *mens rea* of the person acting for a legal entity is the *mens rea* of the entity itself, without requiring any further evidence.[252] This is also the stance of those scholars who assume that individual negligence should entail State negligence, whilst individual intent should imply State intent.[253] In the second case on the *Application of the Genocide Convention*, the ICJ upheld this approach, holding that, in the absence of a State plan or policy, it is necessary to prove collective *dolus specialis* based on individual intent.[254] The limit of this theory is that it tends to only apply to high-ranking agents,[255] whose 'state of mind' would be 'the state of mind' of the organisation.[256]

247 ICLA, Projet de Code (1981) Partie générale – Applicable à une CPI – Système d'application directe, art VI, 3.1, 217–219.

248 Allen Weiner, 'Working the System: A Comment on Andre Nollkaemper's System Criminality in International Law (2010) 8(1) *Santa Clara JIL* 360–362, arguing that this approach can go as far as to prevent domestic criminal prosecution; Drumbl, 'Accountability' (2010) 380; Ollivier, 'International Criminal Responsibility' (2010) 711.

249 Pella, De l'influence (1926) 394; Nollkaemper, 'Systemic Effects' (2010) 324–326.

250 De Maglie, 'Models' (2005) 553; Eser and Rettenmeier, 'Criminality' (2009) 230 and 232; Dubber and Hörnle, *Criminal Law* (2014) 336.

251 Thomas Meron, 'Is International Law Moving towards Criminalization?' (1998) 9(1) *EJIL* 20; Stoitchkova, *Towards Corporate Liability* (2010) 9.

252 Stephen Tully, 'Process and Procedure', in Tully (ed), *International Corporate Legal Responsibility* (Wolters Kluwer, 2012) 82–83.

253 Ago, 'Le délit' (1939) 486.

254 *Application of the Convention* [2015] 66, para 145.

255 *TESCO Supermarkets* [1972] 169–171; Wells, 'Corporate Criminal Responsibility' (2005) 152.

256 *HL Bolton Engineering Co v TJ Graham & Sons, Ltd* [1957] 1 QB 172; Stephen Tully, 'Introduction', in Tully, *International Corporate Legal Responsibility* (2012) 35. Some scholars consider this model outdated and inadequate to address corporate crimes (De Maglie, 'Models' (2005) 560).

By contrast, some legal orders adopt the 'aggregate intent' model, which postulates that a legal entity has *mens rea* per se.[257] Within this framework, it is still possible to take a bottom-up approach, whereby corporate *mens rea* arises as the aggregation of the *mens rea* of individuals acting on behalf of the State.[258] Alternatively, it is possible to adopt a top-down approach, determining the *mens rea* of a legal entity based on its own characteristics.[259]

Under the corporate policy model, collective *mens rea* may arise according to any collective policy that intentionally or foreseeably enables unlawful conduct. Thus, collective policies may be unlawful because they compel, authorise, encourage or tolerate criminal conduct. *Mens rea* would thus arise because of the personality of a legal entity, that is, the collective environment, encouraging its agents to commit crimes. This model progressively emerged in the US in the 1970s.[260] Along these lines, the 1995 Australia Criminal Code Act provides that '[c]orporate culture means an attitude, policy, rule, course of conduct or practice existing within the body corporate generally or in the part of the body corporate in which the relevant activities take place.'[261] At the lower end of the spectrum, the preventive fault model sets a minimum threshold for liability and assumes that collective *mens rea* arises when a corporation fails to adopt an adequate internal system of controls for crime prevention and sanctioning.[262] Thus, in the US the existence of an effective compliance programme is a prerequisite for avoiding corporate negligence.[263] Along these lines, some scholars assume that it is possible to hold the people of a State negligently or intentionally responsible for not preventing the commission of aggravated wrongful acts by their representatives.[264] Whilst, therefore, individual criminal responsibility would deter and punish individual crimes, based on collective *mens rea* State criminal responsibility would deter and punish collective acquiescence.[265]

The changing organisation of legal entities, which are no longer strictly hierarchically organised, but rather decentralised based on the division of tasks, prompted a different approach to the theory of aggregate *mens rea*: even when there is no individual responsibility, aggregated tasks can give rise to collective criminal responsibility.[266] Thus, in the context of a crime involving elements A,

257 Stoitchkova, *Towards Corporate Liability* (2010) 30–32 and 37; Stephen Tully, 'International Criminal Law, in Tully, *International Corporate Legal Responsibility* (2012) 449.

258 *US v Bank of New England* 821 F.2d 844 (1st Cir 1987); Tully, 'Process' (2012) 84.

259 Eser and Rettenmeier, 'Criminality' (2009) 231 and 233–234.

260 Pamela Bucy, 'Corporate Ethos: A Standard for Imposing Corporate Criminal Liability' (1990–91) 75(4) *Min L Rev* 1095–1184, 1101; Stoitchkova, *Towards Corporate Liability* (2010) 30–31.

261 Australian Criminal Code Act (1995) ch 2, div 12.3(6).

262 Wells, 'Corporate Criminal Responsibility' (2005) 153; De Maglie, 'Models' (2005) 559; Stoitchkova, *Towards Corporate Liability* (2010) 26.

263 US Sentencing Guidelines Manual (2016) para 8B2.1(a)(6)(B).

264 Bassiouni, *Introduction* (2013) 105.

265 Secretary General, Draft Code (1950) 317, para 75. See also Crawford, First Report (1998) 21–22, para 83; ILC, Report (1998) 79, para 353; Drumbl, 'Accountability' (2010) 380–381.

266 De Maglie, 'Models' (2005) 560.

B and C, whereby officer A possibly knows element A, officer B possibly knows element B and officer C possibly knows element C, supposedly the organisation will possibly know elements A, B and C for the purpose of criminal imputation. Whilst individual *mens rea* does not subsist, aggregate *mens rea* allows criminalising a legal entity, thus avoiding impunity.

Since the debate on attribution of responsibility to the State for internationally wrongful acts has mostly focused on the dualism opposing objective responsibility and fault from a bottom-up perspective, the possibility of applying the aggregate model to the State has not been extensively explored. In light of the gross and systematic nature of breaches of peremptory norms, the organisational approach to State *mens rea* would facilitate establishing State intention for aggravated responsibility, when conduct of its organs or agents only subsists at best in terms of recklessness or negligence. This particularly applies to the systematic nature of crimes against humanity. To the extent that international criminal tribunals infer individual intent from the existence of a collective policy,[267] it can be said that aggregate *mens rea* already applies in international practice.

2.2.2.3 Assessing State fault on a case-by-case basis under the ILC's DASR

In principle, there is no absolutely valid approach to the relationship between attribution of conduct of an organ or agent of the State as criminal to the individual based on intent and knowledge and as criminal or non-criminal to the State based on intent and knowledge rather than objective responsibility. It is possible to apply different mechanisms and the ultimate reference in this respect is the ILC's DASR.

The ILC avoided explicitly addressing the question of fault in State responsibility. In fact, the general provisions concerning the elements of an internationally wrongful act do not elucidate the issue, notably 2001 DASR 2. Specific provisions concerning the attribution of conduct to a State, notably DASR 4–11, also do not clarify the question. The same can be said of 1996 DASR 3 and 5–15. However, it is considered that the fault element underpins attribution of responsibility in the DASR with respect to both ordinary offences and aggravated breaches.[268] The 2001 DASR take a case-by-case approach to the matter, based on the content of the primary obligation breached. The ILC upheld such an 'eclectic' stance in its Commentary to 2001 DASR 2:

> Whether there has been a breach of a rule may depend on the intention or knowledge of relevant State organs or agents and in that sense [the question] may be 'subjective' […] In other cases, the standard for the breach of an

267 See ss 2.3.2.2, 2.3.3.2 and 2.3.4.2.

268 Arangio-Ruiz, Second Report on State Responsibility, UN Doc A/CN.4/425 and Add.1 (1989) 48–55, paras 164–190; Arangio-Ruiz, Eighth Report (1996) 8–9, paras 48–55.

> obligation may be 'objective', in the sense that the advertence or otherwise of relevant State organs or agents may be irrelevant. Whether responsibility is 'objective' or 'subjective' in this sense depends on the circumstances, including the content of the primary obligation in question [...] The same is true of other standards, whether they involve some degree of fault, culpability, negligence or want of due diligence. Such standards vary from one context to another for reasons which essentially relate to the object and purpose of the treaty provisions or other rule giving rise to the primary obligation [...] Establishing these is a matter for the interpretation and application of the primary rules engaged in the given case.[269]

Different rules of the 2001 DASR support the assumption that a State can act or fail to act intentionally rather than negligently. For instance, DASR 39 provides that reparation is determined by taking into account the contribution to the injury 'by wilful or negligent action or omission of the injured State'. Similarly, the possibility of invoking *force majeure* under DASR 23 depends on a State acting involuntarily. Even more explicitly, 1996 DASR 42 subjected the determination of reparation to 'the negligence or the wilful act or omission' of the 'injured State'. It is indeed clear that, if knowledge and intent are taken into account with respect to the injured State, they should also be considered with respect to the injurer. Moreover, 2001 DASR 23, governing *force majeure* and corresponding to 1996 DASR 31, excludes responsibility based on the absence of intent, when a wrongful act is 'beyond the control of the State'.

Most importantly, it is precisely with respect to the different gravity of State responsibility that knowledge and intention have a role to play, notably with regard to State aggravated responsibility. In fact, purpose and intention to harm are crucial elements that determine the 'seriousness' of the infringement of an obligation protecting fundamental interests in the international community.[270] Scholars interpret such intent as the malice or intention to harm of the State as an international legal person, rather than the individual mental attitude of a number of State officials or agents per se.[271] This is particularly meaningful, in light of the paucity of references to knowledge and intention throughout the ILC's DASR. According to this approach, the choice of the drafters of the 2001 DASR is therefore to envisage State aggravated responsibility based on fault, notably intent.[272] In this regard, given that 'individual fault' may 'transgress into the domain of State responsibility',[273] scholars note that a positive or negative

269 ILC, Report (2001) 34, para 3. See also Cançado Trindade, 'Complementarity' (2005) 258; Crawford, *State Responsibility* (2013) 61–62.

270 ILC, Report (2001) 113, paras 7–9. See also s 2.1.1.1 and Costelloe, *Legal Consequences* (2017) 188.

271 Giuseppe Palmisano, 'Fault', in Rüdiger Wolfrum (ed), *Max Planck Encyclopedia of Public International Law* (2007) para 38, http://opil.ouplaw.com/home/EPIL.

272 Crawford, *State Responsibility* (2013) 381.

273 Nollkaemper, 'Concurrence' (2003) 634.

finding by the ICTY on the intent of Slobodan Milošević to commit genocide would have been 'directly relevant' to determining 'State intent' in the *Bosnian Genocide* case.[274]

However, whilst the DASR seem to favour dual attribution based on *mens rea*, the question is far from being answered in detail. Indeed, State aggravated responsibility requires 'intent', whilst individual responsibility may subsist for either 'intent' or 'negligence'. It is thus impossible to simply assume that the same *mens rea* applies to a State organ or agent and the State itself. For instance, this is the case of a superior responsible for negligently supervising subordinates, when he 'should have known that the [subordinate] forces were committing or about to commit' a crime under ICC Statute Article 28. It therefore seems necessary to assume that the ILC's DASR implement aggregate intent, whereby State intent is the overall intent of individuals acting as State organs or agents. This is consistent with a systemic approach to the proof of individual *mens rea*, which often entails recklessness, at least in the form of willful blindness, possibly overlapping with advertent negligence, based on the context of the offence.[275] Similarly, aggregate intent fits with the possibility that a State has genocidal intent, whereas some State organs or agents do not, absent *dolus specialis*, as in the case of *Krstić*.[276]

In light of the possibility of applying fault to the State, some scholars criticise the dualistic approach that individual criminal responsibility for breaches of core non-severable *erga omnes* obligations 'only' generates State aggravated responsibility. In fact, the same conduct should give rise to identical responsibility at the individual and collective level.[277] However, there is no uniform approach to the question. In fact, other commentators assume that it is perfectly consistent to differentiate State aggravated responsibility from individual criminal responsibility for the same conduct, despite the application of fault to the State.[278] Whilst the first approach would ensure uniformity, the second preserves the specific nature of international responsibility as opposed to domestic law. Both approaches are viable, as the debate that animated the ILC until the adoption of the final version of the ILC's DASR in 2001 proves.[279] Eventually, the choice of the ILC shows that, under current international law, there is no room for the criminal responsibility of the State and thus the same conduct generates a different type of responsibility for the individual and the State. Whereas the terminology has important implications, it does not fundamentally alter the mechanisms underpinning attribution of responsibility.

274 Ibid.

275 *Blăskić* (2000) 82–83, paras 247 and 251; *Karadžić* (2016) 184, para 479. See also Knoops, Mens Rea (2017) 119–123.

276 *Krstić*, IT-98-33, Appeals Chamber, Judgment of 19 April 2004, 46, para 134.

277 ILC, Summary Records (1976) 73, para 6, 84, para 44; Arangio-Ruiz, Fifth Report (1993) 54, paras 250 ff; Arangio-Ruiz, Seventh Report (1995) 26, para 124; ILC, Report (1998) 69, para 276; Cançado Trindade, 'Complementarity' (2005) 258–259.

278 Barboza, 'International Criminal Law' (1999) 81 and 106.

279 See ss 1.2.2.3 and 1.2.3.5.

2.3 Dual *erga omnes* offences

2.3.1 Aggression

Owing to legal and political reasons, the definition of aggression is problematic in international law.[280] Different international instruments define aggression. Concerning States, the basic definition is embedded in a soft law instrument, notably UN General Assembly Resolution 3314 (XXIX) of 14 December 1974:

> Article 2
> Aggression is the use of armed force by a State against the sovereignty, territorial integrity or political independence of another State, or in any other manner inconsistent with the Charter of the United Nations...

Article 3 spells out specific State aggressive conduct:

> Article 3
> Any of the following acts, regardless of a declaration of war, shall, subject to and in accordance with the provisions of article 2, qualify as an act of aggression:
> (a) The invasion or attack by the armed forces of a State of the territory of another State, or any military occupation, however temporary, resulting from such invasion or attack, or any annexation by the use of force of the territory of another State or part thereof,
> (b) Bombardment by the armed forces of a State against the territory of another State or the use of any weapons by a State against the territory of another State;
> (c) The blockade of the ports or coasts of a State by the armed forces of another State;
> (d) An attack by the armed forces of a State on the land, sea or air forces, or marine and air fleets of another State;
> (e) The use of armed forces of one State which are within the territory of another State with the agreement of the receiving State, in contravention of the conditions provided for in the agreement or any extension of their presence in such territory beyond the termination of the agreement;
> (f) The action of a State in allowing its territory, which it has placed at the disposal of another State, to be used by that other State for perpetrating an act of aggression against a third State;
> (g) The sending by or on behalf of a State of armed bands, groups, irregulars or mercenaries, which carry out acts of armed force against another State of such gravity as to amount to the acts listed above, or its substantial involvement therein.

280 See Julius Stone, 'Hopes and Loopholes in the 1974 Definition of Aggression' (1977) 71(2) *AJIL* 225–226; Bengt Broms, 'The Definition of Aggression' (1977) 154(1) *RCADI* 336; Kirsten Sellars, *Crimes against Peace in International Law* (CUP, 2013) 87 ff; Kreß, 'On the Activation' (2018) 1–5.

Along the lines of Resolution 2625 (XXVI) adopted by the UN General Assembly on 24 October 1970, Article 5(a) of Resolution 3314 (XXIX) further qualifies a 'war of aggression' as 'a crime against international peace'. According to most commentators, Article 5 establishes both State aggravated responsibility and individual criminal responsibility for aggressive war.[281] Literally, however, the Resolution simply qualifies aggressive war as 'criminal'.[282]

More recently, the Bruges Declaration adopted by the Institute of International Law (IIL) on 2 September 2003 restated that 'a war of aggression constitutes an international crime'.[283] The UN Security Council, instead, usually does not explicitly associate the terms 'aggression' and 'crime'. For instance, Resolution 660/1990 'condemns' the 'Iraqi invasion of Kuwait'.[284]

The definition of State aggression provides a basis for the individual crime of aggression in international law. Indeed, the Statute of the ICC provides:

> Article 8bis (Crime of Aggression)
>
> 1. For the purpose of this Statute, 'crime of aggression' means the planning, preparation, initiation or execution, by a person in a position effectively to exercise control over or to direct the political or military action of a State, of an act of aggression which, by its character, gravity and scale, constitutes a manifest violation of the Charter of the United Nations.
> 2. For the purpose of paragraph 1, 'act of aggression' means the use of armed force by a State against the sovereignty, territorial integrity or political independence of another State, or in any other manner inconsistent with the Charter of the United Nations [...] in accordance with United Nations General Assembly Resolution 3314 (XXIX) of 14 December 1974.

Point 3 of the Elements of Crimes underscores the necessity of inter-State armed force for individual responsibility to subsist.[285]

A list of acts follows under ICC Statute Article 8bis(2), which is identical to Article 3 of Resolution 3314 (XXIX). However, unlike Article 5(2) of Resolution 3314 (XXIX), which criminalises 'aggressive war', ICC Statute Article 8bis criminalises more broadly an 'act of aggression'.[286] Furthermore, Article 8bis(1) establishes the restrictive condition of the 'manifest' nature of aggression as a violation of the UN Charter.

281 Bonafè, *The Relationship* (2009) 111–112.

282 Dupuy, 'International Criminal Responsibility' (2002) 1088; Ronald C Kramer, 'State-Organized Crime, International Law and Structural Contradictions' (2016) 24(2) *Crit Crim* 231–245, 236. See also s 1.2.2.2 and Saldaña, 'La justice' (1925) 308–312.

283 IIL, Declaration on the Use of Force, Bruges, 2 September 2003, 1.

284 Security Council, Iraq-Kuwait, UN Doc SC/RES/660, 2 August 1990, para 1.

285 Elements of Crimes (2010), art 8 bis (Crime of aggression) elements, 3. See also Astrid Reisinger Coracini and Pål Wrange, 'The Specificity of the Crime of Aggression', in Kreß and Barriaga, *The Crime* (2017) 312–313.

286 Wolf, 'Individual Responsibility' (2016) 26.

The Special Working Group on the Crime of Aggression, which was established to submit to the Assembly of the State Parties to the ICC an 'acceptable provision on the crime of aggression for inclusion in the Statute', finally achieved this result after much work.[287] Since the beginning of preparatory work for the ICC Statute, the definition of aggression seemed problematic, notably because of the link between individual and State responsibility and the role of the UN Security Council.[288] However, fifty years after the Nuremberg process it was considered unrealistic to exclude individual criminal responsibility for such conduct from the Statute of the ICC.[289] Although different proposals were formulated during preparatory work for the ICC Statute in order to define the crime of aggression, none were accepted.[290] This ultimately led to relying upon the definition outlined in Resolution 3314 (XXIX).[291]

Whilst no international treaty harmonises the crime of aggression domestically, national tribunals have adjudicated upon the crime of aggression. This was the case, for instance, of the US Military Tribunal in Nuremberg in *Krupp*.[292]

2.3.1.1 State conduct as a basis for individual conduct (and vice versa)

ICC Statute Article 8bis is based on the stance adopted by the ILC in the 1996 DCCPSM, qualifying participation in State aggression as an individual act of aggression: '[a]n individual who, as leader or organizer, actively participates in or orders the planning, preparation, initiation or waging of aggression committed by a State shall be responsible for a crime of aggression.'[293]

By criminalising 'aggression', ICC Statute Article 8bis is not only broader than Resolution 3314 (XXIX), which criminalises 'aggressive war', but is also broader than the Charters of the IMTs of Nuremberg and Tokyo, which defined the planning, preparation, initiation or waging of a 'war of aggression' as a 'crime against peace' respectively under Articles 6(a) and 5(a).[294] Article 8bis of

287 ICC Assembly of States Parties, Report on the First Session, UN Doc ICC-ASP/1/3 (2002) ICC-ASP/1/Res.1, 328.

288 Matthias Schuster, 'The Rome Statute and the Crime of Aggression: A Gordian Knot in Search of a Sword' (2003) 14(1) *Crim LF* 19 ff.

289 ILC, Report (1994) 38, para 1; *Ad Hoc* Committee, Report, A/50/22 (1995) 13, para 63; PCEICC, Report, A/51/22 (1996) 18, para 66; Kreß, 'On the Activation' (2018) 5.

290 PCEICC, Report, A/51/22/A (1996) 58–59; PCEICC, Draft Statute (1998) 12–14.

291 Gerhard Kemp, *Individual Criminal Liability for the International Crime of Aggression* (CUP, 2nd edn, 2017) 144 ff.

292 *US v Alfried Felix Alwyn Krupp von Bohlen und Halbach* et al, US Military Tribunal, Nuremberg, Case n° 10, Judgment of 30 June 1948 ('Krupp') (1949) 10 *LRTWC* 69–158.

293 ILC, Report (1996) 42–43. See also Mauro Politi, 'The Debate within the Preparatory Commission of the International Criminal Court', in Mauro Politi and Giuseppe Nesi (eds), *The International Criminal Court and the Crime of Aggression* (Ashgate, 2004) 46–48.

294 Andreas Zimmermann and Elisa Freiburg, 'Article 8bis: Crime of Aggression', in Triffterer and Ambos, *Commentary* (2016) 586–587; Carrie McDougall, 'The Crimes against Peace Precedent', in Kreß and Barriaga, *The Crime* (2017) 105.

the ICC Statute thus also covers sporadic acts of aggression, not sustained by the continuity of a war. Some scholars, however, propose a contextual interpretation, whereby 'acts of aggression' under ICC Statute Article 8bis should be confined to 'aggressive war', in line with Resolution 3314 (XXIX).[295]

In any case, the material element of aggression under the ICC Statute necessarily involves the use of armed force by a State against another State, in accordance with Article 3 of Resolution 3314 (XXIX).[296] This approach is consistent with uniform case law and scholarly opinions on aggression.[297] This stance is also in line with the views expressed by the ICJ in *Military and Paramilitary Activities in and against Nicaragua*, where the Court clarified that the concept of use of 'force' by States refers to 'armed force'.[298] It is also considered that 'armed force' includes cyber operations and some scholars propose to make this element explicit in the definition of aggression.[299]

Whether Article 8bis of the ICC Statute also criminalises threatened use of force depends on the interpretation of the words 'planning', 'preparation' and 'initiation' under ICC Statute Article 8bis. Working on the DCCPSM, the ILC clarified that the use of force must be serious enough to trigger both the aggravated responsibility of a State and the criminal responsibility of natural persons.[300] Furthermore, it is unclear what the reference to the 'manifest' nature of aggression as a violation of the UN Charter entails.[301] The purpose of the requirement is outlining a quantitative and qualitative threshold for liability, based on the gravity, scale and nature of individual conduct,[302] which matches the seriousness of State responsibility under 2001 DASR 40. A case-by-case assessment is therefore required.

From the standpoint of the perpetrator, individual aggression necessarily entails State aggression.[303] Indeed, individual aggression is the act of a State organ

295 Elizabeth Wilmshurst, 'Definition of the Crime of Aggression: State Responsibility or Individual Criminal Responsibility?', in Politi and Nesi, *The International Criminal Court* (Ashgate, 2004) 94–96.

296 Prior to the adoption of Resolution 3314 (XXIX) in 1974, the ILC's DCOPSM adopted in 1954 took a broader stance on the issue, criminalising 'any act of aggression', including 'coercive measures of an economic or political character' (art 2(2) and (9)): ILC, Report (1954) 151.

297 *Von Ribbentrop*, Judgment of 1st October 1946 (1947) 1 *Trial of War Criminals before the International Military Tribunal, Nuremberg* 285–286; *Dönitz*, Judgment of 1st October 1946, ibid, 310–311. See also ILC, Report (1996) 43; *Legal Consequences* [2004] 194, para 139. For a scholarly opinion, see Nollkaemper, 'Systemic Effects' (2010) 318; Zimmermann and Freiburg, 'Article 8bis' (2016) 592.

298 *Military and Paramilitary Activities* [1986] 103–104, para 195, 118, para 228. See also Claus Kreß, 'The State Conduct Element', in Kreß and Barriaga, *The Crime* (2017) 424–425.

299 Schmitt, *Tallin Manual* (2017) 329–339, rules 68–70; David Scheffer, 'Amending the Crime of Aggression under the Rome Statute', in Kreß and Barriaga, *The Crime* (2017) 1488.

300 ILC, Report (1996) 43, para 5.

301 Andreas Paulus, 'Second Thoughts on the Crime of Aggression' (2012) 20(4) *EJIL* 1122–1124.

302 Kreß, 'The State' (2017) 425 and 508–509; Id, 'On the Activation' (2018) 6.

303 Dupuy, 'International Criminal Responsibility' (2002) 1088; Roger Clark, 'The Crime of Aggression', in Stahn, *The Law and Practice* (2015) 781. But see Cassese, *International Criminal*

or agent exercising effective control or directing the political or military action of a State: aggression is a 'leadership' crime.[304] This is recalled in Article 25(3bis) of the ICC Statute, governing complicity in aggression:

> In respect of the crime of aggression, the provisions of this article [individual criminal responsibility] shall apply only to persons in a position effectively to exercise control over or to direct the political or military action of a State.

An organic relationship is therefore required for the individual crime to subsist.[305] Although some scholars do not exclude the possibility of a private individual committing aggression,[306] it is preferable to assume that a natural person needs to act as a State organ or agent.[307]

In *Farben*, a US military Tribunal in Nuremberg held that only 'major war criminals' may be liable for aggressive war, because a different approach would entail general guilt, including 'the private soldier on the battlefield' and 'the entire manpower of Germany'.[308] This approach complements that of the IMTs of Nuremberg and Tokyo, which only tried 'high public officials' and 'high military officers' for waging aggressive war. Therefore, lower-ranking officers should not be held responsible for the crime of aggression, although a case-by-case assessment is required. This approach is also interpreted as a defence granted to subordinates receiving superior orders to commit aggression.[309]

It is thus necessary to assume that aggression entails two aspects: individual and State responsibility.[310] There can be no individual responsibility without State responsibility: only if a State is responsible for aggression can an individual acting as a State organ or agent be held liable for aggression. In this respect, scholars speak of 'dual' responsibility generated by 'the same conduct'.[311]

Law (2013) 140, arguing that entities other than States, such as terrorist groups, with particular regard to 9/11, can commit aggression.

304 Clark, 'The Crime' (2015) 782.

305 Sergey Sayapin, *The Crime of Aggression in International Criminal Law: Historical Development, Comparative Analysis and Present State* (Asser Press, 2014) 261.

306 Luigi Condorelli, 'Conclusions générales', in Politi and Nesi, *The International Criminal Court* (2004) 156–157.

307 Mohammed Gomaa, 'The Definition of the Crime of Aggression and the ICC Jurisdiction over That Crime', in Politi and Nesi, *The International Criminal Court* (2004) 64 ff.

308 *US v Krauch*, US Military Tribunal, Nuremberg, Case n° 6, 30 July 1948 ('Farben') (1949) 10 *LRTWC* 38.

309 Bonafè, *The Relationship* (2009) 140.

310 For a detailed analysis of individual and State responsibility with respect to aggression, see PCEICC, Working Group on the Crime of Aggression, Historical Review of Developments Relating to Aggression, Doc PCNICC/2002/WGCA/L.1 (2002) and related Add.1 for comparative tables.

311 Dupuy, 'International Criminal Responsibility' (2002) 1089; Bonafè, *The Relationship* (2009) 27 and 114.

The ILC further held that there is no individual criminal responsibility for aggression, but only for 'aggression committed by a State'.[312] Individual aggression thus necessarily requires a systemic context.[313] Procedurally, this means that the ICC cannot prosecute an individual for the crime of aggression without a prior determination of State aggression.[314] This has led to proposing that the jurisdiction of the ICC be subject to a prior assessment on aggression by the Security Council or the ICJ.[315] In this respect, however, it should also be noted that there can be no State responsibility without action by its individual organs or agents, which generates circular reasoning.[316]

With regard to victims, the offence is so structured that the planning, preparation, initiation or execution of an act of aggression directly breaches a legal relationship vis-à-vis a State as the victim of the crime.[317] In other words, aggression necessarily establishes a relationship between the aggressor and a collective victim.[318] Such a structure is atypical, because other international crimes breach the rights of individual victims first and further offend the international community as such, thus attracting criminal prosecution. Whilst the aggressed State is the direct victim of the crime of aggression, individual and State aggression indirectly affects all the State and non-State subjects of the international community. This approach fits with the *erga omnes* and peremptory status of the prohibition of aggression.[319]

2.3.1.2 Leadership and mens rea

The required *mens rea* for an individual committing the crime of aggression is intent, necessitating knowledge and intention.[320] Indeed, ICC Statute Article 8bis and the Elements of Crimes do not set negligence as a standard of attribution for the crime of aggression.[321] However, some scholars envisage at least the possibility of *dolus eventualis*.[322] The aggressive context, that is, the material element consisting of the use of armed force, is likely to prove decisive

312 ILC Report (1996) 43, para 4.
313 Nollkaemper, 'Systemic Effects' (2010) 317–318.
314 ICC Assembly of States Parties, Report on the Second Session, UN Doc ICC-ASP/2/10 (2003) 234. See also Politi, 'The Debate' (2004) 48–51.
315 Philippa Webb, *International Judicial Integration and Fragmentation* (OUP, 2013) 131–133. Critically, see Carrie McDougall, *The Crime of Aggression under the Rome Statute of the International Criminal Court* (CUP, 2013) 208 ff.
316 ILC, Report (1996) 43, para 4; Gattini, ''A Historical Perspective' (2009) 123.
317 Reisinger Coracini and Wrange, 'The Specificity' (2017) 317–318.
318 Erin Pobjie, 'Victims of the Crime of Aggression', in Kreß and Barriaga, *The Crime* (2017) 821.
319 See s 2.1.1.5.
320 Kreß, 'The State' (2017) 425–426.
321 Werle and Jeßberger, *Principles* (2014) 544; Knoops, Mens Rea (2017) 155 and 157; Roger Clark, 'Individual Conduct', in Kreß and Barriaga, *The Crime* (2017) 586–587.
322 Glaser, 'Culpabilité' (1960) 490; Antonio Cassese, *International Criminal Law* (OUP, 2003) 115.

in establishing whether knowledge subsists.[323] In their judgments, the IMT and IMTFE required knowledge of aggression or participation in aggression. Thus, the IMT acquitted Borman, a high-ranking officer of the Third *Reich*, on the count of aggression for lack of evidence on his knowledge of Hitler's aggressive plans.[324] By contrast, the Tribunal convicted Von Neurath for having knowledge of the same plans.[325]

In order to establish State responsibility for aggression, it is either considered that no fault is required or intent is necessary.[326] This depends on whether the doctrine of objective liability applies, or rather that of fault. Given that the aggravated regime of State responsibility under 2001 DASR 40 requires for the 'seriousness' of the violation to subsist 'intent to violate the norm', which should apply to the State per se, the fault doctrine is preferable.[327] Alternatively, it ought to be assumed that the intent of the State leaders is indispensable to proving the objective gross and systematic character of the breach, which would be attributed to the State without fault.

Assuming State fault, since aggression is a 'leadership' crime, it has been argued that the *mens rea* of individual leaders can be easily identified with that of the State, according to the '*alter ego*' doctrine. Thus, there would be 'identity' between individual and State responsibility not only from the material standpoint, but also from the viewpoint of imputation.[328] This is true if it is presumed that the *mens rea* of a State organ or agent is that of the State. Otherwise, it is necessary to ascertain whether the people of the aggressor State aggregately knew, or could have known, the intent of their leaders so as to possibly prevent aggression.

Whilst it is usually assumed that specific intent (*dolus specialis*) is not a requisite for aggression,[329] according to a particular interpretation, the specific intent of occupying or annexing foreign territory is required.[330] If this approach applies to individuals and intent is also required at the State level, scholars assume that specific intent should also be proved at the State level.[331] This further strengthens the link between individual and State responsibility for aggression. Alternatively, it is assumed that specific intent should only be demonstrated at the individual level, thus splitting individual and collective *mens rea*,[332] which fits

323 Bonafè, *The Relationship* (2009) 141; Knoops, Mens Rea (2017) 162.
324 *Bormann*, Judgment of 1st October 1946 (1947) 1 *Trial of War Criminals* 339.
325 *Von Neurath*, Judgment of 1st October 1946, ibid, 334–336.
326 Bonafè, *The Relationship* (2009) 141.
327 ILC, Report (2001) 113, para 8. See also s 2.2.2.3.
328 Bonafè, *The Relationship* (2009) 142–143; Knoops, Mens Rea (2017) 156–157.
329 Werle and Jeßberger, *Principles* (2014) 545.
330 PCEICC, Proceedings of the Preparatory Commission at Its Seventh Session, Doc PCNICC/2001/L.1/Rev.1 (2001) 17, variation 2. See also Glaser, 'Culpabilité' (1960) 504–505; Cassese, *International Criminal Law* (2013) 142; Jeßberger, 'The Modern Doctrinal Debate' (2017) 298.
331 Bonafè, *The Relationship* (2009) 142.
332 Cassese, *International Criminal Law* (2013) 142.

with the theory of State objective liability. In contrast, by applying the doctrine of State fault, requiring proof of specific intent solely at the individual level is only possible by assuming that the intent of a State leader does not necessarily coincide with that of its people, splitting State and individual responsibility.

2.3.1.3 Self-defence as a dual excuse

Although absolutely prohibited under primary international law rules, the use of force is exceptionally permitted under secondary international law norms. The main justification is self-defence: under general international law, in the case of an armed attack by a State (A), the attacked State (B) can lawfully react. This has been a well-established principle under customary international law since the *Caroline* case and is embedded in UN Charter Article 51.[333] In this respect, the ICJ has clarified that customary and conventional international law are complementary.[334]

Article 21 of the 2001 DASR explicitly provides that self-defence is a circumstance precluding wrongfulness, thus excluding State responsibility. Since all countermeasures are subject to the principles set out in DASR 49–52, self-defence must fulfil the requisites of necessity and proportionality. 'Necessity' implies that no conduct other than the use of force (last resort) is a viable response to an unlawful armed attack. 'Proportionality' constrains the intensity of armed force in self-defence, which must be commensurate with that of the attack.[335] The *erga omnes* and peremptory nature of the prohibition of aggression further entails the possibility of collective self-defence, which was clearly upheld under customary international law by the ICJ in *Nicaragua* and is codified in UN Charter Article 51.[336]

Since a State act of aggression is necessary for individual responsibility to subsist, self-defence provides a justification for both States and individuals. Given that it is the only clear case of a justification that applies at the same time to State aggravated responsibility and individual criminal responsibility, self-defence confirms the unitary nature of aggression at the individual and State level.[337]

2.3.2 Core war crimes

Unlike the crime of aggression, international law defines war crimes at the individual level as serious violations of customary or conventional international humanitarian law. The Statute of the ICC provides:

333 *Caroline (Great Britain v US)* (1841–42) 30 *BFSP* 193–202.
334 *Military and Paramilitary Activities* [1986] 94, para 176.
335 *Oil Platforms (Iran v US)* [2003] ICJ Rep 198–199, paras 76–78.
336 *Military and Paramilitary Activities* [1986] 27, para 34, 102, para 193, 103–104, para 195, 105, para 199.
337 Bonafè, *The Relationship* (2009) 156 and 165.

Article 8 – War crimes

1. The Court shall have jurisdiction in respect of war crimes in particular when committed as part of a plan or policy or as part of a large-scale commission of such crimes.
2. For the purpose of this Statute, 'war crimes' means:
   (a) Grave breaches of the Geneva Conventions of 12 August 1949, namely, any of the following acts against persons or property protected under the provisions of the relevant Geneva Convention:
      (i) Wilful killing;
      (ii) Torture or inhuman treatment, including biological experiments;
      (iii) Wilfully causing great suffering, or serious injury to body or health;
      (iv) Extensive destruction and appropriation of property, not justified by military necessity and carried out unlawfully and wantonly;
      (v) Compelling a prisoner of war or other protected person to serve in the forces of a hostile Power;
      (vi) Wilfully depriving a prisoner of war or other protected person of the rights of fair and regular trial;
      (vii) Unlawful deportation or transfer or unlawful confinement;
      (viii) Taking of hostages.
   (b) Other serious violations of the laws and customs applicable in international armed conflict, within the established framework of international law, namely, any of the following acts:
      (i) Intentionally directing attacks against the civilian population as such or against individual civilians not taking direct part in hostilities;
      (ii) Intentionally directing attacks against civilian objects, that is, objects which are not military objectives

      [...]
   (c) In the case of an armed conflict not of an international character, serious violations of article 3 common to the four Geneva Conventions of 12 August 1949, namely, any of the following acts committed against persons taking no active part in the hostilities, including members of armed forces who have laid down their arms and those placed *hors de combat* by sickness, wounds, detention or any other cause:
      (i) Violence to life and person, in particular murder of all kinds, mutilation, cruel treatment and torture;
      (ii) Committing outrages upon personal dignity, in particular humiliating and degrading treatment;
      (iii) Taking of hostages;
      (iv) The passing of sentences and the carrying out of executions without previous judgement pronounced by a regularly constituted court, affording all judicial guarantees which are generally recognized as indispensable.

      [...]

(e) Other serious violations of the laws and customs applicable in armed conflicts not of an international character, within the established framework of international law, namely, any of the following acts:
   (i) Intentionally directing attacks against the civilian population as such or against individual civilians not taking direct part in hostilities;
   (ii) Intentionally directing attacks against buildings, material, medical units and transport, and personnel using the distinctive emblems of the Geneva Conventions in conformity with international law …

Such a detailed rule criminalises breaches of the 1949 Geneva Conventions on international humanitarian law and violations of customary law of war in international and non-international armed conflicts. Unlike aggression, which violates *jus ad bellum*, war crimes are breaches of human rights in time of war, that is, *jus in bello*, whereby a nexus must exist between the crime and an armed conflict.[338]

More specifically, ICC Statute Article 8(2)(a) is based on grave breaches of the Geneva Conventions and ICC Statute Article 8(2)(b) criminalises other serious violations of the rules governing international armed conflicts. Concerning non-international armed conflicts, ICC Statute Article 8(2)(c) criminalises serious violations of Article 3 common to the Geneva Conventions committed against 'persons taking no active part in the hostilities'. This rule is complemented by ICC Statute Article 8(2)(e), which further criminalises serious violations of rules governing hostilities in non-international armed conflicts, when there is a 'protracted armed conflict between governmental authorities and organized armed groups or between such groups' (ICC Statute Article 8(2)(f)). Offences under ICC Statute Article 8(2)(e) partly replicate those under Article 8(2)(b). Therefore, the ICC Statute relies expressly upon the regulation of non-international armed conflicts as interpreted by international courts.[339] Nonetheless, important restrictions on means and methods of warfare, for instance, the use of prohibited weapons, starvation of civilians and other war crimes embedded in ICC Statute Article 8(2)(b), are missing in Article 8(2)(e).[340]

By contrast, there is no definition of 'war crimes' at the State level in international law. Overlap between individual and State responsibility may exist particularly when war crimes are part of a plan or policy or of a large-scale commission,[341] since centralised State organs often define such a plan or policy.[342]

338 *Haradinaj* (2012) 146, para 397. See also Mary Ellen O'Connell, 'Historical Development and Legal Basis: Definition of the Term "Humanitarian Law"', in Dieter Fleck (ed), *The Handbook of International Humanitarian Law* (OUP, 3rd edn, 2013) 1.

339 *Harun and Abd-Al-Rahman*, ICC-02/05-01/07, Decision on the Prosecution Application under Article 58(7) of the Statute, 27 April 2007, 10 ff, paras 31 ff; *Al Bashir*, ICC-02/05-01/09, Decision on the Prosecution's Application for a Warrant of Arrest, 4 March 2009 20, paras 58 ff. See also s 1.2.2.2.

340 De Beco, 'War Crimes' (2008) 324.

341 Kelsen, *Peace* (1973) 115; Simpson, 'Men and Abstract Entities' (2009) 90; Gattini, 'A Historical Perspective' (2009) 126.

342 Elies van Sliedregt, *The Criminal Responsibility of Individuals for Violations of International Humanitarian Law* (TMC Asser Press, 2003) 4–5; Nollkaemper, 'Systemic Effects' (2010) 317.

However, under ICC Statute Article 8(1) this is not a necessary component of the crime, but rather an additional requirement specifically grounding the jurisdiction of the ICC.[343] This approach follows the jurisprudence of the ICTY, which confirms that individual responsibility for war crimes does not necessarily require a plan or policy.[344]

2.3.2.1 Individual conduct as a basis for collective responsibility

Since there is no independent definition of war crimes at the State level, State responsibility is triggered by the same conduct as that of individuals.[345] Thus, for instance, Article 91 of Protocol I Additional to the Geneva Conventions provides that a State 'shall be responsible for all acts committed by persons forming part of its armed forces'. Therefore, overlap between individual and State responsibility is limited to conduct of State organs or agents. In this context, unlike aggression, no distinction is drawn between superior and inferior organs and agents of the State. By contrast, war crimes committed by private individuals, for instance, members of armed opposition groups, do not engage State responsibility, to the extent that they are not controlled by the State according to 2001 DASR 8. Thus, moving from *jus ad bellum* to *jus in bello* involves a critical difference, since war crimes do not automatically entail State responsibility.[346] At the same time, there can be no individual responsibility for war crimes without State responsibility for waging aggressive war.[347] This has raised issues of consistency between the ICJ and international criminal tribunals concerning the qualification of an armed conflict as an international rather than non-international one.[348]

The common core of a few provisions of the Geneva Conventions outline grave breaches of international humanitarian law as:[349]

> [T]hose involving any of the following acts, if committed against persons or property protected by the Convention: wilful killing, torture or inhuman treatment, including biological experiments, wilfully causing great suffering or serious injury to body or health, and extensive destruction and appropriation of property, not justified by military necessity and carried out unlawfully and wantonly.

343 Knoops, Mens Rea (2017) 74.
344 *Tadić* (1997) 198, para 573.
345 Roger O'Keefe, *International Criminal Law* (OUP, 2015) 135.
346 Dupuy, 'International Criminal Responsibility' (2002) 1091.
347 *Lubanga Dyilo* (2012) 231, para 504; *Tolimir* (2012) 308, para 682. See also Condorelli and Kreß, 'The Rules' (2010) 234; Tom Dannenbaum, 'Why Have We Criminalized Aggressive War?' (2016–17) 126(5) *Yale LJ* 1274.
348 Webb, *International Judicial Integration* (2013) 134 ff.
349 Article 50 of 1949 Geneva Convention I, art 51 of Geneva Convention II, art 130 of Geneva Convention III, art 147 of Geneva Convention IV and art 85 of Additional Protocol I.

At least some of these offences, notably torture, are in breach of *erga omnes* and peremptory obligations.[350] In light of their peremptory nature, at least some serious breaches of international humanitarian law should trigger an aggravated regime of State responsibility under 2001 DASR 40. In such a case, besides the persons directly injured by the violation, all State and non-State entities of the international community are indirectly affected by the breach. By contrast, it is worth noting that 1996 DASR 19 did not refer to war crimes as a cause of State criminal responsibility.

In *Furundžija*, the ICTY recognised the *erga omnes* and imperative nature of the prohibition of torture as part of Article 3 common to the Geneva Conventions, with respect to both natural persons and the State:[351]

> Under current international humanitarian law, in addition to individual criminal liability, State responsibility may ensue as a result of State officials engaging in torture or failing to prevent torture or to punish torturers. If carried out as an extensive practice of State officials, torture amounts to a serious breach on a widespread scale of an international obligation of essential importance for safeguarding the human being, thus constituting a particularly grave wrongful act generating State responsibility.[352]

A gross or systematic failure to comply is not a necessary requisite for the commission of war crimes by natural persons. However, breaches that are not gross or systematic will not easily satisfy the gravity threshold required for prosecution under ICC Statue Article 17(1)(d).[353] Such offences will also not fulfil the threshold of seriousness necessary to trigger State aggravated responsibility under 2001 DASR 40(2), requiring a relevant number of victims or organised breaches.[354] In practice, the fact that war crimes are often committed by the military facilitates systemic perpetration.[355] Examples of systemic war crimes include atrocities committed during World War II in the 1940s, the Balkan Wars in the 1990s, the conflict in the Darfur area of Sudan and the practice of torture by the US after 9/11.[356] Currently, Omar Al Bashir is on indictment before the ICC, inter alia, on counts of systematic war crimes for intentionally directing attacks against a civilian population as such or against individual civilians not taking part in hostilities (ICC Statute Article 8(2)(e)(i)), as well as pillaging (ICC Statute Article 8(2)(e)(v)).[357]

350 *Kupreskić* (2000) 203, para 520. See also s 2.1.2.2.
351 *Furundžija* (1998) 54, para 140. See also s 1.2.3.3.
352 *Furundžija* (1998) 54, para 142.
353 Knoops, Mens Rea (2017) 74–75 and 77.
354 ILC, Report (2001) 113, para 8. See also s 2.1.1.1.
355 Sreenivasa Rao, 'International Crimes' (2005) 77; Bonafè, *The Relationship* (2009) 92; Nollkaemper, 'Systemic Effects' (2010) 317; Wolf, 'Individual Responsibility' (2016) 51.
356 International Commission of Inquiry on Darfur, Report to the UN Secretary-General Pursuant to Security Council Resolution 1564 of 18 September 2004 (2005) 5; *Al Bashir* (2009) 25, para 72; Nollkaemper, 'Systemic Effects' (2010) 316–317.
357 *Al Bashir* (2009) 27, para 77.

2.3.2.2 *Systemically proving individual* mens rea

Consistently with the nature of core war crimes, intent is generally required for imputation, according to ICC Statute Article 30.[358] However, specific elements, such as the status of a 'civilian' under ICC Statute Article 8(2)(b)(i), can be attributed based on negligence.[359] Furthermore, specific offences, such as conscripting or enlisting children under the age of 15 years (ICC Statute Article 8(2)(e)(vii)), are also attributable based on mere negligence. In fact, the Elements of Crimes provide that imputation may take place if '[t]he perpetrator knew or should have known that such person or persons were under the age of 15 years.'[360] Moreover, with respect to the 'plan or policy' or 'large-scale commission' of war crimes knowledge may simply subsist in terms of recklessness (*dolus eventualis*), which is close to advertent negligence, based on mere possibility.[361] Concerning the existence of a war context and the link between offensive conduct and war, in *Boškoski* the ICTY demanded 'knowledge' or 'a reason to know', based on the minimum threshold of negligence.[362]

At the State level, since 2001 DASR 40 requires intent for the purpose of the existence of 'gross' and 'systematic' State conduct, it should be assumed that the determination of individual intent is key to attributing aggravated responsibility for war crimes to the State, following the '*alter ego*' doctrine. The theory of 'aggregate' responsibility, by contrast, fits with the establishment of individual intent based on the systemic context of the offence adopted by the ICTY in *Galić* and with the reckless or negligent knowledge of the systematic aspects of the offence.[363]

2.3.3 *Core crimes against humanity*

Crimes against humanity are outlined at the individual level in international law. The Statute of the ICC provides a definition based on the following elements:

> Article 7 – Crimes against humanity
> 1. For the purpose of this Statute, 'crime against humanity' means any of the following acts when committed as part of a widespread or systematic attack directed against any civilian population, with knowledge of the attack:
>   (a) Murder;
>   (b) Extermination;
>   (c) Enslavement;

358 Knoops, Mens Rea (2017) 79–80, 83 and 85.

359 *Strugar*, IT-01-42-A, Appeals Chamber, Judgment of 17 July 2008, 101, para 271. See also Knoops, Mens Rea (2017) 91.

360 *Lubanga Dyilo* (2007) 124, para 365.

361 *Blaskić* (2000) 83, para 251; *Id* (2004) 16, para 41.

362 *Boškoski and Tarčulovski*, IT-04-82-T, Trial Chamber, Judgment of 10 July 2008, 134, para 295.

363 See s 2.3.5.2.

(d) Deportation or forcible transfer of population;
(e) Imprisonment or other severe deprivation of physical liberty in violation of fundamental rules of international law;
(f) Torture;
(g) Rape, sexual slavery, enforced prostitution, forced pregnancy, enforced sterilization, or any other form of sexual violence of comparable gravity;
(h) Persecution against any identifiable group or collectivity on political, racial, national, ethnic, cultural, religious, gender as defined in paragraph 3, or other grounds that are universally recognized as impermissible under international law, in connection with any act referred to in this paragraph or any crime within the jurisdiction of the Court;
(i) Enforced disappearance of persons;
(j) The crime of apartheid;
(k) Other inhumane acts of a similar character intentionally causing great suffering, or serious injury to body or to mental or physical health.

2. For the purpose of paragraph 1:
(a) 'Attack directed against any civilian population' means a course of conduct involving the multiple commission of acts referred to in paragraph 1 against any civilian population, *pursuant to or in furtherance of a State or organizational policy to commit such attack* ...[364]

This provision codifies customary international law, save a few components. In certain respects, the ICC Statute is narrower. For instance, under customary international law crimes against humanity committed with persecutory intent may also target military personnel.[365] Most importantly, ICC Statute Article 7(2)(a) narrows customary law by requiring that criminal conduct be 'pursuant to or in furtherance of a State or organizational policy'. On the other hand, the ICC Statute is broader than customary law to the extent that it includes conduct such as 'enforced disappearance of persons' (Article 7(1)(i)) or extends persecutory motives to 'cultural', 'gender' and 'other grounds' (Article 7(1)(h)).

Instruments defining State responsibility for human rights breaches refer to international regulation in the field concerning individuals. Specifically, 1996 DASR 19(3)(c) referred to State criminal responsibility for 'a serious breach on a widespread scale of an international obligation of essential importance for safeguarding the human being, such as those prohibiting slavery, genocide and apartheid'.[366]

364 Emphasis added.
365 *Barbie*, French Court of Cassation, Judgment of 20 December 1985 (1988) 78 *ILR* 140.
366 See ss 1.2.2.3 and 1.2.3.5.

2.3.3.1 Systemic conduct

Crimes against humanity are acts in violation of fundamental rights that cause great suffering or serious physical or mental injury.[367] Unlike war crimes, however, such acts must be part of a widespread or systematic attack.[368] In this respect, according to customary international law the widespread or systematic character of the breach is alternative.[369]

A widespread breach entails a large-scale offence, usually in accordance with a common policy.[370] This policy, which is a compulsory requirement under ICC Statute Article 8(2)(a), but not under customary law,[371] can be a State or non-State one.[372] The widespread character of the violation should also include a single act or omission affecting a plurality of victims, although this is not uncontroversial.[373] For instance, the Trial Chamber of the ICTY held Erdemović guilty for 'killing between 10 and 100 people' within 5 hours on 16 July 1995.[374] This matches the 'gross' nature of a State violation under 2001 DASR 40.

The systematic character of the breach includes a plurality of unlawful acts or omissions carried out methodically as a pattern, normally under a policy or plan.[375] The systematic context allows the qualification of a single act as a crime against humanity,[376] provided a link is established between the act and the context.[377] This facilitates establishing a connection between individual and State responsibility, when State organs or agents commit crimes against humanity.[378]

367 *Erdemović*, IT-96-22, Trial Chamber, Judgment of 29 November 1996, para 28; *Kambanda*, ICTR-97-23, Trial Chamber, Judgment of 4 September 1998, para 15; *Situation in the Republic of Kenya*, ICC-01/09, Pre-Trial Chamber, Decision Pursuant to Article 15 of the Rome Statute on the Authorization of an Investigation, 31 March 2010, 31, para 72.

368 *Lukić*, IT-98-32/1-T, Trial Chamber, Judgment of 20 July 2009, 274, para 872.

369 *Akayesu* (1998) para 579; *Blaskić* (2000) 70, para 207; *Lukić* (2009) 274, para 875; *Situation in the Republic of Kenya* (2010) 40–41, para 94; *Tolimir* (2012) 314, para 698. See also PCEICC, Report, A/51/22 (1996) 22, para 85.

370 *Katanga and Ngudjolo Chui*, ICC-01/04-01/07, Pre-Trial Chamber, Decision on the Confirmation of Charges, 30 September 2008, 126, para 396; *Bagosora and Nsengiyumva*, ICTR-98-41-A, Appeals Chamber, Judgment of 14 December 2011, 133, para 389; *Tolimir* (2012) 314, para 698. See also Dupuy, 'International Criminal Responsibility' (2002) 1089.

371 O'Keefe, *International Criminal Law* (2015) 144.

372 *Situation in the Republic of Kenya* (2010) 37–38, paras 89–90. See also Knoops, Mens Rea (2017) 117–118.

373 *Tadić* (1997) 236, para 649; *Akayesu* (1998) para 580; *Kupreskić* (2000) 216, para 543.

374 *Erdemović* (1996) para 85.

375 *Blaskić* (2000) 67, para 203; *Katanga and Ngudjolo Chui* (2008) 127, para 397; *Al Bashir* (2009) 29 ff, paras 80 ff; *Bagosora and Nsengiyumva* (2011) 133–134, para 389; *Blé Goudé*, ICC-02/11-02/11, Pre-Trial Chamber, Decision on the Confirmation of Charges, 11 December 2014, 62-63, para 132; *Katanga* (2014) 420, para 1111. In *Tolimir* (2012) 314, para 698, the ICTY did not consider the existence of a policy an essential requirement to establish the systematic nature of crimes against humanity.

376 *Kunarac*, IT-96-23 & 23/1, Trial Chamber, Judgment of 22 February 2001, 144, para 431.

377 *Id*, IT-96-23 & 23/1-A, Appeals Chamber, Judgment of 12 June 2002, 29, para 96.

378 Simpson, 'Men and Abstract Entities' (2009) 90; Gattini, 'A Historical Perspective' (2009) 106; Wolf, 'Individual Responsibility' (2016) 20.

Indeed, in practice the systematic nature of the violation particularly attracts a centralised policy, which is only a compulsory requirement under ICC Statute Article 8(2)(a), not under customary law.[379] The State can afford such a policy.[380]

The widespread or systematic nature of crimes against humanity facilitates inferring the seriousness of the offence required to establish State aggravated responsibility under 2001 DASR 40.[381] In fact, the ICTY considered that a State 'can most easily and efficiently marshal the resources to launch an attack against a civilian population on a "widespread" scale, or upon a "systematic" basis'.[382] In this regard, some scholars have elaborated the notion of 'system criminality'.[383] Others refer to 'State-enabled crimes', for instance, with respect to acts of torture that reportedly have been systemically committed upon instruction across State-run detention centres throughout Syria and in Abu-Ghraib.[384] However, the ICTY did not exclude the possibility that a non-State policy underpins crimes against humanity or that such offences are committed without a policy or plan.[385]

The primary victims of crimes against humanity are the persons directly injured. Nonetheless, in light of the seriousness of such violations, it is possible to envisage the *erga omnes* nature of crimes against humanity and possibly their peremptory prohibition.[386] This is certainly the case of the prohibition of torture, which is *erga omnes* and peremptory for both the individual and the State, in light of the jurisprudence developed by the ICTY in *Furundžija*.[387] CAT Article 1 defines 'torture' as the unlawful infliction of severe mental or physical pain or suffering for the purposes of obtaining information, punishment, intimidation or coercion. Torture must be committed by a public official or a person acting in an official capacity, or, at least, under his instigation or with his consent or acquiescence. Therefore, torture as a crime by nature entails a specific relationship between individual and State responsibility. The ILC's commentary to the 2001 DASR also confirms the peremptory nature of the prohibition of

379 O'Keefe, *International Criminal Law* (2015) 144.

380 *Kayshema and Ruzindana* (1999) 43, para 94; *Kupreskić* (2000) 21–20, para 551; *Situation in the Republic of Kenya* (2010) 36–37, paras 86 and 89. See also Dupuy, 'International Criminal Responsibility' (2002) 1089; Sreenivasa Rao, 'International Crimes' (2005) 77; Guénaël Mettraux, 'The Definition of Crimes against Humanity and the Question of a "Policy" Element', in Leila Nadya Sadat (ed), *Forging a Convention for Crimes against Humanity* (CUP, 2011) 176; Wolf, 'Individual Responsibility' (2016) 51.

381 Costelloe, *Legal Consequences* (2017) 189.

382 *Limaj*, IT-03-66, Trial Chamber, Judgment of 30 November 2005, 69 para 191. See also *Stakić* (2003) 111, para 400, 170, para 601, 225, paras 822-823; *Id*, IT-97-24, Appeals Chamber, Judgment of 22 March 2006, 29, para 75, 107–108, para 330.

383 Nollkaemper, 'Systemic Effects' (2010) 316–317; Drumbl, 'Accountability' (2010) 374–375.

384 Nollkaemper, 'Systemic Effects' (2010) 318; Rebecca Hamilton, 'State-Enabled Crimes' (2016) 41(2) *Yale JIL* 302; Alshdaifat, *International Law* (2017) 91.

385 *Kunarac* (2002) 29–30, para 98; *Limaj* (2005) 69, para 191.

386 Patricia Wald, 'Genocide and Crimes against Humanity' (2007) 6(3) *Wash UGSLR* 624.

387 *Furundžija* (1998) 58, paras 151 and 153.

torture at the State level.[388] Furthermore, the ILC envisages the peremptory nature of the prohibition against slavery, slave trade, racial discrimination and apartheid,[389] which 1996 DASR 19 classified as 'State crimes'.

Crimes against humanity can be committed in time of peace or war.[390] This entails overlap between crimes against humanity and war crimes.[391] Thus, for instance, torture committed in time of war in a systematic context qualifies as both a war crime and a crime against humanity. This entails a further connection between crimes against humanity and aggression, so much so that scholars maintain that aggression should be seen not only as a violation of territorial sovereignty, but first and foremost as a breach of human rights obligations.[392]

2.3.3.2 Systemically proving individual mens rea

Mens rea for natural persons concerns the underlying offence, for instance, murder or torture, and the existence of a widespread or systematic practice.

The underlying offence usually requires intent, that is, knowledge and intention.[393] However, superiors might only be aware of the potential risk of the consequences of violations committed by subordinates in terms of recklessness (*dolus eventualis*), possibly overlapping with advertent negligence, which is sufficient for imputation.[394] Specific intent (*dolus specialis*) is only required for specific crimes against humanity, notably those having a persecutory purpose, for instance, persecution under ICC Statute Article 7(1)(g).[395]

Unlike war crimes, knowledge of the link between a specific act in breach of human rights and a widespread or systematic attack is necessary for a crime against humanity to subsist.[396] In this respect, awareness of the risk of the widespread or systematic nature of the breach is sufficient for imputation, which thus requires the minimum threshold of recklessness, possibly overlapping with advertent

388 ILC Report (2001) 113, para 5.

389 Ibid 112, para 4.

390 Convention on the Non-Applicability of Statutory Limitations to War Crimes and Crimes against Humanity, adopted 26 November 1968, 754 UNTS 73, in force 11 November 1970, art I(b). See also *Blaskić* (2000) 25, para 66; *Dordević* (2011) 631, para 1587. For a scholarly opinion, see O'Keefe, *International Criminal Law* (2015) 143; Reisinger Coracini and Wrange, 'The Specificity' (2017) 323.

391 ILC, Report to the General Assembly on the Work of the Thirty-Ninth Session, A/42/10 (1987) 16, para 4. See also Jean Graven, 'Les crimes contre l'humanité' (1950) 76(1) *RCADI* 542; Micaela Frulli, 'Are Crimes against Humanity More Serious than War Crimes?' (2001) 12(2) *EJIL* 330, note 3; Vera Gowlland-Debbas and Gloria Gaggioli, 'The Relationship between International Human Rights and Humanitarian Law: An Overview', in Robert Kolb and Gloria Gaggioli (eds), *Research Handbook on Human Rights and Humanitarian Law* (Edward Elgar, 2013) 78–79.

392 Larry May, 'Just War Theory and the Crime of Aggression', in Kreß and Barriaga, *The Crime* (2017) 289–290; Jeßberger, 'The Modern Doctrinal Debate' (2017) 300.

393 Knoops, Mens Rea (2017) 123 ff.

394 Cassese, *International Criminal Law* (2013) 189.

395 Knoops, Mens Rea (2017) 139.

396 *Blaskić* (2000) 263, para 798; *Lukić* (2009) 278, para 889; *Tolimir* (2012) 315, para 700.

negligence.[397] In fact, subordinates might only have a general perception of a systematic attack in light of the context of their conduct, without full knowledge of the details of the attack.[398] It is possible to prove such awareness based on the 'political environment' and 'common plan' in which conduct occurs.[399]

At the State level, in light of the commentary to 2001 DASR 40, which requires intent for the purpose of the existence of 'gross' and 'systematic' State conduct, determining individual intent is crucial to attributing aggravated responsibility for crimes against humanity to the State, according to the '*alter ego*' doctrine. The theory of 'aggregate' responsibility fits with the policy element underpinning crimes against humanity, which facilitates the reckless or negligent imputation of the systemic aspects of the offence to individuals.

2.3.4 *Genocide*

ICC Statute Article 6 defines the crime of genocide as follows:

> Article 6 – Genocide
> For the purpose of this Statute, 'genocide' means any of the following acts committed with intent to destroy, in whole or in part, a national, ethnical, racial or religious group, as such:
> (a) Killing members of the group;
> (b) Causing serious bodily or mental harm to members of the group;
> (c) Deliberately inflicting on the group conditions of life calculated to bring about its physical destruction in whole or in part;
> (d) Imposing measures intended to prevent births within the group;
> (e) Forcibly transferring children of the group to another group.

This provision is identical to Article II of the Genocide Convention, according to which State Parties must criminalise and punish genocide domestically under Article V.[400] As we have seen,[401] the Genocide Convention has implications at the level of State responsibility. In fact, Article IX establishes the 'responsibility of a State for genocide or for any of the other acts enumerated in Article III', triggering the compulsory jurisdiction of the ICJ. Article IX thus postulates that State genocidal conduct materially emulates individual genocidal conduct.[402]

397 Christopher Hall and Kai Ambos, 'Article 7: Crimes against Humanity', in Triffterer and Ambos, *Commentary* (2016) 176.
398 *Kunarac* (2001) 145, para 434; *Lukić* (2009) 275, para 877; *Karadžić* (2016) 184, para 479. See also Cassese, *International Criminal Law* (2013) 99; Knoops, Mens Rea (2017) 119–121.
399 *Katanga and Ngudjolo Chui* (2008) 129, para 402; *Blé Goudé* (2014) 72, paras 154–156.
400 Nasour Koursami, *The 'Contextual Elements' of the Crime of Genocide* (Asser Press, 2018) 6.
401 See s 1.2.1.3.
402 *Application of the Convention* [1996] 616, para 32.

2.3.4.1 Individual genocidal conduct without State responsibility?

Although it is governed by a separate provision in the ICC Statute, genocide is a specific crime against humanity. Indeed, it is a necessarily widespread or systematic violation of human rights.[403] Along these lines, 1996 DASR 19(3)(c) referred to genocide as a State crime involving 'a serious breach on a widespread scale of an international obligation of essential importance for safeguarding the human being'.[404] More specifically, genocide is the most serious form of persecution:[405] the targeted group is the principal victim and only in this context can an individual become a victim of genocide.[406] Furthermore, in light of the peremptory nature of the prohibition,[407] genocide affects the entire international community.

Whilst the existence of a plan or policy is not required for individual responsibility to subsist,[408] genocide is by nature a collective crime.[409] Indeed, historically genocide has been committed under State planning. However, since genocide does not expressly require widespread or systematic conduct, it ought to be assumed that theoretically also the single act of an individual can constitute genocide. In *Jelisić*, the ICTY held:

> [T]he drafters of the [Genocide] Convention did not deem the existence of an organisation or a system serving a genocidal objective as a legal ingredient of the crime. In so doing, they did not discount the possibility of a lone individual seeking to destroy a group as such.[410]

Given the identical nature of individual and State conduct under Article III of the Genocide Convention, the same approach should apply to State responsibility. Scholars indeed assume the necessary dual responsibility of the State and its organs and agents.[411] The hypothesis of a single genocidal act is not inconsistent with the general regime of State aggravated responsibility, which presupposes that State organs or agents act in a gross *or* systematic way, according to 2001 DASR 40. Therefore, hypothetically, from the standpoint of the material element of the offence, it cannot be absolutely excluded that the single act of a State organ

403 *Tadić*, IT-94-1, Trial Chamber, Judgment of 14 July 1997, 6, para 8. For a scholarly viewpoint, see Egon Schwelb, 'Crimes against Humanity' (1946) 23 *BYBIL* 213; William Schabas, *Genocide in International Law: The Crime of Crimes* (CUP, 2nd edn, 2009) 13–14.

404 See ss 1.2.2.3 and 1.2.3.5.

405 *Jélisic*, IT-95-10, Trial Chamber, Judgment of 14 December 1999, 21, para 68.

406 Werle and Jeßberger, *Principles* (2014) 293–295.

407 ILC, Report (2001) 112–113, para 4. See also s 2.1.1.5.

408 *Popović* et al, IT-05-88-A, Appeals Chamber, Judgment of 30 January 2015, 144, para 430. See also Koursami, *The 'Contextual Elements'* (2018) 33.

409 Aquilina and Mulaj, 'Limitations' (2018) 124.

410 *Jélisic* (1999) 31, para 100. See also *Kayshema and Ruzindana*, ICTR-95-1, Appeals Chamber, Judgment of 1 June 2001, 63, para 163.

411 Webb, 'Binocular Vision' (2012) 124–125, 128 and 147. Critically, see Koursami, *The 'Contextual Elements'* (2018) 64 ff.

or agent entails State responsibility for genocide. Concretely, this hypothesis is quite improbable and State genocide involves systematic conduct.[412]

In practice, the ICTR relied on collective responsibility to establish individual responsibility for genocide. Notably, in *Karemera* the Tribunal held that genocide occurring in Rwanda in 1994 was a collective offence and consequently took into account the general context in establishing individual responsibility.[413] Thus, the ICTR determined State responsibility prior to individual responsibility, which also involved high-ranking officers. The ICC upheld this approach when it confirmed an arrest warrant against Sudanese President Omar Al Bashir.[414]

2.3.4.2 Collective specific intent as a basis for individual intent (and vice versa)

Individually, the crime of genocide requires specific intent (*dolus specialis*).[415] Indeed, genocide is the most aggravated form of persecution and it is precisely the persecutory intent that differentiates genocidal murder from murder committed as another crime against humanity or a war crime. Thus, the perpetrator must act with the specific intent to destroy, in whole or in part, a targeted group, notably on national, ethnic, racial or religious grounds.[416] This approach also applies to State responsibility, which was explicitly confirmed by the ICJ in the cases concerning the *Application of the Genocide Convention*.[417]

The systematic perpetration of the crime facilitates establishing specific intent, which is largely presumed from the collective context.[418] Notably, in *Akayesu* the ICTR held:

> [I]t is possible to deduce the genocidal intent inherent in a particular act charged from the general context of the perpetration of other culpable acts systematically directed against that same group, whether these acts were committed by the same offender or by others. Other factors, such as the scale of atrocities committed, their general nature, in a region or a country, or furthermore, the fact of deliberately and systematically targeting victims on account of their membership of a particular group, while excluding the

412 *Blagojević and Jokić*, IT-02-60, Trial Chamber, Judgment of 17 January 2005, 235, para 638. See also Dupuy, 'International Criminal Responsibility' (2002) 1089 and 1093; Nollkaemper, 'Systemic Effects' (2010) 317; Koursami, *The 'Contextual Elements'* (2018) 33.

413 *Karemera*, ICTR-98-44, Trial Chamber, Decision on Prosecutor's Interlocutory Appeal of Decision on Judicial Notice, 16 June 2006, 15, para 36.

414 *Al Bashir* (2009) 44, paras 23–24, 53–54, para 149.

415 *Tolimir* (2012) 329, para 746. See also Aquilina and Mulaj, 'Limitations' (2018) 129.

416 *Karadžić* (2016) 207, para 549. See also Knoops, Mens Rea (2017) 101.

417 *Application of the Convention* [2007] 196–197, para 373; *Application of the Convention* [2015] 66, para 373. See also Dupuy, 'International Criminal Responsibility' (2002) 1095.

418 *Akayesu* (1998) paras 477, 523–524 and 728–730; *Karemera*, ICTR-98-44, Trial Chamber, Judgment of 2 February 2012, 292, para 1607; *Application of the Convention* [2015] 121, para 413; *Karadžić* (2016) 209, para 550. See also Koursami, *The 'Contextual Elements'* (2018) 28.

> members of other groups, can enable the Chamber to infer the genocidal intent of a particular act.[419]

Thus, whilst not a necessary element of the crime of genocide, in practice a genocidal plan or policy becomes a critical element for establishing genocidal intent.[420] Accordingly, the ICTY held that it can be quite difficult to establish individual genocidal intent if there are no widespread crimes and an organisation does not systemically support individual conduct.[421] In fact, there are no cases where individual genocidal intent has been declared in the absence of a genocidal context. More specifically, in *Ndindabahizi* the ICTR relied heavily on the genocidal context and the position of the accused as a Governmental Minister to prove individual genocidal intent, according to the theory of aggregate responsibility.[422] In some trials, the ICTY and ICTR excluded the necessity of demonstrating specific genocidal intent for superiors, being satisfied with knowledge of contextual genocidal acts committed by subordinates.[423] However, proof of individual specific intent may still be problematic, since international tribunals mostly require evidence that an individual shares the general intent.[424] Thus, in *Krstić*, reversing the first instance judgment,[425] the Appeals Chamber of the ICTY held that the accused was aware of the genocidal context aiming at the destruction of the Bosnian Muslim population in Srebrenica, but did not share the general genocidal purpose.[426] In *Bagilishema*, the ICTR took a restrictive approach and only relied on the genocidal context after assessing specific intent in relation to the individual conduct of the accused.[427]

Conversely, as we have seen,[428] in the first case concerning the *Application of the Genocide Convention* the ICJ considered that proof of individual responsibility, and thus of specific individual intent, was not necessary to establish State responsibility.[429] However, not fully consistently with this premise, the Court followed the '*alter ego*' doctrine and took into account individual genocidal intent to determine *dolus specialis* at the State level.[430] Even more explicitly, in the second case on the *Application of the Genocide Convention* the ICJ clearly held

419 *Akayesu* (1998) para 523.
420 *Jelisić*, IT-95-10A, Appeals Chamber, Judgment of 5 July 2001, 18, para 48.
421 *Id* (1999) 32, para 101.
422 *Ndindabahizi*, ICTR-01-71, Trial Chamber, Judgment of 15 July 2004, 110, paras 462–463; *Simba* (2005) 97, para 416.
423 *Ntagerura*, ICTR-99-46-T, Trial Chamber, Judgment of 25 February 2004, 174, para 654; *Brdanin*, IT-99-36, Trial Chamber, Judgment of 1 September 2004, 254, para 718; *Blagojević and Jokić* (2005) 251, para 686.
424 *Akayesu* (1998) paras 544 ff; *Jelisić* (1999) 27–28, para 86, 33, para 107.
425 *Krstić* (2001) 225, para 633.
426 *Id* (2004) 46, para 134.
427 *Bagilishema*, ICTR-95-1A, Trial Chamber, Judgment of 7 June 2001, 29, para 63.
428 See s 1.2.4.1.
429 *Application of the Convention* [2007] 119–120, para 182.
430 Ibid 155, para 277.

that, in the absence of a plan or policy, it is necessary to prove State persecutory intent based on individual intent or a pattern of conduct:

> In the absence of a State plan expressing the intent to commit genocide, it is necessary, in the Court's view, to clarify the process whereby such an intent may be inferred from the individual conduct of perpetrators of the acts contemplated in Article II of the Convention.[431]

Within this framework, the (hypothetical) question arises as to whether sporadic conduct of a single State organ or agent acting with genocidal intent can be attributed to the State and generate collective aggravated responsibility for genocide.[432] Indeed, absent a widespread or systematic context, attribution of responsibility based on the 'aggregate' model cannot apply. The answer will be negative if it is assumed that the *mens rea* of the organs or agents of a State cannot be automatically attributed to its people. It is indeed difficult that people have knowledge of sporadic genocidal conduct of a single State organ or agent. By contrast, State responsibility for sporadic genocidal conduct of one of its organs or agents should not be absolutely excluded under the doctrine of objective State responsibility, nor by assuming that the *mens rea* of a State organ or agent is at the same time that of the State, according to the '*alter ego*' doctrine. In this respect, assessing the responsibility of Serbia in the second case on the *Application of the Genocide Convention*, the ICJ held that '[i]t is difficult [but not impossible] to infer anything from one isolated instance [event].'[433] However, despite such a premise the Court did not even try to determine the persecutory intent of Serbia for genocide based on a speech delivered by Zeljko Raznatovic ('Arkan') to a Serb paramilitary group he commanded in order to direct attacks against the Croatian population on 1 November 1991.[434]

2.3.5 *Terrorism*

Although there is no crystallised international definition of terrorism at the individual and State level, the possible inclusion of terrorism as a crime in the ICC Statute was discussed during preparatory work. Thus, the ICC Draft Statute proposed by the Preparatory Committee in 1998 provided:

> Crimes of Terrorism
> For the purposes of the present Statute, crimes of terrorism means:
> (1) Undertaking, organizing, sponsoring, ordering, facilitating, financing, encouraging or tolerating acts of violence against another State directed at persons or property and of such a nature as to create terror, fear or

431 *Application of the Convention* [2015] 66, para 145.
432 International Commission of Inquiry on Darfur, Report (2005) 132, para 520.
433 *Application of the Convention* [2015] 128, para 438.
434 Bonafè, 'Reassessing' (2016) 31.

insecurity in the minds of public figures, groups of persons, the general public or populations, for whatever considerations and purposes of a political, philosophical, ideological, racial, ethnic, religious or such other nature that may be invoked to justify them;

(2) An offence under the following Conventions:
   (a) Convention for the Suppression of Unlawful Acts against the Safety of Civil Aviation;
   (b) Convention for the Suppression of Unlawful Seizure of Aircraft;
   (c) Convention on the Prevention and Punishment of Crimes against Internationally Protected Persons, including Diplomatic Agents;
   (d) International Convention against the Taking of Hostages;
   (e) Convention for the Suppression of Unlawful Acts against the Safety of Maritime Navigation;
   (f) Protocol for the Suppression of Unlawful Acts against the Safety of Fixed Platforms located on the Continental Shelf;

(3) An offence involving use of firearms, weapons, explosives and dangerous substances when used as a means to perpetrate indiscriminate violence involving death or serious bodily injury to persons or groups of persons or populations or serious damage to property.[435]

Although there is currently no exhaustive binding definition of terrorism under treaty law, some scholars argue that terrorism is prohibited under customary international law, at least in time of peace.[436]

Article 2 of the UN Draft Comprehensive Convention against International Terrorism provides:

1. Any person commits an offence within the meaning of the present Convention if that person, by any means, unlawfully and intentionally, causes:
   (a) Death or serious bodily injury to any person; or
   (b) Serious damage to public or private property, including a place of public use, a State or government facility, a public transportation system, an infrastructure facility or to the environment; or
   (c) Damage to property, places, facilities or systems referred to in paragraph 1(b) of the present article resulting or likely to result in major economic loss; when the purpose of the conduct, by its nature or context, is to intimidate a population, or to compel a Government or an international organization to do or to abstain from doing any act.
2. Any person also commits an offence if that person makes a credible and serious threat to commit an offence as set forth in paragraph 1 of the present article.

435 PCEICC, Draft Statute (1998) 27–28.

436 Antonio Cassese, 'Terrorism Is also Disrupting Some Crucial Legal Categories of International Law' (2001) 12(5) *EJIL* 994; Id, *International Criminal Law* (2013) 148–149 and 154.

3. Any person also commits an offence if that person attempts to commit an offence as set forth in paragraph 1 of the present article.
4. Any person also commits an offence if that person:
   (a) Participates as an accomplice in an offence as set forth in paragraph 1, 2 or 3 of the present article; or
   (b) Organizes or directs others to commit an offence as set forth in paragraph 1, 2 or 3 of the present article; or
   (c) Contributes to the commission of one or more offences as set forth in paragraph 1, 2 or 3 of the present article by a group of persons acting with a common purpose. Such contribution shall be intentional and shall either:
      (i) Be made with the aim of furthering the criminal activity or criminal purpose of the group, where such activity or purpose involves the commission of an offence as set forth in paragraph 1 of the present article; or
      (ii) Be made in the knowledge of the intention of the group to commit an offence as set forth in paragraph 1 of the present article.

In light of the political purpose involved and the practice of State-sponsored terrorism, individual responsibility may entail State responsibility.[437]

Transnationally, the main international conventions on terrorism define specific offences and consistently compel States to criminalise them domestically. These conventions regulate conduct such as taking hostages, hijacking aircraft, terrorist financing and acts against internationally protected persons or the safety of maritime navigation. For instance, Article 2(1) of the International Convention for the Suppression of Terrorist Bombings provides:

> Any person commits an offence within the meaning of this Convention if that person unlawfully and intentionally delivers, places, discharges or detonates an explosive or other lethal device in, into or against a place of public use, a State or government facility, a public transportation system or an infrastructure facility:
> (a) With the intent to cause death or serious bodily injury; or
> (b) With the intent to cause extensive destruction of such a place, facility or system, where such destruction results in or is likely to result in major economic loss.

437 Vincent-Joël Proulx, *Transnational Terrorism and State Accountability* (Hart, 2012) 16; Id, *Insitutionalizing State Responsibility: Global Security and UN Organs* (OUP, 2016) 44 ff; Mosa Zahed, The Evolution and Ascension of Iran's Terror Apparatus', in Paulo Casaca and Sigfried Wolf (eds), *Terrorism Revisited: Islamism, Political Violence and State Sponsorship* (Springer, 2017) 51; Sigfried Wolf, 'Pakistan State-Sponsored Terrorism in South Asia', ibid, 117; Alshaidafat, *International Law* (2017) 80.

Article 2(1) of the 1999 International Convention for the Suppression of the Financing of Terrorism[438] provides:

> Any person commits an offence within the meaning of this Convention if that person by any means, directly or indirectly, unlawfully and wilfully, provides or collects funds with the intention that they should be used or in the knowledge that they are to be used, in full or in part, in order to carry out:
> (a) An act which constitutes an offence within the scope of and as defined in one of the treaties listed in the annex [Convention on Terrorist Bombings and other conventions against terrorism]; or
> (b) Any other act intended to cause death or serious bodily injury to a civilian, or to any other person not taking an active part in the hostilities in a situation of armed conflict, when the purpose of such act, by its nature or context, is to intimidate a population, or to compel a government or an international organization to do or to abstain from doing any act.

2.3.5.1 Political or ideological purpose as a distinguishing material element

Scholars have singled out a few components of the crime of terrorism:

1 Conduct criminalised under domestic law, involving violence
2 Intent to provoke terror in the population or to compel a government or an organisation to follow a certain course of conduct
3 A political or ideological motivation[439]

The customary definition of terrorism proposed by the STL is similarly based on the perpetration or threat of a criminal act (1) and intent to spread fear among the population (2), when such conduct has a transnational nature.[440]

Other elements encompass the indiscriminate nature of conduct, to the extent that the direct victims are chosen randomly and are not the ultimate target of the act, and the fact that violence intentionally addresses civilians as opposed to combatants.[441] This is all quite effectively summarised by the proposed definition of terrorism under the 1998 ICC Draft Statute, whereby protection is largely anticipated, given the tendency to criminalise sponsoring, ordering, facilitating, financing, encouraging or tolerating terrorism and its threat.

438 Adopted 9 December 1999, 2178 UNTS 197, in force 10 April 2002.
439 Cassese, *International Criminal Law* (2013) 149–150 and 155–156. See also Gilbert Guillaume, 'Terrorisme et droit international' (1989) 215(3) *RCADI* 295 ff.
440 *Ayyash* et al (2011) 49 ff, paras 83 ff. See also s 1.2.4.2.
441 Cohen, 'Prosecuting Terrorists' (2012) 230.

When committed on a gross or systematic basis by State organs or agents, terrorism has the potential to trigger not only individual responsibility, but also State aggravated responsibility.[442] In this respect, scholars have envisaged the possibility of relaxing the 'effective control' and 'complete dependence' tests when attributing conduct of private individuals to the State in the case of terrorist acts under 2001 DASR 8.[443] Alternatively, Crawford conceives of a State duty of prevention.[444]

Specific conduct such as murder, causing serious bodily harm and hijacking overlaps with crimes against humanity, war crimes and genocide.[445] Thus, terrorism might already be included within the competence of the ICC under Article 7(1)(k) of its Statute as '[o]ther inhumane acts of a similar [to other crimes against humanity] character intentionally causing great suffering, or serious injury to body or to mental or physical health'. It goes without saying that, in order to constitute crimes against humanity, acts of terrorism must be committed as part of a widespread or systematic attack against civilian population. The banning of terrorism in time of war is specifically underscored in Article 33(1) of 1949 Geneva Convention IV, as well as in Article 51(2) of Additional Protocol I, Article 4(2)(d) and Article 13(2) of Additional Protocol II. The jurisprudence of the ICTY also confirms this approach.[446] The Yazidi genocide committed by the Islamic State of Iraq and Syria (ISIS) in 2014 and Iraqi ethnic cleansing against minorities such as the Mandaeans indicate that conduct aiming to eliminate large groups of people also seeks to terrorise societies.[447]

Whilst the customary definition of terrorism focuses on individual conduct, the Draft Comprehensive Convention focuses more specifically on the organisational aspects of terrorism, governing direction, contribution and group purposes. This should facilitate holding a State responsible, when State agents or organs are involved in the commission of acts of terrorism. The clearest example is that of the 9/11 attacks, which were committed by Al-Qaeda, with the logistical support of the Taliban regime in Afghanistan.[448] In this case, it is not impossible to assume that, by involving the use of armed force, terrorism overlaps with aggression, which can trigger the use of force in self-defence.[449]

442 This was a critical element of terrorism under the 1937 Convention for the Prevention and Punishment of the Crime of Terrorism (see s 1.1.2.4). See also Nollkaemper, 'Systemic Effects' (2010) 332.

443 Trapp, *State Responsibility* (2011) 42. See also s 2.2.1.1.

444 Crawford, *State Responsibility* (2013) 158–159.

445 Giovanni Battaglini, 'War against Terrorism *Extra Moenia*, Self-Defence and Responsibility: A Pure Judicial Approach', in Ragazzi, *International Responsibility* (2005) 146; Cohen, 'Prosecuting Terrorists' (2012) 239–249.

446 *Galić* (2003) paras 113 ff; *Karadžić* (2016) 177, para 460.

447 Paulo Casaca, 'The Conceptual Discussion on Terrorism', in Casaca and Wolf, *Terrorism* (2017) 6–7.

448 Christine Gray, *International Law and the Use of Force* (OUP, 4th edn, 2018) 209. Critically, see Alshdaifat, *International Law* (2017) 190 ff.

449 Michael Byers, 'Terrorism, the Use of Force and International Law after 11 September' (2002) 51(2) *ICLQ* 411–412; Trapp, *State Responsibility* (2011) 24–34; Crawford, *State Responsibility* (2013) 159; Ozcan Ozkan, 'The Changing Nature of Global Armed Conflict', in Alexander

In *Legal Consequences of the Construction of a Wall in the Occupied Palestinian Territory*, the ICJ ruled out the possibility of reacting in self-defence against a private terrorist group:

> Article 51 of the Charter thus recognises the existence of an inherent right of self-defence in the case of armed attack by one State against another State. However, Israel does not claim that the [terrorist] attacks against it are imputable to a foreign State [...] and therefore Israel could not in any event invoke those resolutions in support of its claim to be exercising a right of self-defence.[450]

However, the doctrine of self-defence is evolving in the matter. The ongoing State intervention against ISIS in Syria, notably by a US-led coalition of Western and Arab countries, seems to prove that the use of armed force in self-defence against a terrorist group as such is possible when a State is unwilling or unable to curb the threat of a terrorist attack carried out by a group operating in its territory.[451] Furthermore, terrorism can constitute a threat to peace and security, triggering UN procedures, particularly action by the Security Council under Chapter VII of the UN Charter.[452]

Terrorism entails a plurality of victims at both the State and individual levels. In fact, besides the victims directly targeted by a terrorist attack, terrorism affects the State or organisation whose conduct it ultimately aims to constrain. Therefore, terrorism infringes upon a range of obligations. Within this framework, as we have seen,[453] the prohibition of terrorism is evolving as a peremptory norm in international law.[454] More generally, overlap between terrorism, aggression and at least some war crimes or crimes against humanity, including genocide,[455] might entail the breach of an *erga omnes* and peremptory obligation, notably according to the Preamble to the ICC Statute.[456] From this perspective, terrorism affects all State and non-State subjects of the international community. Along these lines, affirming the customary nature of the prohibition of terrorism under

---

Dawoody (ed), *Eradicating Terrorism from the Middle East: Policy and Administrative Approaches* (Springer, 2016) 159; Alshdaifat, *International Law* (2017) 177 ff.

450 *Legal Consequences* [2004] 194, para 139.

451 Michael Scharf, 'How the War against ISIS Changed International Law' (2016) 48(1–2) *Case W Res J Intl L* 20 ff; Marja Lehto, 'The Fight against ISIL in Syria. Comments on the Recent Discussion of the Right of Self-Defence against Non-state Actors' (2018) 87(1) *Nordic JIL* 24. See s 3.2.4.4.

452 Byers, 'Terrorism' (2002) 412; Cohen, 'Prosecuting Terrorists' (2012) 249–250.

453 See s 2.1.1.5.

454 Weatherall, Jus Cogens (2015) 249.

455 Ciara Damgaard, *Individual Criminal Responsibility for Core International Crimes* (Springer, 2008) 375 ff; Scheffer, 'Amending' (2017) 1485 and 1491.

456 Thomas Weatherall, 'The Status of the Prohibition of Terrorism in International Law: Recent Developments' (2014–15) 46(2) *Geo JIL* 616 ff.

general international law, the STL has held that terrorism is subject to (non-compulsory) universal jurisdiction.[457]

2.3.5.2 Specific intent and collective responsibility

At the individual level, terrorism entails specific intent (*dolus specialis*), which implies the purpose of either provoking terror in the population or compelling a government or an organisation to perform or abstain from performing specific conduct.[458] This can go as far as to aim at destabilising or destroying the stability of a country.[459]

Within the context of international humanitarian law, in *Galić* the ICTY required specific intent (*dolus specialis*) for the commission of the war crime of terror against the civilian population. Galić was accused of ordering a protracted campaign of shelling and sniping over the civilian population in Sarajevo, so as to inflict terror and mental suffering. The Tribunal held that specific intent should cover the element of causing terror among civilians and can be proved based on the systematic context of the offence.[460] The ICTY subsequently upheld this stance in *Popović* and *Karadžić*.[461]

Concerning attribution of responsibility to sponsoring States, non-widespread and systematic acts of terrorism should be attributed to the State based on the '*alter ego*' doctrine, in light of the *mens rea* of individuals acting on behalf of the State. By contrast, the aggregate model facilitates attribution of responsibility in the case of widespread or systematic acts of terrorism, such as 9/11, according to preventive fault or collective *mens rea*.

From the standpoint of motive, terrorism is grounded in political reasons. For instance, the 9/11 terrorist attacks were aimed at compelling the US to review its policy in the Middle East. Political reasons can be a manifestation of collective criminality, so much so that individuals often commit terrorist acts by acting on behalf of groups or organisations.[462] This facilitates State implication, as in the case of the 9/11 attacks involving Al-Qaeda backed by Afghanistan. In such circumstances, the group motive, particularly a State motive, becomes an indispensable element in determining individual responsibility, along the lines of the aggregate model.

Conclusion

From the standpoint of the material element of the offence, individual international crimes and State aggravated offences overlap, to the extent that they

457 *Ayyash* et al (2011) 65–66, para 102. See also Weatherall, 'The Status' (2014–15) 622.
458 Cassese, *International Criminal Law* (2013) 150 and 156.
459 Article I(2) of the Convention of the Organisation of the Islamic Conference on Combating International Terrorism, adopted 1 July 1999, in force 7 November 2002.
460 *Galić* (2003) para 72.
461 *Popović* (2015) 255, para 737; *Karadžić* (2016) 178–179, paras 464–466.
462 Alshdaifat, *International Law* (2017) 308.

are both serious breaches of non-severable *erga omnes* obligations, which are necessarily peremptory rules. In light of international practice, it is sensible to assume that such obligations include the prohibition of aggression, genocide, core war crimes, core crimes against humanity and prospectively terrorism.

From the viewpoint of attribution of responsibility, international law attributes the conduct of an individual acting as an organ or agent of a State to the State itself. It is unclear, nevertheless, whether individual criminal responsibility should generate criminal responsibility rather than aggravated liability at the State level. Both approaches are theoretically viable. In fact, the experience of domestic legal orders demonstrates that applying the doctrine of objective liability to the State does not necessarily lead to excluding collective criminal responsibility. *A fortiori*, a criminal approach to State responsibility cannot be excluded by applying the doctrine of fault to the State. Under the ILC's 2001 DASR, responsibility is attributed to the State on a case-by-case basis, in light of either fault or objective liability, but aggravated responsibility requires intent under Article 40. This approach discloses the necessity of applying 'aggregate' intent at the State level, so as to justify possible discrepancies with a lower degree of fault, notably recklessness or negligence, at the level of the individuals acting on behalf of the State. However, grounding State aggravated responsibility in fault has not led to positing the criminal nature of collective responsibility.

Concerning specific offences, the individual prohibition of aggression is based on the State prohibition outlined in UN General Assembly Resolution 3314 (XXIX). Individual aggression is a leadership crime and necessitates State aggression. Within this framework, the individual *mens rea* of a leader tends to identify with that of the State. At the same time, individual intent is contextually determined based on the existence of State aggression.

Relevant international legal instruments only define core war crimes and core crimes against humanity with respect to individuals. It must therefore be assumed that the same prohibitions that trigger individual criminal responsibility also generate State aggravated responsibility. The systemic context in which these offences take place establishes a link between individual and State responsibility and helps to prove individual intent, along the lines of aggregate fault.

Exceptionally, Article III of the Genocide Convention outlines the prohibition of genocide with respect to both natural persons and the State. Whilst theoretically it is not a necessary requirement for the commission of genocide, in practice a policy is an indispensable component of the offence and prompts international criminal tribunals to presume individual intent on an aggregate basis. Vice versa, the ICJ assumes that individual specific intent is not a prerequisite for State genocidal intent. However, in practice the Court establishes State intent based on that of its individual organs or agents, according to the '*alter ego*' doctrine.

International law defines terrorism as a crime first and foremost with respect to natural persons. However, relevant transnational and international instruments also underscore implications at the State level, given that political reasons often motivate acts of terrorism. Non-widespread and systematic acts of State-sponsored terrorism should be attributed to the State based on the '*alter ego*' doctrine. In contrast, the aggregate model facilitates attribution of responsibility for widespread or systematic acts of terrorism, such as 9/11.

3 Secondary norms

Dispute settlement, sanctions and enforcement

Introduction

State aggravated offences and individual criminal violations generate procedures for dispute settlement. These lead to adopting particular sanctions, whose breach triggers enforcement via specific mechanisms. This chapter explores dispute settlement, sanctions and enforcement procedures and highlights consistency and inconsistency raised by the different regimes of individual criminal responsibility and State aggravated responsibility. The analysis thus moves from the breach of a primary norm to secondary and tertiary substantive and procedural norms.

It is usually assumed that international law establishes a uniform regime of responsibility for States. However, given that it breaches non-severable *erga omnes* obligations, State aggravated responsibility affects all the subjects of the international community. This triggers a universal reaction, which is institutionalised via the UN, notably the Security Council, or implemented by States under general international law. Sanctions also have, in principle, a non-severable *erga omnes* scope, and their breach triggers institutionalised or non-institutionalised universal countermeasures. Similarly, individual criminal responsibility for breaches of peremptory norms affects the entire international community. Domestically, this entails (compulsory) universal jurisdiction, whilst at the supranational level it leads to applying international criminal proceedings.

The systemic investigation of dispute settlement, sanctions and enforcement procedures for individual criminal responsibility and State aggravated responsibility focuses particularly on the DASR, the ICC Statute and complementary instruments, notably the UN Charter and procedures under its Chapter VII. The research developed in this chapter thus completes the analysis carried out in Chapter 2. In light of the principle that the individual conduct of State organs or agents triggers dual *erga omnes* responsibility, the first part of the chapter starts with an illustration of secondary and tertiary rules addressing State aggravated responsibility and then moves to considering norms governing the criminal responsibility of natural persons. The second part of the chapter underscores that, although conduct of State organs and agents vicariously triggers State responsibility, the latter is assessed prior to the liability of natural persons. In light of this premise, the research explores systemic interactions between State and individual proceedings. The implications of such a theoretical framework are tested in the context of critical situations, notably the Bosnian genocide, the interventions of the North Atlantic Treaty Organisation (NATO) in the Former Yugoslavia and Libya, the Iraq wars and counterterrorism in Afghanistan, Syria and Iraq.

3.1 Secondary and tertiary implications of dual *erga omnes* offences

3.1.1 State aggravated responsibility

3.1.1.1 Institutionalised and non-institutionalised (compulsory) universal invocation of responsibility: 2001 DASR 41(1), 42(b), 48(1)(b) and 59

When a State breaches a peremptory rule, specific procedural consequences apply under the ILC's 2001 DASR. In fact, Article 42 provides:

> Article 42
> Invocation of Responsibility by an Injured State
> A State is entitled as an injured State to invoke the responsibility of another State if the obligation breached is owed to:
> (*a*) that State individually; or
> (*b*) a group of states including that State, or the *international community as a whole*, and the breach of the obligation:
> (i) specially affects that State; or
> (ii) is of such a character as radically to change the position of all the other States to which the obligation is owed with respect to the further performance of the obligation.[1]

Therefore, in the case of a breach of a peremptory norm, besides a State directly affected by the breach under Article 42(b)(i), all other indirectly affected States can invoke the responsibility of the injurer under Article 42(b)(ii).[2]

Article 48(1) and (2) of the 2001 DASR governs invocation of responsibility by a State other than an injured State:

> Article 48
> Invocation of Responsibility by a State Other than an Injured State
> 1. Any State other than an injured State is entitled to invoke the responsibility of another State in accordance with paragraph 2 if:
> (*a*) the obligation breached is owed to a group of States including that State, and is established for the protection of a collective interest of the group; or
> (*b*) the obligation breached is owed to the *international community as a whole.*

1 ILC, Report (2001) 117, emphasis added.
2 Ibid 118–119, paras 11–12. See also Dupuy, 'The Deficiencies' (2012) 214–215.

2. Any State entitled to invoke responsibility under paragraph 1 may claim from the responsible State:
   (*a*) cessation of the internationally wrongful act, and assurances and guarantees of non-repetition in accordance with article 30; and
   (*b*) performance of the obligation of reparation in accordance with the preceding articles, in the interest of the injured State or of the beneficiaries of the obligation breached.[3]

According to Iain Scobbie, these remedies apply to system crimes.[4]

A State entitled to invoke responsibility under Article 48 does not act in its individual capacity because of individual injury, but rather in its capacity as a member of a group of States having correlative rights, or as a member of the international community as a whole. In fact, Article 48 assumes that, in the case of a breach of a specific obligation protecting the collective interest of a group of States (non-severable *erga omnes partes* obligation) or the interest of the international community as a whole (non-severable *erga omnes* obligation), States that are not injured in the sense of Article 42 may invoke responsibility.

In this respect, the ILC stated:

> Article 48 complements the rule contained in article 42. It deals with the invocation of responsibility by States other than the injured State *acting in the collective interest*. A State which is entitled to invoke responsibility under article 48 is acting not in its individual capacity by reason of having suffered injury but in its capacity as a member of a group of States to which the obligation is owed, or indeed as a member of the international community as a whole. The distinction is underlined by the phrase "[a]ny State other than an injured State" in paragraph 1 of article 48.[5]

The idea is that States are entitled to invoke responsibility not because they suffer from material injury, but rather to protect the common interest embodied in a non-severable *erga omnes* obligation under Article 48(1)(b) or an obligation *erga omnes partes contractantes* under Article 48(1)(a).[6]

Concerning non-severable *erga omnes* obligations, the ILC refers to the ICJ case-law and indicates the prohibition of aggression, genocide, basic human rights and the right to self-determination of peoples.[7] This approach substantially matches the indications on *jus cogens* rules that the ILC provides in its

3 Ibid 126, emphasis added.
4 Scobbie, 'Assumptions' (2009) 277.
5 ILC, Report (2001) 126, para 1, emphasis added. See also Scobbie, 'Assumptions' (2009) 278; Crawford, *State Responsibility* (2013) 67.
6 Vaurs Chaumette, 'The International Community' (2010) 1027.
7 ILC, Report (2001) 127, para 9.

commentary to DASR 40,[8] which confirms that non-severable *erga omnes* obligations are necessarily peremptory. In the case of a breach of such obligations, each State is entitled in its capacity as a member of the international community as a whole to invoke the responsibility of the responsible State in order to protect a collective interest. Thus, not only an individually injured State, for instance, a State victim of aggression, but also all other States can invoke responsibility.

Theoretically, responsibility may be invoked in favour of an injured State or in favour of non-injured States. However, invocation of responsibility by non-injured States should mainly concern cessation and non-repetition under 2001 DASR 30. A directly injured State, such as Kuwait in the case of the 1990 Iraqi invasion, should invoke reparation for the injury caused (restitution, compensation and satisfaction) under DASR 31–39, or, at least, other States should make a request on its behalf.[9] This approach is consistent with the assumption that in the case of State aggravated offences all States have an obligation to cooperate in invoking responsibility. In fact, 2001 DASR 41(b) provides that 'States shall cooperate to bring to an end through lawful means' a breach of *jus cogens*: the expression 'lawful means' could be interpreted so as to also encompass invocation of responsibility.

Based on material damage, 2001 DASR 48(2)(b) mentions 'injured' and 'non-injured' States, which conceals the breach of an international legal obligation. For instance, it is true that in the case of aggression a State whose territory is attacked suffers from material injury, whereas other States do not suffer from such injury. Consider again the invasion of Kuwait by Iraq in 1990. However, given that, based on relevant international case law, a non-severable *erga omnes* obligation is unitary, that is, owed to the international community 'as a whole', all States are legally affected.[10]

Within such a horizontal framework, 2001 DASR 59 introduces a relevant vertical exception. Indeed, the rule subjects the application of the DASR to the provisions of the UN Charter. Besides classical dispute resolution mechanisms such as negotiation, enquiry, mediation, conciliation, arbitration and judicial settlement under Chapter VI of the Charter, this triggers centralised UN procedures, particularly via the Security Council under Chapter VII, notably in the case of aggression, genocide, core war crimes, core crimes against humanity and terrorism.[11]

8 Ibid 112–113, paras 4–5. See also s 2.1.1.1.

9 Arangio-Ruiz, Fifth Report (1993) 39–40, paras 150–157; Crawford, *State Responsibility* (2013) 67; Dawidowicz, *Third-Party Countermeasures in International Law* (CUP, 2017) 300–304.

10 Linos-Alexandre Sicilianos, 'Countermeasures in Response to Grave Violations of Obligations Owed to the International Community', in Crawford, Pellet, Olleson and Parlett, *The Law* (2010) 1138–1139; Dupuy, 'The Deficiencies' (2012) 216; Dawidowicz, *Third-Party Countermeasures* (2017) 90.

11 See s 3.2.2.

General invocation of responsibility does not necessarily entail the ability of injured and non-injured States to bring a unilateral action in international jurisdictions, as the ICJ pointed out in the *Bosnian Genocide* case:

> The jurisdiction of the Court in this case is based solely on Article IX of the Convention [agreement] [...] [The Court] has no power to rule on alleged breaches of other obligations under international law, not amounting to genocide, particularly those protecting human rights in armed conflict. That is so even if the alleged breaches are of obligations under peremptory norms, or of obligations which protect essential humanitarian values, and which may be owed *erga omnes.*[12]

Schematically, the 2001 DASR outline this pattern for invocation of State aggravated responsibility:

> Breach of a peremptory obligation (VCLT and VCLTIO Article 53 and 2001 DASR 40)
> Aggression, genocide, core war crimes, core crimes against humanity, prospectively terrorism)
> → UN collective action (2001 DASR 59)
> → Invocation of responsibility by the injured State(s) (2001 DASR 42(b))
> → (Compulsory) universal invocation of responsibility by non-injured States (2001 DASR 41(1) and 48(1)(b))

Within this context, James Crawford noted that 'some centralized judicial process' would have been 'beyond the scope of the present text', requiring 'a special regulatory regime which is presently lacking, and which the draft articles cannot realistically create'.[13] According to the Special Rapporteur, it would have been necessary to establish State criminal liability, including secondary implications, outside the DASR, which only define a general theory of State responsibility.[14]

3.1.1.2 Non-punitive erga omnes *sanctions? 2001 DASR 28–39 and UN Charter Articles 39–42*

Sanctions are secondary obligations applying to the breach of a primary duty. They therefore provide essential information on the nature of the primary obligation breached. The 2001 DASR do not establish any specific sanctions for State aggravated offences. Therefore, the classical duties of cessation, non-repetition and reparation, including restitution, compensation and satisfaction,

12 *Application of the Convention* [2007] 104, para 147. See also s 2.1.1.2.
13 Crawford, Third Report (2000) 107, para 409.
14 Id, 'Revisiting' (1999) 443, note 32.

apply according to DASR 28–39. This approach is nonetheless problematic with respect to the observation that the gravity of the sanction should be grounded in the gravity of the offence. Notably, different State breaches can entail different degrees of fault, rather than objective liability.[15]

Whilst the 2001 DASR focus on reparation,[16] during preparatory work Crawford proposed to elaborate on 1996 DASR 52, concerning the specific consequences of a State crime, so as to establish punitive interests and damages.[17] In light of the *erga omnes* nature of State aggravated responsibility, the Special Rapporteur held that, despite the absence of a centralised mechanism for adjudicating on State crimes, it would have still been possible to envisage punitive damages. Crawford considered that 'it can be envisaged that an injured State could be held entitled to demand punitive damages', since 'following gross and systematic breaches of community obligations, there will always be a much wider group of persons indirectly affected, and major restoration work to be done.'[18] This approach followed the indications of the Sixth Committee of the UN General Assembly.[19] Accordingly, 2000 DASR 42(1), governing the consequences of serious breaches of obligations owed to the international community as a whole,[20] provided that '[a] serious breach within the meaning of article 41' might have involved 'for the responsible State, [punitive] damages reflecting the gravity of the breach'.[21]

More specifically, some members of the ILC proposed to introduce in the 2000 version of the DASR a collective monetary sanction owed by the responsible State to the international community as a whole in the case of State aggravated responsibility.[22] This would have been a proportionate measure marking a clear difference between ordinary sanctions and aggravated sanctions, not necessarily characterising State aggravated responsibility as 'criminal'. However, according to Cançado Trindade punitive damages are the appropriate sanction for State crimes,[23] although international law currently does not acknowledge either notion.[24]

15 Arangio-Ruiz, Second Report (1989) 53 ff, paras 183 ff; Arangio-Ruiz, Eighth Report (1996) 8–9, paras 48–55; Andrea Gattini, 'Smoking/No Smoking: Some Remarks on the Current Place of Fault in the ILC Draft Articles on State Responsibility' (1999) 10(2) *EJIL* 402–404. See also ILC, Report (1990) 81–82, paras 408–412; Arangio-Ruiz, Seventh Report (1995) 13–14, paras 46–54.

16 Scobbie, 'Assumptions' (2009) 272–273.

17 Crawford, Third Report (2000) 107, paras 408–409. See also Stephan Wittich, 'Punitive Damages', in Crawford, Pellet, Olleson and Parlett, *The Law* (2010) 672–674.

18 Crawford, Third Report (2000) 107, para 409. See also ILC, Report (2000) 59–60, paras 358–363, 61–62, paras 374–383.

19 Sixth Committee of the General Assembly, Topical Summary of the Discussion Held during the Fifty-Second Session on the Work of the ILC of Its Forty-Ninth Session, UN Doc A/CN.4/483 (1998) 13, para 96.

20 See s 1.2.3.5.

21 ILC, Report (2000) 59, note 110, and 69. See also the Sixth Committee, Topical Summary (2001) 23, paras 110–112.

22 Spinedi, 'La responsabilité' (2000) 101.

23 Francisco García Amador, 'State Responsibility – Some New Problems' (1958) 94(2) *RCADI* 409; Cançado Trindade, 'Complementarity' (2005) 267.

24 Zimmermann and Teichmann, 'State Responsibility' (2009) 306–307.

The commentary to 2000 DASR 45, concerning satisfaction, specified that a link could have been established between the consequences of State aggravated responsibility and individual prosecution for international crimes.[25] Along the same lines, discussing the consequences of a serious breach of a peremptory norm under 2000 DASR 42, some members of the Sixth Committee of the UN General Assembly considered that:

> [The] implementation of the heightened regime of international responsibility when a "serious breach" [of an obligation owed to the international community as a whole] was committed [...] should include an express reference to the international rules on individual criminal responsibility, such as the Rome Statute of the International Criminal Court.[26]

Whilst the 2001 DASR do not embed any difference between State aggravated offences and ordinary responsibility as concerns the content of sanctions, the question arises as to whether international sanctions have a 'non-punitive' character, rather than a 'punitive' nature.[27] Scholars are divided as concerns the possibility of recognising punitive sanctions in international law.[28] As a starting point for this discussion, it should be considered that sanctions in general may have a punitive and non-punitive aim, so that it is difficult to establish a neat divide. Thus, for instance, 'punitive damages' can also have reparatory implications.[29]

Some scholars assume that all international sanctions have both a punitive and reparatory aim.[30] The dual nature of international sanctions would be particularly necessary within a system of uniform responsibility and would allow the criminal responsibility of the State to be realised, regardless of vertically centralised adjudication proceedings. Within this context, criminal offences should entail sanctions that are mainly punitive and residually reparatory, whilst non-criminal offences should entail sanctions that are mainly reparatory and residually punitive.[31] Other scholars simply assume that international law includes sanctions that have a merely punitive nature.[32] Although the debate has mostly focused on the punitive nature of the sanction, the same logic can extend to other implications, notably the pre-emptive and re-socialising purposes of the sanction.

25 ILC, Report (2000) 42, para 217.

26 Sixth Committee, Topical Summary (2001) 23, para 107.

27 Ago, 'Le délit' (1939) 524; Roberto Ago, Second Report on State Responsibility: The Origin of International Responsibility, UN Doc A/CN.4/233 (1970) 2(1) *YBILC* 181–183, paras 16–18; Cançado Trindade, 'Complementarity' (2005) 262.

28 ILC, Report (1994) 144, paras 289–290; Crawford, Fourth Report (2001) 12, para 45.

29 See, for instance, *Rainbow Warrior (New Zealand v France)*, Award of 30 April 1990 (1990) XX *RIAA* 267, paras 108–110; Cançado Trindade, 'Complementarity' (2005) 265.

30 Anzilotti, *Cours* (1929) 522; Arangio-Ruiz, Second Report (1989) 41, para 137; Alain Pellet and Alina Miron, 'Sanctions', in Wolfrum, *Max Planck Encyclopedia* (2013) para 8.

31 Ago, Fifth Report (1976) 42–43, para 127; Spinedi, 'La responsabilité' (2000) 108.

32 Sreenivasa Rao, 'International Crimes' (2005) 77.

Concerning specific sanctions, cessation aims to halt continuous or repetitive conduct, whilst assurances of non-repetition seek to prevent reiteration: both measures bar unlawful conduct. Some scholars assume that these sanctions have a neutral nature.[33] In contrast, establishing a parallel with imprisonment, which halts and pre-empts unlawful conduct, other commentators assume that these sanctions, notably assurances of non-repetition, may have a punitive nature.[34] This is also arguable in light of the fact that assurances of non-repetition can be a form of satisfaction.[35] According to Joachim Wolf, the prosecution of responsible State agents is a punitive form of guarantee of non-repetition.[36] Other scholars underscore that the guarantees of non-repetition are crucial to State aggravated responsibility, since they entail the taking of measures such as ensuring effective control of military and security forces, strengthening the independence of the judiciary and suppressing laws that facilitate systemic human rights breaches and war crimes.[37] It is also debated whether system criminality should lead to a regime change as a guarantee of non-repetition, altering the constitutional structure of the responsible State.[38] In light of this, it is arguable that system criminality entails specific guarantees of non-repetition.[39]

Restitution and compensation seem to have mainly a reparatory function.[40] However, a different approach is taken, for instance, with respect to reparation in the case of aggression.[41] Notably, reparation would have a punitive function when imposed by third States, as in the case of the decisions taken by the Compensation Commission established by the UN Security Council after the war in Kuwait in the 1990s.[42]

Restitution and compensation also imply a satisfactory nature, particularly when material damage involves moral and political damage.[43] A Mixed Claim

33 Karl Zemanek, 'The Legal Foundations of the International System' (1997) 266 *RCADI* 268; Christian Tomuschat, 'Reparation in Cases of Genocide' (2007) 5(4) *JICJ* 911; Weiner, 'Working the System' (2010) 358–359; Olivier Corten, 'The Obligation of Cessation', in Crawford, Pellet, Olleson and Parlett, *The Law* (2010) 545 and 548. See also Crawford, *State Responsibility* (2013) 461 ff.

34 Lauterpacht, 'Règles générales' (1937) 352; Cançado Trindade, 'Complementarity' (2005) 266; Gattini, 'A Historical Perspective' (2009) 110.

35 Sandrine Barbier, 'Assurances and Guarantees of Non-Repetition', in Crawford, Pellet, Olleson and Parlett, *The Law* (2010) 555–556.

36 Wolf, 'Individual Responsibility' (2016) 46.

37 Nollkaemper, 'Systemic Effects' (2010) 341–342.

38 Zimmermann and Teichmann, 'State Responsibility' (2009) 301–302.

39 Ibid 301.

40 Gilbert, 'The Criminal Responsibility' (1990) 352; Christine Gray, 'The Different Forms of Reparation: Restitution', in Crawford, Pellet, Olleson and Parlett, *The Law* (2010) 589; John Barker, 'The Different Forms of Reparation: Compensation', ibid, 599.

41 Gerald Fitzmaurce, 'The Juridical Clauses of the Peace Treaties' (1948) 73(2) *RCADI* 325 ff.

42 Vera Gowlland-Debbas, 'Security Council Enforcement Action and Issues of State Responsibility' (1994) 43(1) *ICLQ* 82–83; Gattini, 'A Historical Perspective' (2009) 118–119.

43 Lauterpacht, 'Règles générales' (1937) 355–356; Eustathiadès, 'Les sujets' (1953) 434–436; Jørgensen, *The Responsibility* (2000) 200; Crawford, *State Responsibility* (2013) 523 ff.

Commission awarded monetary compensation for moral damages in the *Lusitania* case, where a German U-boat sunk an ocean liner owned by the Cunard Steamship Company in a war zone off the coast of Ireland in 1915, causing the death of 128 US nationals and other victims of various nationalities.[44] The satisfactory value of monetary compensation has been particularly underscored with respect to genocide.[45] In some circumstances, notably in the case of intra-State genocide, restitution and compensation would bind a State vis-à-vis its own population and thus have mainly an internal nature.[46] Concerning the *Bosnian Genocide* case,[47] it is argued that the ICJ could have awarded reparation as a form of restorative justice for collective responsibility by imposing specific measures such as the financing of psychotherapy treatment.[48]

The nature of satisfaction is certainly quite ambivalent.[49] Whilst it is classified as a form of reparation under the 2001 DASR, satisfaction may easily entail punitive implications.[50] In addition to monetary compensation,[51] satisfaction implies punitive consequences such as the acknowledgment of a wrongful act by State officials or international jurisdictions, apologies, expression of regret by ranking officials and punishment of responsible individuals.[52] Some scholars consider individual punishment a compulsory measure in the case of State aggravated responsibility,[53] which would allow the crossing of the bridge between individual and State responsibility.[54]

Since the 2001 DASR do not embed any distinctions as concerns sanctions, punitive sanctions may apply to non-criminal responsibility. This is consistent with the suppression of the notion of a 'State crime'. The uniform regime of sanctions thus further excludes State criminal responsibility. A case-by-case assessment is therefore necessary to establish whether sanctions have more a punitive, pre-emptive and re-socialising nature, rather than a reparatory character. Logically, in the case of offences that entail State aggravated responsibility, notably aggression, genocide, core war crimes, core crimes against humanity and prospectively terrorism, it is possible that sanctions, entailing, for instance, particularly extensive compensation, are more satisfactory and

44 *Lusitania (US v Germany)*, Mixed Claims Commission, Award of 1 November 1923 (1923) VII *RIAA* 36–37. See also Scobbie, 'Assumptions' (2009) 283–284; Crawford, *State Responsibility* (2013) 517; Kolb, *The International Law* (2017) 166–167.

45 Tomuschat, 'Reparation' (2007) 909.

46 Webb, 'Binocular Vision' (2012) 135.

47 See s 3.2.4.1.

48 Gattini, 'A Historical Perspective' (2009) 124–125.

49 Crawford, *State Responsibility* (2013) 527 ff.

50 Gilbert, 'The Criminal Responsibility' (1990) 353–354; Cançado Trindade, 'Complementarity' (2005) 266; Eric Wyler and Alain Papaux, 'The Different Forms of Reparation: Satisfaction', in Crawford, Pellet, Olleson and Parlett, *The Law* (2010) 623.

51 Crawford, *State Responsibility* (2013) 528.

52 Trapp, *State Responsibility* (2011) 245–246; Webb, 'Binocular Vision' (2012) 136.

53 Zimmermann and Teichmann, 'State Responsibility' (2009) 302–306.

54 Nollkaemper, 'Systemic Effects' (2010) 331–332.

pre-emptive than reparatory. For example, sanctions imposed on the Axis forces at the end of World War II as a consequence of aggression under the Paris Peace Treaties included obligations ranging from heavy compensation to military restrictions, which had a particularly relevant punitive and pre-emptive nature.[55] In *Armed Activities on the Territory of the Congo*, involving questions of aggression and gross human rights violations, satisfaction and punishment were crucial to determining reparation, also in the light of reparation proceedings in relation to convictions in the cases of *Lubanga Dyilo* and *Katanga* before the ICC.[56]

Furthermore, 2001 DASR 59 provides the application of sanctions outlined in UN Charter Article 39 in the case of a threat or breach to the peace or act of aggression. The terminology of UN Charter Article 39 is not crystal clear, since it refers to the power of the UN Security Council to 'make recommendations' or to 'decide what measures shall be taken in accordance with Articles 41 and 42'. Similarly, UN Charter Articles 41 and 42 provide that the Security Council 'may decide what measures [...] are to be employed to give effect to its decisions'. This language seems to refer to institutionalised countermeasures, without focusing on the content of the decisions and recommendations of the Council. However, in light of such broad terminology it should be assumed that the Security Council has an extensive power to impose sanctions via 'decisions', including cessation, assurances of non-repetition and reparation.

DASR 59 definitely outlines a regime of open-ended aggravated sanctions for State aggravated responsibility, since Articles 39–42 of the UN Charter certainly encompass aggression, genocide, core war crimes, core crimes against humanity and terrorism.[57] Moreover, persistent violations of the principles embedded in the Charter may entail the expulsion of a Member State from the UN under Article 6. This measure, which has mainly a punitive character, has nevertheless been criticised as allowing a State to avoid the obligations and procedures embedded in the Charter, particularly as concerns aggravated offences.[58] More generally, the nature of UN sanctions as punitive rather than reparatory is also debatable.[59]

55 See also s 1.2.1.2.

56 *Armed Activities on the Territory of the Congo (Democratic Republic of the Congo v Uganda)* [2005] ICJ Rep 190, para 26, 257, para 259; *Lubanga Dyilo*, ICC-01/04-01/06, Appeals Chamber, Judgment of 3 March 2015, 23 ff, paras 57 ff; *Katanga*, ICC-01/04-01/07, Trial Chamber, Order for Reparations Pursuant to Article 75 of the Statute, 24 March 2017, 32 ff, paras 64 ff. See also Carla Ferstman, 'The International Court of Justice and the Question of Reparations' (2015), http://asiapacific.anu.edu.au/regarding-rights/2015/07/17/the-international-court-of-justice-and-the-question-of-reparations.

57 White, 'Responses' (2009) 315–316.

58 ILC, Summary Records (1976) 85, para 5; Dupuy, 'Observations' (1980) 477.

59 See ILC, Summary Records (1976) 85, para 5. For a scholarly viewpoint, see Eustathiadès, 'Les sujets' (1953) 441–442 and 444–449; Jeremy Matam Farrall, *United Nations Sanctions and the Rule of Law* (CUP, 2007) 106 ff; Proulx, *Institutionalizing* (2016) 211. Pierre-Marie Dupuy considers that the UN security system establishes a clear divide between interstate 'civil'

From the viewpoint of the scope of secondary obligations, a difference exists between State aggravated and ordinary responsibility. Indeed, along the lines of the universal structure of State aggravated breaches, cessation, non-repetition and reparation should also have a general scope. This is specified in 2001 DASR 33:

> Article 33
> Scope of international obligations set out in this Part [Sanctions]
> 1. The obligations of the responsible State set out in this Part may be owed to another State, to several States, or to the *international community as a whole*, depending in particular on the character and content of the international obligation and on the circumstances of the breach.
> 2. This Part is without prejudice to any right, arising from the international responsibility of a State, which may accrue directly to any person or entity other than a State.[60]

Article 33(1) envisages the possibility of a sanction being a non-severable *erga omnes* obligation, depending on the nature and content of the primary obligation breached, as well as the circumstances of the breach, thus particularly including serious violations of *jus cogens*. This is also implicit in 2001 DASR 54, allowing countermeasures by a State other than the injured one(s).[61] Article 33(2) envisages the possibility of a non-severable *erga omnes* obligation between a State and non-State entities. Therefore, whilst sanctions for ordinary wrongful acts of States are mostly bilateral, sanctions for serious breaches of peremptory norms should also have a peremptory nature.[62]

3.1.1.3 Institutionalised and non-institutionalised universal enforcement: 2001 DASR 41(1), 54 and 59

If a responsible State does not comply with a sanction imposed by means of an agreed procedure or unilateral invocation of responsibility, that sanction can be enforced. According to 2001 DASR 49(1), countermeasures, which were once defined as 'reprisals',[63] aim to implement sanctions. Therefore, countermeasures are actions taken to enforce secondary obligations, when these are breached, which entails their limited application in time, reversibility and proportionality.[64]

---

responsibility, which is mostly concerned with restitution and compensation, and State responsibility vis-à-vis the international community as a whole, which protects the most important international interests and particularly aims to prevent the use of armed force (Pierre-Marie Dupuy, 'Observations' (1980) 473).

60 Emphasis added.

61 See s 3.1.1.3.

62 Cançado Trindade, 'Complementarity' (2005) 257; Orakhelashvili, *Peremptory Norms* (2006) 242; Crawford, *State Responsibility* (2013) 106.

63 Ago, 'Le délit' (1939) 524; Hans Kelsen, *Principles of International Law* (Holt, Rinehart and Winston, 2nd edn, 1966) 20; Kolb, *The International Law* (2017) 174.

64 ILC, Report (2001) 116 ff.

Action in countermeasure is necessarily, or possibly, in breach of an international obligation, but it is justified as a secondary measure under 2001 DASR 49(2). This establishes a difference with respect to retaliation.[65] In fact, the breach of a primary obligation and of an ensuing substitute obligation 'justifies' the taking of countermeasures and is thus a 'circumstance precluding wrongfulness' under 2001 DASR 22.

In light of their function as an instrument for compelling a responsible State to comply with a breached sanction, countermeasures fundamentally have a mixed nature.[66] Along the lines of the debate on sanctions, whilst some scholars assume that countermeasures mostly have a reparatory function, others contend that they mostly have a punitive character.[67] A case-by-case assessment is therefore required.

Consistently with the scope of the sanction for a serious breach of a peremptory norm as a non-severable *erga omnes* obligation under Article 33, 2001 DASR 54 establishes the right of any States other than the injured one to take 'lawful measures' against the responsible State. Such measures aim to 'ensure cessation of the breach and reparation in the interest of the injured State or of the beneficiaries of the obligation breached.' Article 54 is equivocal as concerns the possibility of 'general', or 'collective', countermeasures.[68] In fact, the mention of 'lawful measures', instead of 'countermeasures', might be interpreted as a reference to measures of 'retaliation', which are hostile but lawful.[69] According to this interpretation, non-injured States would not be allowed to adopt countermeasures.

Alternatively, the expression 'lawful measures' in Article 54 may be interpreted as a reference to both 'retaliation' and 'countermeasures', since the latter are primarily unlawful but secondarily lawful. This is the prevailing interpretation,[70] which is supported by the reference to self-defence as a 'lawful measure' in 2001 DASR 21. According to this approach, general countermeasures are permitted in the case of a violation of a non-divisible *erga omnes* obligation.[71] For instance, when Argentina unlawfully took control over part of the Falkland Islands (*Las Malvinas*) in April 1982, the United Kingdom, Australia, Canada, New Zealand and EC Member States adopted trade sanctions, which included a

65 Kolb, *The International Law* (2017) 175.

66 Ollivier, 'International Criminal Responsibility' (2010) 707–708.

67 See Eustathiadès, 'Les sujets' (1953) 442; André De Hoog, *Obligations* Erga Omnes *and International Crimes* (Kluwer, 1996) 216–217; Jørgensen, 'The Concept' (2015) 201; Dawidowicz, *Third-Party Countermeasures* (2017) 292–297.

68 Dawidowicz, *Third-Party Countermeasures* (2017) 108; Costelloe, *Legal Consequences* (2017) 216.

69 Sicilianos, 'The Classification' (2002) 1143; Martin Dawidowicz, *Third-Party Countermeasures* (2017) 27.

70 ILC, Report (2001) 138–139, paras 3–4; Sicilianos, 'Countermeasures' (2010) 1145.

71 Giorgio Gaja, First Report to the Institute of International Law on Obligations and Rights *Erga Omnes* in International Law (2005) 71(1) *YBIIL* 128 and 147; Cassese, 'The Character' (2010) 418–419.

temporary prohibition on all imports of Argentine products. These were secondary lawful countermeasures, but primarily in breach of Article XI of the General Agreement on Tariffs and Trade.[72]

In the specific case of an 'armed attack', 2001 DASR 21 allows the use of necessary and proportionate armed force in individual or collective self-defence. Although this provision refers to 'lawful measures', separately from the justification of 'countermeasures' under Article 22, self-defence should be considered a countermeasure, since it is secondarily lawful action otherwise prohibited under primary international norms. In any case, as we have seen,[73] Article 21 reflects international customary practice established since the *Caroline* case and codified in Article 51 of the UN Charter. Notably, collective self-defence under DASR 21 entails resort to armed force not only by the attacked State, but also by third (non-injured) States. In light of the observation that the prohibition on the use of force is a peremptory norm,[74] collective self-defence under DASR 21 is *lex specialis*, spelling out the normative pattern established for State aggravated responsibility under 2001 DASR 40, 41, 48 and 54.

As we have seen, 2001 DASR 41 provides 'particular' consequences for breaches of peremptory norms.[75] Article 41 is grounded in 1996 DASR 53.[76] Consistently with VCLT Article 71, 2001 DASR 41 establishes two specific consequences for breaches of *jus cogens*. First, States must cooperate to bring to an end any serious breach of a peremptory norm through lawful means (DASR 41(1)).[77] Second, States must not recognise a situation created by a serious breach of a peremptory norm as lawful, nor render aid or assistance in maintaining that situation (DASR 41(2)). Whilst cooperative action under DASR 41(1) marks a significant difference with respect to the ordinary regime of State responsibility, consequences under DASR 41(2) have been criticised, to the extent that all wrongful acts should entail non-recognition and the obligation for States not to assist in maintaining an unlawful situation.[78]

The obligation to cooperate and end breaches of peremptory norms under 2001 DASR 41(1) allows, or even compels ('shall'),[79] reading Article 54, that is, universal enforcement, in a cooperative sense, meaningfully establishing collective enforcement.[80] Despite hesitation, Crawford included Article 41(1)

72 ILC, Report (2001) 138.
73 See s 2.3.1.3.
74 See s 2.1.1.5.
75 See s 1.2.3.5.
76 Crawford, Third Report (2000) 108, para 412; ILC, Report (2001) 114–116. See also s 3.1.1.6.
77 Scobbie, 'Assumptions' (2009) 284.
78 ILC, Report (1995) 54, para 302; Crawford, Third Report (2000) 107, para 410; Costelloe, *Legal Consequences* (2017) 222. But see Zimmermann and Teichmann, 'State Responsibility' (2009) 307–310.
79 Giorgio Gaja, 'Do States Have a Duty to Ensure Compliance with Obligations *Erga Omnes* by Other States?', in Ragazzi, *International Responsibility* (2005) 34.
80 ILC, Report (2001) 113–116 and 137–139. See also Nina Jørgensen, 'The Obligation of Cooperation', in Crawford, Pellet, Olleson and Parlett, *The Law* (2010) 697.

in the final version of the DASR, along the lines of the proposals for 2000 DASR 40-bis(2), 51, 50A and 50B.[81] Actually, it is sensible to assume that Article 41(1) is *lex specialis* with respect to Article 54, and thus compels the adoption of general countermeasures, which is only a right under Article 54. In fact, mentioning that 'States shall cooperate to bring to an end through lawful means' the breach of a peremptory norm should be interpreted as a reference to both retaliation and countermeasures, consistently with Article 54. In this respect, the ILC acknowledged that State aggravated responsibility is a matter of progressive international law development and therefore additional consequences could further evolve.[82]

The obligation not to recognise the lawfulness of a situation created by the breach of a peremptory norm under 2001 DASR 41(2) is in line with instruments such as Article 5(3) of UN General Assembly Resolution 3314 (XXIX) on the Definition of Aggression, providing that territorial acquisition resulting from the threat or use of force cannot be recognised as lawful.[83] In practice, for example, international organisations and States clearly declared the unlawfulness of the 1990 annexation of Iraq by Kuwait.[84]

The obligation not to cooperate in maintaining the effects of the breach of a peremptory norm also codifies international practice. For instance, following the decision of Israel to support Israeli settlements in Arab territories occupied since 1967, by means of Resolution 465/1980 the UN Security Council called upon all States 'not to provide Israel with any assistance to be used specifically in connexion with the occupied territories'.[85]

Besides these particular implications, 2001 DASR 59 envisages specific consequences under the UN Charter, notably institutionalised collective action under the guidance of the Security Council based on Chapter VII, in the case of a threat to or breach of the peace. In particular, enforcement measures can go as far as to allow the use of armed force under UN Charter Article 42, which marks a critical difference with respect to enforcement measures for State ordinary responsibility. In this respect, it has been noted that, since the 2001 DASR are subordinated to the UN Charter, priority given to collective enforcement under Chapter VII of the UN Charter by virtue of both DASR 59 and UN Charter Article 103 overrides universal enforcement procedures for State aggravated

81 Crawford, Third Report (2000) 39, para 119, 108–109, para 413; ILC, Report (2000) 59–62, paras 358 and 364–383.

82 Crawford, Third Report (2000) 108, para 411; ILC, Report (2001) 114, para 3. See also Cassese, 'The Character' (2010) 419, underscoring the progressive nature of 2001 DASR 41(1) with respect to international practice.

83 Arangio-Ruiz, Fifth Report, Add.3 (1993) 24, para 134.

84 Martin Dawidowicz, 'The Obligation of Non-Recognition of an Unlawful Situation', in Crawford, Pellet, Olleson and Parlett, *The Law* (2010) 682.

85 Territories Occupied by Israel, S/RES/465, 1 March 1980, para 7. See Arangio-Ruiz, Fifth Report, Add.3 (1993) 25–26, paras 136–140; Nina Jørgensen, 'The Obligation of Non-Assistance to the Responsible State', in Crawford, Pellet, Olleson and Parlett, *The Law* (2010) 690 ff.

offences under 2001 DASR 54 (and 41(1) and 48).[86] However, it is possible to read procedures under the UN Charter as part of the general remedies envisaged under 2001 DASR 41(1), 48 and 54.[87]

In practice, combined enforcement by States under general international law and the UN Charter took place when, on 2 August 1990, Iraqi troops invaded and occupied Kuwait. Following the Iraqi announcement of a permanent merger with Kuwait, the UN Security Council declared the annexation null and void.[88] The US and other States adopted trade embargoes and froze Iraqi assets with the consent of the Government of Kuwait.[89] Further collective action was undertaken under the institutional guidance of the UN Security Council, leading to the use of force in order to free the occupied territory of Kuwait.[90]

More recently, a significant example of universal enforcement is the reaction to the humanitarian crisis that unfolded in Libya in 2011 under the regime of Muammar Gaddafi. In this case, States such as Switzerland and the US first adopted countermeasures such as the freezing of assets of Colonel Gaddafi and the Central Bank of Libya in response to serious breaches of human rights.[91] Subsequently, States undertook collective action, including the use of force, under the guidance of the UN Security Council.[92]

States have also undertaken collective enforcement against Russia, including measures such as investment limitations and embargoes, as a reaction to the occupation of Ukraine that took place in 2014.[93]

3.1.1.4 Rejecting compulsory jurisdiction

The 1996 DASR did not embed a specific provision on invocation of responsibility, but rather defined the notion of an 'injured State' and allowed invocation of responsibility under customary international law. According to 1996

86 Arangio-Ruiz, 'The "Federal Analogy"' (1997) 25, note 38; White, 'Responses' (2009) 316; Crawford, *State Responsibility* (2013) 107–108. According to Riphagen, '[a]ctually, in all the cases mentioned by way of (possible) examples of international crime in article 19, paragraph 3, of part 1 of the draft, the United Nations system has been involved in some way or another' (Willem Riphagen, Third Report on the Content, Forms and Degrees of International Responsibility (Part 2 of the Draft Articles), UN Doc A/CN.4/354 and Add.1 and 2 (1982) 2(1) *YBILC* 49, para 14). See also Arangio-Ruiz, Fifth Report, Add.2 (1993) 30 ff, paras 51 ff; ILC, Report (1995) 50, para 272.

87 Crawford, *State Responsibility* (2013) 386.

88 S/RES/660; Security Council, Iraq-Kuwait, UN Doc S/RES/662, 9 August 1990.

89 See US Secretary of State, *Note Verbale* to the UN Secretary-General, UN Doc S/21525, 15 August 1990, 1–2.

90 See Dawidowicz, *Third-Party Countermeasures* (2017) 159–162.

91 See President Obama's Executive Order 13566: Libya, 25 February 2011.

92 Security Council, Libya, UN Doc S/RES/1973, 17 March 2011. See Dawidowicz, *Third-Party Countermeasures* (2017) 216–220.

93 See, in particular, EU Council, Decision 2014/512/CFSP of 31 July 2014 concerning Restrictive Measures in View of Russia's Actions Destabilising the Situation in Ukraine (2014) OJ L 229 14–15. See also Dawidowicz, *Third-Party Countermeasures* (2017) 231–238.

DASR 40(3), all States of the international community could invoke responsibility for a State crime:

> Article 40
> Meaning of injured State
> 1. For the purposes of the present articles, 'injured State' means any State a right of which is infringed by the act of another State, if that act constitutes, in accordance with Part One, an internationally wrongful act of that State.
> 2. In particular, 'injured State' means:
>   [...]
>   (e) if the right infringed by the act of a State arises from a multilateral treaty or from a rule of customary international law, any other State party to the multilateral treaty or bound by the relevant rule of customary international law, if it is established that:
>   (i) the right has been created or is established in its favour;
>   (ii) the infringement of the right by the act of a State necessarily affects the enjoyment of the rights or the performance of the obligations of the other States parties to the multilateral treaty or bound by the rule of customary international law; or
>   (iii) the right has been created or is established for the protection of human rights and fundamental freedoms;
>   (f) if the right infringed by the act of a State arises from a multilateral treaty, any other State party to the multilateral treaty, if it is established that the right has been expressly stipulated in that treaty for the protection of the collective interests of the States parties thereto.
> 3. In addition, 'injured State' means, if the internationally wrongful act constitutes an *international crime*, *all other States*.[94]

This rule was based on a different assumption compared to the 2001 DASR, notably Article 48. Indeed, 1996 DASR 40 posited no distinction between (legally) injured and non-injured States. Thus, either a State was injured by an internationally wrongful act, in which case it was allowed to invoke responsibility, or not, with a consequent preclusion of the faculty of invoking responsibility.

Article 40(2)(e) of the 1996 DASR established that the breach of a non-severable obligation *erga omnes contractantes* affected all State parties to a treaty, whilst the breach of a non-severable *erga omnes* obligation affected all States of the international community, allowing general invocation of responsibility. Article 40(3) provided that a crime would affect all States of the international community, thus implying the breach of a non-severable *erga omnes* obligation, allowing general invocation of responsibility.[95] In this respect, the wording of

94 Emphasis added.
95 Pellet, 'Can a State' (1999) 432.

1996 DASR 53(d), referring to State cooperation '*in the application of measures* designed to eliminate the consequences of the crime' was more restrictive than 2001 DASR 41(1), generally referring to cooperation 'to *bring to an end* through lawful means' serious breaches of peremptory norms.[96] Therefore, it would have been more difficult to rely on 1996 DASR 53(d) to compel State coordination in invoking responsibility.

It has been observed that, whilst invocation of responsibility in the 1996 DASR was general, it remained decentralised.[97] According to some scholars, this would not have allowed the establishment of an accomplished system of State criminal responsibility.[98] The 1996 DASR were indeed considered unaccomplished as concerns the procedural implications of the notion of a 'State crime'. In particular, the absence of a central authority mandated to adjudicate upon State criminal responsibility and the lack of an organised police force would have prevented the establishment of an international criminal procedure for assessing State responsibility.[99] Institutional adjudication for State criminal responsibility was considered a *conditio sine qua non* for the establishment of substantive criminal responsibility.[100] Indeed, the nature of dispute settlement would have had no specific characteristics of vertical criminal procedures. Such features could have only been introduced by establishing compulsory jurisdiction.[101]

During preparatory work, the Sixth Committee of the UN General Assembly developed innovative procedural solutions for State crimes.[102] Thus, the ILC envisaged, as a minimum form of institutional adjudication, an *ex ante* consent to collective countermeasures by the ICJ and an *ex post* control by the same Court.[103] Article 4 of the Third Part of the DASR drafted by Willem Riphagen was particularly advanced in the matter of compulsory jurisdiction. Indeed, Article 4(a) of his Project established the possibility for a State of unilaterally resorting to the ICJ in the case of a breach of a peremptory norm. Article 4(b) allowed a State to bring the breach of a peremptory norm to the attention of the UN Secretary General, who could then submit it to a Conciliation Commission. Article 4(c) allowed any State to unilaterally resort to the ICJ in the case of a State crime.[104] Alternatively, the ILC envisaged arbitration for State crimes,[105]

96 Emphasis added.
97 Pellet, 'Remarques' (1996) 25–26.
98 Marek, 'Criminalizing'(1978–79) 481.
99 Gilbert, 'The Criminal Responsibility' (1990) 351.
100 Acosta Estévez, 'Normas' (1995) 21; Crawford, 'On Re-Reading' (1998) 296.
101 Crawford, First Report (1998) 9, para 43, 22, para 86. See also Spinedi, 'La responsabilité' (2000) 101.
102 Sixth Committee, Report (1978) 55, para 152; Id, Topical Summary, Add.1 (1996) 22 ff, paras 78 ff.
103 ILC, Report (1995) 57, paras 314–316.
104 Riphagen, Sixth Report (1985) 18, paras 32–33; Id, Seventh Report (1986) 4–5. See also Arangio-Ruiz, Fifth Report, Add.3 (1993) 15, para 107; Arangio-Ruiz, Seventh Report (1995) 20, para 89, 24, para 109.
105 ILC, Report (1995) 57, para 314.

or the competence of the UN General Assembly, based upon a prior compulsory advisory opinion by the ICJ or a subsequent faculty of applying to the Court.[106] A proposal was also put forward to establish the competence of an independent Commission of Jurists nominated by the General Assembly or the Security Council for investigating State crimes.[107] The commentary to the 1996 DASR envisaged the possibility of introducing a mechanism whereby a State could ask the Conciliation Commission established under DASR 57 to assess the commission of a State crime. In the case of a positive assessment, the responsible State or the injured State could resort unilaterally to arbitration.[108]

Some scholars conceived of a system whereby a compulsory assessment by a Committee of Jurists would have preceded the competence of the UN Security Council to decide upon State crimes.[109] Others thought about the establishment of an *ad hoc* criminal court having jurisdiction over State crimes,[110] or envisaged the criminal competence of the ICJ.[111] According to Arangio-Ruiz, this raised the question of excluding the influence of the Security Council over the Court.[112] During preparatory work, the ILC also envisaged the possibility of conferring jurisdiction on State crimes to the ICC.[113] This solution, nonetheless, would have required a significant amendment of the UN Charter. In this respect, Vespasian Pella underscored that establishing State criminal responsibility without an appropriate system of adjudication is tantamount to making the implementation of such liability dependent upon unstable military power.[114]

Arangio-Ruiz envisaged a system to allow any State to unilaterally resort to the ICJ.[115] Initially, Arangio-Ruiz thought about a system whereby a Public Prosecutor would have been competent to refer an international crime to the ICJ.[116] Along these lines, Article 17(1) included in the Second Part of the DASR

106 Ibid.
107 Ibid 56, para 312.
108 ILC, Report (1996) 71, para 12:

> [Proposals] envisaging a two-step procedural mechanism for determining disputes as to whether a crime has been committed are based on the idea that such disputes are too important to be left to the general procedures of part three […] disputes to which the application of article 19 might give rise should be submitted to an impartial third party with decision-making power.

For a scholarly viewpoint, see Bowett, 'Crimes' (1998) 168 ff.
109 Bowett, 'Crimes' (1998) 170.
110 ILC, Report (1995) 57, para 314.
111 Dupuy, 'Observations' (1980) 485; Gilbert, 'The Criminal Responsibility' (1990) 351; Abi-Saab, 'The Uses' (1999) 343. See also ILC, Summary Records (1976) 77–78, para 39.
112 Arangio-Ruz, Seventh Report (1995) 20, para 88, 23, paras 101–102.
113 ILC, Report (1995) 57, para 314.
114 Pella, 'La codification' (1952) 415.
115 On compulsory jurisdiction as the key element for the implementation of State aggravated offences, see also Franz Przetacznik, 'The Compulsory Jurisdiction of the International Court of Justice as a Prerequisite for Peace' (1990) 68(1) *RDISPD* 61 and 65.
116 Arangio-Ruiz, Fifth Report, Add.3 (1993) 16, para 108; Id, Seventh Report (1995) 34, para 89; ILC, Report (1995) 56, para 310.

proposed by Arangio-Ruiz subjected the collective action of States in countermeasure to a declaration on the existence of a crime by the ICJ.[117] More specifically, Arangio-Ruiz proposed the establishment of a mechanism allowing States to bring an alleged State crime to attention of the UN Security Council or the General Assembly. The Council or Assembly could adopt a resolution by a qualified majority, authorising a State to submit the case to the ICJ in order to obtain a consultative opinion or a judgment in a contentious procedure open to the intervention of all States. The ICJ would have then been vested with the power to impose sanctions upon the responsible State under Article 16, notably (disproportionate) cessation and reparation, and to allow States to adopt general countermeasures under Articles 16–18.[118] Arangio-Ruiz also suggested that countermeasures could go as far as to entail the use of armed force,[119] with a preference for centralised enforcement, which facilitates arms control,[120] rather than a decentralised one.[121]

The adjudication system outlined by Arangio-Ruiz was the natural consequence of the non-severable *erga omnes* nature of the obligations affected by an international crime committed by a State.[122] This system elaborated on the proposals submitted in 1920 by the Advisory Committee of Jurists to the League of Nations and certain mechanisms established by the 1928 ICLA Draft Statute for an ICC.[123] Pierre-Marie Dupuy later described such a system as an 'international criminal procedure'.[124] These proceedings would have entailed a 'political' assessment in the first phase of the adjudication process and a judicial assessment in the second phase.[125] Within the context of such a procedure, all States were allowed to take pre-emptive measures under Article 17(2).[126]

Arangio-Ruiz also proposed that the UN Security Council or Assembly appoint a Prosecution body to investigate State crimes subject to the jurisdiction of the ICJ.[127] However, Article 20 of the Project provided that such a system would

117 Arangio-Ruiz, Seventh Report, Add.1 (1995) 2, para 139.

118 Id, Fifth Report, Add.3 (1993) 18 ff, paras 117 ff; Id, Seventh Report (1995) 24, paras 108–112.

119 Id, Fifth Report, Add.3 (1993) 8–9, paras 84–86, also raising the question of the use of armed force to obtain sufficient assurances of non-repetition.

120 Kelsen, *Peace* (1973) 19 and 51.

121 Arangio-Ruiz, Fifth Report, Add.3 (1993) 10 ff, paras 89 ff. See also Dawidowicz, *Third-Party Countermeasures* (2017) 82.

122 Arangio-Ruiz, Seventh Report (1995) 11–12, para 35; Arangio-Ruiz, Eighth Report (1996) 4, paras 18–19.

123 See ss 1.1.2.2–1.1.2.4.

124 Dupuy, 'L'unité' (2002) 369.

125 Arangio-Ruiz, Seventh Report (1995) 22 ff, paras 100 ff; ILC, Report (1995) 54–56, paras 304–311; Arangio-Ruiz, Eighth Report (1996) 5 ff, paras 27 ff. See also Arangio-Ruiz, 'The "Federal Analogy"' (1997) 24.

126 Arangio-Ruiz, Seventh Report (1995) 13, para 42, 29, para 139; ILC, Report (1995) 53, para 299; Arangio-Ruiz, Eighth Report (1996) 4, para 20. See also Arangio-Ruiz, Fifth Report, Add.3 (1993) 19–20, paras 119–121; ILC, Report (1995) 56, para 309; Bowett, 'Crimes' (1998) 169.

127 ILC, Report (1995) 56–57, para 313.

not have affected action undertaken by the Security Council under Chapter VII of the UN Charter.[128] Alternatively, the Rapporteur thought about imposing a compulsory advisory opinion by the ICJ for the UN Security Council or General Assembly making decisions on State crimes, or allowing appeals against a decision of the UN Security Council on such offences.[129] This would have nevertheless raised tension between the Council, as a political organ, and the ICJ, as a judicial body. Within this framework, Arangio-Ruiz and the ILC conceived of a reform of the Security Council that could make it more democratic and representative.[130]

Although the ILC eventually rejected such 'vertical' proposals, some critical observations are necessary. First, universal reaction to State crimes under general international law is a meaningful exception to the ordinary regime of State responsibility. Since international law is by nature horizontal, universal reaction is the only viable difference.[131] In fact, Cançado Trindade noted that State criminal responsibility should not necessarily be identical to domestic criminal liability.[132] After all, individual criminal liability is different in international law and domestic law, owing to the specific features of the international legal system.[133]

Second, 1996 DASR 58(2) provided the possibility for a State affected by countermeasures to submit unilaterally a dispute to an arbitral tribunal. This mechanism thus established for State crimes the possibility of unilaterally resorting to an international jurisdiction. Some scholars assume that such a revolutionary mechanism would have ultimately led to a possible recourse by the injured State to the ICJ against the arbitral decision triggered by the offender.[134] However, it would have been unlikely that a responsible State would initially bring its own responsibility to the attention of an international jurisdiction, unless it believed it was not responsible.[135]

Third, the DASR ultimately included a meaningful 'vertical' exception under Article 39, which referred to the provisions of the UN Charter relevant to the maintenance of international peace and security. This is a critical provision. Indeed, in addition to negotiation, enquiry, mediation, conciliation, arbitration and judicial settlement under Chapter VI of the Charter, aggression, genocide,

128 Arangio-Ruiz, Seventh Report (1995) 30.

129 Arangio-Ruiz, Seventh Report (1995) 93, para 103. See also Giorgio Gaja, 'Réflexions sur le rôle du Conseil de sécurité dans le nouvel ordre mondial. À propos des rapports entre maintien de la paix et crimes internationaux des États' (1993) 97(2) *RGDIP* 315.

130 Arangio-Ruiz, Fifth Report, Add.3 (1995) 16 ff, paras 110 ff; ILC, Report (1996) 306–307, paras 55–56.

131 ILC, Summary Records (1976) 90, para 30; Dupuy, 'Observations' (1980) 486; Arangio-Ruiz, 'Fine prematura' (1998) 125. See also Sreenivasa Rao, 'International Crimes' (2005) 78–79.

132 Cançado Trindade, 'Complementarity' (2005) 264.

133 See, for instance, Douglas Guilfoyle, *International Criminal Law* (OUP, 2018) 3. See also s 3.1.2.

134 Crawford, Fourth Report (2001) 4–5, para 10.

135 Bowett, 'Crimes' (1998) 169.

core war crimes, core crimes against humanity and terrorism could trigger centralised UN action, particularly via the Security Council, under Chapter VII of the Charter. In fact, the procedures under Chapter VII of the UN Charter have been interpreted as a punitive reaction to State criminal responsibility under 1996 DASR 19.[136]

Of course, unlike general international law, 'vertical' procedures can be implemented within the context of 'particular' international organisations, which can be (quasi-)universal, as in the case of the UN. Thus, whilst they eventually put forward no new solutions to establish compulsory jurisdiction over State crimes, the 1996 DASR codified existing centralised UN practice.

3.1.1.5 Punitive erga omnes *sanctions? 1996 DASR 41–46 and 52*

The distinction between State crimes and delicts embedded in the First Part of the 1996 DASR entailed complementary consequences in terms of sanctions in the Second Part of the Project.[137] Articles 41–46 envisaged sanctions common to all offences, whilst Article 52 envisaged specific sanctions for international crimes.[138] Articles 41–46 included cessation of wrongful conduct, restitution, compensation, satisfaction and assurances of non-repetition. Within such a context, some scholars underscored the criminal nature of the assurances of non-repetition.[139] Article 45(2)(d) established a significant link between individual and State criminal responsibility, providing that satisfaction would include 'in cases where the internationally wrongful act arose from the serious misconduct of officials or from criminal conduct of officials or private parties, disciplinary action against, or punishment of, those responsible.' In this case, individual criminal punishment was also a form of State sanction.[140]

136 ILC, Summary Records (1976) 69, para 26, 70 ff, paras 30 ff; Dupuy, 'Observations' (1980) 472. See also Paula Escarameia, 'The ICC and the Security Council on Aggression: Overlapping Competencies?', in Politi and Nesi, *The International Criminal Court* (2004) 139.

137 According to Roberto Ago, 'a discernible tendency to distinguish between international crimes and international delicts [...] should lead to the establishment of more severe regimes of responsibility for the former and, ultimately, to a system for the application of sanctions' (ILC, Summary Records (1976) 91, para 34). See also Gaetano Arangio-Ruiz, Preliminary Report on State Responsibility, UN Doc A/CN.4./416 and Add.1 (1988) 9, para 15; Arangio-Ruiz, Fifth Report, Add.2 (1993) 5–6, paras 8–9.

138 Arangio-Ruiz, Seventh Report (1995) 8, paras 9–11.

139 Alain Pellet, '"Vive le crime"! Remarques sur les degrés de l'illicite en droit international', in Christian Tomuschat (ed), *International Law on the Eve of the 21st Century – Le droit international à l'aube du XXI siècle)* (UN, 1997) 309.

140 Arangio-Ruiz, Fifth Report, Add.3 (1993) 21, para 126. See also Arangio-Ruiz, Seventh Report (1995) 17, para 68, 29, para 140, art 18(e); ILC, Report (1998) 73, para 300. See also Shabtai Rosenne, 'State Responsibility and International Crimes: Further Reflections on Article 19 of the Draft Articles on State Responsibility' (1997–98) 30(1) *NYU JILP* 163–164; Nollkaemper, 'Systemic Effects' (2010) 339.

In addition to sanctions under Articles 41–46, 1996 DASR 51 provided for the application of particular obligations in the case of State crimes,[141] notably under Article 52:

> Article 52 (Specific consequences [of an international crime])
> Where an internationally wrongful act of a State is an international crime:
> (a) an injured State's entitlement to obtain restitution in kind is not subject to the limitations set out in subparagraphs (c) and (d) of article 43 [Restitution in kind];
> (b) an injured State's entitlement to obtain satisfaction is not subject to the restriction in paragraph 3 of article 43 [Satisfaction].

Article 52(a) excluded the necessity that restitution should not involve a burden out of all proportion to the benefit of the injured State under Article 43(c). It also excluded that restitution should not seriously jeopardize the political independence or economic stability of the State under Article 43(d).[142] The exclusion of limits to compensation out of all proportion with respect to its benefits was grounded in the necessity of re-establishing the fundamental interests of the international community breached by a State crime, overriding the interest of the responsible State.[143] Loss of political independence was meant to address the choice of government, not the existence and territorial integrity of the State.[144] Economic destabilisation was considered particularly appropriate if a responsible State increased its prosperity via criminal conduct.[145] However, a clause safeguarding the preservation of the vital needs of the responsible State should have moderated the exclusion of economic destabilisation.[146] Such a clause was eventually embedded in 1996 DASR 42(3).

141 The commentary to DASR 51 (Consequences of an International Crime) stated:

> The effect of the introduction of article 19 of part one has been to recognize a category of wrongful acts to which, because of their seriousness, special consequences should attach. Whether that category is called "crimes", or "exceptionally grave delicts" is immaterial in the sense that, however termed, special consequences should attach.
>
> (ILC, Report (1996) 70, para 1)

142 DASR 52(a) corresponds to art 16(2) of the Second Part of the DASR proposed by Arangio-Ruiz in 1995 (Arangio-Ruiz, Seventh Report, Add.1 (1995) 2, para 139). On the punitive function of such a provision and related issues, see Arangio-Ruiz, Fifth Report, Add.3 (1993) 5, paras 72–73, 21, paras 123–125; ILC, Report (1995) 52, paras 283–294; Arangio-Ruiz, Eighth Report (1996) 3–4, paras 11–17. For a critique of the idea of renouncing proportionality for *restitutio in integrum* in the case of a State crime, see Pellet, 'Remarques' (1996) 24.

143 Arangio-Ruiz, Seventh Report (1995) 9, para 19; ILC, Report (1996) 72, paras 3 and 5.

144 Arangio-Ruiz, Seventh Report (1995) 9–10, paras 23–25.

145 Ibid 9, para 22; ILC, Report (1996) 72, para 3.

146 Ibid 9, para 21.

DASR 52(b) excluded, in the case of a State crime, the necessity that satisfaction should not impair the dignity of the responsible State under Article 45(3).[147] In Article 16(3) of its Seventh Report on State Responsibility, Arangio-Ruiz envisaged extending the exclusion of such a limitation to assurances of non-repetition, permitting that guarantees of non-repetition affect the political independence of a State, whilst safeguarding the vital needs of the population.[148] The ILC, nevertheless, rejected this extension.[149]

The aggravation of sanctions complemented the serious nature of State crimes.[150] Whilst some scholars assume that sanctions under 1996 DASR 52 intentionally had a punitive character,[151] others consider them either too light,[152] or definitely excessive.[153] Among those who assumed that there was no significant difference between sanctions for State crimes and delicts, some scholars maintained that this was due to the indistinct application of fault to both State crimes and delicts, whereas, more appropriately, fault should only have applied to State crimes.[154] Thus, taking into account negligence or intent in determining reparation would have been excessive for State delicts and would have unduly extended the notion of punitive damages to State ordinary responsibility.[155] At the same time, the Project would have unduly excluded specific sanctions for State crimes,[156] such as the possibility of a fine vis-à-vis the international community as a whole.[157]

Some scholars proposed heavier duties, such as the suspension of the status of a State as a Member of the UN.[158] However, although this measure in the end was not explicitly included in the 1996 DASR, it would have applied anyway by virtue of DASR 39, which referred to the UN Charter, whose Article 6 provides for the faculty of expelling from the Organisation a Member in breach of the principles of the Charter. More generally, by subjecting the application of

147 DASR 52(b) corresponds to art 16(3) of the Second Part of the DASR proposed by Arangio-Ruiz in 1995 (Arangio-Ruiz, Seventh Report, Add.1 (1995) 2, para 139). On the punitive function of such a provision and related issues, see Arangio-Ruiz, Fifth Report, Add.3 (1993) 5, paras 73–74, 21, paras 123–125; ILC, Report (1995) 53, para 295.

148 Arangio-Ruiz, Fifth Report, Add.3 (1993) 5, para 74; Id, Seventh Report (1995) 10–11, paras 29–33.

149 ILC, Report (1996) 72, paras 7–8; Sixth Committee of the General Assembly, Topical Summary (1997) 22–23, paras 67–69.

150 ILC, Summary Records (1976) 64, para 28; Arangio-Ruiz, Fifth Report, Add.2 (1995) 5, para 6.

151 Bowett, 'Crimes' (1998) 171–172.

152 Crawford, First Report (1998) 9, para 43, 22, para 86; Id, 'On Re-Reading' (1998) 297; Pellet, 'Can a State' (1999) 430–431.

153 Understandably, Crawford defined the measures 'trivial, incidental and unreal' (Crawford, Third Report (2000) 107, para 408).

154 ILC, Report (1998) 66, para 255, 79, para 353. See also ILC, Report (1995) 50, paras 264–266.

155 Pellet, 'Remarques' (1996) 24, n 90.

156 Id, 'Can a State' (1999) 431.

157 ILC, Report (1994) 142, para 274.

158 Arangio-Ruiz, Fifth Report, Add.2 (1993) 11, para 19(VI).

proceedings under Part 2 of the 1996 DASR to the procedures outlined in the UN Charter, DASR 39 subjected State crimes to the regime of open sanctions provided for in Article 40 of the Charter.

Those commentators who assumed that sanctions under Article 52 were too harsh requested a further elaboration of the norm. Indeed, these scholars pointed out that, whilst under Article 52 the substance of sanctions was not different for State crimes and delicts, quantitative implications were particularly meaningful. Article 52 tended to quantitatively aggravate uniform sanctions in the case of a State crime, so as to mark a clear difference between the substantive implications of State crimes and delicts. Arguably, it is not necessary to justify the existence of State crimes by aggravating ordinary sanctions beyond proportion. Whilst sanctions have a deterrent effect and a differential regime for international crimes is possible, it should always be inspired by the fundamental principle of proportionality.[159]

In any case, no provisions in the 1996 DASR employed the word 'punishment' or 'penalty', which created a terminological mismatch with respect to the word 'crimes' embedded in primary norms. Overall, with respect to both the terminology and gravity of sanctions, it should not be forgotten that DASR 19 only tentatively outlined State crimes, which prevented the clear definition of their implications from the perspective of sanctions in the Second Part of the Project.[160]

The text of the 1996 DASR did not explicitly govern the scope of sanctions for State crimes. However, DASR 40(3) provided that a State crime injured 'all States'. According to Arangio-Ruiz, this implied that sanctions for international crimes should be non-severable *erga omnes* obligations.[161]

3.1.1.6 Universal punitive enforcement? 1996 DASR 53

The 1996 DASR did not fully develop the consequences of State crimes in terms of tertiary procedural measures. These were quite similar to those currently outlined in 2001 DASR 41 for breaches of *jus cogens*. In fact, 1996 DASR 53 provided:

> Article 53
> Obligations for all States
> An international crime committed by a State entails an obligation for every other State:
> (a) not to recognize as lawful the situation created by the crime;
> (b) not to render aid or assistance to the State which has committed the crime in maintaining the situation so created;

159 Crawford, Third Report (2000) 52, para 167, 56, para 193, 107, para 408.
160 Arangio Ruiz, 'Fine prematura' (1998) 125–126.
161 Id, Seventh Report (1995) 8, para 13, 29, para 140.

(c) to cooperate with other States in carrying out the obligations under subparagraphs (a) and (b); and
(d) to cooperate with other States in the application of measures designed to eliminate the consequences of the crime.[162]

Like 2001 DASR 41, the State obligation to cooperate under 1996 DASR 53(d) covered measures aiming to eliminate the consequences of a crime. Furthermore, 1996 DASR 53(a)–(c) compelled State cooperation to implement the duties not to recognise the lawfulness of the situation created by a crime and not to render aid or assistance in maintaining the situation created by the breach.

In the specific case of an 'armed attack', 1996 DASR 34 allowed the use of necessary and proportionate armed force in individual or collective self-defence against an act of aggression, consistently with international practice codified in UN Charter Article 51. DASR 34 thus established *lex specialis*, spelling out for armed force the pattern defined for State criminal responsibility in Articles 19, 40 and 53. By contrast, no rule in the 1996 DASR matched the content of general countermeasures outlined in 2001 DASR 54, so that some scholars concluded that universal countermeasures for State crimes were an implied possibility in the 1996 DASR, notably under Article 53(d).[163]

The collective obligation to cooperate under 1996 DASR 53(d) created a meaningful difference with respect to bilateral enforcement for ordinary State responsibility, and thus established a 'vertical' element in the procedure for enforcing State crimes. Indeed, according to some scholars general countermeasures would have had an essentially punitive nature,[164] involving not only the subject directly affected by the violation, but all States of the international community affected by the offence.[165] Universal enforcement was indeed considered to be the natural consequence of the breach of a non-severable *erga omnes* sanction, whereby all the subjects of the international community would have been affected as victims, triggering State general reaction, according to a criminal law logic.[166]

162 See Willem Riphagen, Third Report (1982) 38–39, paras 100–101, 48–49, paras 1–13; ILC, Report (1994) 142–144, paras 275–288; Arangio-Ruiz, Seventh Report (1995) 16–17, paras 61–69; ILC, Report (1995) 53–54, paras 297–303; Sixth Committee, Topical Summary (1997) 23–25, paras 70–76; Crawford, Third Report (2000) 107, para 410.

163 Sicilianos, 'Countermeasures' (2010) 1143.

164 Pellet, 'Remarques' (1996) 26; Spinedi, 'La responsabilité' (2000) 111; Dawidowicz, *Third-Party Countermeasures* (2017) 291–292.

165 ILC, Report (1996) 72–73. See also Dominicé, 'The International Responsibility' (1999) 363.

166 Roberto Ago in ILC, Topical Summary (1976) 90, para 30; Dupuy, 'Observations' (1983) 538; ILC, Report (1998) 67, para 265. But see ILC, Report (1998) 67–68, para 266; Spinedi, 'La responsabilité' (2000) 97, considering that the notion of *erga omnes* responsibility does not necessarily entail State criminal responsibility.

Furthermore, 1996 DASR 39 gave priority to collective countermeasures under the UN Charter, notably Chapter VII.[167] These would have also had a punitive function,[168] whereby the use of armed force marked a critical difference with respect to enforcement for State ordinary responsibility.[169] Some scholars further assume that in practice universal action under DASR 53 entailed coordination by the UN Security Council, according to the UN Charter.[170] This approach is consistent with the assumption that action by the UN Security Council encompassed State crimes under DASR 19(3).[171] In this respect, scholars underscored that institutionalised collective countermeasures excluded the risk of disparate and uncoordinated reactions and were therefore preferable in the case of serious breaches of fundamental international obligations.[172] The ILC similarly considered that allowing States to respond separately and in different ways to a crime would have entailed 'an unacceptable multiplicity of claims' and 'anarchy', in cases where only collective action is appropriate, notably under the guidance of the UN Security Council.[173]

It is also worth noting that Article 18 of the Second Part of the DASR presented by Arangio-Ruiz in 1996 provided:

> Where an internationally wrongful act is an international crime, all States shall [...] [f]ully implement the *aut dedere aut judicare* principle, with respect to any individuals accused of crimes against the peace and security of mankind the commission of which has brought about the international crime of the State or contributed thereto.[174]

This norm established a link between individual criminal responsibility envisaged in the DCCPSM and State criminal responsibility under DASR 19, but the 1996 version of the DASR did not include such a provision.

Consistently with its competence to adjudicate upon State crimes under Article 17 of the Second Part of his Project,[175] Arangio-Ruiz also vested the ICJ

167 Arangio-Ruiz, Fifth Report, Add.2 (1993) 18, para 31(IV)–(V), 22–23, para 39(IV). On the ability of the UN Security Council and General Assembly to decide on international crimes, see ILC, Report (1994) 145–147, paras 298–312.

168 ILC, Report to the General Assembly on the Work of the Thirty-First Session, UN Doc A/34/10 (1979) 116, para 3; Arangio-Ruiz, Fifth Report, Add.3 (1993) 12 ff, paras 98 ff; Id, Sixth Report, Add.1 (1996) 4 ff, paras 7 ff; Gowlland-Debbas, 'Security Council' (1994) 63.

169 Arangio-Ruiz, Fifth Report, Add.2 (1993) 19, para 31(VI).

170 Bowett, 'Crimes' (1998) 172–173.

171 ILC, Summary Records (1976) 68, para 9; Gowlland-Debbas, 'Security Council' (1994) 64; Arangio-Ruiz, 'The "Federal Analogy"' (1997) 24.

172 Gowlland-Debbas, 'Security Council' (1994) 73.

173 ILC, Report (1995) 50, para 274; ILC, Report (2000) 31, para 128.

174 Arangio-Ruiz, Seventh Report (1995) 17, para 68, 29–30, para 140. See also ILC, Report (1994) 85, para 195; Id, Report (1995) 54, para 302.

175 See s 3.1.1.4.

with the power to decide on issues arising at the stage of the enforcement of State criminal responsibility.[176] However, this proposal was also excluded from the final text of the 1996 DASR.

3.1.2 Individual criminal responsibility

3.1.2.1 (Compulsory) universal jurisdiction and complementary international adjudication

Serious breaches of peremptory obligations give rise to individual criminal responsibility: international criminal law governs the ensuing procedures via two different responses. Adjudication can take place (1) transnationally, at the level of domestic jurisdictions or (2) supranationally, at the level of international jurisdictions. These proceedings interact, so that supranational procedures complement transnational procedures. Interaction can go as far as to establish 'hybrid' tribunals, including a mix of domestic prosecutors and judges and applying both domestic and international law. Within this framework, the Serious Crimes Panels in the East Timor District Court of Dili, the Mixed Panels in the Courts of Kosovo, the Special Tribunal for Iraq and the War Crimes Chamber of the Court of Bosnia-Herzegovina are 'internationalised domestic courts'. The SCSL, the Extraordinary Chambers in the Courts of Cambodia and the STL are 'domesticated international courts'.[177]

In addition to classical customary grounds determining jurisdiction upon domestic and international crimes, notably territoriality, active and passive personality, as well as State interest in proceeding, transnationally harmonised crimes in breach of peremptory norms are subject to universal jurisdiction.[178] However, the presence of the accused person in the proceeding State can be a restrictive requirement.[179] Grave breaches of the Geneva Conventions, including torture, are customarily subject to universal jurisdiction.[180] Core crimes against humanity and genocide should also be subject to universal adjudication, in light of the *erga omnes* nature of these violations.[181] Notably, according to the ICTY, a crucial

176 Arangio-Ruiz, Seventh Report, Add.2 (1995) 3, paras 145–146; ILC, Report (1995) 57–58, para 320.

177 Guilfoyle, *International Criminal Law* (2018) 97. See also s 1.2.3.3.

178 Zdzislaw Galicki, Preliminary Report on the Obligation to Extradite or Prosecute (*Aut Dedere aut Judicare*), UN Doc A/CN.4/571 (2006) 2(1) *YBILC* 263, para 20; Orakhelashvili, *Peremptory Norms* (2006) 264–265 and 288 ff. However, legal commentators and domestic courts tend to acknowledge universal competence restrictively and subject to the existence of a specific conventional provision (see Dupuy, 'International Criminal Responsibility' (2002) 1097; Zdzislaw Galicki, Third Report on the Obligation to Extradite or Prosecute (*Aut Dedere aut Judicare*), UN Doc A/CN.4/603 (2008) 126, para 87).

179 *Arrest Warrant of 11 April 2000 (Democratic Republic of the Congo v Belgium)* [2002] ICJ Rep 3, Joint Separate Opinion of Higgins, Kooijmans and Buergenthal JJ 68, para 19.

180 *Furundžija* (1998) 18–19, paras 42–44, 60, para 156.

181 *Eichmann*, Supreme Court of Israel, Judgment of 29 May 1962 (1968) 36 *ILR* 298–304; *Regina v Bow Street Metropolitan Stipendiary Magistrate; Ex parte Pinochet Ugarte (No 3)*, House of Lords, 13 January 1999 [2000] 1 AC 288. See also Payam Akhavan, 'The Universal

consequence of the peremptory nature of the prohibition of torture is that 'every State is *entitled* to investigate, prosecute and punish or extradite individuals accused of torture.'[182] Such a conclusion is based on a parallelism with the invalidity of norms inconsistent with *jus cogens*, since the Tribunal considered that it would be unreasonable to outlaw torture and not to allow its universal prosecution.[183] Therefore, once again a link brings together the non-derogability of peremptory obligations and the possibility of a general reaction in the case of a breach.[184] Furthermore, it can be assumed that universal jurisdiction applies to aggression.[185] International conventions mostly subject terrorism to universal jurisdiction, a stance that the STL upheld.[186]

Considering the relationship between individual criminal responsibility and State aggravated responsibility, universal jurisdiction may be regarded as a specific implication of 2001 DASR 54, which provides that all States of the international community are 'entitled' to 'take lawful measures' against a State responsible for breaching a peremptory duty and ensure cessation. Punishing the individuals acting on behalf of the State could indeed be considered a 'lawful measure' ensuring not only cessation, in light of the identity of individual and State conduct, but also non-repetition, given the pre-emptive nature of criminal proceedings.

Furthermore, transnationally harmonised crimes breaching peremptory norms are often subject to compulsory jurisdiction (*aut dedere aut judicare*), entailing an obligation for a State to either prosecute or extradite the accused person.[187] This is explicitly established in different provisions of the Geneva Conventions,[188] the CAT (Article 8(1)) and the Convention for the Suppression of Terrorist Bombings (Article 7(4)). According to some scholars, in light of their universal nature, crimes against humanity should be subject to compulsory universal jurisdiction, at least prospectively.[189] The ICJ held that the

---

Repression of Crimes against Humanity before National Jurisdictions', in Sadat, *Forging* (2011) 29.

182 *Furundžija* (1998) 60, para 156, emphasis added. See also s 1.2.3.3.

183 Ibid.

184 Dupuy, 'International Criminal Responsibility' (2002) 1098.

185 Michael Scharf, 'Universal Jurisdiction and the Crime of Aggression' (2012) 53(2) *Harv ILJ* 388; Kemp, *Individual Criminal Liability* (2017) 231 ff; Pål Wrange, 'The Crime of Aggression, Domestic Prosecutions and Complementarity', in Kreß and Barriaga, *The Crime* (2017) 720.

186 *Ayyash* et al (2011) 65–66, para 102. See also s 2.3.5.1 and Jackson Nyamuya Maogoto, 'War on the Enemy: Self-Defence and State-Sponsored Terrorism' (2003) 4(2) *Mel JIL* 417.

187 ILC, Report to the General Assembly on the Work of the Fifty-Sixth Session, UN Doc A/59/10 (2004) 2(2) *YBILC* 123, para 1; Working Group on the Obligation to Extradite or Prosecute (*Aut Dedere aut Judicare*), Report, UN Doc A/CN.4/L.829 (2013) 5 ff, paras 11 ff; Id, Final Report, UN Doc A/CN.4/L.844 (2014) 4 ff, paras 9 ff. See also Bassiouni, *Introduction* (2013) 246.

188 Article 49 of Geneva Conventions I and II, art 129 of Geneva Convention III, art 146 of Geneva Convention IV.

189 Akhavan, 'The Universal Repression' (2012) 36–37; Michael Scharf, '*Aut Dedere aut Judicare*', in Wolfrum, *Max Planck Encyclopedia* (2012) para 21; Kriangsak Kittichaisaree, *The Obligation to Extradite or Prosecute* (OUP, 2018) 217.

(non-severable) *erga omnes* duties embedded in the Genocide Convention imply that 'each State' has 'the *obligation* to prevent and *punish* the crime of genocide'.[190]

The obligation to punish or prosecute individual crimes can be considered an implication of 2001 DASR 41(1), providing that States '*shall cooperate* to bring to an end through lawful means' any serious breaches of peremptory norms.[191] In fact, along the lines of Article 18 of the Second Part of the DASR presented by Arangio-Ruiz in 1996, the duty under 2001 DASR 41(1) can be read as entailing an obligation for States to cooperate in enforcing not only State liability but also underpinning individual responsibility, by implementing the principle *aut dedere aut judicare*.[192]

Ad hoc or permanent international criminal proceedings complement domestic proceedings for core individual crimes in breach of peremptory obligations. Article VI of the Genocide Convention clearly envisages such a mechanism. Whilst the IMT, IMTFE, ICTY and ICTR carried out *ad hoc* prosecutions, the ICC has permanent jurisdiction. Under Article 12 of its Statute, the ICC has competence over genocide, crimes against humanity, war crimes and aggression when committed by natural persons in the territory of a State Party or by its nationals. The ICC complements national courts: its jurisdiction is only triggered if national tribunals are unwilling or unable to prosecute genuinely (ICC Statute Article 17).

International criminal proceedings fundamentally include a preliminary analysis, investigation, confirmation hearing, trial, appeal and revision.[193] Proceedings are mainly grounded in the adversarial model, confronting prosecution and defence, but they also include inquisitorial elements, particularly a pro-active role of the judge in collecting evidence.[194] Given that supranational jurisdiction overrides State sovereignty, personal and functional immunities do not apply before supranational courts and tribunals, as several conventional provisions expressly recognise.[195]

190 *Application of the Convention* [1996] 616, para 31, emphasis added; See also *Application of the Convention* [2007] 111, para 162; *Application of the Convention* [2015] 68, para 153. According to Pierre-Marie Dupuy, not only the prohibition of genocide, but also the obligation of States to cooperate in preventing and punishing genocide is part of *jus cogens* (see Dupuy, 'Normes', in Ascensio, Decaux and Pellet, *Droit* (2000) 79).

191 Emphasis added.

192 Arangio-Ruiz, Seventh Report (1995) 17, para 68, 29, para 140, art 18(e) and s 3.1.1.6. See also Nollkaemper, 'Systemic Effects' (2010) 339–340.

193 Christoph Safferling, *Towards an International Criminal Procedure* (OUP, 2001) 54 ff; Geert-Jan Alexander Knoops, *Theory and Practice of International and Internationalised Criminal Proceedings* (Kluwer, 2005) 101 ff; Goran Sluiter *et al*, *International Criminal Procedure: Principles and Rules* (OUP, 2013) 39 ff; Guilfoyle, *International Criminal Law* (2018) 123 ff.

194 ICC, Regulations of the Court, 5th Plenary Session, ICC Doc ICC-BD/01-01-04 (2004) reg 48.

195 Genocide Convention art 4, IMT Charter art 7, IMTF Charter art 6, ICTY Statute art 7(2), ICRT Statute art 6(2), ICC Statute art 27.

3.1.2.2 (Erga omnes) *imprisonment, fines and forfeiture*

Transnationally harmonised crimes in breach of peremptory norms are subject to harmonised domestic sanctions, having a punitive character. For instance, CAT Article 4 provides that '[e]ach State Party shall make these offences [acts of torture] punishable by appropriate penalties which take into account their grave nature.' Article V of the Genocide Convention stipulates that Member States 'provide effective penalties for persons guilty of genocide or of any of the other acts enumerated in article III [punishable acts]'.

As regards sanctions for international crimes, unlike domestic law, which usually determines specific punishment for specific crimes, international law takes a comprehensive approach and defines uniformly punitive sanctions for all international crimes.[196] Thus, Articles 27–28 of the IMT Charter established the penalties of 'death' or any other 'just punishment', as well as the expropriation of stolen property. Article 16 of the IMTFE Charter outlined similar penalties. Article 9 of the IMT Charter also embedded the possible declaration of the criminal nature of organisations. Nuremberg Principle 1 and Article 3 of the 1996 DCCPSM confirm this broad approach.[197] ICTY Statute Article 24 and ICTR Statute Article 23 instituted the penalties of imprisonment, based on the regulation and practice respectively applying in the former Yugoslavia and Rwanda, and expropriation of property and proceeds criminally acquired.

More comprehensively, ICC Statute Article 77 sets out the penalties of life imprisonment, imprisonment up to 30 years, fines and forfeiture of proceeds, property and assets criminally acquired. ICC Statute Article 79 also establishes compensation for victims via a Trust Fund. As we have seen,[198] early proposals for an international criminal code and court were more exhaustive and often outlined ancillary sanctions, such as forfeiture of public offices.

Considering mixed jurisdictions, Article 19 of the SCSL Statute provides for the penalties of imprisonment and forfeiture of criminally acquired property, proceeds and assets. Articles 24 and 25 of the STL Statute outline the penalties of imprisonment and compensation for victims, taking into account the specific implications of terrorism.

From the standpoint of secondary substantive rules, the universal nature of the breach should also imply the universality of consequent sanctions.[199] However, the identity, or duplication, of non-severable *erga omnes* obligations breached by individual crimes and State aggravated wrongful acts is not replicated from the standpoint of the sanction.[200] In fact, secondary *erga omnes* obligations have a different content for individuals and States. In this respect, the ILC underscored

196 Emmanuel Decaux, 'The Definition of Traditional Sanctions: Their Scope and Characteristics' (2008) 90 *IRRC* 253–255.
197 Spiropoulos, Formulation (1950) 191; ILC, Report (1996) 22.
198 Section 1.1.
199 Orakhelashvili, *Peremptory Norms* (2006) 319.
200 See s 2.2.1.1.

that, even if individual criminal responsibility could generate State criminal responsibility, sanctions would necessarily be different.[201] Scholars thus conclude that individual responsibility is 'invisible' in the remedies for State aggravated responsibility.[202] This approach is valid to the extent that it is impossible to assume the absolute identity of sanctions.[203] However, certain similarities, or even overlaps, also exist at the level of the content of the sanction. Indeed, expropriation of the proceeds derived from the crimes and fines apply to both natural persons and States. Compensation in favour of victims equally applies to States and individuals, notably in cases such as the intra-State genocide that took place in Rwanda.[204] Ancillary sanctions, such as disqualification from holding a public office, entail an interesting overlap with the exercise of a public function and thus with acts carried out by public organs or agents.

The crucial difference between sanctions applying to natural persons and States is imprisonment. However, the essence of imprisonment, which is deprivation of liberty, that is, a restriction of the capacity to act, can also apply to a legal person, when certain activities are prohibited, as in the case of demilitarisation imposed on Germany after World War II.[205] According to a theoretical scale of gravity, scholars go as far as to outline a parallel between the death penalty, which was included in the IMT and IMTFE Charters, and the State penalty of loss of independence.[206] In this sense, the variety of sanctions applying to legal persons that are criminally responsible domestically provide a yardstick for comparison. These include a vast array of measures, ranging from heavy fines to the adoption of appropriate compliance and ethics programmes,[207] having retributive, deterrent and rehabilitative purposes.[208]

3.1.2.3 Domestic enforcement

Sentences delivered by domestic courts for international crimes in breach of peremptory obligations are enforced according to domestic rules. In this respect, transnational rules govern interstate cooperation, also known as 'international cooperation in criminal matters'.[209] Cooperation has a horizontal nature and concerns issues such as extradition of natural persons and their transit through a foreign State in relation to the enforcement of sentences. Core rules on mutual

201 ILC, Report (1998) 69, para 276; Nollkaemper, 'Concurrence' (2003) 636.
202 Verhoeven, 'Vers un ordre' (1999) 61; Nollkaemper, 'Concurrence' (2003) 617.
203 Webb, 'Binocular Vision' (2012) 134–135.
204 Ibid 135–136.
205 See s 1.2.1.2.
206 ICLA, 'Plan d'un Code' (1935) tit IV, ch 1, s 1.
207 US Sentencing Guidelines Manual (2016) para 8B2.1.
208 Meron, 'Is International Law' (1998) 20; De Maglie, 'Models' (2005) 563; David Caron, 'State Crime: Looking at Municipal Experience with Organizational Crime', in Ragazzi, *International Responsibility* (2005) 26; Eser and Rettenmeier, 'Criminality' (2009) 233; Weiner, 'Working the System' (2010) 357–358.
209 Cryer, Friman, Robinson and Wilmshurst, *An Introduction* (2014) 90 ff.

assistance are embedded in customary law as well as bilateral and multilateral conventions, which complement domestic rules. For instance, Article 88 of Additional Protocol I to the Geneva Conventions provides that States afford reciprocal assistance in proceedings concerning war crimes, in accordance with other bilateral and multilateral treaties, with particular regard to extradition.

With respect to international criminal jurisdictions, the sentences delivered by the IMT in Nuremberg and the IMTFE in Tokyo were enforced respectively according to the orders of the Control Council for Germany and those of the Supreme Commander for the Allied Powers, according to IMT Charter Article 29 and IMTFE Charter Article 17. Sentences delivered by the ICTY, ICTR and ICC are served in a State according to domestic proceedings, upon designation based on a list of countries that have agreed to accept convicted persons.[210] With regard to mixed jurisdictions, Article 22 of the SCSL Statute provides for the enforcement of sentences of imprisonment in Sierra Leone or other States having concluded a special agreement for that purpose. Similarly, STL Statute Article 29(1) determines that States accepting persons convicted by the Tribunal enforce sentences of imprisonment. In the absence of a 'direct' system of enforcement, States therefore implement individual sentences 'indirectly'.[211]

However, international criminal jurisdictions maintain the role of supervising the execution of sentences, as pointed out in ICTY Statute Article 28, ICTR Statute Article 27 and ICC Statute Article 106. Within this context, Article 80 of the ICC Statute provides that the Court may order the transfer of money and other property collected through fines or forfeiture to a Trust Fund, for the purpose of victims' compensation. Similarly, concerning mixed jurisdictions, Article 22 of the SCSL Statute provides that, whilst the law of Sierra Leone determines enforcement conditions, supervision remains with the Special Court. Along the same lines, STL Statute Article 29(2) establishes that the law of the State of enforcement governs imprisonment, but subject to the supervision of the Special Tribunal. Such a framework underscores that the complementary nature of international criminal jurisdictions makes State cooperation a cornerstone of their functioning.[212]

In light of this framework, it is possible to consider that State collaboration *inter se* and with international criminal tribunals fulfils the duty to 'cooperate to bring to an end through lawful means' any serious breaches of peremptory norms under 2001 DASR 41(1).[213]

210 ICTY Statute art 27; ICTR Statute art 26; ICC Statute arts 103 and 109.

211 Knoops, *Theory* (2005) 282–283.

212 As established in ICTY Statute art 29, ICTR Statute art 28, ICC Statute Part IX (arts 86 ff) and art 17(1) of the Agreement on the SCSL. See Knoops, *Theory* (2005) 282–285 and 309–323.

213 *Application of the Convention* [2007] 229, para 449, 238–239, para 471(8); Webb, 'Binocular Vision' (2012) 136–137.

3.2 Procedural intersections

3.2.1 Systemic patterns and inter-temporality

Concerning States, it ought to be recognised that aggression, genocide, core war crimes, core crimes against humanity and prospectively terrorism breach non-severable *erga omnes* obligations. Based on general international law as codified in the 2001 DASR, in the case of a serious breach of such obligations, all States can (or should) invoke responsibility, preferably via the UN. The ensuing sanction will be a non-severable *erga omnes* obligation, necessarily peremptory (*cogens*).[214] The breach of a sanction requires non-recognition, aid, assistance and cooperation in enforcement by all States of the international community, preferably via the UN:

(1) Serious State breach of a non-severable *erga omnes* obligation (*jus cogens*: VCLT and VCLTIO Article 53 and 2001 DASR 40)
Aggression, genocide, core war crimes, core crimes against humanity, prospectively terrorism
→ (2) UN collective measures (UN Charter Chapters VI-VII; 2001 DASR Article 59)
Universal invocation of responsibility (2001 DASR 41(1), 42(b) and 48(1)(b))
→ (3) Non-severable *erga omnes* sanctions (*jus cogens*)
Cessation, non-repetition, reparation (2001 DASR 28–39)
→ Breach
→ (4) Universal countermeasures
Individual and collective self-defence (UN Charter Article 51 and 2001 DASR 21)
Obligation to cooperate to end the violation through lawful means (2001 DASR 41(1) and 54)
Obligation not to recognise the situation created by the infringement as lawful (2001 DASR 41(2))
Obligation not to render aid or assistance in maintaining the situation created by the infringement (2001 DASR 41(2))

The 1996 DASR provided a similar pattern, whereby the notion of a 'State crime' nevertheless entailed the possibility of disproportionate sanctions.[215] According

214 Crawford, *State Responsibility* (2013) 106.

215 As underscored by Arangio-Ruiz, the two main characteristics of the 'special' regime of 'State crimes' would be: '(a) the "substance" of the consequences, which would be more severe than for other breaches; and (b) the kind of reaction, which, in the case [of] wrongful acts affecting fundamental interests of the international community, would be, one might say, "diffuse", or downright universal' (Arangio-Ruiz, Fifth Report, Add.2 (1993) 6, para 9). Therefore, '[i]t is the weight of the two factors and their interaction which differentiates the regime of

to the proposals of Arangio-Ruiz, a State crime should also have entailed the compulsory jurisdiction of the ICJ:[216]

(1) Serious State breach of a non-severable *erga omnes* obligation: State crime (1996 DASR 19)
Aggression, breach of the right to self-determination, human rights breaches, massive environmental pollution
→ (2) UN collective measures (UN Charter Chapters VI–VII; 1996 DASR 39)
Universal invocation of responsibility (1996 DASR 40)
Unilateral resort to the ICJ (2nd Part, Article 17 Arangio-Ruiz DASR 1995)
→ (3) Non-severable disproportionate *erga omnes* sanctions
Cessation, non-repetition, reparation, individual punishment (1996 DASR 41–46 and 52)
→ Breach
→ (4) Universal countermeasures
Individual and collective self-defence (UN Charter Article 51 and DASR 34)
Measures under UN Charter Articles 40–42
Obligation to cooperate to end the violation through lawful means (1996 DASR 53(d))
Obligation not to recognise the situation created by the infringement as lawful (1996 DASR 53(a) and (c))
Obligation not to render aid or assistance in maintaining the situation (1996 DASR 53(b) and (c))

It is possible to infer from these patterns that, whether the 2001 DASR or the 1996 DASR are taken into account as a basis for State aggravated responsibility, rather than criminal liability, does not make a particularly significant difference in terms of secondary and tertiary norms. In this context, however, opting for, rather than excluding, the compulsory jurisdiction of the ICJ has meaningful implications.

From the perspective of individuals, it ought to be recognised that core international crimes, notably aggression, genocide, core war crimes, core crimes against humanity and prospectively terrorism, breach non-severable *erga omnes* obligations. This triggers (compulsory) universal jurisdiction and complementary international criminal jurisdiction, notably under ICC Statute Article 17. Such jurisdictions apply harmonised or international sanctions, which are implemented domestically:

---

the consequences of crimes from that of the consequences of delicts and justifies treating the former as a special category of wrongful act' (Arangio-Ruiz, Seventh Report (1995) 12, para 36).

216 Arangio-Ruiz, Seventh Report (1995) 30, art 19.

(1) Core individual international crimes in breach of a non-severable *erga omnes* obligation (*jus cogens*) (ICC Statute, Preamble)
Aggression, genocide, core war crimes, core crimes against humanity, prospectively terrorism
→ (2) (Compulsory) universal jurisdiction (for instance, Article 50 of Geneva Conventions I and II; Article 7(4) of the Convention for the Suppression of Terrorist Bombings)
Complementary international criminal jurisdiction (ICC Statute Article 17)
→ (3) Harmonised or international sanctions
→ (4) Domestic implementation
[Fulfilling the State obligation to end the violation through lawful means under 1996 DASR 53 and 2001 DASR 41(1) and 54]

Fundamentally, breaches of non-severable *erga omnes* obligations trigger State universal reaction via institutionalised UN Charter procedures or non-institutionalised procedures under the DASR. States implement ensuing peremptory sanctions collectively via institutionalised or non-institutionalised enforcement. The same breaches trigger State universal reaction in terms of criminal prosecution of individuals via (compulsory) universal jurisdiction or international adjudication, notably by means of the ICC. States implement ensuing harmonised or international sanctions domestically.

Some scholars consider that a 'bifurcated' approach to individual and State responsibility is unbalanced, because it overlooks the question of collective criminal responsibility.[217] Given the priority of the political element in assessing State responsibility, it has been noted that a strictly legal approach is 'just a tool in the toolbox for responding to States involved in international crimes' and 'certainly not the most important one'.[218] The willingness to approach State aggravated responsibility politically is indeed considered to be the fundamental cause of the rejection of the notion of a 'State crime'.[219] This has reignited the debate on the nature of State responsibility and the necessity of envisaging integrated procedural responses to individual and collective liability.[220] Some scholars have therefore dusted off the notion of a 'State crime'.[221]

Substantively, criminal conduct of individuals acting as organs or agents of a State (1) vicariously triggers State aggravated responsibility (2).[222] Theoretically, State responsibility should therefore be inconceivable without individual responsibility. In this context, aggregate responsibility helps to assess individual

217 Nollkaemper, 'Systemic Effects' (2010) 320–322; Drumbl, 'Accountability' (2010) 379.
218 Nollkaemper, 'Systemic Effects' (2010) 335.
219 Ibid.
220 Ibid 322 ff.
221 Cherif Bassiouni, 'Challenges Facing a Rule-of-Law Oriented World Order' (2010) 8(1) *Santa Clara JIL* 9.
222 See s 2.2.1.1.

responsibility.[223] In practice, 'politically sensitive' procedures addressing State aggravated responsibility precede proceedings addressing individual criminal responsibility. In a horizontal context dominated by equal State sovereignty, individual criminal proceedings seem to be 'appendixes' of procedures addressing State responsibility. It has thus been noted that:

> Criminal law is not capable of capturing the complex mechanisms and relations of organizations which engage in mass crimes. It provides a distorted and fragmentized picture of reality in which the blame rests on a few individuals who, understandably, resent their being sacrificed as scapegoats [...] The power of international criminal justice to better respond to the situations of mass atrocities that have inspired its evolution, will largely depend on its ability to transcend individuality and to integrate individual and collective responsibility in a complementary framework that matches the dynamics that cause international crimes to happen in the first place.[224]

3.2.2 The limits of UN procedures

State aggravated responsibility is addressed primarily via UN procedural mechanisms, notably those centred on the Security Council. Such a priority is generally established in 2001 DASR 59 and in specific provisions, notably Article VIII of the Genocide Convention.

Based on UN Charter Article 23, the UN Security Council includes 5 Permanent Members, that is, China, France, the UK, the US and the Soviet Union (USSR). In addition, the Council comprises 10 Non-Permanent Members elected for two years by virtue of their contribution to peace and equitable geographical distribution. The status of a Permanent Member is the result of the emergence of the great powers after World War II. The number of Non-Permanent Members increased from 6 to 10 via UN General Assembly Resolution 1991 (XVIII) in 1963,[225] following the decolonisation process and the improved number of States participating in the General Assembly.[226]

According to UN Charter Article 24(1), the Security Council has the 'primary responsibility for the maintenance of international peace and security' and its decisions are binding on UN Member States under Article 25. Under Article 27 of the Charter, given that any Member has one vote, an affirmative vote of seven Members is necessary to decide all procedural matters, whilst an affirmative vote of nine Members, including the permanent ones, is required to decide all other questions. The veto mechanism in favour of the Permanent Members was initially

223 See ss 2.2.2.2 and 2.2.2.3. The same principle applies in the context of corporate responsibility (see Stoitchkova, *Towards Corporate Liability* (2012) 37).

224 Nollkaemper, 'Systemic Effects' (2010) 352.

225 General Assembly, Questions of Equitable Representation on the Security Council and the Economic and Social Council, UN Doc A/RES/1991 (XVIII), 17 December 1963.

226 Rudolf Geiger, 'Article 23', in Bruno Simma (ed), *The Charter of the United Nations: A Commentary* (OUP, 2012) 754.

not included in the Dumbarton Oak Proposals, but was adopted following the Yalta Proposals and finally embedded in the Charter, despite several critiques.[227] Other UN Members and State parties to a dispute can participate in the meetings of the Council as non-voting Members under UN Charter Articles 31–32.

The Security Council can act within the context of Chapter VI (Pacific Settlement of Disputes) or Chapter VII (Action with respect to Threats to the Peace, Breaches of the Peace, and Acts of Aggression). These are complemented by Chapter VIII (Regional Arrangements), coordinating the action of the Council with that of regional arrangements or agencies.[228] It has nonetheless been critically remarked that the Council uses its powers under Chapter VII more frequently than those under Chapter VI.[229]

Under Chapter VI, UN Charter Article 38 vests the Council with the power to make recommendations to the parties to a dispute that is likely to endanger international peace and security, particularly via classical peaceful settlement means.[230] Within this framework, negotiation, conciliation and jurisdictional means, which indistinctly apply to State aggravated and non-aggravated responsibility, notably via the ICJ, remain voluntary under Articles 33–37 of the Charter.

Under Chapter VII of the UN Charter, when it determines the existence of a 'threat to the peace', 'breach of the peace', or 'act of aggression', the Council has the power to adopt measures not involving or involving the use of armed force to end the violation, according to Articles 41 and 42 of the Charter. For this purpose, the Council relies on the armed forces that UN Member States make available (UN Charter Articles 43–45) and on the assistance of the Military Advice Committee (UN Charter Articles 47). Otherwise, Member States implement the decisions of the Council under Article 48 of the Charter. To the extent that the Council has not taken action under Chapter VII, Member States can act in individual or collective self-defence under Article 51 of the Charter. Under Chapter VIII, the Council can encourage dispute settlement via regional arrangements and can rely on these arrangements to implement coercive measures.

Security Council procedures under Chapter VII of the UN Charter for a threat to or breach of the peace are at least particularly suited to the aggravated regime of international responsibility, entailing countermeasures that can go as far as to involve the use of armed force. In practice, the Security Council has progressively extended its areas of intervention under Chapter VII, and thus the notion of threat to or breach of the peace.[231] Throughout the

227 United Nations Conference on International Organization (UNCIO) vol 11 754, Doc 852, 111/1/37; Andreas Zimmermann, 'Article 27', in Simma, *The Charter* (2012) 877–878.

228 Loraine Sievers and Sam Daws, *The Procedure of the UN Security Council* (OUP, 4th edn, 2014) 6–9.

229 Steven Ratner, 'Image and Reality in the United Nation's Peaceful Settlement of Disputes' (1995) 6(3) *EJIL* 429; Gray, *International Law* (2018) 262.

230 Thomas Giegerich, 'Article 38', in Simma, *The Charter* (2012) 1162.

231 Nayantha Wijesundara, 'Who Will Guard the Guardian of the International Peace and Security – Judicial Review of Chapter VII Resolutions' (2016) 3 *Ind JICL* 378.

Cold War, the conceptualisation of peace-threatening conflicts mostly focused on aggression.[232] However, in January 1992 the Council adopted a Summit Declaration that 'non-military sources of instability in the economic, social, humanitarian and ecological fields have become threats to peace and security.'[233] Along these lines, by means of Resolution 794/1992 the Security Council authorised the use of armed force to end civil war in Somalia, whereby action was justified by the 'magnitude of the human tragedy caused by the conflict'.[234] Resolutions 1368/2001 and 1373/2001 condemned 'terrorism' as a 'threat to international peace and security'.[235] By means of Resolution 2139/2014, the Council 'strongly condemned' widespread violations of human rights and international humanitarian law committed in Syria by the Syrian authorities and armed groups.[236] This expansion tends to correspond to the area of fundamental obligations affected by State crimes under 1996 DASR 19.[237]

Furthermore, some decisions of the Security Council address not only States, but also natural persons. Thus, via Resolution 794/1992 the Council held 'individually responsible' those 'who commit or order the commission' of violations of 'international humanitarian law' in Somalia.[238] In the *Lockerbie* case, the Council requested Libya to cooperate in bringing to justice two Libyan citizens suspected of acts of terrorism via Resolution 731/1992.[239] Subsequently, the Council prompted Libya to cooperate and renounce terrorism as well as support to terrorist organisations via Resolution 784/1992.[240] The trend eventually resulted in the creation of the *ad hoc* international criminal Tribunals for the Former Yugoslavia and Rwanda, the STL and the SCSL.[241] This approach also resulted in the tribunals created by special UN Missions in Kosovo and East Timor, and by the national Government in the Central African Republic.[242] On such a basis, some scholars conclude that under Chapter VII of the UN Charter the Security Council has decisional power on both individual and State criminal responsibility.[243]

232 Gray, *International Law* (2018) 263–272.
233 Note by the President of the Security Council, UN Doc S/23500 (1992) 3. See also Proulx, *Institutionalizing* (2016) 48; Gray, *International Law* (2018) 272 ff.
234 Security Council, Somalia, UN Doc S/RES/794, 3 December 1992, preamble.
235 Id, Threats to International Peace and Security Caused by Terrorist Acts, UN Doc S/RES/1373, 28 September 2001, preamble; Id, UN Doc S/RES/1368, 12 September 2001, preamble.
236 Security Council, Middle East, UN Doc S/RES/2139, 22 February 2014.
237 Barboza, 'International Criminal Law' (1999) 100; Sreenivasa Rao, 'International Crimes' (2005) 77; White, 'Responses' (2009) 328–329; Jørgensen, 'The Concept' (2015) 202.
238 S/RES/794, para 5.
239 Security Council, Libyan Arab Jamahiriya, UN Doc S/RES/731, 21 January 1992.
240 Id, UN Doc S/RES/748, 31 March 1992.
241 See s 1.2.3.3.
242 Ibid.
243 White, 'Responses' (2009) 318; Wijesundara, 'Who Will Guard' (2016) 377–380.

3.2.2.1 Chapter VII procedures: political and enforcement action for State aggravated responsibility?

The procedure under Chapter VII of the UN Charter raises a few questions with respect to State aggravated responsibility.[244] It is indeed quite vague as regards aggravated wrongful acts. In fact, from the substantive viewpoint UN Charter Articles 39, 41 and 42 broadly define international wrongful acts and sanctions, whilst Article 40 does not specify the substantive content of provisional measures. These provisions do not clearly outline (aggravated) offences, dispute settlement, sanctions and enforcement. The approach is consistent with Article 24(1) of the Charter, which vests the Council with a broad responsibility for the maintenance of peace in international relations.[245]

Concerning offences, the notion of 'threat to the peace, breach of the peace, or act of aggression' is quite general. Notably, the notion of 'peace' is so broad that any offence can be considered to threaten such a value, so much so that scholars speak of a 'comprehensive' and 'neutral' definition aiming to extend the power of the Council.[246] In fact, following Immanuel Kant,[247] Kelsen defined international peace as 'a condition of absence of force in the relations among States'.[248] Pella regarded peace as a preliminary condition for the exercise of international rights and duties.[249] Scholars consider that such a broad competence encompasses cyber threats.[250]

Secondary rules confirm the broad margin of discretion that the Security Council enjoys under primary norms. UN Charter Articles 29 and 40 generally mention 'resolutions' and 'decisions', without setting any specific limits to sanctions imposed by the Council. Enforcement procedures are also quite broad, ranging from measures not involving the use of armed force under UN Charter Article 41 to measures implying the use of force under Article 42. Furthermore, it is possible to assume that decisions taken by the Council can be addressed not only to States, but also to non-State subjects, since the Charter does not establish any specific rules on this. However, scholars are divided on the question.[251]

244 Pierre Klein, 'Responsibility for Serious Breaches of Obligations Deriving from Peremptory Norms of International Law and United Nations Law' (2002) 13(5) *EJIL* 1242; White, 'Responses' (2009) 320.
245 Dupuy, 'The Deficiencies' (2012) 219.
246 Gaja, 'Réflexions' (1993) 299; Bardo Fassbender, '*Quis judicabit?* The Security Council, Its Powers and Its Legal Control' (2000) 11(1) *EJIL* 222; White, 'Responses' (2009) 322; Philippa Webb and Christopher Michaelsen, 'Strengthening the Accountability of the UN Security Council' (2014) 19(3) *JC&SL* 385; Proulx, *Institutionalizing* (2016) 189.
247 Immanuel Kant, *On Perpetual Peace* (1795, Broadview Press, 2015) 54.
248 Hans Kelsen, *The Law of the United Nations: A Critical Analysis of Its Fundamental Problems* (Stevens & Sons, 1950) 19.
249 Pella, *La guerre-crime* (1946) 50.
250 Marco Roscini, *Cyber Operations and the Use of Force in International Law* (OUP, 2014) 110–111; Schmitt, *Tallin Manual* (2017) 357, rule 76.
251 Michael Wood, 'Towards New Circumstances in Which the Use of Force May be Authorized?', in Niels Blokker and Nico Schrijver (eds), *The Security Council and the Use of Force* (Martinus Nijhoff, 2005) 83.

The power of the Council ultimately descends from Article 16 of the Covenant of the League of Nations. According to some scholars, this power addressed State criminal responsibility and should have triggered the competence of an international jurisdiction.[252] During preparatory work for the UN Charter in San Francisco, provisions intending to limit the power of the Council, notably via preliminary or subsequent control by the General Assembly, were rejected.[253] The broad authority enjoyed by the Council can be further extended by applying the theory of implied powers, allowing the Council to exercise the command necessary to fulfil its functions.[254]

With regard to legal personality, under Article 23 of the UN Charter the Security Council has a political composition, rather than a strictly legal one. Scholars thus assume that the Council does not deliver strictly legal decisions, but makes political resolutions, thus addressing political disputes rather than legal controversies.[255] For instance, in *Military and Paramilitary Activities in and against Nicaragua*, Judge Schwebel held:

> [T]he Security Council is invested by the Charter with the authority to determine the existence of an act of aggression, it does not act as a court in making such a determination. It may arrive at a determination of aggression – or, as more often is the case, fail to arrive at a determination of aggression – for political rather than legal reasons [...] It may take legal considerations into account but, unlike a court, it is not bound to apply them.[256]

There are some critiques to the assumption that the Security Council politically assesses a threat to or breach of the peace. First, the language of the resolutions adopted by the Council often implies State responsibility. For instance, Resolution 660/1990 'condemns the Iraqi invasion of Kuwait'.[257] Resolution 1973/2011 affirms the 'responsibility' of the Libyan authorities vis-à-vis the

252 Donnedieu De Vabres, *Les principes* (1928) 429. See also s 1.1.1.

253 UNCIO, vol 3, 93, 126, 127, 136, 170–171, vol 4, 223, 649, 680, vol 12, 591–592, 599–600, 624–625, 641. For a scholarly viewpoint, see Nico Krisch, 'Article 41', in Simma, *The Charter* (2012) 1314–1315.

254 *Reparation for Injuries Suffered in the Service of the United Nations (Advisory Opinion)* [1949] ICJ Rep 180. For a critical opinion on the opportunity of applying the doctrine of implied powers to the Security Council, see Arangio-Ruiz, 'The "Federal Analogy"' (1997) 1.

255 White, 'Responses' (2009) 324. Meaningfully, according to Kelsen:

> The purpose of enforcement action under article 39 is not: to maintain or restore the law, but to maintain or restore peace, which is not necessarily identical with the law [...] For the Council would be empowered to establish justice if it considered the existing law as not satisfactory, and hence to enforce a decision which it considered to be just though not in conformity with existing law.
>
> (Kelsen, *The Law* (1950) 294–295)

256 *Military and Paramilitary Activities* [1986] Dissenting Opinion Schwebel 290, para 60.

257 S/RES/660, preamble.

people of Libya.[258] Second, although the notion of 'peace' under UN Charter Article 39 is a broad political concept, the notion of 'aggression' legally outlines an aggravated offence in international law. Third, the decisions of the Council trigger specific legal procedures and sanctions under Chapter VII of the UN Charter. The Council is thus a political organ that exercises a fundamentally juridical function, since it assesses State aggravated responsibility and imposes sanctions.[259] In this respect, during preparatory work for the DASR some Members of the ILC qualified measures under UN Charter Article 41 as 'penalties'.[260]

Scholars have underscored that there is a risk of undue interference by the Council in the matter of State aggravated responsibility.[261] Indeed, the composition of the Council reflects a centralised system of dominance by the Permanent Members, which was established according to the Dumbarton Oaks Proposals after World War II.[262] The Council also applies an undefined standard of proof.[263] Furthermore, the veto mechanism under Article 27 of the Charter introduces an aleatory element that diminishes the certainty of the sanction, thus affecting its pre-emptive effect. A Permanent Member might indeed be prone to offering protection to an allied State.[264]

For example, the Council authorised all necessary measures to repel the invasion of Kuwait by Iraq in 1990.[265] However, it could not take effective action on genocide and gross human rights violations in the SFRY in 1994, because of a Russian veto.[266] Similarly, the Council has not been able to take action in Syria since 2011, because of the opposition of China and Russia.[267] The fact that the General Assembly can replace the Council when it is paralysed by the

258 S/RES/1973, preamble.

259 Oscar Schachter, 'The Quasi-Judicial Role of the Security Council and the General Assembly' (1964) 58(4) *AJIL* 962; Sherif Elgebeily, *The Rule of Law in the United Nations Security Council Decision-Making Process* (Routledge, 2017) 11.

260 ILC, Summary Records (1976) 66, para 45.

261 See Arangio-Ruiz, 'The "Federal Analogy"' (1997) 23–26, arguing in favour of a more equitable distribution of power among the different UN organs and claiming that 1996 DASR 19 would have at least limited the influence of the UN Security Council in the field of State responsibility; Jacovides, 'State Responsibility' (2000) 297; Églantine Cujo and Mathias Forteau, 'Les réactions des organs politiques internationaux', in Ascensio, Decaux and Pellet, *Droit* (2012) 759–760.

262 United Nations Dumbarton Oaks Proposals (1944) ch VI, A. See also Kramer, 'State-Organized Crime' (2016) 241; Elgebeily, *The Rule* (2017) 10.

263 Nollkaemper, 'Concurrence' (2003) 631.

264 ILC, Summary Records (1976) 76, paras 24–26, 83, para 33; White, 'Responses' (2009) 321 and 329–330; Bassiouni, 'Challenges' (2010) 3; Elgebeily, *The Rule* (2017) 10.

265 Security Council, Iraq-Kuwait, UN Doc S/RES/678, 29 November 1990.

266 Id, Draft Resolution Reconfirming the Measures Imposed by the Security Council Resolutions with Respect to All Goods Crossing the Border between Yugoslavia and Bosnia and Herzegovina, Including Goods Destined for the UN Peace Areas in Croatia, UN Doc S/1358, 2 December 1994.

267 See, for instance, Security Council, Middle East, UN Doc S/RES/315, 12 April 2017.

veto mechanism, according to Resolution 377 (V) adopted in 1950,[268] is only a partial response to these critiques.

Alternatively, it has been argued that the measures taken by the Security Council are a form of 'police' action and thus have an enforcement nature, rather than a judicial one, which would exclude the necessity of determining State responsibility.[269] This argument, however, overlooks the fact that enforcement necessitates a prior assessment on responsibility. Even when it undertakes action to halt unlawful conduct, the Council needs to determine responsibility.[270] The 'police enforcement' view entails a determination of State aggravated responsibility in the absence of the full guarantees of judicial proceedings.[271] In this respect, it is noticeable that the Council does not have the independent military force initially envisaged in the Dumbarton Oaks Proposals and provided for in Articles 43–45 of the UN Charter.[272] Thus, the effectiveness of Council action depends on State collaboration on a case-by-case basis, mainly based on the contribution of the Permanent Members.[273]

According to some scholars, the Security Council exercises a jurisdictional role in assessing State aggravated responsibility.[274] In this respect, it has been pointed out that the criminalisation of State aggravated responsibility under 1996 DASR 19 had the critical function of prompting a shift from a political, or police, view of State aggravated responsibility to a judicial approach.[275] Indeed, if a judicial process were in place to assess State aggravated responsibility, notably via compulsory jurisdiction, police enforcement by the Council would be contextualised within such a process to implement pre-emptive measures and the final judgment.[276] Along these lines, commentators have underscored the need for a 'strengthened rule of law quality of the activities of political organs,

268 General Assembly, Uniting for Peace, UN Doc A.RES/377 (V), 3 November 1950. See also White, 'Responses' (2009) 333.

269 Proulx, *Institutionalizing* (2016) 225.

270 Pierre-Marie Dupuy, 'Implications of the Institutionalization of International Crimes of State', in Weiler, Cassese and Spinedi, *International Crimes* (1989) 176–177; Proulx, *Institutionalizing* (2016) 194.

271 ILC, Summary Records (1976) 79, paras 9–10; Martti Koskenniemi, 'The Police in the Temple Order, Justice and the United Nations: A Dialectical View (1995) 6(3) *EJIL* 326; White, 'Responses' (2009) 325; Proulx, *Institutionalizing* (2016) 126 and 223 ff.

272 United Nations Dumbarton Oaks Proposals (1944) ch VIII, B(5)–(10).

273 Rosalyn Higgins, 'Peace and Security: Achievements and Failures' (1995) 6(3) *EJIL* 451; White, 'Responses' (2009) 323–324 and 332–333.

274 According to Cherif Bassiouni, the Security Council would exercise criminal jurisdiction over States, raising the question of the conviction of innocent citizens together with the State (Cherif Bassiouni, *Introduction au droit pénal international* (Bruylant, 2002) 58). See also White, 'Responses' (2009) 316–318 and 332; Ollivier, 'International Criminal Responsibility' (2010) 711–712.

275 Arangio-Ruiz, 'The "Federal Analogy"' (1997) 24.

276 This was the purpose of the proposals elaborated by Gaetano Arangio Ruiz in his Seventh Report on State Responsibility (Arangio-Ruiz, Seventh Report (1995) 17 ff, paras 70 ff).

notably the Security Council, in regard to system criminality'.[277] The Council of the League of Nations gave rise to analogous concerns.[278]

Similar considerations may be developed with respect to the UN General Assembly, when it subrogates the Council in the exercise of powers under Chapter VII of the Charter, according to Resolution 377 (V). It is indeed because of the political nature of both the Council and the Assembly that the Second Part of the DASR proposed by Arangio-Ruiz in his Seventh Report envisaged their action as preliminary to the final decision of the ICJ on State criminal responsibility, upon unilateral recourse by a State.[279] However, according to Resolution 377 (V) the Assembly can only address States by means of recommendations, consistently with Article 10 of the UN Charter. Furthermore, the Assembly represents all UN Member States as the plenary organ of the Organisation. It thus ensures more impartiality, deciding by a simple or qualified majority, according to Article 18 of the Charter.[280]

3.2.2.2 The limited role of consensual jurisdiction, particularly the International Court of Justice

The function of international jurisdictions is quite limited with respect to State aggravated responsibility. Indeed, based on the essential tenet of equal sovereignty, States must consent to submit a dispute to international adjudication,[281] save the meaningful exception established in Article IX of the Genocide Convention. In fact, ICJ Statute Article 36 provides for the competence of the Court over 'cases which the parties refer to it'. UN Charter Article 95 allows States to submit disputes to tribunals other than the ICJ by means of agreement. Preparatory work for the UN Charter in San Francisco shows that compulsory jurisdiction was rejected as an obstacle to the achievement of a universal agreement.[282] Whilst this may be understandable if compulsory jurisdiction is implemented as a general solution, such a critique is less convincing if compulsory jurisdiction is limited to State aggravated responsibility, notably for aggression and genocide.

The establishment of compulsory jurisdiction would be an indispensable step for creating an effective procedural regime for State aggravated responsibility. The current absence of compulsory jurisdiction ultimately compels the adoption of alternative general reactions to State aggravated offences via the UN Security Council or State universal countermeasures.[283] The question therefore arises as

277 Nollkaemper, 'Systemic Effects' (2010) 352.
278 Donnedieu De Vabres, *Les principes* (1928) 426–427.
279 Arangio-Ruiz, Seventh Report (1995) 23, para 101. See also s 3.1.1.4.
280 White, 'Responses' (2009) 333–334; Proulx, *Institutionalizing* (2016) 116.
281 Scobbie, 'Assumptions' (2009) 285.
282 UNCIO, vol 13, 416, Report by the Rapporteur of Committee IV/I, Doc 913, IV/I/74(I).
283 Josef Kunz, 'Compulsory International Adjudication and Maintenance of Peace' (1944) 38(4) *AJIL* 678; Barboza, 'International Criminal Law' (1999) 108; Scobbie, 'Assumptions' (2009) 285.

to how such actions can be coordinated, particularly those of the ICJ as the principal judicial organ of the UN and those of the Security Council as the main UN organ dealing with State aggravated responsibility as a police or political body. In fact, with particular regard to UN action under Article VIII of the Genocide Convention, it has been remarked that it is 'sparse, ineffective or belated'.[284]

It is possible that the Security Council and the ICJ are seized of State aggravated responsibility simultaneously, giving rise to 'parallel competence'.[285] This could eventually lead to adopting different decisions on the same matter. In fact, according to Article 36(6) of its Statute the ICJ is free to decide on its own competence. Within the framework of proceedings under Chapter VI of the UN Charter, Article 36 provides that the Security Council has an obligation to take into account any dispute settlement procedures already adopted, prioritising the competence of the ICJ. This, nonetheless, does not exclude the possibility of the Council recommending other dispute settlement means under Chapter VI of the Charter. Such limits are also not applicable to proceedings under Chapter VII of the Charter.[286] *De facto*, it is not impossible that the Council could establish its competence in the matter of State aggravated responsibility before the ICJ does.

In the absence of specific normative mechanisms coordinating the decisions of the Security Council and the ICJ, the Court maintains that a prior decision of the Council or the Court prevails, according to a temporal logic. Indeed, decisions taken by the Council and the Court have the same hierarchical status. They override non-UN obligations, at least according to an extensive interpretation of UN Charter Article 103 as applying not only to obligations arising under the Charter, but also to those deriving from decisions of UN organs.[287] However, obligations established by the Charter and decisions of UN organs are limited by peremptory norms, which are absolutely non-derogable. In fact, peremptory rules are fundamentally embedded in the Charter itself, notably under Articles 1 and 2, which posit the general principles of the UN. Therefore, the temporal paradigm outlined by the ICJ should have limited application in the matter of State aggravated responsibility, allowing the Court to review prior decisions taken by the Council that are inconsistent with peremptory obligations.[288]

284 Webb, 'Binocular Vision' (2012) 126.

285 *United States Diplomatic and Consular Staff in Tehran (US v Iran)* [1980] ICJ Rep 21, para 40; *Armed Activities* [2005] ICJ Rep 168, Separate Opinion Elaraby 329, para 11. See also Chehrazad Krari-Lahya, 'Cooperation and Competition between the International Court of Justice and the Security Council', in Giorgio Gaja and Jenny Grote Stoutenberg (eds), *Enhancing the Rule of Law through the International Court of Justice* (Brill, 2014) 56; Proulx, *Institutionalizing* (2016) 145.

286 Preparatory work confirms that UN Charter art 36 is not meant to limit the power of the Security Council vis-à-vis the ICJ (UNCIO, vol 12, 73–74, Doc 530, III/2/30).

287 *Questions of Interpretation and Application of the 1971 Montreal Convention Arising from the Aerial Incident at Lockerbie (Libyan Arab Jamahiriya v US)* [1992] ICJ Rep 126, paras 39–42.

288 Dapo Akande, 'The ICJ and the Security Council: Is There Room for Judicial Control of Decisions of the Political Organs of the United Nations?' (1997) 46(2) *ICLQ* 317 and 322; Elgebeily, *The Rule* (2017) 42–43.

In light of the minimum normative hierarchy established by *jus cogens*, the question as to whether the ICJ can control the legality of decisions taken by the Council should be answered positively in the case of State aggravated offences,[289] despite the absence of any explicit provisions to this effect in the UN Charter.[290] In practice, the question is quite delicate, since it may entail a revision of 'police', or 'policy', action, going as far as to involve the use of armed force under Chapter VII of the Charter. In fact, the Court has not yet reviewed any decisions of the Council and might also have refrained from pronouncing on the use of force in the absence of a prior decision by the Council.[291] Similar problems arise with respect to measures adopted by the UN General Assembly.[292]

Concerning enforcement, under UN Charter Article 94, if a party to a dispute fails to comply with obligations imposed by a judgment of the ICJ, it is possible for another party to have recourse to the Security Council. Consequently, if it 'deems necessary', the Council may 'make recommendations' or 'decide upon measures to be taken to give effect to the judgment'. In light of this terminology, it is questionable whether ICJ judgments are effectively enforceable. A proposal aiming to compel action by the Council in support of a State accepting the jurisdiction of the Court was indeed rejected during preparatory work for the UN Charter.[293] Suggestions aiming to extend enforcement by the Council to all decisions made by international jurisdictions suffered the same negative outcome.[294] It is thus uniformly assumed that the Security Council is free to decide whether or not to enforce ICJ judgments in the case of a breach,[295] unlike the Council of the League of Nations under prior Article 13(4) of the Covenant of the League. The power of the Security Council is unrestrained in this respect and subject to the veto mechanism, by virtue of UN Charter Article 27.[296] In light of ICJ Statute Article 41, according to which the ICJ 'indicates' provisional

289 *Questions of Interpretation* [1992] Separate Opinion Shahabuddeen 28–29; *Armed Activities* [2005] 168, Separate Opinion Simma, 335, para 3. See also José Alvarez, 'Judging the Security Council' (1996) 90(1) *AJIL* 39; Robert Kolb, *The International Court of Justice* (Hart, 2013) 894–895; Proulx, *Institutionalizing* (2016) 137–141.

290 Costelloe, *Legal Consequences* (2017) 139. At the Conference in San Francisco, Committee IV/2 considered that, when the Charter was drafted, the nature of the UN and its competences did not prompt the inclusion of a provision conferring upon the ICJ competence to ultimately determine the correct interpretation of the Charter, thus vesting each organ with the power to decide what type of procedure would suit for resolving a question of interpretation of the Charter (UNCIO, vol 13, 709, Doc 933, IV/2/42(2)).

291 Webb, *International Judicial Integration* (2013) 130; Giorgio Gaja, 'Preventing Conflicts between the Court's Orders on Provisional Measures and Security Council Resolutions', in Gaja and Stoutenberg, *Enhancing* (2014) 89–90.

292 Rosa Möhrlein, 'Act-Dependent Judicial Review of Security Council and General Assembly Resolutions', in Gaja and Stoutenberg, *Enhancing* (2014) 110.

293 UNCIO, vol 4, 695.

294 Id, vol 4, 515, vol 12, 293 and 313.

295 Attila Tanzi, 'Problems of Enforcement of Decisions of the International Court Justice and the Law of the United Nations' (1995) 6(4) *EJIL* 541; Kolb, *The International Court* (2013) 849.

296 Kolb, *The International Court* (2013) 855. See also s 3.2.2.

measures and gives 'notice' to the Council, it is also considered that the Council has a discretionary power to implement provisional measures.[297] The enforcement of obligations imposed by the ICJ for State aggravated offences thus remains ultimately subject to political scrutiny.

3.2.3 Decentralised State action under general international law

Outside the quasi-universal system established by the UN Charter, the 2001 DASR codify specific remedies for State aggravated responsibility, in addition to voluntary settlement of international disputes indistinctly applying to all State wrongful acts. These complement procedures under the Charter, by virtue of DASR 59 and UN Charter Article 103:[298] third-party countermeasures are available to the extent that the action of the Security Council is ineffective.[299]

Substantively, the DASR clearly outline sanctions, which indistinctly apply to all State wrongful acts, but they do not precisely define State aggravated responsibility. Based on *jus cogens*, the definition of State aggravated responsibility under 2001 DASR 40 is certainly more specific than under the UN Charter. However, it still allows States to decide, on a case-by-case basis, what conduct is actually a serious breach of a peremptory norm.[300]

Procedurally, 2001 DASR 41(1), 48 and 54 seek to coordinate universal reactions to State aggravated responsibility by compelling cooperation, arguably at the level of both invocation of responsibility and countermeasures. Although these are meaningful remedies,[301] the assessment of State aggravated responsibility is left to States themselves, which can proceed on a political basis, not necessarily following strict legal criteria. Whereas it is consistent with the horizontal structure of international law, this approach defines an enforcement phase that ultimately depends on State interests and power.[302] Some scholars speak, in this regard, of a 'Westphalian model' that 'reflects the Hobbesian state of nature governing international relations whereby each State pursues its own interests'.[303] This regulation has given rise to different doctrines, particularly those of humanitarian intervention, responsibility to protect, anticipatory self-defence and implied authorisation.[304]

The theory of 'humanitarian intervention' provides that a State is authorised to resort to necessary and proportionate measures, including the use of force, in order to end human rights crises. In fact, given that at least some human

297 Kolb, *The International Court* (2013) 636–637.
298 Dupuy, 'The Deficiencies' (2012) 211.
299 Dawidowicz, *Third-Party Countermeasures* (2017) 261.
300 Ollivier, 'International Criminal Responsibility' (2010) 710.
301 Zimmermann and Teichmann, 'State Responsibility' (2009) 312–313; White, 'Responses' (2009) 316.
302 Nollkaemper, 'Systemic Effects' (2010) 345–347; Kramer, 'State-Organized Crime' (2016) 239.
303 Bassiouni, 'Challenges' (2010) 2. See also Scobbie, 'Assumptions' (2009) 296.
304 Alshdaifat, *International Law* (2017) 163 ff.

rights, such as the prohibition of torture, may be regarded as non-severable *erga omnes* obligations, their gross or systematic breach would affect all States of the international community, which would consequently be allowed to end the violation. Fundamentally, massive human rights infringements, such as genocide, affect the international community as a whole and justify a universal reaction, including secondary derogations from the prohibition on the use of force.[305] The doctrine of humanitarian intervention can also justify a State universal reaction when massive breaches of human rights are carried out by means of a terrorist attack.

The notion of humanitarian intervention is nonetheless controversial and State practice is evolving in the matter.[306] In the aftermath of the Kosovo war, it was suggested that the doctrine be extended so as to make intervention compulsory, in light of the stricter notion of 'responsibility to protect'.[307] This doctrine postulates that third States have not only a right but also a responsibility to end grave humanitarian crises, when a State fails to protect people in its own territory.[308] Such a view is supported by the text of 2001 DASR 41, which compels ('shall') State cooperation in bringing State aggravated responsibility to an end. However, States seem to be reluctant to accept this concept both within and outside the UN context,[309] which compels a case-by-case approach.[310]

Another theory is that of anticipatory self-defence. In fact, under general international law self-defence is allowed as a reaction to a 'threat' or an actual 'armed attack', according to the *Caroline* doctrine.[311] This is confirmed by UN Charter Article 2(4), prohibiting the 'threat or use of force'. UN Charter Article 51, however, refers to an 'armed attack' and its 'occurrence', and thus takes a narrower approach that departs from customary international law. On this basis, it is controversial whether it is possible to extend the limits of (collective) self-defence so as to include anticipated action forestalling a danger before it materialises, encompassing potential threats, in addition to effectively threatened force. The doctrine particularly addresses terrorism and the use of weapons

305 Chris O'Meara, 'Should International Law Recognize a Right of Humanitarian Intervention?' (2017) 66(2) *ICLQ* 448.

306 SC, Report on the 3988th Meeting, UN Doc S/PV 3988 (1999) 2 and 7; O'Meara, 'Should International Law' (2017) 442.

307 International Commission on Intervention and State Sovereignty, The Responsibility to Protect (2001) 11 ff; General Assembly, World Summit Outcome, UN Doc RES/A/60/L1, 24 October 2005, 30, para 139; Secretary General, Implementing the Responsibility to Protect, UN Doc A/63/677 (2009) 5, paras 3–4; O'Meara, 'Should International Law' (2017) 446.

308 Sassan Gholiagha, 'To Prevent Future Kosovos and Future Rwandas: A Critical Constructivist View of the Responsibility to Protect' (2015) 19(8) *IJHR* 1075–1078.

309 White, 'Responses' (2009) 331; Botte, 'Redefining' (2015) 1030.

310 Spencer Zifcak, 'Falls the Shadow: The Responsibility to Protect from Theory to Practice', in Charles Sampford and Ramesh Thajur, ***Responsibility to Protect and Sovereignty*** (Ashgate, 2013) 35.

311 See s 2.3.1.3.

of mass destruction,[312] but goes against a strict interpretation of the limits of self-defence, notably in light of UN Charter Article 51.[313]

The doctrine of 'implied authorisation' assumes that, when the UN Security Council is paralysed by a veto, all States may act in countermeasure against State aggravated offences, including the use of force, based on prior resolutions adopted by the Council.[314] This theory is also controversial, since in principle the Council should explicitly authorise States to act on a case-by-case basis.[315]

3.2.4 A controversial practice

In practice, the regulatory framework established under the UN Charter and general international law as codified in the 2001 DASR has spawned decentralised and non-uniform approaches to aggravated wrongful acts of States.[316] It is considered that the system has a low remedial and pre-emptive effect,[317] which has prompted the conclusion that the absence of a sufficiently organised reaction is the main cause of war.[318]

Nigel White underscores that action by the UN Security Council is an expression of '*Realpolitik*', but 'manifests insufficient concern for the fundamental norms of the international community' and 'has failed thus far to provide an effective centralized organ to ensure those norms are respected and enforced'.[319] Iain Scobbie maintains that invoking State responsibility as a reaction to system criminality 'guarantees neither remedy nor resolution' and 'might simply be an exercise in talking to the profoundly deaf'.[320] Pierre Marie Dupuy considers that the system is 'far from stable' and State aggravated offences, echoing State crimes, 'leave room for the sporadic development of unilateral or collective

312 Kinga Tibori Szabó, *Anticipatory Action in Self-Defence: Essence and Limits under International Law* (Springer, 2011) 2, 6, 196–199 and 203; Ryan Hayward, 'Evaluating the "Imminence" of a Cyber Attack for Purposes of Anticipatory Self-Defence' (2017) 117(2) *Col L Rev* 414 ff; Gray, *International Law* (2018) 170–173.

313 *Military and Paramilitary Activities* [1986] ICJ Rep 102 ff, paras 193 ff. See also Tom Ruys, *'Armed Attack' and Article 51 of the UN Charter* (CUP, 2010) 250; Gray, *International Law* (2018) 174–175.

314 Olivier Corten and François Dubuisson, 'L'hypothèse d'une règle émergente fondant une intervention militaire sur une "autorisation implicite" du Conseil de sécurité' (2000) 104(4) *RGDIP* 900; Gray, *International Law* (2018) 361 ff; Monica Hakimi, 'The *Jus ad Bellum*'s Regulatory Form' (2018) 112(2) *AJIL* 166.

315 Erika De Wet, *The Chapter VII Powers of the United Nations Security Council* (Hart, 2004) 290 and 295; Gray, *International Law* (2018) 382.

316 White, 'Responses' (2009) 316.

317 Dawidowicz, *Third-Party Countermeasures* (2017) 278.

318 Saldaña, 'La justice' (1925) 370; Sreenivasa Rao, 'International Crimes' (2005) 79–80; Battaglini, 'War' (2005) 149.

319 White, 'Responses' (2009) 329.

320 Scobbie, 'Assumptions' (2009) 296–297.

initiatives more or less inspired by the provisions set out in Article 48(2) of the ILC Articles'.[321]

The Bosnian genocide, humanitarian crises in Kosovo, Libya and Syria, the Iraq wars and the use of force to counter terrorism in Afghanistan, Syria and Iraq are critical examples of controversial reactions to State aggravated offences under the UN Charter and general international law. Some scholars assume that these are actions entailing punitive sanctions for State crimes.[322]

3.2.4.1 Bosnian genocide

In 1992, a conflict erupted in Bosnia-Herzegovina between Bosnians, having declared independence from the SFRY, and Serbians, organised as the Republika Srpska and controlling the dissolved Yugoslav armed forces, aiming to ensure the independence of Serbians living in Bosnia. This conflict was particularly ferocious, as shown by the sieges of Sarajevo and Srebrenica, which lasted years. Within this context, on 20 March 1993 Bosnia and Herzegovina unilaterally seized the ICJ under Article IX of the Genocide Convention to adjudicate upon the responsibility of Serbia and Montenegro for genocide, use of force, and violations of human rights and international humanitarian law.[323] Bosnia and Herzegovina also asked the Court to adopt preliminary measures, notably to waive a 'general and complete embargo on all deliveries of weapons and military equipment to Yugoslavia' imposed by the UN Security Council on the SFRY by means of Resolution 713/1991.[324] The aim was for Bosnia and Herzegovina to be enabled to exercise their (temporary) right to self-defence under UN Charter Article 51, so as to enforce the cessation of aggression and genocide.[325] Since it prevented the cessation of aggression and genocide, the embargo was considered to be in breach of the fundamental (peremptory) principles of the UN Charter.[326]

By a decision of 8 April 1993, in the *Bosnian Genocide* case the ICJ ordered the SFRY (Serbia and Montenegro) to 'take all measures within its power to prevent commission of the crime of genocide'.[327] Such a prudent decision is consistent with Article V of the Genocide Convention and anticipates the outcome of the final judgment. The Court delivered the final judgment in 2007,[328] long after the perpetration of the genocide, the initial Resolutions of the Security

321 Dupuy, 'The Deficiencies' (2012) 220.

322 Sreenivasa Rao, 'International Crimes' (2005) 77.

323 *Application of the Convention*, Application by the Republic of Bosnia and Herzegovina Instituting Proceedings versus Yugoslavia (Serbia and Montenegro), 20 March 1993, paras 32 ff.

324 Security Council, Socialist Federal Republic of Yugoslavia, UN Doc S/RES/713, 25 September 1991; *Application of the Convention*, Application (1993) paras 116 and 125–126.

325 *Application of the Convention*, Application (1993) paras 110 and 122–123.

326 Ibid, para 124.

327 *Application of the Convention*, Request for Indication of Provisional Measures [1993] ICJ Rep 24, para 52.

328 *Application of the Convention* [2007] 43.

Council, NATO air strikes against Serbian armed forces and the negotiation of the Dayton Agreement settling the conflict in 1995. Notably, in its order for preliminary measures the Court did not make a decision on the lawfulness of the embargo imposed by the Security Council, in light of peremptory international law.

However, the Court could have taken a much more courageous approach under Article VIII of the Genocide Convention, which allows UN organs to take 'such action under the Charter of the United Nations as they consider appropriate for the prevention and suppression of acts of genocide'.[329] The Court could have thus pre-emptively imposed on the SFRY an order for cessation of aggression and genocide, which States and the UN Security Council could have enforced under Article 41 of the ICJ Statute. Instead, the Court simply followed the policy already outlined by the Council.[330] The Court could also have anticipated satisfaction, prompting universal prosecution of the individual organs and agents of the SFRY responsible for genocide, but decided to separate completely individual criminal liability and State aggravated responsibility. The prudent orders of the ICJ proved to be ineffective and the Srebrenica genocide followed.[331] Scholars underscore that the *Bosnian Genocide* case demonstrates the 'need for rethinking of the connection between international law and system criminality'.[332]

In its final judgment of 26 February 2007, the ICJ held Serbia and Montenegro indirectly responsible for breaching the obligation to prevent and punish the commission of genocide by natural persons. The Court reached this conclusion considering that Serbia and Montenegro could not be unaware of a grave risk of genocide once the forces of the Republika Srpska had decided to take possession of the city of Srebrenica.[333] The Court also considered Serbia and Montenegro in breach of the 1996 preliminary measures requiring the taking of any possible actions to prevent the crime of genocide.[334] Concerning the obligation to punish the perpetrators, the ICJ held Serbia responsible for not collaborating

329 See s 1.2.1.3.

330 Rafaelle Maison, 'Les ordonnances de la CIJ dans l'affaire relative à la Convention pour la prévention et la répression du crime de génocide (1994) 5(3) *EJIL* 399–400.

331 Geoffrey DeWesee considered:

> In reading the ICJ's orders and judgments concerning this case it is too easy to forget what is really at issue – the lives of thousands of innocent people. Twice in 1993 the ICJ ordered that nothing be done to exacerbate the situation in Bosnia, yet two years later, a year before the Court was to finally establish its jurisdiction, Srebrenica fell and thousands were killed. It is the ghastly events which took place in Srebrenica that haunt me every time I think about the role of the ICJ in the dispute. What good is the ICJ, I ask myself, if it cannot even get to the merits on a case of such urgency as this one?
>
> (Geoffrey DeWeese, 'The Failure of the ICJ to Effectively Enforce the Genocide Convention' (1997–98) 26(4) *Denv J Intl L & Pol* 653)

332 Nollkaemper, 'Systemic Effects' (2010) 336.

333 *Application of the Convention* [2007] 219–229, paras 425–450.

334 Ibid 230 ff, paras 451 ff.

with the ICTY, notably in transferring General Mladić to the Tribunal.[335] The ICJ considered that the recognition of the responsibility of Serbia for failing to prevent and punish genocide constituted adequate satisfaction in favour of Bosnia and Herzegovina.[336] Scholars have underscored the inadequacy of the sanction, notably the absence of monetary compensation for victims, given the devastation suffered in Srebrenica.[337]

In reaching its conclusions, the ICJ excluded that Serbia and Montenegro were directly liable for the conduct of organs of the Republika Srpska acting in Bosnia. In fact, the Court considered that the standard for attribution of individual conduct to the State under 2001 DASR 8 is that of a 'complete dependence',[338] following the 'effective control' test previously established in *Nicaragua*.[339] The Court disregarded the broader 'overall control' test established by the ICTY in *Tadić*,[340] which would have permitted the direct responsibility of Serbia and Montenegro for genocidal conduct of members of the Republika Srpska operating in Bosnia to be affirmed.

It is therefore clear that the ICJ, as the organ competent to adjudicate upon State responsibility, and the ICTY, as the organ having jurisdiction over individuals, reached diametrically opposed conclusions on the issue of attribution of responsibility to the State for genocidal conduct of its organs or agents.[341] Subsequently, in the case of *Lubanga Dyilo*, the ICC upheld the 'overall control' test to determine the attribution of conduct of Mr Dyilo and the *Union des patriots congolais* to the State of Rwanda.[342] This was a preliminary step to establishing the international nature of a conflict taking place in the territory of the Democratic Republic of the Congo.

3.2.4.2 Humanitarian crises in Kosovo, Libya and Syria

Military action carried out in the SFRY by NATO Member States as a reaction to the inhumane treatment of Albanian people in the autonomous province of Kosovo is a typical example of humanitarian intervention. From 26 March to 10 June 1999, NATO Member States conducted aerial bombing operations in Belgrade and other parts of the territory of Serbia. The aim was to free Kosovo from the Serbian army, which was considered responsible for the commission of serious human rights violations within the context of ethnic cleansing against

335 Ibid 229, para 449.
336 Ibid 233 ff, paras 462 ff.
337 Tomuschat, 'Reparation' (2007) 906 ff; Webb, 'Binocular Vision' (2012) 135.
338 *Application of the Convention* [2007] 167, paras 379 ff.
339 *Military and Paramilitary Activities* [1986] 64–65, para 115.
340 *Application of the Convention* [2007] 209–210, paras 403–404; *Tadić* (1999) 50, para 122, 56, para 131, 171–172, paras 160 and 162. See also s 2.2.1.1.
341 Webb, 'Binocular Vision' (2012) 137 ff; Alain Pellet, 'Should We (Still) Worry about Fragmentation?', in Andreas Follesdal and Geir Ulfstein (eds), *The Judicialization of International Law* (OUP, 2018) 231.
342 *Lubanga Dyilo* (2012) 248, para 541.

the Kosovar population. Bombing covered residential areas, which raised doubts on the proportionality of the intervention. Russia, China, India and other non-aligned States condemned the use of force in Kosovo as unlawful.[343] After the intervention, the UN Mission in Kosovo established internationalised courts to try inter-ethnic war crimes and humanitarian crimes via Regulation 6/2000, based on the consideration that local judges did not offer adequate guarantees of impartiality.[344]

In *Legality of Use of Force (1999–2004)*, Serbia and Montenegro, having succeeded the SFRY, challenged the lawfulness of the humanitarian campaign with an action in the ICJ against nine NATO Member States.[345] Serbia and Montenegro invoked, inter alia, a breach of the prohibition on the use of force and unlawful attacks against civilian targets.[346] As a ground for jurisdiction, Serbia and Montenegro invoked Article 36(2) of the ICJ Statute, Article IX of the Genocide Convention and Article 4 of the 1930 Convention of Conciliation, Judicial Settlement and Arbitration concluded between Yugoslavia and some of the defendants.[347] The complaint also raises the question of the division of responsibility between NATO as an international organisation and its Member States.

In the course of oral arguments in the case of *Serbia and Montenegro v Belgium*, responding to a request for provisional measures by the plaintiff,[348] Belgium argued that 'NATO, and the Kingdom of Belgium in particular, felt obliged to intervene to forestall an ongoing humanitarian catastrophe, acknowledged in Security Council Resolutions.'[349] In the view of Belgium, the intervention aimed to safeguard 'essential values which also rank as *jus cogens*', such as 'the right to life, physical integrity, the prohibition of torture', according to the principle of an 'armed humanitarian intervention'.[350] The ICJ took a stance opposite to the one it adopted in the dispute concerning the *Bosnian Genocide* case and dismissed the disputes on jurisdictional grounds, because Serbia and Montenegro were not parties to the ICJ Statute as well as other invoked treaties. The Court assumed that there was no continuity between the plaintiffs and the SFRY.[351]

343 Richard Falk, 'Kosovo, World Order, and the Future of International Law' (1999) 93(4) *AJIL* 850; Antonio Cassese, '*Ex Iniuria Ius Oritur*: Are We Moving towards International Legitimation of Forcible Humanitarian Countermeasures in International Law?' (1999) 10(1) *EJIL* 28–29.

344 Williams, *Hybrid* (2012) 83; Sarah Williams, 'The Specialist Chambers of Kosovo: The Limits of Internationalization?' (2016) 14(1) *JICJ* 51.

345 *Legality of Use of Force (Serbia and Montenegro v Belgium* et al*)*, Application Instituting Proceedings, 29 April 1999.

346 Ibid 4 ff.

347 Ibid 3.

348 *Legality of Use of Force*, Request for the Indication of Provisional Measures, 29 April 1999.

349 Public Sitting Held on Monday 10 May 1999, CR 99/15.

350 Ibid.

351 See, for instance, *Legality of Use of Force (Serbia and Montenegro v Belgium)* [2004] ICJ Rep 327, para 125.

A critical application of the doctrine of 'humanitarian intervention', extensively interpreted according to the 'responsibility to protect' theory, took place in Libya in 2011. Within the context of the 'Arab Awakening', Libyan security forces opened fire on protesters in Benghazi and anti-government movements that had spread across Libya against Muammar Gaddafi.[352] Following these events, Colonel Gaddafi delivered radio broadcasts that were reminiscent of the 1994 Rwandan genocide and government forces allegedly attacked indiscriminately civilian targets.[353] The situation prompted the UN Human Rights Council (HRC) to call for Libya to cease human rights violations.[354] By means of Resolution 1970/2011, the UN Security Council referred the situation in Libya to the ICC under Article 13(b) of its Statute and called on States to apply sanctions, including arms embargoes, travel bans and asset freezing.[355] The European Union (EU) and States, including the UK, the US, Switzerland, Australia and Canada, consequently adopted sanctions against Libya.[356] On 17 March 2011, the UN Security Council passed Resolution 1973, establishing a no-fly zone and authorising States to take 'all necessary measures' to 'protect civilians and civilian populated areas under threat in the Libyan Arab Jamahiriya'.[357] The Resolution prompted the establishment of a NATO-led coalition of Western and Arab States, which implemented a no-fly zone, conducted air strikes on areas under governmental control and provided support to rebel forces. The coalition eventually defeated the regime of Colonel Gaddafi on 14 October 2011.[358]

Although at the outset the situation in Libya was a serious breach of *jus cogens* and seemed to fulfil all the requirements to compel humanitarian action,[359] it has been argued that countermeasures not involving the use of force would have been a sufficient remedy.[360] Furthermore, since UN Security Council Resolution 1973/2011 only allowed the use of force to protect civilians, by overthrowing the regime of Colonel Gaddafi the NATO-led coalition stretched its mandate.[361] On 20 October 2011, rebel forces reportedly captured Gaddafi in a drainpipe, killed him and allegedly committed mass murder of members of Gaddafi's forces, which was never appropriately investigated.[362] As a consequence of the

352 Spencer Zifcak, 'The Responsibility to Protect after Libya and Syria' (2012) 13(1) *Mel JIL* 62.
353 Ibid 63.
354 HRC, Situation of Human Rights in the Libyan Arab Jamahiriya, Resolution S-15/2, 25 February 2011. See also HRC, Report of the International Commission of Inquiry on Libya, UN Doc A/HRC/19/68 (2012).
355 S/RES/1973, 3 ff, paras 4 ff.
356 See, for instance, EU Council, Restrictive Measures in View of the Situation in Libya, Decision 2011/137/CFSP.
357 S/RES/1973, 3, paras 4 and 6.
358 Zifcak, 'The Responsibility' (2012) 65–66.
359 Weatherall, Jus Cogens (2015) 414 and 419.
360 Security Council Meeting of 17 March 2011, UN Doc S/PV.6498 (2011) 8.
361 Zifcak, 'The Responsibility' (2012) 66; Christian Henderson, *The Use of Force and International Law* (CUP, 2018) 138–139.
362 Human Rights Watch, Libya: New Proof of Mass Killings at Gaddafi Death Site (2011), https://www.hrw.org/news.

intervention, Libya is experiencing a legitimacy crisis, whereby a government established in the eastern city of Tobruk, representing the elected Parliament and backed by an armed group called 'Operation Dignity', opposes another government established in Tripoli and supported by the armed group 'Operation Dawn'.[363] In light of these circumstances, some scholars maintain that Libya was a lost opportunity to show how to appropriately rely on the responsibility to protect, based on a minimum use of force.[364] However, analysis generally shows that the doctrine applies flexibly according to the situation and is developing progressively.[365]

Similar to the situation in Libya, crimes against humanity committed by both the State and individuals have been reported in Syria since 2011, in the framework of a conflict between the government and anti-government armed groups.[366] A UN Independent Commission of Inquiry underscored the peremptory nature of such violations and the obligation of the Syrian Arab Republic to punish individual perpetrators.[367] By 2013, the situation had deteriorated to an extent that prompted the Commission to affirm the responsibility of governmental and non-governmental forces for crimes against humanity and war crimes.[368] At the same time, the Commission invoked the notion of 'responsibility to protect', reminding Syria's Government of its 'primary role in protecting the rights of its citizens'.[369] In 2015, the Commission underscored the inaction of the UN Security Council and pointed out that, given 'the manifest failure of the Government to protect its population from gross human rights abuses, the international community, through the United Nations, bears the responsibility of protecting the Syrian population from such crimes.'[370] In 2016, the UN HRC called for an immediate cessation of violations of human rights and international humanitarian law.[371] The HRC also pointed out the need to ensure the prosecution of responsible individuals via national or international jurisdictions, noting the critical role of the ICC.[372] The UN General Assembly

363 Gray, *International Law* (2018) 62.

364 Sigmund Simonsen, 'The Intervention in Libya in a Legal Perspective: R2P and International Law', in Dag Henriksen and Ann Karin Larssen (eds), *Political Rationale and International Consequences of the War in Libya* (OUP, 2016) 263–264; Gray, *International Law* (2018) 63.

365 Maggie Powers, 'Responsibility to Protect: Dead, Dying, or Thriving?' (2015) 19(8) *IJHR* 1269.

366 Independent International Commission of Inquiry on the Syrian Arab Republic, First Report to the Human Rights Council, UN Doc A/HRC/S-17/2/Add.1 (2011) 20 ff, paras 109 ff.

367 Ibid 21, para 110.

368 Independent International Commission of Inquiry on the Syrian Arab Republic, Sixth Report to the Human Rights Council, UN Doc A/HRC/24/46 (2013) 23, paras 192 and 194.

369 Ibid 23, para 192.

370 Independent International Commission of Inquiry on the Syrian Arab Republic, Ninth Report to the Human Rights Council, UN Doc A/HRC/28/69 (2015) 20, para 133.

371 HRC, The Deteriorating Situation of Human Rights in the Syrian Arab Republic, and the Recent Situation in Aleppo, UN Doc A/HRC/RES/S-25/1, 21 October 2016, 2, para 1.

372 Ibid 3, para 8.

subsequently upheld the same stance.[373] In 2011, this situation prompted some States and international organisations, including Canada, Germany the UK and the EU, to establish a Commission for International Justice and Accountability. The Commission has collected evidence against senior Syrian leaders for future use by courts in assessing criminal responsibility for serious human rights violations, raising concerns of partiality.[374] In 2016, the UN General Assembly established the International, Impartial and Independent Mechanism for Syria and mandated it to collect evidence assisting future national, regional or international criminal proceedings against persons responsible for serious crimes under international law.[375]

Following the probable use of chemical weapons by Syrian armed forces in Eastern Damascus in August 2013, the UK qualified '[t]he use of chemical weapons by the Syrian regime' as 'a serious crime of international concern', as well as 'a war crime and a crime against humanity', attracting 'humanitarian intervention'.[376] In 2013, the UN General Assembly reiterated the responsibility to protect of the Syrian Government via Resolution 67/262.[377] In this context, scholars have articulated the theoretical framework of 'humanitarian reprisals' or 'humanitarian sanctions', whereby States should act collectively to end breaches of peremptory norms in Syria, according to 2001 DASR 40, 41 and 48.[378] Collective State action should be grounded in both humanitarian interests and punitive purposes, in light of the theories of humanitarian intervention, responsibility to protect and State crimes.[379] Joseph Weiler has thus stated that 'State crimes are back on the agenda.'[380]

Whilst initially paralysed by the opposition of Russia and China, the Security Council condemned Syria via Resolution 2139/2014.[381] However, China and Russia vetoed a referral of the situation to the ICC.[382] In 2017, Russia vetoed a draft resolution condemning the use of chemical weapons by Syria.[383]

373 General Assembly, Middle East, UN Doc A/RES/71/248, 21 December 2016. See also Christian Wenaweser and James Cockayne, 'Justice for Syria? The International, Impartial and Independent Mechanism and the Emergence of the UN General Assembly in the Realm of International Criminal Justice' (2017) 15(2) *JICJ* 214.

374 Melinda Rankin, 'Investigating Crimes against Humanity in Syria and Iraq: The Commission for International Justice and Accountability' (2017) 9(4) *GRP* 420.

375 A/RES/71/248, 2, para 4.

376 UK Prime Minister's Office, Chemical Weapon Use by the Syrian Regime: UK Government Legal Position, Policy Paper (2013).

377 General Assembly, The Situation in the Syrian Arab Republic, UN Doc A/RES/67/262, 15 May 2013.

378 Jørgensen, 'The Concept' (2015) 198.

379 Ibid 199; Botte, 'Redefining' (2015) 1031–1032; Alise Coen, 'R2P, Global Governance, and the Syrian Refugee Crisis' (2015) 19(8) *IJHR* 1051.

380 Joseph Weiler, 'Crime and Punishment: The Reification and Deification of the State (A Footnote to the Syria Debate)' (2013) 24(4) *EJIL* 996.

381 S/RES/2139.

382 Id, Middle East, UN Doc S/RES/348, 22 May 2014.

383 S/315/2017.

Since 2014, a US-led international coalition established to counter the Islamic State in Iraq and The Levant (ISIL) has conducted airstrikes in Syria against ISIL, as well as against government and pro-government targets.[384] Russia has conducted military operations in support of the Government since September 2015. In April 2018, the alleged use of chemical weapons by the Syrian Government against civilians in Douma was considered to be a 'pretext' by Russia, but the situation prompted the US, the UK and France to launch strikes against chemical weapons facilities.[385] Such disparate reactions perfectly summarise the anarchical response of the international community to a situation involving both individual criminal responsibility and State aggravated responsibility.[386]

3.2.4.3 Iraq wars

When, on 2 August 1990, Iraqi troops, then governed by Saddam Hussein, crossed the border of Kuwait, a small and oil-rich neighbouring country, an international crisis unfolded. Occupation, aiming at annexation, entailed the use of force in flagrant violation of the basic principle of sovereignty recognised in Article 2(4) of the UN Charter. Reportedly, Iraqi troops systematically committed human rights violations and breaches of international humanitarian law. In response, seized of the question by then US President George Bush, acting under UN Charter Articles 39 and 40 the UN Security Council adopted Resolution 660/1990, condemning Iraq for aggression and demanding its withdrawal from Kuwait.[387] Following non-compliance, the Council passed Resolution 661/1990, compelling all States to impose a financial and trade embargo on Iraq.[388] Subsequently, still acting under Chapter VII of the UN Charter the Council passed Resolution 678/1990, requesting that 'Iraq comply fully with Resolution 660 (1990)' and allowing UN Member States to 'use all necessary means' in order to 'restore international peace and security'.[389]

Within the legal framework created by the Security Council, a US-led coalition, including Western and Arab States, freed Kuwait from Iraqi troops in a quick combat operation named 'Iraqi Storm'. The legality of Resolution 678/1990 has been criticised, both because the Resolution was adopted without the consensus of the five Permanent Members of the Security Council and because it is not uncontroversial that economic sanctions would have been insufficient to end the

384 See further s 3.2.4.4.
385 Security Council, Letter from the Secretary General, S/2018/732, 25 July 2018, 84 ff; Hakimi, 'The *Jus ad Bellum*' (2018) 180–181.
386 Gabriele Lombardo, 'The Responsibility to Protect and the Lack of Intervention in Syria between the Protection of Human Rights and Geopolitical Strategies' (2015) 19(8) *IJHR* 1194; Elgebeily, *The Rule* (2018) 83.
387 S/RES/660, paras 1 and 2.
388 Security Council, Iraq-Kuwait, UN Doc S/RES/661, 6 August 1990, paras 3–4.
389 Id, Iraq-Kuwait, UN Doc S/RES/678, 29 November 1990, para 4.

invasion of Kuwait.[390] Other scholars, by contrast, consider that the first Iraq war is one of the few occasions where there was a consistent invocation of international law to justify the use of military force.[391]

Whilst the legality of the first Iraq war is disputed, the second Iraq war, also known as 'Operation Iraqi Freedom', is the most controversial case of pre-emptive self-defence.[392] In 2003, a combined force including troops from the US, the UK, Australia and Poland invaded Iraq and toppled the regime of Saddam Hussein after three weeks of combat operations. Action was justified as a form of anticipatory self-defence, assuming that Iraq was in possession of weapons of mass destruction. In fact, Iraq had obstructed work of UN weapons inspectors for more than a decade, in breach of the obligations imposed by UN Security Council Resolution 687/1991, which had been adopted after the liberation of Kuwait from Iraqi occupation. Despite the absence of a specific UN authorisation, the US and Allied Powers sought to justify the use of force based on an implied permission by the UN Security Council under Resolution 678/1990, which allowed resort to 'all necessary means' to implement not only prior Resolution 660/1990 but also 'all subsequent relevant resolutions'.[393]

After the end of combat in May 2003, only degraded remnants of abandoned chemical weapons were found in Iraq, so that the US-led Iraq Survey Group concluded that in 1991 Iraq had terminated its nuclear, chemical and biological programmes and had no active plans at the time of occupation.[394] Not being justified under 2001 DASR 21 as a secondary reaction to an anticipated armed attack, the use of force by the US-led coalition could thus correctly qualify as an act of aggression under international law.[395] However, no response has so far ensued not only at the collective level but also in terms of individual prosecution for aggression.[396]

On 10 December 2003, the Iraqi Governing Council created by the Coalition Provisional Authority established the Iraqi Special Tribunal. The Tribunal has jurisdiction over Iraqi nationals or residents accused of genocide, crimes against

390 John Quigley, 'The United States and the United Nations in the Persian Gulf War: New Order or Disorder' (1992) 25(1) *Cornell Intl LJ* 32.

391 Paul Kahn, 'Lessons for International Law from the Gulf War' (1992–93) 45(2) *Stan L Rev* 433.

392 Carsten Stahn, 'Enforcement of the Collective Will after Iraq' (2003) 97(4) *AJIL* 814; Abraham Sofaer, 'On the Necessity of Pre-emption' (2003) 14(2) *EJIL* 220 ff; Gray, *International Law* (2018) 367.

393 William Taft and Todd Buchawald, 'Pre-emption, Iraq and International Law' (2003) 97(3) *AJIL* 559 ff; Gray, *International Law* (2018) 368–370.

394 Iraq Survey Group, Final Report: Weapons of Mass Destruction (2004), http://www.globalsecurity.org/wmd/library/report/2004/isg-final-report.

395 On the second Iraq war as an international crime, see Ronald Kramer and Raymond Michalowski, 'War, Aggression and State Crime: A Criminological Analysis of the Invasion and Occupation of Iraq' (2005) 45(4) *Br J Crim* 448 ff; Kramer, 'State-Organized Crime' (2016) 236; Alshdaifat, *International Law* (2017) 209–210.

396 John Hagan, Joshua Kaiser and Anna Hanson, *Iraq and the Crimes of Aggressive War: The Legal Cynicism of Criminal Militarism* (CUP, 2015) 2–3; Tom Ruys, 'Justiciability, Complementarity and Immunity: Reflections on the Crime of Aggression' (2017) 13(1) *Utr L Rev* 27.

humanity, war crimes, or other violations of Iraqi laws committed between 17 July 1968 and 1 May 2003.[397] These dates span the period from the coup d'état that brought the Ba'athists to power to the end of major hostilities declared by US President Bush. In 2005, the sovereign Iraqi Government amended the Statute of the Tribunal to include the death penalty.

On 13 May 2014, upon receipt of new information the ICC Prosecutor re-opened a preliminary examination of Operation Iraqi Freedom which was terminated on 9 February 2006.[398] The Prosecutor is currently considering the situation of members of the UK military forces for allegations of war crimes, including civilian casualties and ill-treatment.[399]

3.2.4.4 Counter-terrorism in Afghanistan, Syria and Iraq

State practice also seems to have controversially evolved towards the acknowledgment of the legality of the use of pre-emptive armed force against terrorism, especially since the 9/11 attacks on the US.[400] In fact, defining a general framework for international counter-terrorism via Resolutions 1368 and 1373, in 2001 the UN Security Council acknowledged the 'inherent right of individual or collective self-defence', as well as 'the need to combat by all means, in accordance with the Charter of the United Nations, threats to international peace and security caused by terrorist acts'.[401] The Resolutions thus authorised States to 'take the necessary steps to prevent the commission of terrorist acts'.[402] Hence, a terrorist attack is considered a 'threat' or 'use' of force, which, if (pre-emptively) attributable to a State, could trigger resort to armed force in self-defence.[403]

Following this logic, Al-Qaeda, a private organisation, was held mainly responsible for the 9/11 attacks. However, based on UN Security Council Resolutions 1368/2001 and 1373/2001, in October 2001 a US-led coalition undertook military operations against the Taliban regime, suspected of protecting Al-Qaeda terrorists in Afghanistan.[404] Some scholars, nonetheless, argue that the use of force was immediately directed against Al-Qaeda, not against the Taliban regime ruling Afghanistan.[405] In any case, the use of force in this context is considered to be an application of the State obligation to cooperate in

397 Michael Newton, 'Legal Authorities for the Creation of the Iraqi High Tribunal', in Michael Scharf and Gregory McNeal (eds), *Saddam on Trial: Understanding and Debating the Iraqi High Tribunal* (Carolina Academic Press, 2006) 20.

398 ICC Prosecutor, Report on Preliminary Examination Activities (2015) 7, https://www.icc-cpi.int/iccdocs/otp/otp-pe-rep-2015-eng.pdf.

399 Ibid 8–10.

400 Sofaer, 'On the Necessity' (2003) 225; Gray, *International Law* (2018) 249.

401 S/RES/1368 and S/RES/1373, preamble.

402 S/RES/1368, 1, para 5; S/RES/1373, 2, para 2(b).

403 John Dauth, 'Defence Cooperation: Terrorism' (2002) 22 *Aust YBIL* 355; Gray, *International Law* (2018) 206–207.

404 Dupuy, 'L'unité' (2002) 345–349; Gray, *International Law* (2018) 208–209.

405 Scharf, 'How the War' (2016) 40–41.

ending breaches of peremptory norms under 2001 DASR 41. In fact, Resolution 1368/2001 called on 'the international community to redouble their efforts to prevent and suppress terrorist attacks including by increased cooperation'.[406] Since 2007, the ICC Prosecutor has been examining war crimes and crimes against humanity allegedly committed during the conflict in Afghanistan by members of the Taliban regime, on the one hand, and members of the US military and Central Intelligence Agency, on the other.[407]

This approach further evolved with the intervention of a coalition of Western and Arab States led by the US to counter the terrorist activities of the Islamic State based in Iraq and Syria.[408] ISIS has its roots in the Sunni and Ba'athist-dominated Iraqi army of Saddam Hussein, which was defeated via operation 'Iraqi Freedom' in 2003 and subsequently oppressed by the Shi'ite-dominated Iraqi Government of Prime Minister Nouri al-Maliki. This situation prompted members of the former Sunni army to become insurgents under the name of 'Al-Qaeda in Iraq', which was later changed to the 'Islamic State of Iraq' (ISI). When protests against the regime of Bashar al-Assad in Syria escalated into a civil war in 2014, ISI occupied territory across the border, established its 'capital' in al-Raqqa and further modified the group's name to 'ISIS'. In the occupied lands, ISIS has imposed repressive conditions, similar to the former Taliban regime in Afghanistan, beheading thousands of Christians, Kurds and Shi'ites and destroying Shi'ite shrines and archaeological sites.[409]

Counter-terrorist action against ISIS has taken place particularly via targeted airstrikes. Whilst Iraq consented to such action in its territory, Syria did not. Counter-terrorist action was first justified based on humanitarian intervention and the right to use force in a failed State,[410] but justifications eventually settled on self-defence. The arguments elaborated in the aftermath of 9/11 thus evolved so as to assume that, when a government is unable or unwilling to suppress the (potential) threat of an armed attack posed by a non-State actor operating within its borders, the use of force in (pre-emptive) self-defence by third States is justified.[411] Major Powers such as China, Russia and the UK initially opposed this argument, but consensus was achieved after ISIS attacked a Russian jetliner over the Sinai desert, as well as a stadium and concert hall in Paris in 2015. Indeed, on 2 December 2015 the UN Security Council adopted Resolution 2249.[412] The Resolution called on States 'to take all necessary measures, in compliance with international law, in particular with the United Nations Charter, as well as international human rights, refugee and humanitarian law, on the territory

406 S/RES/1368, 1, para 4. See Weatherall, 'The Status' (2014–15) 624.

407 ICC Prosecutor, Report on Preliminary Examination (2015) 26–31.

408 Gray, *International Law* (2018) 238.

409 Ibid 237.

410 Jørgensen, 'The Concept' (2015) 174.

411 Scharf, 'How the War' (2016) 17–18.

412 Security Council, Threats to International Peace and Security Caused by Terrorist Acts, UN Doc S/RES/2249, 20 November 2015.

under the control of ISIL'.[413] Following the logic of peremptory obligations, the Resolution also called States to 'redouble and coordinate their efforts to prevent and suppress terrorist acts committed specifically by ISIL' as well as 'ANF [Al-Nusrah Front], and all other individuals, groups, undertakings, and entities associated with Al Qaeda, and other terrorist groups', so as to 'eradicate the safe haven they have established over significant parts of Iraq and Syria'.[414] Some scholars claim that this approach prompted a critical paradigm shift in favour of self-defence against non-State actors, establishing a new international customary practice comparable to the change prompted by the establishment of the IMTs in Nuremberg and Tokyo, and the ICTY and ICTR.[415]

3.2.5 State and individual immunities as a bar to domestic jurisdiction?

3.2.5.1 State and individual immunities?

Domestic jurisdiction raises issues of justiciability with respect to both States and natural persons. States, indeed, enjoy immunity from domestic jurisdiction by virtue of the principle of sovereign equality.[416] In the context of State sovereign immunity, individuals enjoy immunity for functional conduct and temporary personal immunity for non-functional conduct.[417] However, given the peremptory nature of the rights that State aggravated offences and some individual crimes infringe, a conflict arises between non-derogable *erga omnes* obligations and immunity from domestic jurisdiction. It is therefore possible to assume that the peremptory nature of the infringed obligations overrides immunity, which would thus subject the State and its organs or agents to domestic jurisdiction.

Concerning States, domestic courts have sought to erode the inviolability of the principle of absolute immunity in the case of a serious breach of a peremptory norm. Notably, this was the approach taken by the Italian Supreme Court of Cassation in *Ferrini*. This case concerned gross human rights violations committed by German occupying forces against Italians between 1943 and 1945, including mass killing, the deportation of large numbers of civilians for use as forced labour and denial of prisoner of war status for thousands of soldiers. Whilst the Trial Chamber and Appeals Court declined jurisdiction based on

413 Ibid, para 5.

414 Ibid.

415 Michael Scharf, 'How the War' (2016) 64–67. But see Gray, *International Law* (2018) 192 and 242–248.

416 Convention on Jurisdictional Immunities of States and Their Property, adopted 2 December 2004, A/RES/59/38, not yet in force, art 5. See also Hazel Fox and Philippa Webb, *The Law of State Immunity* (OUP, 3rd edn, 2013) 2–3 and 89; Hamilton, 'State-Enabled Crimes' (2016) 319–320.

417 Ramona Pedretti, *Immunity of Heads of State and State Officials for International Crimes* (Brill, 2015) 8.

the doctrine of *acta jure imperii*,[418] the Supreme Court held that, although customary law prescribes the immunity from jurisdiction of a foreign State for acts that are an expression of its sovereign authority, immunity is waived when such acts amount to international crimes.[419] Indeed, according to the Court, international crimes violate peremptory norms, which override the principle of State immunity.[420] The Court further broadly identified international crimes committed by State organs or agents, such as deportation and forced labour, as grave breaches of peremptory norms under 2001 DASR 40(2).[421] Some scholars interpret this stance as a form of compliance with the State obligation not to recognise the lawfulness of a serious breach of a peremptory norm under DASR 41(2).[422]

The decision of the Italian Supreme Court in *Ferrini* prompted several actions by Italian civilians against Germany for compensation. Whilst the identification of individual international crimes as breaches of peremptory norms and State responsibility under DASR 40 seems quite broad, the decision of the Court disclosed the possibility of subjecting State aggravated responsibility to domestic adjudication, and possibly prosecution, when, unlike Italy, domestic law recognises the criminal responsibility of legal entities.

The *Ferrini* judgment prompted Germany to act in the ICJ, which, in *Jurisdictional Immunities of the State*, rebutted the *Ferrini* decision and held Germany immune from the jurisdiction of Italian courts for offences committed in the Italian territory during World War II. The ICJ took a more conservative stance and held that 'under customary international law as it presently stands, a State is not deprived of immunity by reason of the fact that it is accused of serious violations of international human rights law or the international law of armed conflict.'[423] As a consequence, the Italian Constitutional Court reacted by declaring that the principle of State sovereign immunity cannot trump supreme constitutional principles, such as those shielding victims of international crimes.[424] The case underscores that, whilst there is an evident tension between State aggravated responsibility and jurisdictional immunity, it is clear that domestic action against a State is quite problematic, at least for the time being. In

418 *Ferrini v Germany*, Trial Chamber (Arezzo), Decision of 3 November 2000; *Id*, Court of Appeals (Firenze), Decision of 14 January 2002.

419 *Id*, Italian Court of Cassation, Case 5044/2004, Judgment of 6 November 2003, Registered 11 March 2004 (2006) 128 *ILR* 659.

420 Ibid 669, para 9.1.

421 Ibid 668, para 2.

422 Zimmermann and Teichmann, 'State Responsibility' (2009) 311–312.

423 *Jurisdictional Immunities of the State (Germany v Italy: Greece Intervening)* [2012] ICJ Rep 139, para 91. See also Costelloe, *Legal Consequences* (2017) 285.

424 *Immunità degli Stati esteri da giurisdizione*, Italian Constitutional Court, Judgment 238 of 22 October 2014 (2015) 98(1) *RDI* 255, para 3.5. For a scholarly viewpoint, see Michaela Frulli, '"Time Will Tell Who Just Fell and Who's Been Left Behind": On the Clash between the International Court of Justice and the Italian Constitutional Court' (2016) 14 *JICJ* 589.

this respect, some scholars assume that the notion of a 'State crime' under 1996 DASR 19 would have waived State immunity before domestic courts.[425]

With respect to individuals, the principle of immunity for functional acts (*ratione materiae*) before domestic jurisdictions has actually been eroded for international crimes and transnationally harmonised crimes in breach of peremptory norms. Notably, in *Pinochet* the UK House of Lords held that a former head of State can be prosecuted domestically for international crimes committed in the exercise of his functions.[426] The Draft Articles on the Immunity of State Officials from Foreign Criminal Jurisdiction (DAISOFCJ) exclude functional immunity for genocide, crimes against humanity and war crimes, including torture and enforced disappearances.[427] This shows that peremptory obligations have the potential to trump individual immunity and discloses the possibility of prosecuting individuals acting on behalf of the State in domestic courts.[428] Alternatively, it has been argued that State officials cannot be immune from the criminal jurisdiction of other States because international crimes cannot be considered official sovereign acts.[429] This interpretation, however, excludes State responsibility for serious breaches of *jus cogens* and challenges the principle that conduct of State organs or agents is attributable to the State itself, regardless of its lawful or unlawful nature.[430] *A fortiori*, these arguments should apply to personal immunities.[431] In any case, it is not settled which State officials are actually entitled to claim jurisdictional immunities. In fact, the immunity of individuals other than heads of States and senior government officials is quite controversial.[432]

3.2.5.2 Intersections

Considering the intersection between individual criminal responsibility and State aggravated responsibility, the question of State immunity is particularly relevant to the establishment of the individual crime of aggression. In fact, the

425 Pellet, 'Can a State' (1999) 432.

426 *Regina v Bartle and the Commissioner of Police for the Metropolis* et al *(Appellants), Ex Parte Pinochet (Respondent); Regina v Evans and Another and the Commissioner of Police for the Metropolis* et al *(Appellant), Ex Parte Pinochet (Respondent) (No 3)*, Judgment of 24 March 1999, 38 ILM 661.

427 ILC, Immunity of State Officials from Foreign Criminal Jurisdiction, UN Doc A/CN.4/L.893 (2017) 1, art 7.

428 Alexander Orakhelashvili, 'Immunities of State Officials, International Crimes and Foreign Domestic Courts' (2011) 22(3) *EJIL* 855; Pedretti, *Immunity* (2015) 404.

429 Andrea Bianchi, 'Immunity versus Human Rights: The *Pinochet* Case' (1999) 10(2) *EJIL* 265. But see Brad Roth, 'Coming to Terms with Ruthlessness: Sovereign Equality, Global Pluralism, and the Limits of International Criminal Justice' (2010) 8(1) *Santa Clara JIL* 281.

430 See s 2.2.1 and 2.2.2.

431 But see Pedretti, *Immunity* (2015) 398–399.

432 *Ex Parte Pinochet (No 3)* [2000] 201–202; *Certain Questions of Mutual Assistance in Criminal Matters (Djibouti v France)* [2008] ICJ Rep 243–244, para 194. See also Pedretti, *Immunity* (2015) 48–52.

possibility of prosecuting natural persons acting as State organs or agents raises the problem of coordinating domestic adjudication on individual criminal responsibility and State responsibility. National courts should not be able to decide on individual criminal responsibility without a prior assessment on State responsibility for aggression.[433] Thus, the question has been raised as to whether the individual crime of aggression can actually be subject to domestic adjudication, in light of the fact that it is interwoven with State responsibility, which is covered by jurisdictional immunity.[434]

Interestingly, the DAISOFCJ do not exclude immunity from foreign jurisdiction for State officials committing the crime of aggression.[435] According to Concepción Escobar Hernández, Special Rapporteur to the ILC on the issue, a customary exception to immunity has not yet emerged with regard to aggression.[436] However, the Rapporteur envisaged the possibility of excluding immunity for aggression via the territorial tort exception.[437] The 1996 DCCPSM sought to avoid the complexity of the issue by excluding domestic jurisdiction over aggression and conferring it exclusively to the then-proposed ICC, with the exception of an aggressor State prosecuting its own nationals.[438]

Scholars argue that the case law has eroded the principle of immunity for aggression before domestic courts since the Nuremberg trials.[439] In fact, domestic courts have adjudicated upon the responsibility of foreign State officials for aggression, for instance, Chinese courts with regard to Japanese officers and Russian tribunals with respect to German officers in the aftermath of World War II.[440] The ICC Statute currently does not exclude aggression from the scope of complementarity, which implies that aggression should primarily be subject to domestic adjudication, as should all other crimes included in the Statute.[441] In this context, the conviction of a foreign official by a national court for aggression implies an incidental *de facto* finding on State responsibility, which nonetheless does not exclude State procedural immunity from foreign jurisdiction.[442]

Moreover, national tribunals adjudicating on war crimes have determined the existence of international or non-international armed conflicts, thus

433 Ruys, 'Justiciability' (2017) 19.
434 Kemp, *Individual Criminal Liability* (2017) 231; Ruys, 'Justiciability' (2017) 28–29.
435 ILC, Immunity (2017) 1, art 7.
436 Concepción Escobar Hernández, Fifth Report on the Immunity of State Officials from Foreign Criminal Jurisdiction, UN Doc A/CN.4/701 (2016) 87–88, para 222.
437 Ibid 89, para 227.
438 ILC, Report (1996) 27, art 8.
439 Nidal Nabil Jurdi, 'The Domestic Prosecution of the Crime of Aggression after the International Criminal Court Review Conference: Possibilities and Alternatives' (2013) 14(1) *Mel JIL* 132–133 and 135; Ruys, 'Justiciability' (2017) 31–32.
440 Clark, 'The Crime' (2015) 795. See also s 2.3.1.
441 Zimmermann and Freiburg, 'Article 8bis' (2016) 618; Wrange, 'The Crime' (2017) 730 ff. See also Kreß and Barriaga, *The Crime* (2017) 1115 ff.
442 Ruys, 'Justiciability' (2017) 29.

incidentally deciding *de facto* on aggression.[443] For example, this was the case of the US Military Tribunal in Nuremberg in the 'Farben' and 'Krupp' trials.[444] The same reasoning should apply to the crime of genocide, at least to the extent that there is no practice where individuals have been considered responsible for genocide in the absence of State responsibility.[445] Similar arguments can be put forward with respect to core crimes against humanity and terrorism, in light of their systemic and ideological nature,[446] but the inference is less compelling.

Assuming that domestic courts can assess not only individual criminal responsibility but also State responsibility, at least incidentally for aggression and genocide, the further question arises as to what margin of discretion is left to invoke responsibility for the UN Security Council, under UN Charter Chapter VII, and for States, under 2001 DASR 41(1), 42(2) and 48(1)(b).[447] Should the UN Security Council and States take into account domestic proceedings and their outcome? Reciprocally, should domestic courts take into account decisions of the Security Council and States in determining individual responsibility? To what extent would this be consistent with the presumption of innocence?[448] Indeed, in light of dual responsibility generated by conduct of individuals acting as State organs or agents, a State can only be responsible for aggression if one or some of its organs or agents are responsible. If a State is held responsible based on a non-judicial process, one or some individuals must necessarily be liable. A different outcome, whereby no individual is liable, would disclose a scenario whereby countermeasures adopted under Chapter VII of the UN Charter or DASR 41(1), 42(2) and 48(1)(b) are wrongfully decided. Such a scenario is difficult to envisage and could give rise to massive consequences in terms of reparation.

3.2.6 Ad hoc *criminal jurisdictions: victors' justice?*

3.2.6.1 Power and organic dependence

Critically, *ad hoc* tribunals are bound by an organic relationship to the States or bodies that create them.[449] *Ad hoc* proceedings have thus been criticised as po-

443 Ruth Rissing-van Saan, 'The German Federal Supreme Court and the Prosecution of International Crimes Committed in the Former Yugoslavia' (2005) 3(2) *JICJ* 389–390.

444 *Farben* 19 ff; *Krupp* 132 ff.

445 See ss 2.3.4.1 and 2.3.4.2.

446 Wrange, 'The Crime' (2017) 714.

447 Ruys, 'Justiciability' (2017) 20.

448 Wrange, 'The Crime' (2017) 726–727.

449 Timothy McCormack and Gerry Simpson, 'A New International Criminal Law Regime?' (1995) 42(2) *NILR* 183; Frédéric Mégret, 'The Anxieties of International Criminal Justice' (2016) 29(1) *LJIL* 202; Silje Aambø Langvatn and Theresa Squatrito, 'Conceptualising and Measuring the Legitimacy of International Criminal Tribunals', in Nobuo Hayashi and Cecilia Baillet (eds), *The Legitimacy of International Criminal Tribunals* (CUP, 2017) 42.

litical trials implementing victors' justice.[450] Notably, the IMT was established in Nuremberg according to the Statute embedded in the London Agreement signed by the Allied Powers on 8 August 1945.[451] Articles 2 and 14 of the IMT Charter vested the Allied Powers with the capacity to appoint the Judges of the Tribunal and Chief Prosecutors. Article 29 of the IMT Charter conferred the power to review sentences on the Control Council for Germany, including representatives from the Allied Powers, according to the Agreements reached at the Potsdam Conference on 2 August 1945.

The IMTFE was established by means of an order of General MacArthur as the Supreme Commander of the Allied Powers in the Far East on 19 January 1946.[452] The IMTFE Charter vested General MacArthur with relevant powers within the process. Article 2 allowed the Supreme Commander to appoint Judges based on the names submitted by the Signatories to the Instrument of Surrender. Under IMTFE Charter Article 8, the Supreme Commander designated the Chief of Counsel for prosecution. Article 17 of the IMTFE Charter vested the Supreme Commander with the power to review sentences. The distribution of 'judicial' power among non-judicial organs casts doubts on the impartiality of proceedings.[453]

Issues of neutrality also arise with respect to mixed tribunals established by States. This is notably the case of the Iraqi Special Tribunal, known as the Iraqi High Criminal Court. The Tribunal is an internationalised domestic jurisdiction that has tried acts such as genocidal campaigns against Kurdish populations committed by Iraqi officials between 1968 and 2003, applying the death penalty.[454] Particularly in light of the fact that it was established following the rejection of proposals for an international forum and a neutral venue for trials, the Iraqi Special Tribunal has been criticised as a body established by belligerent occupants in an effort to insulate proceedings from objectivity.[455] Similar critiques have been raised with regard to the impartiality of domestic proceedings against suspected Afghan terrorists kept in detention and prosecuted before domestic courts in the US.[456]

With regard to *ad hoc* jurisdictions created by the UN, concerns particularly focus on tribunals instituted by the Security Council. Scholars have debated

450 Mégret, 'The Anxieties' (2016) 201.

451 Ronen Steinke, *The Politics of International Criminal Justice* (Hart, 2012) 59–60; Larry May and Shannon Fyfe, 'The Legitimacy of International Criminal Tribunals', in Hayashi and Baillet (eds), *The Legitimacy* (2017) 30. See also s 1.2.1.2.

452 Fujita Hisakazu, 'The Tokyo Trial: Humanity's Justice v Victors' Justice', in Yuki Tanaka, Timothy McCormack and Gerry Simpson (eds), *Beyond Victors' Justice? The Tokyo War Crimes Trial Revisited* (Martinus Nijhoff, 2011) 20. See also s 1.2.1.2.

453 Danilo Zolo, *Victors' Justice: From Nuremberg to Baghdad* (Verso, tr Weir, 2009) 142.

454 Ilias Bantekas, 'The Iraqi Special Tribunal for Crimes against Humanity' (2005) 54(1) *ICLQ* 242–246. See also s 3.2.4.3.

455 Ibid 252; Zolo, *Victors' Justice* (2009) 161.

456 Kai Ambos and Annika Maleen Poschadel, 'Terrorists and Fair Trial: The Right to a Fair Trial for Alleged Terrorists Detained in Guantánamo Bay' (2013) 9(4) *Utr L Rev* 111 ff.

the question whether the Council actually has the power to create criminal jurisdictions, notably the ICTY and ICTR.[457] At first glance, the Council has competence to institute criminal jurisdictions in light of UN Charter Article 29, which allows the creation of subsidiary organs.[458] Alternatively, the faculty of creating international criminal jurisdictions could be grounded in UN Charter Articles 24 and 25, which vest the Council with a general power in the matter of peace and security. Chapter VII of the Charter has also been invoked, notably Articles 39 and 41, which would allow the creation of *ad hoc* tribunals as a measure to re-establish peace, not implying the use of force. [459] In fact, these rules are open-ended and could thus be extensively interpreted so as to justify the creation of criminal jurisdictions.[460]

In a more restrictive sense, however, it should be noted that measures under Chapter VII of the UN Charter should primarily address States, not the creation of jurisdictional organs with implications for individuals. Furthermore, it has been reasoned that the Security Council has the power to establish subsidiary organs in order to carry out functions that are within the scope of its power, but not judicial functions, which would be outside its competence.[461] In fact, within Chapter VI of the UN Charter Articles 36(1) and 37(2) expressly outline the power of the Council in jurisdictional matters by referring to the recommendation of appropriate procedures and methods of dispute adjustment, without providing for the power to create *ad hoc* jurisdictions. There is thus room for the view that the creation of international criminal jurisdictions by the Council is *ultra vires*.[462]

However, the ICTY rejected any negative stance, holding that, whilst it has no judicial power, the Security Council can establish jurisdictional organs for the purpose of maintaining peace.[463] Furthermore, the absence of a formal

457 Sean Murphy, 'Progress and Jurisprudence of the ICTY' (1999) 93(1) *AJIL* 63–64; Michael Matheson and David Scheffer, 'The Creation of the International Criminal Tribunals for the Former Yugoslavia and Rwanda' (2016) 110(2) *AJIL* 178–182.

458 Secretary General, Report Pursuant to Paragraph 2 (1993) 8, para 28; Matheson and Scheffer, 'The Creation' (2016) 179.

459 Secretary General, Report Pursuant to Paragraph 2 (1993) 7, para 22; Matheson and Scheffer, 'The Creation' (2016) 179–180; May and Fyfe, 'The Legitimacy' (2017) 39.

460 Frederic Kirgis Jr, 'The Security Council's First Fifty Years' (1995) 89(3) *AJIL* 522; Matheson and Scheffer, 'The Creation' (2016) 179.

461 Matheson and Scheffer, 'The Creation' (2016) 181.

462 Wijesundara, 'Who Will Guard' (2016) 379.

463 In *Tadić*, the ICTY held:

> The argument that the Security Council, not being endowed with judicial powers, cannot establish a subsidiary organ possessed of such powers is untenable: it results from a fundamental misunderstanding of the constitutional set-up of the Charter. Plainly, the Security Council is not a judicial organ and is not provided with judicial powers (though it may incidentally perform certain quasi-judicial activities such as effecting determinations or findings) [...] The establishment of the International Tribunal by the Security Council does not signify, however, that the Security Council has delegated to it some of its own functions or the exercise of some of its own powers. Nor does it mean, in reverse, that the Security

opposition by States to the establishment of *ad hoc* tribunals by the Council can constitute a form of tacit acquiescence.[464] Overall, the competences of the Council are quite broadly defined, particularly under the UN Charter, and it is therefore not impossible to interpret them so as to include all sorts of powers, particularly in light of the expanding activism of the organ.[465] This approach requires nonetheless stretching the limits of the theory of implied powers and entails a strict relationship between *ad hoc* tribunals as judicial organs and the Council as a political organ.[466]

Considerations developed with respect to *ad hoc* tribunals directly created by the Security Council extend to hybrid tribunals established by the special UN Missions in Kosovo and East Timor, which were ultimately based on UN Security Council Resolutions 1244/1999 and 1272/1999.[467] The same argument is put forward with respect to the STL, which is ultimately grounded in Security Council Resolution 1757/2007.[468] In this regard, questioned about the legality of its constitution, the STL Trial Chamber and Appeals Chamber confirmed the power of the UN Security Council to establish an international criminal jurisdiction, but denied the possibility of reviewing such a power.[469] This has been interpreted as a regressive stance with respect to the legacy of the ICTY in *Tadić*.[470]

By contrast, although the Security Council fundamentally prompted the creation of the SCSL via Resolution 1315/2000, it is considered that the legitimacy of the SCSL is actually grounded in a treaty concluded between the UN Secretary General and the local Government.[471] The competence of the UN as such to establish *ad hoc* mixed or international jurisdictions is less questionable, in light of the universal nature of the organisation. Thus, the legitimacy of the Extraordinary Chambers in the Courts of Cambodia is also less problematic. In fact, the UN Secretary General established the Chambers by means of an

---

> Council was usurping for itself part of a judicial function [...] The Security Council has resorted to the establishment of a judicial organ in the form of an international criminal tribunal as an instrument for the exercise of its own principal function of maintenance of peace and security ...
>
> (*Tadić* (1995) 12–13, paras 37–38)

See also *Kajelijeli*, ICTR-98-44, Trial Chamber, Judgment of 1 December 2003, 1, para 2; Mohamed Shahabuddeen, *International Criminal Justice at the Yugoslav Tribunal: A Judge's Recollection* (OUP, 2012) 26.

464 Matheson and Scheffer, 'The Creation' (2016) 175; May and Fyfe, 'The Legitimacy' (2017) 37.

465 May and Fyfe, 'The Legitimacy' (2017) 39–40.

466 Williams, *Hybrid* (2012) 44; Wijesundara, 'Who Will Guard' (2016) 400–402.

467 Williams, *Hybrid* (2012) 259–260.

468 Ibid 270.

469 *Ayyash* et al, Trial Chamber, Decision on the Defence Challenge to the Jurisdiction and Legality of the Tribunal, 27 July 2012, 18, para 55, 23, para 69; *Ayyash* et al, Appeals Chamber, Decision on the Defence Appeals against the Trial Chamber's Decision on the Defence Challenges to the Jurisdiction and Legality of the Tribunal, 24 October 2012, 15, para 31, 26, para 53.

470 Proulx, *Institutionalizing* (2016) 142.

471 Williams, *Hybrid* (2012) 271 ff.

Agreement concluded with the Cambodian Government based on UN General Assembly Resolution 57/228, that is, a universal instrument, which is a guarantee of impartiality.[472]

3.2.6.2 Ex post *jurisdictions*

Concerning the time element, *ad hoc* tribunals are established *post factum*. This is problematic with respect to the fundamental principles of non-retroactivity and legality: *nullum crimen, nulla poena sine praevia lege poenali*.[473] Whilst this effect is mitigated by the fact that substantive provisions applied by *ad hoc* tribunals largely codify customary law,[474] or even natural law,[475] the same is not necessarily true of procedural rules. This approach means that *ad hoc* tribunals have a repressive nature, rather than a pre-emptive character.

Furthermore, *ad hoc* tribunals adjudicate upon individual criminal responsibility after State aggravated responsibility has been determined and countermeasures have been taken against responsible States.[476] Since such a temporal discrepancy is a problem in the context of domestic courts,[477] *a fortiori* it raises concerns within the framework of *ad hoc* jurisdictions. In this regard, in the *Bosnian Genocide* case the SFRY pointed out that 'the *conditio sine qua non* for establishing State responsibility is the prior establishment, according to the rules of criminal law, of the individual responsibility of a perpetrator engaging the State's responsibility.'[478] As we have seen,[479] however, this stance was rejected by the ICJ:

> The different procedures followed by, and powers available to, this Court and to the courts and tribunals trying persons for criminal offences, do not themselves indicate that there is a legal bar to the Court itself finding that genocide or the other acts enumerated in Article III [of the Genocide Convention] have been committed.[480]

472 For the details of the founding instruments of the different Tribunals, see s 1.2.3.3.
473 Langvatn and Squatrito, 'Conceptualising' (2017) 42.
474 *Galić*, IT-98-29-A, Appeals Chamber, Judgment of 30 November 2006, 38, para 83; Hans Ehard, 'The Nuremberg Trial against the Major War Criminals and International Law' (1949) 43(2) *AJIL* 232; Williams, *Hybrid* (2012) 323.
475 Roth, 'Coming to Terms' (2010) 250.
476 Lauri Mälskoo, 'Great Powers Then and Now: Security Council Reform and Responses to Threats to Peace and Security', in Peter Danchin and Horst Fischer (eds), *United Nations Reform and the New Collective Security* (CUP, 2010) 102–103.
477 Georgina Fitzpatrick, 'War Crimes Trials, "Victors' Justice" and Australian Military Justice in the Aftermath of the Second World War', in Kevin John Heller and Gerry Simpson (eds), *The Hidden History of War Crimes Trials* (OUP, 2013) 331. See also s 3.2.5.2.
478 *Application of the Convention* [2007] 119, para 180.
479 See s 1.2.4.1.
480 *Application of the Convention* [2007] 119, para 181.

It is true that, particularly in the case of aggression and genocide, there is a circular situation, whereby State responsibility becomes theoretically or *de facto* indispensable to determining individual liability. However, the temporal discrepancy whereby State aggravated responsibility is determined prior to individual criminal liability compels *ad hoc* tribunals to take into account the prior assessment on State responsibility made by political entities. It would indeed not be easy for an *ad hoc* tribunal to challenge the assessment on State responsibility made by the Security Council, another body or States, in light of the legal and political implications of such a decision.[481] This affects the impartiality of criminal proceedings and ultimately the basic principle of the presumption of innocence, particularly as concerns high-ranking State officers.[482]

There is therefore a major loophole in adjudicating individual criminal responsibility after State aggravated responsibility. In this respect, scholars have pointed out that the presumption of innocence is 'the first and foremost principle of international criminal proceedings', having a '*jus cogens* nature',[483] so much so that:

> [T]he politically charged inception of international courts and its tribunals does pose a challenge to the semblance of judicial impartiality and the mantle of presumption of innocence worn by the accused. In the case of the tribunals for the Former Yugoslavia, Rwanda and Sierra Leone, they were created pursuant to a Security Council Resolution which expressly states that certain atrocities have been committed and in some instances attributes these atrocities to specific members of an ethnic group. It is thus arguable that there is a danger that the public might reach an implicit assumption that by virtue of the fact that these courts and tribunals were established to prosecute identified atrocities by identified ethnic groups and political oragnizations, persons indicted by them *must* be guilty of something.[484]

A situation whereby an *ad hoc* tribunal negates individual responsibility for aggression or genocide allegedly committed by organs or agents of a State affected by countermeasures could go as far as to entail the criminal responsibility of those same individuals who have taken countermeasures by acting as organs or agents of the Security Council, another body or States. Such countermeasures might imply the use of armed force.

A critical case in this respect concerns the legality of certain actions carried out by NATO Member States against Serbia during the humanitarian intervention in Kosovo, which emerged before the ICTY. In fact, a Committee was appointed to investigate attacks against civilians allegedly committed in Grdelica Gorge,

481 Mark Osiel, 'The Banality of Good: Aligning Incentives against Mass Atrocity' (2005) 105(6) *Col L Rev* 1815.

482 Kelsen, *Peace* (1973) 114–115.

483 Knoops, *Theory* (2005) 25.

484 Ibid 26–27.

Djakovica, Koica and Belgrade. However, the Report of the Committee resulted in a recommendation not to prosecute and a subsequent decision not to investigate.[485] Scholars have argued that the Committee undermined the impartiality of the ICTY's decision, covering-up the responsibility of individuals, in contrast to decisions taken by domestic tribunals.[486]

Similarly, the absence of prosecution for atomic bombing in Hiroshima and Nagasaki, two events that inspired scholarly reflections on State criminal responsibility,[487] has raised concerns of one-sided prosecution by the Military Tribunals established in Nuremberg and Tokyo after World War II.[488]

3.2.7 The independence of the International Criminal Court

3.2.7.1 Permanency as a guarantee of independence?

The establishment of a permanent international criminal court via the ICC Statute was supposed to resolve the problem of victors' justice raised by *ad hoc* jurisdictions. Indeed, a permanent ICC is considered impartial, since it is in principle respectful of the tenet of legality from the standpoint of both substance and procedure.[489] Furthermore, such a Court allows the problem of immunities to be permanently overcome. The ICC should thus effectively have both a pre-emptive and retributive function.

In practice, so far the ICC has only prosecuted representatives of African countries,[490] which has raised concerns with respect to the impartiality of the Court.[491] Furthermore, because of the substantive overlap between individual criminal responsibility and State aggravated responsibility, the ICC raises

485 Review Committee, Final Report to the Prosecutor on the NATO Bombing Campaign against the Federal Republic of Yugoslavia (2000) paras 90–91, http://www.icty.org/en/press/final-report-prosecutor-committee-established-review-nato-bombing-campaign-against-federal; Office of the Prosecutor for the ICTY, Press Release of 13 June 2000, PR/PIS/510-e, http://www.icty.org/en/press/prosecutors-report-nato-bombing-campaign.

486 Paolo Benvenuti, 'The ICTY Prosecutor and the Review of the NATO Bombing Campaign against the Federal Republic of Yugoslavia' (2001) 12(3) *EJIL* 505 ff; Anne-Sophie Massa, 'NATO's Intervention in Kosovo and the Decision of the Prosecutor of the International Criminal Tribunal for the Former Yugoslavia Not to Investigate: An Abusive Exercise of Prosecutorial Discretion? (2006) 24(2) *Berkeley J Intl L* 643.

487 Jørgensen, *The Responsibility* (2000) ix.

488 Richard Minear, *Victors' Justice: The Tokyo War Crimes Trial* (Princeton University Press, 1972) 93; Bert Röling, 'The Nuremberg and the Tokyo Trials in Retrospect', in Guénaël Mettraux (ed), *Perspectives on the Nuremberg Trial* (OUP, 2008) 456.

489 *Ad Hoc* Committee, Report, A/50/22 (1995) 4, para 18; Sandra Jamison, 'A Permanent International Criminal Court: A Proposal that Overcomes Past Objections' (1994–95) 23(2) *Denv J Intl L & Pol* 420; Mégret, 'The Anxieties' (2016) 201.

490 ICC, Situations and Cases, https://www.icc-cpi.int; Lyal Sunga, 'Has the ICC Unfairly Targeted Africa or Has Africa Unfairly Targeted the ICC?', in Triestino Mariniello (ed), *The International Criminal Court in Search of Its Purpose and Identity* (Routledge, 2015) 154.

491 Kamari Maxine Clarke, 'Why Africa?', in Richard Steinberg (ed), *Contemporary Issues Facing the International Criminal Court* (Brill, 2016) 331 ff; James Nyawo, *Selective Enforcement*

problems of coordination with respect to action undertaken by States, the Security Council and the ICJ. Similar to *ad hoc* jurisdictions, the fundamental issue is that States, the Security Council and the ICJ can react to State aggravated responsibility independently from the ICC, notably prior to the exercise of the jurisdiction of the Court over natural persons. More specifically, the Statute of the ICC does not include any norms addressing issues of coordination with State enforcement and the ICJ. This approach does not exclude possible inconsistencies between procedures for individual and State responsibility, such as those raised by the genocide committed in Srebrenica.[492] In contrast, complex norms have been adopted to coordinate ICC proceedings and action undertaken by the Security Council, notably ICC Statute Articles 13(b), 16, 15bis and 15ter.

Unlike the ICTY and ICTR, currently the ICC is not an organ of the UN. The ILC debated the possibility of integrating the ICC into the UN during early preparatory work for the ICC Statute.[493] Article 2 of the Project proposed by the Working Group on a Draft Statute for an ICC in 1993 envisaged integration.[494] However, the proposal to make the ICC an organ of the UN was eventually abandoned.[495] Within this framework, at a later stage of preparatory work for the ICC Statute the Permanent Members of the UN Security Council supported the idea of a strong influence of the Council on the Court.[496] Such a stance revolutionises the ideas underpinning most pre-World War II proposals for an international criminal code and court as well as some of those put forward after World War II. These proposals subordinated the executive action of the Council of the League of Nations or the UN Security Council to the judicial power of an international criminal court.[497]

3.2.7.2 The UN Security Council and the International Criminal Court

Articles 13 and 16 of the ICC Statute are particularly concerned with the coordination between the ICC and the UN Security Council. Whilst these provisions

---

and International Criminal Law: The International Criminal Court and Africa (Intersentia, 2017) 253 ff.

492 See s 3.2.4.1.

493 ILC, Report (1994) 22–23, paras 53–55, Commentary to Article 2 (Relationship of the Court to the United Nations), 73, Appendix III.

494 Thiam, Eleventh Report (1993) 115, para 20, art 2 (The Court, Judicial Organ of the United Nations); ILC, Report (1993) 101.

495 *Ad Hoc* Committee, Report, A/50/22 (1995) 3–4, paras 12–17; PCEICC, Report, A/51/22 (1996) 9–10, paras 29–31; PCEICC, Report, A/51/22/A (1996) 4 (Article 2 – Relationship of the Court to the United Nations – Proposals); PCEICC, Draft Statute (1998) 10 (Article 2 – Relationship of the Court to the United Nations).

496 Philippe Kirsch and John Holmes, 'The Rome Conference on an International Criminal Court: the Negotiating Process' (1999) 93(1) *AJIL* 4; David Scheffer, 'The United States and the International Criminal Court', ibid, 13–15.

497 See ss 1.1, 1.2.1 and 1.2.3.1.

vest the Council with the power to influence the action of the Court, they do not reciprocally provide a similar faculty in favour of the Court.

ICC Statute Article 13(b) provides that the Security Council, acting under Chapter VII of the UN Charter, can refer to the Court any situations possibly entailing a crime under its jurisdiction:

> Article 13 (Exercise of jurisdiction)
> The Court may exercise its jurisdiction with respect to a crime referred to in article 5 in accordance with the provisions of this Statute if:
> [...]
> (b) A situation in which one or more of such crimes appears to have been committed is referred to the Prosecutor by the Security Council acting under Chapter VII of the Charter of the United Nations ...

This provision is consistent with Article 23(1) of the ILC's 1994 Draft Statute[498] and Article 10 of the 1998 Draft Statute adopted by the ICC Preparatory Committee.[499] By contrast, Article 25 of the 1993 Draft Statute adopted by the ILC's Working Group provided the broader possibility for the Council to refer a situation to the Court without the necessity of acting under Chapter VII of the Charter.[500] It should therefore be excluded that referring a situation to the Court is intrinsically an act under Chapter VII of the Charter. Within this framework, the veto mechanism may play an unpredictable role, allowing or preventing a referral under ICC Statute Article 16, so much so that the ILC underscored that the veto affects the principles of non-discrimination and equality underpinning justice.[501]

Scholars have interpreted Article 13(b) so as to allow the Council to also refer to the Court the situation of a natural person outside the national and territorial limits outlined in ICC Statute Article 12.[502] Indeed, Article 12 confines the jurisdiction of the ICC to nationals of a State Party or committing a crime in the territory of a State Party only upon referral by a State Party or when the Prosecutor investigates *proprio motu* under ICC Statute Article 13(a) and (c). Thus, under Article 13(b) the UN Security Council adopted Resolution 1593 (2005) and referred to the ICC the situation in Darfur, which led to formulating charges against

498 ILC, Report (1994) 43, para 9.

499 PCEICC, Draft Statute (1998) 34–35 (Article 10(1) – [[Action by] [Role of] The Security Council] [Relationship between the Security Council and the International Criminal Court]). See also *Ad Hoc* Committee, Report, A/50/22 (1995) 27, paras 120–121; PCEICC, Report, A/51/22 (1996) 31–32, paras 132–136; PCEICC, Report, A/51/22/A (1996) 75 (Article 23 – Action by the Security Council – Proposals).

500 ILC, Report (1993) 109.

501 Id, Report (1994) 24, para 65. For critical insights on the debate preceding the adoption of ICC Statute art 13(b), see Fanny Benedetti, Karine Bonneau and John Washburn, *Negotiating the International Criminal Court* (Martinus Nijhoff, 2014) 165–166; William Schabas, *The International Criminal Court: A Commentary on the Rome Statute* (OUP, 2nd edn, 2016) 367–371.

502 William Schabas and Giulia Pecorella, 'Article 13: Exercise of Jurisdiction', in Triffterer and Ambos, *Commentary* (2016) 696.

President Omar Al Bashir and other Sudanese officers for genocide, crimes against humanity and war crimes.[503] Darfur is a region of Sudan, which is not a Party to the ICC Statute. Similarly, via Resolution 1970 (2011) the Council unanimously referred the situation in Libya to the ICC,[504] where the forces of Muammar Gaddafi allegedly committed gross human rights violations against civilians from 15 February 2011. These prosecutions are examples of 'system criminality', whereby action against State officials has profound implications for a State government.[505]

In referring situations to the ICC under Article 13(b) of the ICC Statute, the Security Council has often resorted to safeguard clauses, limiting the jurisdiction of the Court. Thus, Resolution 1593 (2005), referring the situation in Sudan, and Resolution 1970 (2011), referring the situation in Libya, excluded the competence of the ICC over personnel from a State not a party to the Rome Statute.[506] This approach has been criticised as affecting the integrity of ICC proceedings, particularly because powerful States on the Security Council could apply a double standard, whereby the Court 'can be used to attack some while protecting others'.[507]

It has also been considered that a referral by the Council under ICC Statute Article 13(b) compels a competent State to dismiss a case in favour of the ICC, notably because of the obligatory nature of the decisions of the Council by virtue of UN Charter Articles 48 and 103, overriding ICC Statute Articles 1 and 17.[508] These views are not unanimously shared.[509] However, in the case of *Al Bashir* the ICC held that its jurisdiction overrides third States' procedures based on a referral by the Council.[510] A fortiori, when backed by the Council the Court should be able to override the competence of State Parties. In light of this, some scholars conclude that ICC Statute Article 13(b) repeals the power of the Council to create *ad hoc* tribunals.[511] Thus, it has been critically pointed out that the action of the Court is subordinated to that of the Council.[512]

503 Security Council, Sudan, UN Doc S/RES/1593, 31 March 2005.

504 Id, Peace and security in Africa, UN Doc S/RES/1970, 26 February 2011. See also s 3.2.4.2.

505 Julian Ku, 'How System Criminality Could Exacerbate the Weaknesses of International Criminal Law' (2010) 8(1) *Santa Clara JIL* 371.

506 S/RES/1593, 2, para 6; S/RES/1970, 2, para 6.

507 Deborah Ruiz Verduzco, 'The Relationship between the ICC and the United Nations Security Council', in Stahn, *The Law and Practice* (2015) 37.

508 Louise Arbour and Morten Bergsmo, 'Conspicuous Absence of Jurisdictional Overreach', in Herman von Hebel, Johan Lammers and Jolien Schukking (eds), *Reflections on the International Criminal Court* (TMC Asser Press, 1999) 139–140; Schabas, *The International Criminal Court* (2016) 375; Schabas and Pecorella, 'Article 13' (2016) 697.

509 Arsanjani, 'The Rome Statute' (1999) *AJIL* 28; Nidal Nabil Jurdi, *The International Criminal Court and National Courts: A Contentious Relationship* (Ashgate, 2011) 259; Schabas, *The International Criminal Court* (2016) 375.

510 *Al Bashir*, ICC-02/05-01/09, Pre-Trial Chamber, Decision on the Cooperation of the Democratic Republic of the Congo Regarding Omar Al Bashir's Arrest and Surrender to the Court, 9 April 2014, 13–14, para 29.

511 Ruiz Verduzco, 'The Relationship' (2015) 32; Sarah Babaian, *The International Criminal Court: A Criminal World Court* (Springer, 2018) 39 and 41.

512 Rosa Aloisi, 'A Tale of Two Institutions: The United Nations Security Council and the International Criminal Court' (2013) 13(1) *Intl CLR* 159–160.

Critiques concerning subordination, however, can be rejected, at least if one assumes that the ICC Statute is *lex specialis* with respect to the UN Charter and thus applies to the extent that it is not inconsistent with it. In fact, upon a referral by the Council, the ICC Prosecutor remains free to initiate or not to initiate prosecutions under ICC Statute Article 53.[513] It is true, nonetheless, that the ICC Preliminary Chamber can examine the decision of the Prosecutor *proprio motu* or upon request by a State or the Council under ICC Statute Article 53(3). This affords an avenue for the Council to exercise political pressure on the Court.

Furthermore, ICC Statute Article 19 provides that the Court 'shall satisfy itself that it has jurisdiction in any case brought before it', including conditions under Article 17, according to the *Kompetenz-Kompetenz* principle. Consistently, ICC Statute Article 13 provides that the Court 'may exercise its jurisdiction', thus establishing in favour of the ICC an ability, not a duty, to proceed in the case of a referral by the Security Council. The Court can thus scrutinise the grounds of a referral, including whether, in referring a situation to the Court, the Council acted under Chapter VII of the UN Charter. In this case, the question arises as to what the consequences would be of a decision of the Court inconsistent with a referral by the Council. Particularly, in a situation where the Council has already taken action against a State, a decision not to proceed by the ICC could theoretically compel a review of the action undertaken by the Council, with critical consequences in terms of cessation and reparation.[514]

ICC Statute Article 16 vests the Security Council with the power to defer prosecutions for a renewable period of 12 months, by adopting a Resolution under Chapter VII of the UN Charter:

> ICC Statute (Article 16)
> Deferral of investigation or prosecution
> No investigation or prosecution may be commenced or proceeded with under this Statute for a period of 12 months after the Security Council, in a resolution adopted under Chapter VII of the Charter of the United Nations, has requested the Court to that effect; that request may be renewed by the Council under the same conditions.

The Preparatory Committee for the ICC elaborated the current formulation of Article 16 in the 1998 Draft Statute.[515] The fact that a deferral must be embedded in a Resolution under Chapter VII of the UN Charter requires that, in order to defer prosecutions, the Security Council must, at least, adopt a Resolution under Chapter VII of the Charter, determining the existence of a threat to or

513 Schabas, *The International Criminal Court* (2016) 375.
514 Ibid 375–376.
515 PCEICC, Draft Statute (1998) 34–35 (Article 10(3)).

breach of the peace.[516] Given the broad scope of application of Chapter VII, by means of ICC Statute Article 16 the Council can thus exclude the competence of the ICC over any crimes falling within the jurisdiction of the Court under its Statute.[517] In this respect, unlike ICC Statute Article 13(b), the text of Article 16 should allow the Council to defer a situation by means of an *ad hoc* Resolution adopted under Chapter VII of the UN Charter, regardless of the adoption of actual measures under Article 41 or 42 of the Charter.

Legal commentators have criticised such a broad power as a means to subject criminal proceedings to political interests,[518] whereby the Security Council becomes the 'gatekeeper to the activities of the Court'.[519] Indeed, in practice the Permanent Members of the Council have gone as far as to request the adoption of a resolution excluding the competence of the ICC under Article 16 of its Statute before consenting to action under Chapter VII of the UN Charter. Notably, before consenting to Resolution 1420/2002, extending the mandate of the UN Mission in Bosnia-Herzegovina under Chapter VII of the Charter,[520] the US demanded the adoption of Resolution 1422/2002.[521] This Resolution excluded the jurisdiction of the ICC over UN peacekeeping personnel from States Non-Parties to the ICC Statute for a twelve-month period.[522] Resolution 1487/2003 subsequently renewed the immunity for twelve additional months.[523] However, following allegations of acts of torture committed in Abu-Ghraib by State officials and contracted personnel the US accepted the advice of the UN Secretary General and withdrew the proposal for a further renewal.[524] More recently, the Government of Sudan prompted African States on the UN Security Council to seek a deferral of prosecution against President Omar Al Bashir under ICC Statute Article 16. The request was nonetheless unsuccessful.[525]

516 Jennifer Trahan, 'The Relationship between the International Criminal Court and the UN Security Council: Parameters and Best Practices' (2013) 24(4) *Crim LF* 435; Morten Bergsmo, Jelena Pejic and Dan Zhu, 'Article 16: Deferral of Investigation or Prosecution', in Triffterer and Ambos, *Commentary* (2016) 778–779.

517 White, 'Responses' (2009) 325; Babaian, *The International Criminal Court* (2018) 70.

518 PCEICC, Report, A/51/22 (1996) 32, para 130; Benedetti, Bonneau and Washburn, *Negotiating* (2014) 166–167.

519 Ruiz Verduzco, 'The Relationship' (2015) 53.

520 Security Council, Bosnia and Herzegovina, UN Doc S/RES/1420, 30 June 2002.

521 Id, United Nations Peacekeeping, UN Doc S/RES/1422, 12 July 2002, para 1.

522 Ibid, para 2. Mohamed El Zeidy, 'The United States Dropped the Atomic Bomb of Article 16 on the ICC Statute: Security Council Power of Deferrals and Resolution 1422' (2002) 35(5) *Vand J Transnatl L* 1517 ff; Babaian, *The International Criminal Court* (2018) 71.

523 Security Council, United Nations Peacekeeping, UN Doc S/RES/1487, 12 June 2003.

524 Coalition for the ICC, Chronology of the Adoption of Security Council Resolutions 1422/1487 and Withdrawal of the Proposed Renewal in 2004, Factsheet (2004), http://www.iccnow.org/documents/FS-1422and1487Chronology_26March2008.pdf. See also s 2.3.3.1.

525 Annalisa Ciampi, 'The Proceedings against President Al Bashir and the Prospects of Their Suspension under Article 16 ICC Statute' (2008) 6(5) *JICJ* 885 ff; Max Du Plessis and Christopher Gevers, 'The Role of the Assembly of States Parties for the ICC', in Steinberg, *Contemporary Issues* (2016) 171.

Some scholars acknowledge the possibility of the ICC reviewing a deferral by the Council.[526] More restrictively, it is possible to assume that such an option only extends to procedural issues, but not to the substance of a deferral. In fact, the word 'request' in Article 16 is balanced by the ensuing 'impossibility' of commencing an investigation or prosecution following such a demand.[527] Therefore, in assessing individual criminal responsibility involving State aggravated responsibility, the balance of power can shift from a judicial organ to a political body.

3.2.7.3 Jurisdictional autonomy over aggression?

With respect to the crime of aggression, concerning investigations commenced *proprio motu* or following a State submission under ICC Statute Article 13(a) and (c), a State Party will be able to exclude the jurisdiction of the ICC by lodging a declaration with the Registrar, according to Article 15bis(4).

Furthermore, Article 15bis(5) excludes the jurisdiction of the ICC over aggression committed by the nationals of a third State or in the territory of a third State. Read in conjunction with ICC Statute Article 12, this provision excludes the jurisdiction of the Court over aggression committed by nationals of a State Party in the territory of a third State.[528] Jurisdiction is thus restricted to aggression committed by nationals of a State Party to the ICC Statute in the territory of a State Party.

Upon finding a reasonable basis to proceed, the Prosecutor must ascertain whether the UN Security Council made a determination on State responsibility and must further notify the Secretary General, including any relevant information and documents (ICC Statute Article 15bis(6)). This is the logical consequence of the inextricable link between individual and State responsibility for aggression.[529] Only when such a determination has been made, can the Prosecutor initiate investigations under ICC Statute Article 15bis(7). Otherwise, according to Article 15bis(8), absent a determination by the Security Council within six months from the notification, the Prosecutor may only proceed if authorised by the Pre-Trial Division of the Court in accordance with ICC Statute Article 15. In this context, it has been argued that, by affirming that no act of aggression occurred in a particular situation, the Security Council should be able to steer the Court away from aggression charges.[530] The Council can also defer prosecution under ICC Statute Article 16.

526 Babaian, *The International Criminal Court* (2018) 73.

527 Abel Knottnerus, 'The Security Council and the International Criminal Court: The Unsolved Puzzle of Article 16' (2014) 61(2) *NILR* 200.

528 Andreas Zimmermann and Elisa Freiburg, 'Article 15bis: Exercise of Jurisdiction over the Crime of Aggression (State Referral, *proprio motu*)', in Triffterer and Ambos, *Commentary* (2016) 758.

529 See ss 2.3.1.1 and 2.3.1.2 and Ruys, 'Justiciability' (2017) 24.

530 Scheffer, 'Amending' (2017) 1492.

It is true that, under ICC Statute Article 15bis(9), the determination of an act of aggression by an organ other than the Court does not prejudice the Court's own findings. However, the mechanism established under Article 15bis can go as far as to subordinate the Court's proceedings to the will of the Security Council. This is particularly due to the reference to the possibility of a deferral under ICC Statute Article 16. The Council thus has a broad power to interfere with the jurisdictional competence of the Court.[531] In fact, scholars underscore the 'complementary' role of the ICC's jurisdiction over aggression with respect to the mandate of the Council.[532] The provision, however, is progressive, compared to Article 23(3) of the 1994 Draft Statute, which simply excluded the possibility for the ICC to prosecute a situation addressed by the Council under Chapter VII of the UN Charter, save express authorisation.[533] This proposal was subject to a fierce debate[534] and encountered the opposition of several members of the Sixth Committee of the UN General Assembly, who considered that, by 'making the judicial process subject to the political process' the norm 'curtailed the independence of the Court', particularly in light of the veto mechanism.[535]

It should be assumed that investigations commenced following a submission by the UN Security Council under ICC Statute Article 13(b) also extend to nationals of third States or crimes committed on the territory of third States, absent an explicit provision on the matter.[536] Similarly, a deferral by the Security Council should override a declaration by a State Party excluding the jurisdiction of the Court under Article 15bis(4). In this respect, ICC Statute Article 15ter(4) provides for the independence of the Court in determining responsibility for aggression, regardless of external assessments. Scholars thus consider that this rule should help to develop a 'symbiotic relationship between the political role of the Security Council and the institutions of international criminal justice'.[537] It is legitimate to wonder, however, what the consequences would be of a decision of the Court in contrast with measures taken by the Security Council, particularly

531 Muhammad Aziz Shukri, 'Will Aggressors Ever Be Tried before the ICC?', in Politi and Nesi, *The International Criminal Court* (2004) 42; Clark, 'The Crime' (2015) 786; Eleni Chaitidou, Franziska Eckelmans and Barbara Roche, 'The Judicial Function of the Pre-Trial Division', in Kreß and Barriaga, *The Crime* (2017) 773–774.

532 Nicolaos Strapatsas, 'The Practice of the Security Council Regarding the Concept of Aggression', in Kreß and Barriaga, *The Crime* (2017) 204; Reisinger Coracini and Wrange, 'The Specificity' (2017) 325–326.

533 ILC, Report (1994) 43 (Article 23(2)–(3) – Action by the Security Council). See also *Ad Hoc* Committee, Report, A/50/22 (1995) 28–29, paras 122–126; PCEICC, Report, A/51/22 (1996) 32–33, paras 137–144; PCEICC, Report, A/51/22/A (1996) 75 (Article 23 – Action by the Security Council – Proposals).

534 Sienho Yee, 'A Proposal to Reformulate Article 23 of the ILC Draft Statute for an International Criminal Court' (1995–96) 19(3) *Hastings Intl & Comp L Rev* 531 ff.

535 Sixth Committee of the General Assembly, Topical Summary of the Discussion Held during Its Forty-Ninth Session on the Work of the ILC of Its Forty-Sixth Session, UN Doc A/CN.4/464/Add.1 (1995) 28, para 120.

536 See s 3.2.7.2.

537 Kemp, *Individual Criminal Liability* (2017) 182.

in light of the precautions established in ICC Statute Article 15bis. It has indeed been argued that the ICC is compelled not only to determine individual criminal responsibility but also to preliminarily assess State responsibility for aggression.[538]

In any case, at least from a substantive perspective ICC Statute Articles 15bis and 15ter represent important progress with respect to Article 27 of the Draft Statute prepared by the ILC in 1993. This provision established that the ICC could not adjudicate upon an individual criminal act of aggression without the UN Security Council previously establishing State responsibility.[539] Furthermore, Articles 15bis(10) and 15ter(5) of the ICC Statute disjoin the competence of the Court over aggression from jurisdiction over war crimes, crimes against humanity and genocide. This is also an improvement with respect to preparatory work, whereby Article 23(2) of the 1994 ICC Draft Statute excluded the competence of the ICC over aggression or directly related acts without a prior assessment by the Security Council on State responsibility for aggression.[540] Scholars heavily criticised this provision, because it made a decision by the Court ultimately dependent on the political will of the Security Council.[541]

Conclusion

State aggravated responsibility is assessed primarily via UN institutionalised proceedings and residually via non-institutionalised State cooperation. Individual criminal responsibility for core crimes is addressed via compulsory universal jurisdiction and international criminal proceedings, whilst sanctions are enforced domestically. Whereas individual conduct is at the basis of State responsibility, State responsibility is determined via 'politically sensitive' proceedings prior to individual responsibility. To a certain extent, this is understandable in the case of aggression and genocide, where theoretically or practically the relationship between the two forms of responsibility is circular. To a lesser extent, this approach can be explained in light of the systemic nature of core war crimes and core crimes against humanity, or based on the political purpose of terrorism. Such a system, however, affects the individual presumption of innocence.

With respect to State aggravated responsibility, consensual dispute settlement is not necessarily effective. Action by the UN Security Council and, residually, State cooperation, should remedy the inefficacy of voluntary adjudication. However, UN procedures are problematic, to the extent that the Security Council, and the subrogating General Assembly, are political organs enjoying a

538 Akande and Tzanakopoulos, 'The Crime' (2017) 36.

539 ILC, Report (1993) 111, art 27: 'The Working Group was of the view that, if an act of aggression occurs, the responsibility of an individual would presuppose that a State had been held to be guilty of aggression, and such a finding would be for the Security Council to make.'

540 ILC, Report (1994) 43, art 23(2).

541 McCormack and Simpson, 'A New International Criminal Law' (1995) 196; Marie Dumée, 'Le crime d'agression', in Ascensio, Decaux and Pellet, *Droit* (2000) 262.

broad power to determine the most serious State offences. The Security Council, whose operation is subject to the veto mechanism, is also not strictly controlled by the ICJ, which could theoretically revise the acts of the Council based on *jus cogens*. Universal reaction under general international law codified in the ILC's 2001 DASR has given rise to different theoretical approaches that have proven to be anarchical in practice, sometimes leading to paradoxical outcomes, notably in the second Iraq war. In the absence of the notion of a 'State crime', the jurisdictional immunity of the State still prevents domestic prosecution, despite the development of diverging trends in national legal orders. The overall framework entails a multiplication of proceedings addressing broadly defined State aggravated offences.

With regard to individual criminal responsibility, domestic jurisdictions have progressively eroded functional and personal immunity, which nonetheless still hampers prosecution, including the assessment of State responsibility preliminary to individual liability, notably as concerns aggression. *Ad hoc* jurisdictions created by States or the UN, particularly the Security Council, entail the question of *post factum* victors' justice. Theoretically, the ICC, as a permanent jurisdiction, might overcome these problems, but complex normative relations arise with respect to both States and the UN Security Council. With particular regard to the Council, overlapping competence goes as far as to establish the primacy of the political, or executive, organ over the judicial one. In fact, the Council has the power to refer a situation to the Court under ICC Statute Articles 13(b), and, most importantly, to defer its jurisdiction under ICC Statute Article 16. Furthermore, the ICC Statute reinforces such procedural guarantees in the case of aggression under Articles 15bis and 15ter.

Consistently with the peremptory nature of State aggravated responsibility, the 'vertical' mechanisms suggested by Arangio-Ruiz in 1996 under Article 17 of the Second Part of his proposals on State responsibility essentially aimed to re-organise a scattered framework, complementing State crimes under Article 19 of the First Part of the DASR. The proposals compelled coordinated action by the main UN organs, that is, the Council, Assembly and ICJ, whereby State crimes would have been assessed by the Court and enforced by the Council, properly executing police functions. The project sought to bring clearly defined State aggravated offences within an institutionalised judicial context. This would have also guaranteed that individual criminal liability be assessed following an impartial judicial determination of State responsibility.

Conclusion

Antinomies

From a normative standpoint, individual criminal responsibility and State aggravated responsibility are evolving overlapping concepts. Although differences exist, crucial substantive links emerge, particularly because the conduct of State organs or agents generates dual responsibility.

A historical analysis of core regulatory instruments demonstrates that, contrary to the pre-World War II era,[1] a trend emerged after World War II to separate individual criminal liability and State aggravated responsibility in international law, specifically within the context of the UN. A turning point is the non-criminal interpretation of State responsibility under Articles I and IX of the Genocide Convention. This ultimately led to establishing the international criminal responsibility of natural persons via the permanent Statute of the ICC, with particular regard to aggression, war crimes, crimes against humanity and genocide. In contrast, the ILC's DASR eventually adopted in 2001 reject the notion of a 'State crime' posited in 1996 DASR 19[2] and adopt the uniform concept of a 'breach of a peremptory norm of general international law',[3] which generates State 'aggravated' responsibility.

From the standpoint of the material element of the offence, that is, the breach of a primary norm, peremptory rules necessarily encompass non-severable *erga omnes* obligations, which are non-derogable. Thus, as concerns the general structure of State aggravated responsibility, the ILC's 2001 DASR embed the substance of State crimes outlined in 1996 DASR 19. In light of international practice, it ought to be concluded that State aggravated responsibility includes as a minimum the (overlapping) prohibitions of aggression, genocide, core war crimes, core crimes against humanity and prospectively terrorism. These can indeed be serious breaches of non-severable *erga omnes* obligations. Such breaches also entail individual criminal responsibility, giving rise to dual *erga omnes* offences. Like genocide under Articles I and IX of the Genocide Convention,

1 ICLA, Projet de Statut (1928); Id, Plan d'un Code (1935).
2 ILC, Report (1996) 58.
3 Id, Report (2001) 112.

aggression literally qualifies as a 'crime' according to Principle 1 of UN General Assembly Resolution 2625 (XXVI) and Article 5(2) of Resolution 3314 (XXIX); however, it is considered that both aggression and genocide only generate non-criminal State responsibility.

Concerning the subjective element of the offence, under international law the conduct of an individual acting as a State organ or agent is attributed to the State and triggers its responsibility. Whilst individual responsibility is logically preliminary to State responsibility, a circular situation exists, whereby there can be no individual responsibility for aggression without State aggregate responsibility.[4] Similarly, in the case of genocide, individual liability is in practice mostly determined on the aggregate basis of State responsibility, but is also essential to establishing collective liability, as proven by the dialectical development of the jurisprudence of the ICJ in the cases concerning the *Application of the Genocide Convention*.[5] The systemic context also facilitates the aggregate establishment of individual liability for core war crimes and core crimes against humanity. Moreover, an aggregate motive and specific intent underpin individual acts of terrorism.[6]

With respect to implementation, and therefore secondary and tertiary norms, when consensual settlement is impossible, notably via the ICJ, State aggravated responsibility is subject to a response by the UN Security Council complemented by universal State cooperation.[7] Following the *erga omnes* nature of the offence and related sanctions, individual criminal responsibility is (universally) prosecuted first domestically and complementarily by the ICC or *ad hoc* tribunals. Therefore, whereas individual criminal responsibility is subject to a rigorous judicial process, State responsibility undergoes primarily a political response, based on a loose definition of aggravated offences. It has thus been contended that 'if a State commits an international crime – for instance, aggression or genocide – then the orthodox remedial mechanisms afforded by the international legal system often prove inadequate.'[8]

Contrary to the substantive relationship, whereby individual criminal responsibility is preliminary to State aggravated liability, State responsibility is assessed politically prior to the judicial determination of individual liability.[9] This unveils systemic problems with respect to basic legal principles, such as the effectiveness of the law, the impartiality of individual proceedings and the presumption of innocence. In practice, inconsistency is exemplified by situations such as the impossibility of preventing genocide in Srebrenica,[10] the divergent jurisprudence

4 ICC Statute art 8-bis.

5 *Application of the Convention* [2007] 119–120, para 182; *Application of the Convention* [2015] 61, para 129, 67, para 148, 128, para 440.

6 *Karadžić* (2016) 178–179, paras 464–466.

7 UN Charter chs VI and VII; 2001 DASR 41(1), 42(b), 48(1)(b), 54 and 59.

8 White, 'Responses' (2009) 315.

9 Nollkaemper, 'Systemic Effects' (2010) 352.

10 *Application of the Convention* [1993] 24, para 52.

of the ICJ and international criminal tribunals,[11] the disparate reactions to the humanitarian crisis in Syria, the impunity of the Coalition of States and their officials for the second Iraq war, as well as the 'immunity' of NATO members before the ICTY and ICJ.[12] These issues are further illustrated by the difficulty of achieving a satisfying balance between the action of the UN Security Council and that of the ICC.[13]

Ways forward

Ideally, consistently with the substantive relationship between individual criminal responsibility and State aggravated responsibility, the former should be adjudicated upon prior to the latter. Individual criminal proceedings should thus be preliminary to assessing State aggravated responsibility. Accordingly, a unitary system should be established, whereby a permanent ICC determines individual criminal responsibility first. State aggravated responsibility would be assessed subsequently, by the same court deciding on individual criminal responsibility, or, more realistically, by other international jurisdictions, notably the ICJ. The UN Security Council acting as an executive organ would enforce decisions against States. Provisional measures could be implemented against States in the presence of requisite danger in delay (*periculum in mora*) and *prima facie* case (*fumus boni juris*). Such was the model put forward within the framework of the League of Nations, achieved by Bassiouni within the context of the ICLA in 1981[14] and recently revisited in relation to practical developments such as the humanitarian crisis in Syria.[15] However, whilst it is normatively consistent, an absolutely monistic system is a purely theoretical archetype. In practice, the disparate reality of international relations is an impediment to such a model.[16] For instance, not all States are currently parties to the Statute of the ICC, whose jurisdiction is only complementary with respect to that of domestic courts.

Along the lines of Article IX of the Genocide Convention and the proposals put forward by Gaetano Arangio-Ruiz in the context of the DASR,[17] a more realistic approach would be to reorganise proceedings addressing State aggravated responsibility, which currently have a primarily political nature, so as to ensure that they also afford the necessary judicial guarantees.[18] This would entail that, in the case of a breach of a non-severable *erga omnes* obligation, notably the prohibition of aggression and genocide, all States of the international community

11 Webb, 'Binocular Vision' (2012) 138.
12 Review Committee, Final Report (2000) paras 90–91; Office of the Prosecutor for the ICTY, Press Release (2000); *Legality of Use of Force* [2004] 328.
13 ICC Statute arts 13(b) and 16.
14 ICLA, Projet de Code (1981).
15 Hamilton, 'State-Enabled Crimes' (2016) 335.
16 Mark Klamberg, *Power and Law in International Society* (Routledge, 2015) 38, 105–106, 127–128 and 135.
17 Arangio-Ruiz, Seventh Report (1995) 17–26, paras 70–120, and Add.1, 4, art 19.
18 White, 'Responses' (2009) 329.

could react by bringing the offence to the attention of the ICJ, possibly via a preliminary screening by the UN General Assembly.[19] The Court would thus have compulsory jurisdiction over State aggravated responsibility and decide on sanctions, which the UN Security Council would then enforce acting as an executive organ. Requisite *periculum in mora* and *fumus boni juris* would allow the implementation of provisional measures against States. The Court would also be vested with the power to impose satisfaction by compelling the prosecution of responsible individuals acting as organs or agents of a State, according to the principle of compulsory universal jurisdiction and the complementary jurisdiction of the ICC.

It should be possible to imagine a future where breaches such as State aggression and genocide are primarily subject to the competence of the ICJ, the main quasi-universal judicial organ of the international community. This model is not flawless; in particular, it is not fully consistent with the principle that individuals acting as State organs or agents trigger State responsibility. In particular, adjudicating upon the responsibility of a State before that of its organs or agents generates a temporal discrepancy that may affect the presumption of innocence. However, first, in the context of dual *erga omnes* offences State responsibility is a ground for establishing individual responsibility, according to aggregate liability, particularly in the case of aggression and genocide. Second, although it would be assessed via criminal proceedings following non-criminal proceedings for State responsibility, individual criminal responsibility would be determined on the basis of a judicial assessment of State responsibility, not a political one. Decisions taken by the ICJ would thus constitute evidence on State liability as a circumstantial element of individual crimes in domestic criminal proceedings and complementary proceedings before the ICC.

19 Ibid 333–335.

Bibliography

Abi-Saab, Georges, 'The Uses of Article 19' (1999) 10(2) *EJIL* 339–351.

Abtahi, Hirad and Webb, Philippa, *The Genocide Convention: The* Travaux Préparatoires (Martinus Nijhoff Publishers, 2008).

Acosta Estévez, José, 'Normas de *ius cogens*, efecto *erga omnes*, crimen internacional y la téoria de los círculos concéntricos' (1995) 11 *An Der Int* 3–22.

Ago, Roberto, 'Le délit international' (1939) 68(2) *RCADI* 415–554.

———, 'Droit des traités à la lumière de la Convention de Vienne – Introduction' (1971) 134(3) *RCADI* 297–331.

———, 'Obligations *Erga Omnes* and the International Community', in Joseph Weiler, Antonio Cassese and Marina Spinedi (eds), *International Crimes of States* (Walter de Gruyter & Co, 1989) 237–239.

———, 'The Concept of "International Community as a Whole": A Guarantee to the Notion of State Crimes', in Joseph Weiler, Antonio Cassese and Marina Spinedi (eds), *International Crimes of States* (Walter de Gruyter & Co, 1989) 252–253.

Akande, Dapo, 'The ICJ and the Security Council: Is There Room for Judicial Control of Decisions of the Political Organs of the UN?' (1997) 46(2) *ICLQ* 309–343.

Akande, Dapo and Tzanakopoulos, Antonios, 'The Crime of Aggression in the ICC and State Responsibility' (2017) 58 *Harv ILJ (Online)* 33–36.

Akhavan, Payam, 'The Universal Repression of Crimes against Humanity before National Jurisdictions', in Leila Nadya Sadat (ed), *Forging a Convention for Crimes against Humanity* (CUP, 2011) 28–42.

Aksenova, Marina, *Complicity in International Criminal Law* (Hart, 2017).

Allain, Jean and Jones, John, 'A Patchwork of Norms: A Commentary on the 1996 Draft Code of Crimes against the Peace and Security of Mankind (1997) 8(1) *EJIL* 100–117.

Aloisi, Rosa, 'A Tale of Two Institutions: The United Nations Security Council and the International Criminal Court' (2013) 13(1) *Intl CLR* 147–168.

Alshdaifat, Shadi Adnan, *International Law and the Use of Force against Terrorism* (Cambridge Scholars Publishing, 2017).

Alvarez, José, 'Judging the Security Council' (1996) 90(1) *AJIL* 1–39.

Ambos, Kai, 'Command Responsibility and *Organisationsherrschaft*: Ways of Attributing International Crimes to the "Most Responsible"', in André Nollkaemper and Harmen van der Wilt (eds), *System Criminality in International Law* (CUP, 2009) 127–157.

Ambos, Kai and Poschadel, Annika Maleen, 'Terrorists and Fair Trial: The Right to a Fair Trial for Alleged Terrorists Detained in Guantánamo Bay' (2013) 9(4) *Utr L Rev* 109–126.

Anzilotti, Dionisio, *Cours de droit international* (Sirey, 1929, re-published by Panthéon-Assas, 1999).

Aquilina, Kevin and Mulaj, Klejda, 'Limitations in Attributing State Responsibility under the Genocide Convention' (2018) 17(1) *JHR* 123–139.

Arangio-Ruiz, Gaetano, 'The "Federal Analogy" and UN Charter Interpretation: A Crucial Issue' (1997) 8(1) *EJIL* 1–28.

———, 'Fine prematura del ruolo preminente di studiosi italiani nel progetto di codificazione della responsabilità degli Stati: specie a propositio di crimini internazionali e dei poteri del Consiglio di sicurezza' (1998) 81(1) *RDI* 110–129.

Arbour, Louise and Bergsmo, Morten, 'Conspicuous Absence of Jurisdictional Overreach', in Herman von Hebel, Johan Lammers and Jolien Schukking (eds), *Reflections on the International Criminal Court* (TMC Asser Press, 1999) 129–140.

Arsanjani, Mahnoush, 'The Rome Statute of the International Criminal Court' (1999) 93(1) *AJIL* 22–43.

Ascensio, Hervé, Decaux, Emmanuel and Pellet, Alain, *Droit international pénal* (Pedone, 1st edn, 2000).

———, *Droit international pénal* (Pedone, 2nd edn, 2012).

Babaian, Sarah, *The International Criminal Court: A Criminal World Court* (Springer, 2018).

Badar, Mohamed Elewa and Porro, Sara, 'Rethinking the Mental Elements in the Jurisprudence of the ICC', in Carsten Stahn (ed), *The Law and Practice of the International Criminal Court* (OUP, 2015) 649–668.

Bantekas, Ilias, 'The Iraqi Special Tribunal for Crimes against Humanity' (2005) 54(1) *ICLQ* 237–253.

Barak, Greg (ed), *International Handbook of the Crimes of the Powerful* (Routledge, 2015).

Barbier, Sandrine, 'Assurances and Guarantees of Non-Repetition', in James Crawford, Alain Pellet, Simon Olleson and Kate Parlett (eds), *The Law of International Responsibility* (OUP, 2010) 551–561.

Barboza, Julio, 'International Criminal Law' (1999) 278 *RCADI* 9–199.

Bardonnet, Daniel *et al* (eds), *Le droit international: unité et diversité* (Pedone, 1981).

Barker, John, 'The Different Forms of Reparation: Compensation', in James Crawford, Alain Pellet, Simon Olleson and Kate Parlett (eds), *The Law of International Responsibility* (OUP, 2010) 599–611.

Bassiouni, Cherif, *A Draft International Criminal Code and Draft Statute for an International Criminal Tribunal* (Martinus Nijhoff, 1987).

———, 'International Crimes: *Jus Cogens* and *Obligatio Erga Omnes*' (1996) 59(4) *Law & Contemp Probs* 63–74.

———, 'Observations Concerning the 1997–1998 Preparatory Committee's Work' (1996–97) 25(2) *Denv J Intl L & Pol* 397–422.

———, *Introduction au droit pénal international* (Bruylant, 2002).

———, 'Challenges Facing a Rule-of-Law Oriented World Order' (2010) 8(1) *Santa Clara JIL* 1–10.

———, *Introduction to International Criminal Law* (Martinus Nijhoff, 2nd edn, 2013).

Battaglini, Giovanni, 'War against Terrorism Extra Moenia, Self-Defence and Responsibility: A Pure Judicial Approach', in Maurizio Ragazzi (ed), *International Responsibility Today* (Brill, 2005) 137–149.

Beaudouin, Anouche, 'Le maintien par la force d'une domination coloniale', in Hervé Ascensio, Emmanuel Decaux and Alain Pellet (eds), *Droit international pénal* (Pedone, 1st edn, 2000) 427–444.

Bederman, David, 'Article 40 (2) (E) and (F) in the ILC Draft Articles on State Responsibility: Standing of Injured States under Customary International Law and Multilateral Treaties' (1998) 92 *ASIL Proc* 291–294.

Benedetti, Fanny, Bonneau, Karine and Washburn, John, *Negotiating the International Criminal Court* (Martinus Nijhoff, 2014).

Benvenuti, Paolo, 'The ICTY Prosecutor and the Review of the NATO Bombing Campaign against the Federal Republic of Yugoslavia' (2001) 12(3) *EJIL* 503–529.

Berg, Bradley, 'The 1994 ILC Draft Statute for an ICC: A Principled Appraisal of Jurisdictional Structure' (1996) 28(2) *Case W Res J Intl L* 221–264.

Bergsmo, Morten, Pejic, Jelena and Zhu, Dan, 'Article 16: Deferral of Investigation or Prosecution', in Otto Triffterer and Kai Ambos (eds), *Commentary on the Rome Statute of the International Criminal Court* (Nomos, 3rd edn, 2016) 770–780.

Bianchi, Andrea, 'Immunity versus Human Rights: The *Pinochet* Case' (1999) 10(2) *EJIL* 237–277.

Blokker, Niels and Schrijver, Nico (eds), *The Security Council and the Use of Force* (Martinus Nijhoff, 2005).

Boister, Neil, 'Transnational Criminal Law?' (2003) 14(5) *EJIL* 953–976.

Bollecker-Stern, Brigitte, *Le préjudice dans la théorie de la responsabilité internationale* (Pedone, 1973).

Bonafè, Beatrice, *The Relationship between State and Individual Responsibility for International Crimes* (Martinus Nijhoff, 2009).

———, 'Reassessing Dual Responsibility for International Crimes' (2016) 73 *Seqüência* 19–36.

Botte, Auriane, 'Redefining the Responsibility to Protect Concept as a Response to International Crimes' (2015) 19(8) *IJHR* 1029–1043.

Bowett, Derek William, 'Crimes of State and the 1996 Report of the International Law Commission on State Responsibility' (1998) 9(1) *EJIL* 163–173.

Brierly, James Leslie, 'Do We Need an International Criminal Court?' (1927) 8 *BYBIL* 81–88.

Broms, Bengt, 'The Definition of Aggression' (1977) 154(1) *RCADI* 299–399.

Brown, Philip Marshall, 'International Criminal Justice' (1941) 35(1) *AJIL* 118–121.

Brownlie, Ian, *International Law and the Use of Force by States* (Clarendon Press, 1963).

Bruha, Thomas, 'The General Assembly's Definition of an Act of Aggression', in Claus Creß and Stefan Barriaga (eds), *The Crime of Aggression: A Commentary* (CUP, 2017) 142–177.

Bucy, Pamela, 'Corporate Ethos: A Standard for Imposing Corporate Criminal Liability' (1990–91) 75(4) *Min L Rev* 1095–1184.

Byers, Michael, 'Terrorism, the Use of Force and International Law after 11 September' (2002) 51(2) *ICLQ* 401–414.

Cançado Trindade, Antônio Augusto, 'Complementarity between State Responsibility and Individual Responsibility for Grave Violations of Human Rights: The Crime of State Revised', in Maurizio Ragazzi (ed), *International Responsibility Today* (Martinus Nijhoff, 2005) 253–269.

———, *International Law for Humankind: Towards a New Jus Gentium* (Brill, 2nd edn, 2013).

Canizzaro, Enzo (ed), *The Law of Treaties beyond the Vienna Convention* (OUP, 2011).

Carjeu, Pierre-Marie, 'Quelques aspects du nouveau Projet de Statut des Nations Unies pour une juridiction criminelle internationale' (1956) 60(3) *RGDIP* 401–425.

Caron, David, 'State Crimes in the ILC Draft Articles on State Responsibility: Insights from Municipal Experience with Corporate Crimes' (1998) 92 *ASIL Proc* 307–312.

———, 'State Crime: Looking at Municipal Experience with Organizational Crime', in Maurizio Ragazzi, *International Responsibility Today* (Brill, 2005) 23–30.

Carter, Linda, Ellis, Mark and Jalloh, Charles, *The International Criminal Court in an Effective Global Justice System* (Edward Elgar, 2016).

Casaca, Paulo, 'The Conceptual Discussion on Terrorism', in Paulo Casaca and Sigfried Wolf (eds), *Terrorism Revisited: Islamism, Political Violence and State Sponsorship* (Springer, 2017) 3–32.

Casaca, Paulo and Wolf, Sigfried (eds), *Terrorism Revisited: Islamism, Political Violence and State Sponsorship* (Springer, 2017).

Cassese, Antonio, '*Ex Iniuria Ius Oritur*: Are We Moving towards International Legitimation of Forcible Humanitarian Countermeasures in International Law?' (1999) 10(1) *EJIL* 23–30.

———, 'Terrorism Is Also Disrupting Some Crucial Legal Categories of International Law' (2001) 12(5) *EJIL* 993–1001.

———, *International Criminal Law* (OUP, 2003).

———, 'On the Use of Criminal Law Notions in Determining State Responsibility for Genocide' (2007) 5(4) *JICJ* 875–887.

——— (ed), *The Oxford Companion to International Criminal Justice* (OUP, 2009).

———, 'The Character of the Violated Obligation', in James Crawford, Alain Pellet, Simon Olleson and Kate Parlett (eds), *The Law* (OUP, 2010) 415–420.

——— (ed), *Realizing Utopia: The Future of International Law* (OUP, 2012).

———, *International Criminal Law* (OUP, 3rd edn, 2013)

Cassese, Antonio, Gaeta, Paola and Jones, John (eds), *The Rome Statute of the International Criminal Court* (OUP, 2002).

Chaitidou, Eleni, Eckelmans, Franziska and Roche, Barbara, 'The Judicial Function of the Pre-Trial Division', in Claus Kreß and Stefan Barriaga (eds), *The Crime of Aggression: A Commentary* (CUP, 2017) 752–815.

Ciampi, Annalisa, 'The Proceedings against President Al Bashir and the Prospects of Their Suspension under Article 16 ICC Statute' (2008) 6(5) *JICJ* 885–897.

Clark, Roger, 'The Mental Element in International Criminal Law: The Rome Statute of the ICC and the Elements of Offences' (2001) 12(3) *Crim LF* 291–334.

———, 'The Crime of Aggression', in Carsten Stahn (ed), *The Law and Practice of the International Criminal Court* (OUP, 2015) 778–800.

———, 'Individual Conduct', in Claus Creß and Stefan Barriaga (eds), *The Crime of Aggression: A Commentary* (CUP, 2017) 565–589.

Clarke, Kamari Maxine, 'Why Africa?', in Richard Steinberg (ed), *Contemporary Issues Facing the International Criminal Court* (Brill, 2016) 326–332.

Coates, Ken, 'Russell Tribunals', http://www.russfound.org/The_Spokesman/KCTrib104.html.

Coen, Alise, 'R2P, Global Governance, and the Syrian Refugee Crisis' (2015) 19(8) *IJHR* 1044–1058.

Cohen, Aviv, 'Prosecuting Terrorists at the International Criminal Court: Reevaluating an Unused Legal Tool to Combat Terrorism' (2012) 20(2) *Mich St ILR* 219–257.

Condorelli, Luigi, 'L'imputation à l'État d'un fait internationalement illicite: solutions classiques et nouvelles tendances' (1984) 189(6) *RCADI* 9–221.

———, 'Conclusions générales', in Mauro Politi and Giuseppe Nesi (eds), *The International Criminal Court and the Crime of Aggression* (Ashgate, 2004) 151–162.

Condorelli, Luigi and Kreß, Klaus, 'The Rules of Attribution: General Considerations', in James Crawford, Alain Pellet, Simon Olleson and Kate Parlett (eds), *The Law of International Responsibility* (OUP, 2010) 221–236.

Corten, Olivier, 'The Obligation of Cessation', in James Crawford, Alain Pellet, Simon Olleson and Kate Parlett (eds), *The Law of International Responsibility* (OUP, 2010) 545–549.

Corten, Olivier and Dubuisson, François, 'L'hypothèse d'une règle émergente fondant une intervention militaire sur une "autorisation implicite" du Conseil de sécurité' (2000) 104(4) *RGDIP* 873–910.

Costelloe, Daniel, *Legal Consequences of Peremptory Norms in International Law* (CUP, 2017).

Crawford, James, 'The ILC's Draft Statute for an International Criminal Tribunal' (1994) 88(1) *AJIL* 140–152.

———, 'The ILC Adopts a Statute for an International Criminal Court' (1995) 89(2) *AJIL* 404–416.

———, 'The Internationalization of Criminal Law: Remarks' (1995) 89 *ASIL Proc* 301–304.

———, 'On Re-Reading the Draft Articles on State Responsibility' (1998) 92 *ASIL Proc* 295–299.

———, 'Revisiting the Draft Articles on State Responsibility' (1999) 10(2) *EJIL* 435–460.

———, *The International Law Commission's Articles on State Responsibility: Introduction, Text and Commentaries* (CUP, 2002).

———, 'International Crimes of States', in James Crawford, Alain Pellet, Simon Olleson and Kate Parlett (eds), *The Law of International Responsibility* (OUP, 2010) 405–414.

———, *State Responsibility: The General Part* (CUP, 2013).

Crawford, James, Bodeau, Pierre and Peel, Jacqueline, 'The International Law Commission's Draft Articles on State Responsibility: Toward Completion of a Second Reading' (2000) 94(4) *AJIL* 660–674.

Crawford, James, Pellet, Alain, Olleson, Simon and Parlett, Kate (eds), *The Law of International Responsibility* (OUP, 2010).

Creß, Claus and Barriaga, Stefan (eds), *The Crime of Aggression: A Commentary* (CUP, 2017).

Cryer, Robert, Friman, Håkan, Robinson, Darryl and Wilmshurst, Elizabeth, *An Introduction to Criminal Law and Procedure* (CUP, 3rd edn, 2014).

Cujo, Églantine and Forteau, Mathias, 'Les réactions des organs politiques internationaux', in Hervé Ascensio, Emmanuel Decaux and Alain Pellet (eds), *Droit international pénal* (Pedone, 2nd edn, 2012) 755–772.

Czapliński, Władysław, '*Jus Cogens*, Obligations *Erga Omnes* and International Criminal Responsibility', in José Doria, Hans-Peter Gasser and Cherif Bassiouni (eds), *The Legal Regime of the International Criminal Court* (Brill, 2009) 403–420.

Damgaard, Ciara, *Individual Criminal Responsibility for Core International Crimes* (Springer, 2008).

Danchin, Peter and Fischer, Horst (eds), *United Nations Reform and the New Collective Security* (CUP, 2010).

Dannenbaum, Tom, 'Why Have We Criminalized Aggressive War?' (2016–17) 126(5) *Yale LJ* 1242–1318.

Dauth, John, 'Defence Cooperation: Terrorism' (2002) 22 *Aust YBIL* 355.

Dautricourt, Joseph, 'Nature et fondement du droit pénal universel' (1949–50) 30(10) *RDPC* 1023–1061.

David, Eric, 'Primary and Secondary Rules', in James Crawford, Alain Pellet, Simon Olleson and Kate Parlett (eds), *The Law of International Responsibility* (OUP, 2010) 27–33.

Dawidowicz, Martin, 'The Obligation of Non-Recognition of an Unlawful Situation', in James Crawford, Alain Pellet, Simon Olleson and Kate Parlett (eds), *The Law of International Responsibility* (OUP, 2010) 677–686.

Dawoody, Alexander (ed), *Eradicating Terrorism from the Middle East: Policy and Administrative Approaches* (Springer, 2016).

De Beco, Gauthier, 'War Crimes in International versus Non-International Armed Conflicts: New Wine in Old Wineskins?' (2008) 8(1) *Int'l Crim L Rev* 319–329.

De Hoog, André, 'The Relationship between *Jus Cogens*, Obligations *Erga Omnes* and International Crimes: Peremptory Norms in Perspective' (1991) 42(2) *Austrian J Pub Intl L* 183–214.

———, André, *Obligations* Erga Omnes *and International Crimes* (Kluwer, 1996).

De Maglie, Cristina, 'Models of Corporate Criminal Liability in Comparative Law' (2005) 4(3) *Wash UGSLR* 547–566.

De Visscher, Charles, 'Positivisme et "*jus cogens*"' (1971) 75(1) *RGDIP* 5–11.

De Wet, Erika, *The Chapter VII Powers of the United Nations Security Council* (Hart, 2004).

———, '*Jus Cogens* and Obligations *Erga Omnes*', in Dinah Shelton (ed), *Oxford Handbook of International Human Rights Law* (OUP, 2013) 541–561.

Decaux, Emmanuel, 'The Definition of Traditional Sanctions: Their Scope and Characteristics' (2008) 90 *IRRC* 249–257.

Descheemaeker, 'Le tribunal militaire international des grands criminels de guerre' (1946) 50(1) *RGDIP* 210–311.

DeWeese, Geoffrey, 'The Failure of the ICJ to Effectively Enforce the Genocide Convention' (1997–98) 26(4) *Denv J Intl L & Pol* 625–654.

Dominicé, Christian, 'La question de la double responsabilité de l'État et de son agent', in Emile Yakpo and Tahar Boumedra (eds), *Liber amicorum Judge Mohammed Bedjaoui* (Kluwer, 1999) 143–157.

———, 'The International Responsibility of States for Breach of Multilateral Obligations' (1999) 10(2) *EJIL* 353–363.

Donnedieu De Vabres, Henri, 'La Cour permanente de justice internationale et sa vocation en matière criminelle' (1924) 1 *RIDP* 175–201.

———, 'Le procès de Nuremberg devant les principes modernes du droit pénal international' (1947) 70(1) *RCADI* 477–582.

———, *Les principes modernes du droit pénal international* (Sirey, 1928, republished by Pantheon-Assas, 2004).

Doria, José, Gasser, Hans-Peter and Bassiouni, Cherif (eds), *The Legal Regime of the International Criminal Court* (Brill, 2009).

Drumbl, Mark, 'Accountability for System Criminality' (2010) 8(1) *Santa Clara JIL* 373–382.

Du Plessis, Max and Gevers, Christopher, 'The Role of the Assembly of States Parties for the ICC', in Richard Steinberg (ed), *Contemporary Issues Facing the International Criminal Court* (Brill, 2016) 159–172.

Dubber, Markus and Hörnle, Tatjana, *Criminal Law: A Comparative Approach* (OUP, 2014).

Dumée, Marie, 'Le crime d'agression', in Hervé Ascensio, Emmanuel Decaux and Alain Pellet (eds), *Droit international pénal* (Pedone, 2000) 251–264.

Dupuy, Pierre-Marie, 'Observations sur le "crime international de l'État"' (1980) 84(2) *RGDIP* 449–486.

———, 'Observations sur la pratique récente des "sanctions" de l'illicite' (1983) 87(3) *RGDIP* 505–548.

———, 'Le fait générateur de la responsabilité internationale des États' (1984) 188(5) *RCADI* 9–134.

———, 'Implications of the Institutionalization of International Crimes of State', in Joseph Weiler, Antonio Cassese and Marina Spinedi (eds), *International Crimes of States* (Walter de Gruyter & Co, 1989) 170–185.

———, 'Normes internationales pénales', in Hervé Ascensio, Emmanuel Decaux and Alain Pellet (eds), *Droit international pénal* (Pedone, 2000) 71–80.

———, 'A General Stocktaking of the Connections between the Multilateral Dimension of Obligations and Codification of the Law of Responsibility (2002)' 13(5) *EJIL* 1053–1081.

———, 'International Criminal Responsibility of the Individual and International Responsibility of the State', in Antonio Cassese, Paola Gaeta and John Jones (eds), *The Rome Statute of the International Criminal Court* (OUP, 2002) 1085–1099.

———, 'L'unité de l'ordre juridique international' (2002) 297 *RCADI* 9–489.

———, 'Quarante ans de codification du droit de la responsabilité internationale des États: un bilan' (2003) 107(2) *RGDIP* 305–348.

———, 'Normes internationales pénales et droit impératif (*jus cogens*)', in Hervé Ascensio, Emmanuel Decaux and Alain Pellet (eds), *Droit international pénal* (Pedone, 2nd edn, 2012) 81–90.

———, 'The Deficiencies of the Law of State Responsibility Relating to Breaches of "Obligations Owed to the International Community as a Whole": Suggestions for Avoiding the Obsolescence of Aggravated Responsibility', in Antonio Cassese (ed), *Realizing Utopia: The Future of International Law* (OUP, 2012) 210–226.

Eagleton, Clyde, 'Punishment of War Criminals by the United Nations' (1943) 37(3) *AJIL* 495–499.

Ehard, Hans, 'The Nuremberg Trial against the Major War Criminals and International Law' (1949) 43(2) *AJIL* 223–245.

El Zeidy, Mohamed, 'The United States Dropped the Atomic Bomb of Article 16 on the ICC Statute: Security Council Power of Deferrals and Resolution 1422' (2002) 35(5) *Vand J Transnatl L* 1503–1544.

Elgebeily, Sherif, *The Rule of Law in the United Nations Security Council Decision-Making Process* (Routledge, 2017).

Escarameia, Paula, 'The ICC and the Security Council on Aggression: Overlapping Competencies?', in Mauro Politi and Giuseppe Nesi (eds), *The International Criminal Court and the Crime of Aggression* (Ashgate, 2004) 133–143.

Eser, Albin, 'Mental Elements – Mistake of Fact and Mistake of Law', in Antonio Cassese, Paola Gaeta and John Jones (eds), *The Rome Statute of the International Criminal Court* (OUP, 2002) 889–948.

Eser, Albin and Rettenmeier, Felix, 'Criminality of Organizations: Lessons from Domestic Law – A Comparative Perspective', in André Nollkaemper and Harmen van der Wilt (eds), *System Criminality in International Law* (CUP, 2009) 222–237.

Eustathiadès, Constantin, 'La Cour pénale internationale pour la répression du terrorisme et le problème de la responsabilité internationale des États' (1936) 43(1) *RGDIP* 385–415.

———, 'Les sujets du droit international et la responsabilité internationale – Nouvelles tendances' (1953) 84(3) *RCADI* 397–633.

Falk, Richard, 'Kosovo, World Order, and the Future of International Law' (1999) 93(4) *AJIL* 847–857.

Farrall, Jeremy Matam, *United Nations Sanctions and the Rule of Law* (CUP, 2007).

Fassbender, Bardo, '*Quis judicabit*? The Security Council, Its Powers and Its Legal Control' (2000) 11(1) *EJIL* 219–232.

Fathi Sorour, Ahmed, 'Quelques remarques sur la partie générale du projet de code pénal international' (1981) 52(3–4) *RIDP* 507–512.

Fenwick, Charles, 'Germany and the Crime of the World War' (1929) 23(4) *AJIL* 812–815.

———, 'Draft Code of Offences against the Peace and Security of Mankind' (1952) 46(1) *AJIL* 98–100.

Ferencz, Benjamin, 'An International Criminal Code and Court: Where They Stand and Where They're Going' (1992) 30(2) *Col J Transnatl L* 375–399.

Ferstman, Carla, 'The International Court of Justice and the Question of Reparations' (2015), http://asiapacific.anu.edu.au/regarding-rights/2015/07/17/the-international-court-of-justice-and-the-question-of-reparations.

Finch, George, 'The Nuremberg Trial and International Law' (1947) 41(1) *AJIL* 20–37.

———, 'Draft Statute for an International Criminal Court' (1952) 46(1) *AJIL* 89–98.

Fitzmaurce, Gerald, 'The Juridical Clauses of the Peace Treaties' (1948) 73(2) *RCADI* 255–367.

Fitzpatrick, Georgina, 'War Crimes Trials, "Victors' Justice" and Australian Military Justice in the Aftermath of the Second World War', in Kevin John Heller and Gerry Simpson (eds), *The Hidden History of War Crimes Trials* (OUP, 2013) 327–347.

Fleck, Dieter (ed), *The Handbook of International Humanitarian Law* (OUP, 3rd edn, 2013).

Follesdal, Andreas and Ulfstein, Geir (eds), *The Judicialization of International Law* (OUP, 2018).

Fox, Hazel and Webb, Philippa, *The Law of State Immunity* (OUP, 3rd edn, 2013).

Frulli, Micaela, 'Are Crimes against Humanity More Serious than War Crimes?' (2001) 12(2) *EJIL* 329–350.

———, '"Time Will Tell Who Just Fell and Who's Been Left Behind': On the Clash between the International Court of Justice and the Italian Constitutional Court" (2016) 14 *JICJ* 587–594.

Gaeta, Paola, 'The Character of the Breach', in James Crawford, Alain Pellet, Simon Olleson and Kate Parlett (eds), *The Law of International Responsibility* (OUP, 2010) 421–426.

Gaja, Giorgio, '*Jus Cogens* beyond the Vienna Convention' (1981) 172(3) *RCADI* 271–316.

———, 'Obligations *erga omnes*, International Crimes and *Jus Cogens*: A Tentative Analysis of Three Related Concepts', in Joseph Weiler, Antonio Cassese and Marina Spinedi (eds), *International Crimes of States* (Walter de Gruyter & Co, 1989) 151–160.

———, 'Réflexions sur le rôle du Conseil de sécurité dans le nouvel ordre mondial. À propos des rapports entre maintien de la paix et crimes internationaux des États' (1993) 97(2) *RGDIP* 297–320.

———, 'Should all References to International Crimes Disappear from the ILC's Draft Articles on State Responsibility?' (1999) 10(2) *EJIL* 365–370.

———, 'Do States Have a Duty to Ensure Compliance with Obligations *Erga Omnes* by Other States?', in Maurizio Ragazzi (ed), *International Responsibility Today* (2005) 31–36.

———, 'Preventing Conflicts between the Court's Orders on Provisional Measures and Security Council Resolutions', in Giorgio Gaja and Jenny Grote Stoutenberg (eds), *Enhancing the Rule of Law through the International Court of Justice* (Brill, 2014) 87–92.

Gaja, Giorgio and Stoutenberg, Jenny Grote (eds), *Enhancing the Rule of Law through the International Court of Justice* (Brill, 2014).

García-Amador, Francisco, 'State Responsibility in the Light of the New Trends of International Law' (1955) 49(3) *AJIL* 339–346.

———, 'State Responsibility – Some New Problems' (1958) 94(2) *RCADI* 365–491.

Gattini, Andrea, 'Smoking/No Smoking: Some Remarks on the Current Place of Fault in the ILC Draft Articles on State Responsibility' (1999) 10(2) *EJIL* 397–404.

———, 'A Historical Perspective: From Collective to Individual Responsibility and Back', in André Nollkaemper and Harmen van der Wilt (eds), *System Criminality in International Law* (CUP, 2009) 101–126.

Geiger, Rudolf, 'Article 23', in Bruno Simma (ed), *The Charter of the United Nations: A Commentary* (OUP, 2012) 751–760.

Gholiagha, Sassan, 'To Prevent Future Kosovos and Future Rwandas: A Critical Constructivist View of the Responsibility to Protect' (2015) 19(8) *IJHR* 1074–1097.

Giegerich, Thomas, 'Article 38', in Bruno Simma (ed), *The Charter of the United Nations: A Commentary* (OUP, 2012) 1161–1170.

Gilbert, Geoff, 'The Criminal Responsibility of States' (1990) 39(2) *ICLQ* 345–369.

Glaser, Stefan, 'L'État en tant que personne morale est-il pénalement responsable?' (1948–1949) 29(5) *RDPC* 425–452.

———, 'Culpabilité en droit international pénal' (1960) 99(1) *RCADI* 467–593.

Goldstone, Richard and Hamilton, Rebecca, '*Bosnia v Serbia*: Lessons from the Encounter of the International Court of Justice with the International Criminal Tribunal for the Former Yugoslavia' (2008) 21(1) *LJIL* 95–112.

Gomaa, Mohammed,'The Definition of the Crime of Aggression and the ICC Jurisdiction over That Crime', in Mauro Politi and Giuseppe Nesi (eds), *The International Criminal Court and the Crime of Aggression* (Ashgate, 2004) 55–77.

Gómez Robledo, Antonio, 'Le *ius cogens* international' (1981) 172(3) *RCADI* 9–218.

Goodrich, Leland and Hambro, Edvard, *Charter of the United Nations: Commentary and Documents* (Stevens, 2nd edn, 1949).

Gounelle, Max, 'Quelques remarques sur la notion de "crime international de l'État" et sur l'évolution de la responsabilité internationale de l'État', in Daniel Bardonnet *et al* (eds), *Le droit international: unité et diversité* (Pedone, 1981) 315–326.

Gowlland-Debbas, Vera, 'Security Council Enforcement Action and Issues of State Responsibility' (1994) 43(1) *ICLQ* 55–98.

Gowlland-Debbas, Vera and Gaggioli, Gloria, 'The Relationship between International Human Rights and Humanitarian Law: An Overview', in Robert Kolb and Gloria Gaggioli (eds), *Research Handbook on Human Rights and Humanitarian Law* (Edward Elgar, 2013) 77–103.

Graven, Jean, 'Les crimes contre l'humanité' (1950) 76(1) *RCADI* 427–607.

Gray, Christine, 'The Different Forms of Reparation: Restitution', in James Crawford, Alain Pellet, Simon Olleson and Kate Parlett (eds), *The Law of International Responsibility* (OUP, 2010) 589–597.

———, *International Law and the Use of Force* (OUP, 4th edn, 2018).

Grebing, Gerhardt, 'La création d'une Cour pénale internationale: bilan et perspectives' (1974) 45(3–4) *RIDP* 435–452.

Gros, André, 'La condition juridique de l'Allemagne' (1946) 50(1) *RGDIP* 67–78.

Grotius, Hugo, *On the Law of Peace and War* (1625, CUP, Stephen Neff ed, 2012).

Grover, Leena, *Interpreting Crimes in the Statute of the International Criminal Court* (CUP, 2014).

Guest, Anthony (ed), *Oxford Essays in Jurisprudence* (OUP, 1961).

Guilfoyle, Douglas, *International Criminal Law* (OUP, 2018).

Guillaume, Gilbert, 'Terrorisme et droit international' (1989) 215(3) *RCADI* 287–416.

Hagan, John, Kaiser, Joshua and Hanson, Anna, *Iraq and the Crimes of Aggressive War: The Legal Cynicism of Criminal Militarism* (CUP, 2015).

Hakimi, Monica, 'The *Jus ad Bellum*'s Regulatory Form' (2018) 112(2) *AJIL* 151–190.

Hall, Christopher, 'The First Proposal for a Permanent International Criminal Court' (2010) 322 *ICRC* 57–74.

Hall, Christopher and Ambos, Kai, 'Article 7: Crimes against Humanity', in Otto Triffterer and Kai Ambos (eds), *Commentary on the Rome Statute of the International Criminal Court* (Nomos, 3rd edn, 2016) 144–294.

Hameed, Asif, 'Unravelling the Mystery of *Jus Cogens* in International Law' (2013) 84(1) *BYBIL* 52–102.

Hamilton, Rebecca, 'State-Enabled Crimes' (2016) 41(2) *Yale JIL* 301–346.

Hannikainen, Lauri, *Peremptory Norms* (Jus Cogens) *in International Law* (Finnish Lawyers' Publishing, 1988).

Hart, Herbert, 'Negligence, *Mens Rea* and Criminal Responsibility', in Anthony Guest (ed), *Oxford Essays in Jurisprudence* (OUP, 1961) 29–49.

———, *The Concept of Law* (1961, OUP, 3rd edn, 2012).

Hayashi, Nobuo and Baillet, Cecilia (eds), *The Legitimacy of International Criminal Tribunals* (CUP, 2017).

Hayward, Ryan, 'Evaluating the "Imminence" of a Cyber Attack for Purposes of Anticipatory Self-Defence' (2017) 117(2) *Col L Rev* 399–434.

Heller, Kevin John and Simpson, Gerry (eds), *The Hidden History of War Crimes Trials* (OUP, 2013).

Henckaerts, Jean-Marie and Doswald-Beck, Louise, *Customary International Humanitarian Law* (CUP, 2005).

Henderson, Christian, *The Use of Force and International Law* (CUP, 2018).

Henriksen, Dag and Larssen, Ann Karin (eds), *Political Rationale and International Consequences of the War in Libya* (OUP, 2016).

Higgins, Rosalyn, *The Development of International Law through the Political Organs of the United Nations* (OUP, 1963).

———, 'Peace and Security: Achievements and Failures' (1995) 6(3) *EJIL* 445–460.

Hisakazu, Fujita, 'The Tokyo Trial: Humanity's Justice v Victors' Justice', in Yuki Tanaka, Tim McCormack and Gerry Simpson (eds), *Beyond Victors' Justice? The Tokyo War Crimes Trial Revisited* (Martinus Nijhoff, 2011) 3–21.

Hohfeld, Wesley Newcomb, 'Some Fundamental Legal Conceptions as Applied in Judicial Reasoning' (1913–14) 23(1) *Yale LJ* 16–59.

———, 'Fundamental Legal Conceptions' (1916–17) 26(8) *Yale LJ* 710–770.

Hudson, Manley, 'The Proposed International Criminal Court' (1938) 32(3) *AJIL* 549–554.

Jacovides, Andrew, 'State Responsibility: Reflections on the International Law Commission's Draft Articles' (2000) 94 *ASIL Proc* 295–297.

Jamison, Sandra, 'A Permanent International Criminal Court: A Proposal that Overcomes Past Objections' (1994–95) 23(2) *Denv J Intl L & Pol* 419–457.

Jeßberger, Florian, 'The Modern Doctrinal Debate on the Crime of Aggression', in Claus Creß and Stefan Barriaga (eds), *The Crime of Aggression: A Commentary* (CUP, 2017) 287–306.

Jessup, Philip, *A Modern Law of Nations: An Introduction* (Macmillan, 1948).

Jørgensen, Nina, *The Responsibility of States for International Crimes* (OUP, 2000).

———, 'Criminality of International Organisations under International Law', in Nollkaemper and Van der Wilt (eds), *System Criminality in International Law* (2009) 201–221.

———, 'The Obligation of Cooperation', in James Crawford, Alain Pellet, Simon Olleson and Kate Parlett (eds), *The Law of International Responsibility* (OUP, 2010) 695–701.

———, 'The Obligation of Non-Assistance to the Responsible State', in James Crawford, Alain Pellet, Simon Olleson and Kate Parlett (eds), *The Law of International Responsibility* (OUP, 2010) 687–693.

———, 'The Concept of State Crimes in the Context of the Syrian Crisis' (2015) 18 *Pal YBIL* 173–202.

Jurdi, Nidal Nabil, *The International Criminal Court and National Courts: A Contentious Relationship* (Ashgate, 2011).

———, 'The Domestic Prosecution of the Crime of Aggression after the International Criminal Court Review Conference: Possibilities and Alternatives' (2013) 14(1) *Mel JIL* 129–148.

Kadelbach, Stefan, 'Genesis, Function and Identification of *Jus Cogens* Norms' (2015) 46 *NYBIL* 147–172.

Kahn, Paul, 'Lessons for International Law from the Gulf War' (1992–93) 45(2) *Stan L Rev* 425–441.

Kant, Immanuel, *On Perpetual Peace* (1795, Broadview Press, 2015).

Kellor, Frances and Hatvanj, Antonia, *Security against War* (MacMillan, 1924).

Kelsen, Hans, 'Collective Security and Collective Self-Defence under the Charter of the United Nations' (1948) 42(4) *AJIL* 783–796.

———, *The Law of the United Nations: A Critical Analysis of Its Fundamental Problems* (Stevens & Sons, 1950).

———, *Pure Theory of Law* (1934, Peter Smith, tr Max Knight, 1989).

———, *Peace through Law* (1944, North Carolina Press, Garland Edition, 1973).

———, *General Theory of Law and State* (Russell & Russell, 1961).

———, *Principles of International Law* (Holt, Rinehart and Winston, 2nd edn, 1966).

———, *General Theory of Norms* (1979, Clarendon Press, tr Michael Hartney, 1991).

Kemp, Gerhard, *Individual Criminal Liability for the International Crime of Aggression* (CUP, 2nd edn, 2017).

Kirgis, Frederic Jr, 'The Security Council's First Fifty Years' (1995) 89(3) *AJIL* 506–539.

Kirsch, Philippe and Holmes, John, 'The Rome Conference on an International Criminal Court: the Negotiating Process' (1999) 93(1) *AJIL* 2–12.

Kittichaisaree, Kriangsak, *Public International Law of Cyberspace* (Springer, 2017).

———, *The Obligation to Extradite or Prosecute* (OUP, 2018).

Klamberg, Mark, *Power and Law in International Society* (Routledge, 2015).

Klein, Pierre, 'Responsibility for Serious Breaches of Obligations Deriving from Peremptory Norms of International Law and United Nations Law' (2002) 13(5) *EJIL* 1241–1255.

Kleinlein, Thomas, '*Jus Cogens* as the "Highest Law"? Peremptory Norms and Legal Hierarchies' (2015) 46 *NYBIL* 173–210.

Knoops, Geert-Jan Alexander, *Theory and Practice of International and Internationalised Criminal Proceedings* (Kluwer, 2005).

———, Mens Rea *at the International Criminal Court* (Brill, 2017).

Knottnerus, Abel, 'The Security Council and the International Criminal Court: The Unsolved Puzzle of Article 16' (2014) 61(2) *NILR* 195–224.

Kolb, Robert, *The International Court of Justice* (Hart, 2013).

———, *Advanced Introduction to International Humanitarian Law* (Edward Elgar, 2014).

———, *Peremptory International Law* – Jus Cogens (Hart, 2015).

———, *The International Law of State Responsibility: An Introduction* (Edward Elgar, 2017).
Kolb, Robert and Gaggioli, Gloria (eds), *Research Handbook on Human Rights and Humanitarian Law* (Edward Elgar, 2013).
Koskenniemi, Martti, 'The Police in the Temple Order, Justice and the United Nations: A Dialectical View (1995) 6(3) *EJIL* 325–348.
Koursami, Nasour, *The 'Contextual Elements' of the Crime of Genocide* (Asser Press, 2018).
Kramer, Ronald and Michalowski, Raymond, 'War, Aggression and State Crime: A Criminological Analysis of the Invasion and Occupation of Iraq' (2005) 45(4) *Br J Crim* 446–469.
———, 'State-Organized Crime, International Law and Structural Contradictions' (2016) 24(2) *Crit Crim* 231–245.
Krari-Lahya, Chehrazad, 'Cooperation and Competition between the International Court of Justice and the Security Council', in Giorgio Gaja and Jenny Grote Stoutenberg (eds), *Enhancing the Rule of Law through the International Court of Justice* (Brill, 2014) 47–61.
Kreß, Claus, 'The State Conduct Element', in Claus Creß and Stefan Barriaga (eds), *The Crime of Aggression: A Commentary* (CUP, 2017) 412–564.
———, 'On the Activation of ICC Jurisdiction over the Crime of Aggression' (2018) 16(1) *JICJ* 1–17.
Kreß, Claus and Barriaga, Stefan, *The Crime of Aggression: A Commentary* (CUP, 2017).
Krisch, Nico, 'Article 41', in Bruno Simma (ed), *The Charter of the United Nations: A Commentary* (OUP, 2012) 1305–1329.
Krzan, Bartłomiej (ed), *Prosecuting International Crimes: A Multidisciplinary Approach* (Brill, 2016).
Ku, Julian, 'How System Criminality Could Exacerbate the Weaknesses of International Criminal Law' (2010) 8(1) *Santa Clara JIL* 365–372.
Kuhn, Arthur, 'International Criminal Jurisdiction' (1947) 41(2) *AJIL* 430–433.
Kunz, Josef, 'Compulsory International Adjudication and Maintenance of Peace' (1944) 38(4) *AJIL* 673–678.
———, 'Individual and Collective Self-Defense in Article 51 of the Charter of the United Nations' (1947) 41(4) *AJIL* 872–879.
Langvatn, Silje Aambø and Squatrito, Theresa, 'Conceptualising and Measuring the Legitimacy of International Criminal Tribunals', in Nobuo Hayashi and Cecilia M Baillet (eds), *The Legitimacy of International Criminal Tribunals* (CUP, 2017) 41–65.
Lauterpacht, Hersch, 'Règles générales du droit de la paix' (1937) 62(4) *RCADI* 95–422.
Lehto, Marja, 'The Fight against ISIL in Syria. Comments on the Recent Discussion of the Right of Self-Defence against Non-state Actors' (2018) 87(1) *Nordic JIL* 1–25.
Liang, Yuen-Li, 'Notes on Legal Questions Concerning the United Nations – The Question of the Establishment of an International Criminal Jurisdiction' (1949) 43(3) *AJIL* 460–486.
———, 'Notes on Legal Questions Concerning the United Nations – The Question of the Establishment of an International Criminal Jurisdiction: The First Phase' (1952) 46(1) *AJIL* 73–88.
Lombardo, Gabriele, 'The Responsibility to Protect and the Lack of Intervention in Syria between the Protection of Human Rights and Geopolitical Strategies' (2015) 19(8) *IJHR* 1190–1198.

Lopes Peña, Oliver, 'Counter-claims and Obligations *Erga Omnes* before the International Court of Justice' (1998) 9(4) *EJIL* 724–736.

Lord Phillimore, 'An International Criminal Court and the Resolution of the Committee of Jurists' (1922–23) 3 *BYBIL* 79–86.

MacDonald, Ronald St John and Millar Johnston, Douglas (eds), *The Structure and Process of International Law* (Martinus Nijhoff, 1983).

Maison, Rafaelle, 'Les ordonnances de la CIJ dans l'affaire relative à la Convention pour la prévention et la répression du crime de génocide (1994) 5(3) *EJIL* 381–400.

Mälskoo, Lauri, 'Great Powers Then and Now: Security Council Reform and Responses to Threats to Peace and Security', in Peter Danchin and Horst Fischer (eds), *United Nations Reform and the New Collective Security* (CUP, 2010) 94–113.

Maogoto, Jackson Nyamuya, 'War on the Enemy: Self-Defence and State-Sponsored Terrorism' (2003) 4(2) *Mel JIL* 406–438.

Marchuck, Iryna, *The Fundamental Concept of Crime in International Criminal Law* (Springer, 2014).

Marek, Krystyna, 'Criminalizing State Responsibility' (1978–79) 14(2) *RBDI* 460–485.

Mariniello, Triestino (ed), *The International Criminal Court in Search of Its Purpose and Identity* (Routledge, 2015).

Massa, Anne-Sophie, 'NATO's Intervention in Kosovo and the Decision of the Prosecutor of the International Criminal Tribunal for the Former Yugoslavia Not to Investigate: An Abusive Exercise of Prosecutorial Discretion?' (2006) 24(2) *Berkeley J Intl L* 610–649.

Matheson, Michael and Scheffer, David, 'The Creation of the International Criminal Tribunals for the Former Yugoslavia and Rwanda' (2016) 110(2) *AJIL* 173–190.

May, Larry, 'Just War Theory and the Crime of Aggression', in Claus Creß and Stefan Barriaga (eds), *The Crime of Aggression: A Commentary* (CUP, 2017) 273–286.

May, Larry and Fyfe, Shannon, 'The Legitimacy of International Criminal Tribunals', in Nobuo Hayashi and Cecilia Baillet (eds), *The Legitimacy of International Criminal Tribunals* (CUP, 2017) 25–40.

McCormack, Timothy and Simpson, Gerry, 'The ILC's Draft Code of Crimes against the Peace and Security of Mankind: An Appraisal of the Substantive Provisions' (1994) 5(1) *Crim LF* 1–55.

———, 'A New International Criminal Law Regime?' (1995) 42(2) *NILR* 177–206.

———, (eds), *Beyond Victors' Justice? The Tokyo War Crimes Trial Revisited* (Martinus Nijhoff, 2011).

McDougall, Carrie, *The Crime of Aggression under the Rome Statute of the International Criminal Court* (CUP, 2013).

———, 'The Crimes against Peace Precedent', in Claus Creß and Stefan Barriaga (eds), *The Crime of Aggression: A Commentary* (CUP, 2017) 49–112.

Mégret, Frédéric, 'The Anxieties of International Criminal Justice' (2016) 29(1) *LJIL* 197–221.

Meron, Thomas, 'Is International Law Moving towards Criminalization?' (1998) 9(1) *EJIL* 18–31.

Mettraux, Guénaël (ed), *Perspectives on the Nuremberg Trial* (OUP, 2008).

———, 'The Definition of Crimes against Humanity and the Question of a "Policy" Element', in Leila Nadya Sadat (ed), *Forging a Convention for Crimes against Humanity* (CUP, 2011) 142–176.

Minear, Richard, *Victors' Justice: The Tokyo War Crimes Trial* (Princeton University Press, 1972).

Möhrlein, Rosa, 'Act-Dependent Judicial Review of Security Council and General Assembly Resolutions', in Giorgio Gaja and Jenny Grote Stoutenberg (eds), *Enhancing the Rule of Law through the International Court of Justice* (Brill, 2014) 93–111.

Momtaz, Djamchid, 'Attribution of Conduct to the State: State Organs and Entities Empowered to Exercise Elements of Governmental Authority', in James Crawford, Alain Pellet, Simon Olleson and Kate Parlett (eds), *The Law of International Responsibility* (OUP, 2010) 237–246.

Murphy, Sean, 'Progress and Jurisprudence of the ICTY' (1999) 93(1) *AJIL* 57–97.

Napel, Hans-Martien Ten, 'The Concept of International Crimes of States: Walking the Thin Line between Progressive Development and Disintegration of the International Legal Order' (1988) 1(2) *LJIL* 149–169.

Newton, Michael, 'Legal Authorities for the Creation of the Iraqi High Tribunal', in Michael Scharf and Gregory McNeal (eds), *Saddam on Trial: Understanding and Debating the Iraqi High Tribunal* (Carolina Academic Press, 2006) 15–23.

Nollkaemper, André, 'Concurrence between Individual Responsibility and State Responsibility in International Law' (2003) 52(3) *ICLQ* 615–640.

———, 'Systemic Effects of International Responsibility for International Crimes' (2010) 8(1) *Santa Clara JIL* 313–352.

Nollkaemper, André and Van der Wilt, Harmen, 'Conclusions and Outlook', in André Nollkaemper and Harmen van der Wilt (eds), *System Criminality in International Law* (2009) 338–353.

——— (eds), *System Criminality in International Law* (CUP, 2009).

Nolte, Georg, 'From Dionisio Anzilotti to Roberto Ago. The Classical International Law of State Responsibility and the Traditional Primacy of a Bilateral Conception of Inter-State Relations' (2002) 13(5) *EJIL* 1083–1098.

Nyawo, James, *Selective Enforcement and International Criminal Law: The International Criminal Court and Africa* (Intersentia, 2017).

O'Connell, Mary Ellen, 'Historical Development and Legal Basis: Definition of the Term "Humanitarian Law"', in Dieter Fleck (ed), *The Handbook of International Humanitarian Law* (OUP, 3rd edn, 2013) 1–42.

O'Keefe, Roger, *International Criminal Law* (OUP, 2015).

O'Meara, Chris, 'Should International Law Recognize a Right of Humanitarian Intervention?' (2017) 66(2) *ICLQ* 441–466.

Ollivier, Antoine, 'International Criminal Responsibility of the State', in James Crawford, Alain Pellet, Simon Olleson and Kate Parlett (eds), *The Law of International Responsibility* (OUP, 2010) 703–715.

Orakhelashvili, Alexander, 'Immunities of State Officials, International Crimes and Foreign Domestic Courts' (2011) 22(3) *EJIL* 849–855.

Osiel, Mark, 'The Banality of Good: Aligning Incentives against Mass Atrocity' (2005) 105(6) *Col L Rev* 1751–1862.

Ottenhoff, Reynald, 'L'Association internationale de droit pénal et la création de la Cour pénale internationale: de l'utopie à la réalité' (2002) 73(1–2) *RIDP* 15–21.

Ozkan, Ozcan, 'The Changing Nature of Global Armed Conflict', in Alexander Dawoody (ed), *Eradicating Terrorism from the Middle East: Policy and Administrative Approaches* (Springer, 2016) 155–160.

Palmisano, Giuseppe, 'Les causes d'aggravation de la responsabilité des États et la distinction entre "crimes" et "délits" internationaux' (1994) 98(3) *RGDIP* 629–673.

———, 'Fault', in Rüdiger Wolfrum (ed), *Max Planck Encyclopedia of Public International Law* (2007), http://opil.ouplaw.com/home/EPIL.

Paulus, Andreas, 'Second Thoughts on the Crime of Aggression' (2012) 20(4) *EJIL* 1117–1128.

Peaslee, Amos, 'The Sanction of International Law' (1916) 10(2) *AJIL* 328–336.

Pedretti, Ramona, *Immunity of Heads of State and State Officials for International Crimes* (Brill, 2015).

Pella, Vespasian, *La criminalité collective des États et le droit pénal de l'avenir* (Imprimerie de l'État de Romanie, 2nd edn, 1926).

———, 'La répression des crimes contre la personnalité de l'État'(1930) 33(3) *RCADI* 671–837.

———, *La guerre-crime et les criminels de guerre – Réflexions sur la justice pénale internationale ce qu'elle est et ce qu'elle devrait être* (Sottile and Pedone, 1946).

———, 'Towards an International Criminal Court' (1950) 44(1) *AJIL* 37–68.

———, 'La codification du droit pénal international' (1952) 56(3) *RGDIP* 337–459.

Pellet, Alain, 'Remarques sur une révolution inachevée: le Projet d'articles de la CDI sur la responsabilité des États' (1996) 42 *AFDI* 7–32.

———, '"Vive le crime"! Remarques sur les degrés de l'illicite en droit international', in Christian Tomuschat (ed), *International Law on the Eve of the 21st Century – Le droit international à l'aube du XXI siècle)* (UN, 1997) 287–315.

———, 'Can a State Commit a Crime? Definitely, Yes!' (1999) 10(2) *EJIL* 425–434.

———, 'Les articles de la CDI sur la responsabilité de l'État pour fait internationalement illicite: suite - et fin?' (2002) 48 *AFDI* 1–23.

———, 'Should We (Still) Worry about Fragmentation?', in Andreas Follesdal and Geir Ulfstein (eds), *The Judicialization of International Law* (OUP, 2018) 228–242.

Pellet, Alain and Miron, Alina, 'Sanctions', in Rüdiger Wolfrum (ed), *Max Planck Encyclopedia of Public International Law* (2013), http://opil.ouplaw.com/home/EPIL.

Picone, Paolo, 'Distinction between *Jus Cogens* and Obligations *Erga Omnes*', in Enzo Canizzaro (ed), *The Law of Treaties beyond the Vienna Convention* (OUP, 2011) 411–424.

Piragoff, Donald and Robinson, Darryl, 'Article 30: Mental Element', in Otto Triffterer and Kai Ambos (eds), *Commentary on the Rome Statute of the International Criminal Court* (Nomos, 3rd edn, 2016) 1111–1124.

Pobjie, Erin, 'Victims of the Crime of Aggression', in Claus Creß and Stefan Barriaga (eds), *The Crime of Aggression: A Commentary* (CUP, 2017) 816–860.

Politi, Mauro, 'The Debate within the Preparatory Commission of the International Criminal Court', in Mauro Politi and Giuseppe Nesi (eds), *The International Criminal Court and the Crime of Aggression* (Ashgate, 2004) 43–51.

Politi, Mauro and Nesi, Giuseppe (eds), *The International Criminal Court and the Crime of Aggression* (Ashgate, 2004).

Potter, Pitman, 'Offences against the Peace and Security of Mankind' (1952) 46(1) *AJIL* 101–102.

Powers, Maggie, 'Responsibility to Protect: Dead, Dying, or Thriving?' (2015) 19(8) *IJHR* 1257–1278.

Pritchard, John, Zaide, Sonia and Cameron Watt, Donald (eds), *The Tokyo War Crimes Trial* (Garland, 1981).

Proulx, Vincent-Joël, *Transnational Terrorism and State Accountability* (Hart, 2012).

———, *Insitutionalizing State Responsibility: Global Security and UN Organs* (OUP, 2016).

Przetacznik, Franz, 'The Compulsory Jurisdiction of the International Court of Justice as a Prerequisite for Peace' (1990) 68(1) *RDISPD* 39–74.
Quigley, John, 'The International Law Commission's Crime-Delict Distinction: A Toothless Tiger?' (1988) 66(2) *RDISPD* 117–161.
———, 'The United States and the United Nations in the Persian Gulf War: New Order or Disorder' (1992) 25(1) *Cornell Intl LJ* 1–49.
Ragazzi, Maurizio, *The Concept of International Obligation* Erga Omnes (Clarendon Press, 1997).
——— (ed), *International Responsibility Today* (2005).
Rankin, Melinda, 'Investigating Crimes against Humanity in Syria and Iraq: The Commission for International Justice and Accountability' (2017) 9(4) *GRP* 395–421.
Ratner, Steven, 'Image and Reality in the United Nation's Peaceful Settlement of Disputes' (1995) 6(3) *EJIL* 426–444.
Reisinger Coracini, Astrid and Wrange, Pål, 'The Specificity of the Crime of Aggression', in Claus Creß and Stefan Barriaga (eds), *The Crime of Aggression: A Commentary* (CUP, 2017) 307–350.
Riphagen, Willem, 'State Responsibility: New Theories of Obligation in Interstate Relations', in Ronald St John MacDonald and Douglas Millar Johnston (eds), *The Structure and Process of International Law* (Martinus Nijhoff, 1983) 581–625.
Rissing-van Saan, Ruth, 'The German Federal Supreme Court and the Prosecution of International Crimes Committed in the Former Yugoslavia' (2005) 3(2) *JICJ* 381–399.
Röling, Bert, 'The Nuremberg and the Tokyo Trials in Retrospect', in Guénaël Mettraux (ed), *Perspectives on the Nuremberg Trial* (OUP, 2008) 455–472.
Root, Elihu, 'The Outlook for International Law' (1916) 10(1) *AJIL* 1–11.
Roscini, Marco, *Cyber Operations and the Use of Force in International Law* (OUP, 2014).
Rosenne, Shabtai, 'State Responsibility and International Crimes: Further Reflections on Article 19 of the Draft Articles on State Responsibility' (1997–98) 30(1) *NYU JILP* 145–166.
Rosenstock, Robert, 'The Forty-Eight Session of the International Law Commission' (1997) 91(2) *AJIL* 365–374.
Roth, Brad, 'Coming to Terms with Ruthlessness: Sovereign Equality, Global Pluralism, and the Limits of International Criminal Justice' (2010) 8(1) *Santa Clara JIL* 231–288.
Ruiz Verduzco, Deborah, 'The Relationship between the ICC and the United Nations Security Council', in Carsten Stahn (ed), *The Law and Practice of the International Criminal Court* (OUP, 2015) 30–64.
Ruys, Tom, *'Armed Attack' and Article 51 of the UN Charter* (CUP, 2010).
———, 'Justiciability, Complementarity and Immunity: Reflections on the Crime of Aggression' (2017) 13(1) *Utr L Rev* 18–33.
Sadat, Leila Nadya (ed), *Forging a Convention for Crimes against Humanity* (CUP, 2011).
Safferling, Christoph, *Towards an International Criminal Procedure* (OUP, 2001).
Saldaña, Qunitiliano, 'La justice pénale internationale' (1925) 10(5) *RCADI* 223–430.
Sampford, Charles and Thajur, Ramesh (eds), *Responsibility to Protect and Sovereignty* (Ashgate, 2013).
Sandoz, Yves, 'The Dynamic but Complex Relationship between International Penal Law and International Humanitarian Law', in José Doria, Hans-Peter Gasser and Cherif Bassiouni (eds), *The Legal Regime of the International Criminal Court* (Brill, 2009) 1049–1069.
Sassòli, Marco, 'Humanitarian Law and International Criminal Law', in Antonio Cassese (ed), *The Oxford Companion to International Criminal Justice* (OUP, 2009) 111–120.

Sayapin, Sergey, *The Crime of Aggression in International Criminal Law: Historical Development, Comparative Analysis and Present State* (Asser Press, 2014).

Schabas, William, *Genocide in International Law: The Crime of Crimes* (CUP, 2nd edn, 2009).

———, *The International Criminal Court: A Commentary on the Rome Statute* (OUP, 2nd edn, 2016).

Schabas, William and Pecorella, Giulia, 'Article 13: Exercise of Jurisdiction', in Otto Triffterer and Kai Ambos (eds), *Commentary on the Rome Statute of the International Criminal Court* (Nomos, 3rd edn, 2016) 690–702.

Schachter, Oscar, 'The Quasi-Judicial Role of the Security Council and the General Assembly' (1964) 58(4) *AJIL* 960–965.

Scharf, Michael, '*Aut Dedere aut Judicare*', in Rüdiger Wolfrum (ed), *Max Planck Encyclopedia of Public International Law* (2012), http://opil.ouplaw.com/home/EPIL.

———, 'Universal Jurisdiction and the Crime of Aggression' (2012) 53(2) *Harv ILJ* 357–389.

———, 'How the War against ISIS Changed International Law' (2016) 48(1–2) *Case W Res J Intl L* 15–68.

Scharf, Michael and McNeal, Gregory (eds), *Saddam on Trial: Understanding and Debating the Iraqi High Tribunal* (Carolina Academic Press, 2006).

Scheffer, David, 'The United States and the International Criminal Court'(1999) 93(1) *AJIL* 12–22.

———, 'Amending the Crime of Aggression under the Rome Statute', in Claus Creß and Stefan Barriaga (eds), *The Crime of Aggression: A Commentary* (CUP, 2017) 1480–1500.

Schick, F B, 'The Nuremberg Trial and the International Law of the Future' (1947) 41(4) *AJIL* 770–794.

Schmitt, Michael, *Tallin Manual 2.0 on the International Law Applicable to Cyber Operations* (CUP, 2017).

Schuster, Matthias, 'The Rome Statute and the Crime of Aggression: A Gordian Knot in Search of a Sword' (2003) 14(1) *Crim LF* 1–57.

Schwelb, Egon, 'Crimes against Humanity' (1946) 23 *BYBIL* 178–226.

Scobbie, Iain, 'The Invocation of Responsibility for the Breach of "Obligations under Peremptory Norms of General International Law"' (2002) 13(5) *EJIL* 1201–1220.

———, 'Assumptions and Presuppositions: State Responsibility for System Crimes', in André Nollkaemper and Harmen van der Wilt (eds), *System Criminality in International Law* (CUP, 2009) 270–297.

Sellars, Kirsten, *Crimes against Peace in International Law* (CUP, 2013).

———, 'The First World War, Wilhelm II and Article 227: The Origin of the Idea of "Aggression" in International Criminal Law', in Claus Creß and Stefan Barriaga (eds), *The Crime of Aggression: A Commentary* (CUP, 2017) 21–48.

Shahabuddeen, Mohamed, *International Criminal Justice at the Yugoslav Tribunal: A Judge's Recollection* (OUP, 2012).

Shelton, Dinah (ed), *Oxford Handbook of International Human Rights Law* (OUP, 2013).

Shukri, Muhammad Aziz, 'Will Aggressors Ever Be Tried before the ICC?', in Mauro Politi and Giuseppe Nesi (eds), *The International Criminal Court and the Crime of Aggression* (Ashgate, 2004) 33–42.

Sicilianos, Linos-Alexandre, 'The Classification of Obligations and the Multilateral Dimension of the Relations of International Responsibility' (2002) 13(5) *EJIL* 1127–1145.

———, 'Countermeasures in Response to Grave Violations of Obligations Owed to the International Community', in James Crawford, Alain Pellet, Simon Olleson and Kate Parlett (eds), *The Law of International Responsibility* (OUP, 2010) 1137–1148.

Sievers, Loraine and Daws, Sam, *The Procedure of the UN Security Council* (OUP, 4th edn, 2014).

Simma, Bruno, 'From Bilateralism to Community Interest in International Law' (1994) 250(6) *RCADI* 217–384.

——— (ed), *The Charter of the United Nations: A Commentary* (OUP, 2012).

Simonsen, Sigmund, 'The Intervention in Libya in a Legal Perspective: R2P and International Law', in Dag Henriksen and Ann Karin Larssen (eds), *Political Rationale and International Consequences of the War in Libya* (OUP, 2016) 245–266.

Simpson, Gerry, 'Men and Abstract Entities: Individual Responsibility and Collective Guilt in International Criminal Law', in André Nollkaemper and Harmen van der Wilt (eds), *System Criminality in International Law* (2009) 69–100.

Sluiter, Goran, Friman Håkan, Linton, Suzannah, Vasiliev, Sergey and Zappalà, Salvatore, *International Criminal Procedure: Principles and Rules* (OUP, 2013).

Sofaer, Abraham, 'On the Necessity of Pre-emption' (2003) 14(2) *EJIL* 209–226.

Spinedi, Marina, 'La responsabilité de l'État pour "crime": une responsabilité pénale?', in Hervé Ascensio, Emmanuel Decaux and Alain Pellet (eds), *Droit international pénal* (Pedone, 1st edn, 2000) 93–114.

———, 'From One Codification to Another: Bilateralism and Multilateralism in the Genesis of the Codification of the Law of Treaties and the Law of State Responsibility' (2002) 13(5) *EJIL* 1099–1125.

Sreenivasa Rao, Pemmaraju, 'International Crimes and State Responsibility', in Maurizio Ragazzi (ed), *International Responsibility Today* (Brill, 2005) 63–80.

Stahn, Carsten, 'Enforcement of the Collective Will after Iraq' (2003) 97(4) *AJIL* 804–823.

——— (ed), *The Law and Practice of the International Criminal Court* (OUP, 2015).

Steinberg, Richard (ed), *Contemporary Issues Facing the International Criminal Court* (Brill, 2016).

Steinke, Ronen, *The Politics of International Criminal Justice* (Hart, 2012).

Stoitchkova, Desislava, *Towards Corporate Liability in International Criminal Law* (Intersentia, 2010).

Stone, Julius, 'Hopes and Loopholes in the 1974 Definition of Aggression' (1977) 71(2) *AJIL* 224–246.

Strapatsas, Nicolaos, 'The Practice of the Security Council Regarding the Concept of Aggression', in Claus Kreß and Stefan Barriaga (eds), *The Crime of Aggression: A Commentary* (CUP, 2017) 178–213.

Sunga, Lyal, *The Emerging System of International Criminal Law* (Kluwer, 1997).

———, 'Has the ICC Unfairly Targeted Africa or Has Africa Unfairly Targeted the ICC?', in Triestino Mariniello (ed), *The International Criminal Court in Search of Its Purpose and Identity* (Routledge, 2015) 147–173.

Szabó, Kinga Tibori, *Anticipatory Action in Self-Defence: Essence and Limits under International Law* (Springer, 2011).

Taft, William and Buchawald, Todd, 'Pre-emption, Iraq and International Law' (2003) 97(3) *AJIL* 557–563.

Tams, Christian, *Enforcing Obligations* Erga Omnes *in International Law* (CUP, 2005).

Tanaka, Yuki, McCormack, Tim and Simpson, Gerry (eds), *Beyond Victors' Justice? The Tokyo War Crimes Trial Revisited* (Martinus Nijhoff, 2011).

Tanzi, Attila, 'Problems of Enforcement of Decisions of the International Court Justice and the Law of the United Nations' (1995) 6(4) *EJIL* 539–572.

Thirlway, Hugh, *The Sources of International Law* (OUP, 2014).

Tomuschat, Christian, 'Obligations *Erga Omnes* for States without or against Their Will' (1993) 241(4) *RCADI* 195–374.

———, (ed), *International Law on the Eve of the 21st Century – Le droit international à l'aube du XXI siècle*) (UN, 1997).

———, 'Reparation in Cases of Genocide' (2007) 5(4) *JICJ* 905–912.

Trahan, Jennifer, 'The Relationship between the International Criminal Court and the UN Security Council: Parameters and Best Practices' (2013) 24(4) *Crim LF* 417–473.

Trapp, Kimberley, *State Responsibility for International Terrorism* (OUP, 2011).

Triffterer, Otto, 'Efforts to Recognize and Codify International Crimes' (1989) 60(1–2) *RIDP* 31–88.

———, 'Prosecution of States for Crimes of State' (1996) 67(1–2) *RIDP* 341–364.

Triffterer, Otto and Ambos, Kai (eds), *Commentary on the Rome Statute of the International Criminal Court* (Nomos, 3rd edn, 2016).

Tully, Stephen (ed), *Research Handbook on Corporate Criminal Responsibility* (Edward Elgar, 2005).

———, *International Corporate Legal Responsibility* (Wolters Kluwer, 2012).

Twinam Ghoshal, Anamika and Passas, Nikos, 'State and Corporate Drivers of Global Dysnomie: Horrendous Crimes and the Law', in Greg Barak (ed), *International Handbook of the Crimes of the Powerful* (Routledge, 2015) 105–120.

Ulf Linderfalk, 'International Legal Hierarchy Revisited: The Status of Obligations *Erga Omnes*' (2011) 80(1) *Nordic JIL* 1–23.

Van Den Herik, Larissa and Stahn, Carsten (eds), *The Diversification and Fragmentation of International Criminal Law* (Brill, 2012).

Van Sliedregt, Elies, *The Criminal Responsibility of Individuals for Violations of International Humanitarian Law* (TMC Asser Press, 2003).

Vaurs Chaumette, Anne-Laure, *Les sujets du droit international pénal* (Pedone, 2009).

———, 'The International Community as a Whole', in James Crawford, Alain Pellet, Simon Olleson and Kate Parlett (eds), *The Law of International Responsibility* (OUP, 2010) 1023–1028.

Verhoeven, Joe, 'Vers un ordre répressif universel? Quelques réflexions' (1999) 45 *AFDI* 55–71.

Verzijl, Jan Hendrik Willem, *International Law in Historical Perspective* (Martinus Nijhoff, 1973).

Von Hebel, Herman, Lammers, Johan and Schukking, Jolien (eds), *Reflections on the International Criminal Court* (TMC Asser Press, 1999).

Wald, Patricia, 'Genocide and Crimes against Humanity' (2007) 6(3) *Wash UGSLR* 621–633.

Weatherall, Thomas, 'The Status of the Prohibition of Terrorism in International Law: Recent Developments' (2014–15) 46(2) *Geo JIL* 589–627.

———, Jus Cogens: *International Law and Social Contract* (CUP, 2015).

Webb, Philippa, 'Binocular Vision: State Responsibility and Individual Criminal Responsibility for Genocide', in Larissa Van Den Herik and Carsten Stahn (eds), *The Diversification and Fragmentation of International Criminal Law* (Brill, 2012) 117–148.

———, *International Judicial Integration and Fragmentation* (OUP, 2013).

Webb, Philippa and Michaelsen, Christopher, 'Strengthening the Accountability of the UN Security Council' (2014) 19(3) *JC&SL* 385–388.

Weigend, Thomas, 'Problems of Attribution in International Criminal Law' (2014) 12 *JICJ* 253–266.

Weiler, Joseph, 'Crime and Punishment: The Reification and Deification of the State (A Footnote to the Syria Debate)' (2013) 24(4) *EJIL* 993–998.

Weiler, Joseph, Cassese, Antonio and Spinedi, Marina (eds), *International Crimes of States* (Walter de Gruyter & Co, 1989).

Weiner, Allen, 'Working the System: A Comment on Andre Nollkaemper's System Criminality in International Law (2010) 8(1) *Santa Clara JIL* 353–364.

Wells, Celia, 'Corporate Criminal Responsibility', in Stephen Tully (ed), *Research Handbook on Corporate Criminal Responsibility* (Edward Elgar, 2005) 147–158.

Wenaweser, Christian and Cockayne, James, 'Justice for Syria? The International, Impartial and Independent Mechanism and the Emergence of the UN General Assembly in the Realm of International Criminal Justice' (2017) 15(2) *JICJ* 211–230.

Werle, Gerhard and Jeßberger, Florian, *Principles of International Criminal Law* (OUP, 3rd edn, 2014).

White, Nigel, 'Responses of Political Organs to Crimes by States', in André Nollkaemper and Harmen van der Wilt (eds), *System Criminality in International Law* (CUP, 2009) 314–337.

Wijesundara, Nayantha, 'Who Will Guard the Guardian of the International Peace and Security – Judicial Review of Chapter VII Resolutions' (2016) 3 *Ind JICL* (2016) 373–434.

Williams, Sarah, 'The Specialist Chambers of Kosovo: The Limits of Internationalization?' (2016) 14(1) *JICJ* 25–51.

———, *Hybrid and Internationalized Criminal Tribunals: Selected Jurisdictional Issues* (Hart, 2012).

Wilmshurst, Elizabeth, 'Definition of the Crime of Aggression: State Responsibility or Individual Criminal Responsibility?', in Mauro Politi and Giuseppe Nesi (eds), *The International Criminal Court and the Crime of Aggression* (Ashgate, 2004) 93–96.

Wittich, Stephan, 'Punitive Damages', in James Crawford, Alain Pellet, Simon Olleson and Kate Parlett (eds), *The Law of International Responsibility* (OUP, 2010) 667–675.

Wolf, Joachim, 'Individual Responsibility and Collective State Responsibility for International Crimes: Separate or Complementary Concepts under International Law?', in Bartłomiej Krzan (ed), *Prosecuting International Crimes: A Multidisciplinary Approach* (Brill, 2016) 3–52.

Wolf, Sigfried, 'Pakistan State-Sponsored Terrorism in South Asia', in Paulo Casaca and Sigfried Wolf (eds), *Terrorism Revisited: Islamism, Political Violence and State Sponsorship* (Springer, 2017) 109–155.

Wolfrum, Rüdiger (ed), *Max Planck Encyclopedia of Public International Law*, http://opil.ouplaw.com/home/EPIL.

Wood, Michael, 'Towards New Circumstances in Which the Use of Force May be Authorized?', in Niels Blokker and Nico Schrijver (eds), *The Security Council and the Use of Force* (Martinus Nijhoff, 2005) 75–90.

Wrange, Pål, 'The Crime of Aggression, Domestic Prosecutions and Complementarity', in Claus Creß and Stefan Barriaga (eds), *The Crime of Aggression: A Commentary* (CUP, 2017) 704–751.

Wright, Quincy, 'The Law of the Nuremberg Trial' (1947) 41(1) *AJIL* 38–72.

———, 'Proposal for an International Criminal Court' (1952) 46(1) *AJIL* 60–72.

Wyler, Eric, 'From "State Crime" to Responsibility for "Serious Breaches of Obligations under Peremptory Norms of General International Law"' (2002) 13(5) *EJIL* 1147–1160.

Wyler, Eric and Papaux, Alain, 'The Different Forms of Reparation: Satisfaction', in James Crawford, Alain Pellet, Simon Olleson and Kate Parlett (eds), *The Law of International Responsibility* (OUP, 2010) 623–637.

Yahi, Abdelkader, 'La violation d'un traité: l'articulation du droit des traités et du droit de la responsabilité internationale' (1993) 26(2) *RBDI* 437–469.

Yakpo, Emile and Boumedra, Tahar (eds), *Liber amicorum Judge Mohammed Bedjaoui* (Kluwer, 1999).

Yamada, Chusei, 'Revisiting the International Law Commission's Draft Articles on State Responsibility', in Maurizio Ragazzi (ed), *International Responsibility Today* (Brill, 2005) 117–123.

Yee, Sienho, 'A Proposal to Reformulate Article 23 of the ILC Draft Statute for an International Criminal Court' (1995–96) 19(3) *Hastings Intl & Comp L Rev* 529–537.

Zahed, Mosa, The Evolution and Ascension of Iran's Terror Apparatus', in Paulo Casaca and Sigfried Wolf (eds), *Terrorism Revisited: Islamism, Political Violence and State Sponsorship* (Springer, 2017) 57–82.

Zakerhossein, Mohammad Hadi and De Brouwer, Anne-Marie, 'Diverse Approaches to Total and Partial *in Absentia* Trials by International Criminal Tribunals' (2015) 26(2) *Crim LF* 181–224.

Zemanek, Karl, 'The Legal Foundations of the International System' (1997) 266 *RCADI* 9–336.

Zifcak, Spencer, 'The Responsibility to Protect after Libya and Syria' (2012) 13(1) *Mel JIL* 59–93.

———, 'Falls the Shadow: The Responsibility to Protect from Theory to Practice', in Charles Sampford and Ramesh Thajur (eds), *Responsibility to Protect and Sovereignty* (Ashgate, 2013) 11–39.

Zimmermann, Andreas, 'Article 27', in Bruno Simma (ed), *The Charter of the United Nations: A Commentary* (OUP, 2012) 871–938.

Zimmermann, Andreas and Teichmann, Michael, 'State Responsibility for International Crimes', in André Nollkaemper and Harmen van der Wilt (eds), *System Criminality in International Law* (CUP, 2009) 298–313.

Zimmermann, Andreas and Freiburg, Elisa, 'Article 8bis: Crime of Aggression', in Otto Triffterer and Kai Ambos (eds), *Commentary on the Rome Statute of the International Criminal Court* (Nomos, 3rd edn, 2016) 580–618.

———, 'Article 15bis: Exercise of Jurisdiction over the Crime of Aggression (State Referral, *proprio motu*)', in Otto Triffterer and Kai Ambos (eds), *Commentary on the Rome Statute of the International Criminal Court* (Nomos, 3rd edn, 2016) 741–764.

Zolo, Danilo, *Victors' Justice: From Nuremberg to Baghdad* (Verso, tr Weir, 2009).

Index

For Product Safety Concerns and Information please contact our EU representative GPSR@taylorandfrancis.com
Taylor & Francis Verlag GmbH, Kaufingerstraße 24, 80331 München, Germany

www.ingramcontent.com/pod-product-compliance
Ingram Content Group UK Ltd.
Pitfield, Milton Keynes, MK11 3LW, UK
UKHW020015200926
475702UK00014B/1904
* 9 7 8 1 0 3 2 2 4 1 4 7 0 *